There was an extraordinary mixture of comedy and tragedy in the situation which is here described, and those who are affected by the pathos of it will not need to have it explained to them that the comedy was superficial and the tragedy essential.

—Edmund Gosse, introduction to *Father and Son*

He that hath wife and children hath given hostages to fortune; for they are impediments to great enterprises, either of virtue or mischief.

—Francis Bacon

We are pilgrims only, but since the trip's quite long, I tend to look around for suitable accommodations.

—J. F. Powers, June 3, 1952

To the memory of my sister Mary Farl Powers and my parents

Farrar, Straus and Giroux
18 West 18th Street, New York 10011

Library of Congress Cataloging-in-Publication Data
Powers, J. F. (James Farl), 1917–1999.
   [Correspondence. Selections]
   Suitable accommodations : an autobiographical story of family life : the letters of
J. F. Powers, 1942–1963 / edited by Katherine A. Powers. — First edition.
      pages   cm
   Includes index.
   ISBN 978-0-374-26806-0 (hardcover)
   1. Powers, J. F. (James Farl), 1917–1999—Correspondence.   2. Authors,
American—20th century—Correspondence.   I. Powers, Katherine A., 1947– editor
of compilation.   II. Title.
   PS3566.O84 Z48 2013

   813'.54—dc23
   [B]

2013010997

Designed by Jonathan D. Lippincott

Farrar, Straus and Giroux books may be purchased for educational, business, or
promotional use. For information on bulk purchases, please contact the Macmillan
Corporate and Premium Sales Department at 1-800-221-7945, extension 5442, or write
to specialmarkets@macmillan.com.

www.fsgbooks.com
www.twitter.com/fsgbooks • www.facebook.com/fsgbooks

10 9 8 7 6 5 4 3 2 1

Suitable Accommodations

An Autobiographical Story of Family Life: The Letters of J. F. Powers, 1942–1963

Edited by Katherine A. Powers

Farrar, Straus and Giroux

New York

BE A WINNER

Suitable Accommodations

Contents

Introduction

Katherine A. Powers

Jim and George Garrelts, 1952

Well before the publication of his first novel, *Morte D'Urban*, in 1962, my father, J. F. Powers, henceforth called Jim, planned to write a novel about "family life," an intention that persisted for the rest of his life. It was to be, in some fashion, the story of a writer, an artist, with bright prospects, a taste for the good things in life, and an expectation of camaraderie as he made his way in the world. The man falls in love, gets married, has numerous children—but has neither money nor home. He finds no pleasant ease and little of the fellowship of like minds he associated with the literary life he had thought was to be his own. The novel would be called *Flesh*, a word infused with Jansenist distaste, conveying the bleak comedy and terrible bathos of high aesthetic and spiritual aspiration in hopeless contest with human needs and material necessity.

The proposed book took on other names and fused itself with other themes, most notably with the triumph of consumerism in American life: at times it was *The Sack Race*; at other times, *NAB* (*Nationally Advertised Brands*); and, at yet others, *Nobody Home*. (The last two also served as provisional titles for another unwritten novel, while *The Sack Race* became the working title for Jim's second—and final—novel, *Wheat That Springeth Green*, the image serving admirably for both priests and artists.) In one version of the novel—drawn very much from life—the narrator, a "one-book author" who is unable to complete a second novel, has been reduced to living with his populous family in his wife's parents' middle-American home.

In any event, the family-life novel never got beyond a few notes, jottings, and false starts. Or so it seemed. Jim was, in fact, not only living it but creating and embellishing it in his correspondence, a body of writing whose size and extent go some way toward explaining the small number of his published books.

The letters that make up this story begin with Jim at age twenty-five and the acceptance for publication of his first short story. They then leap forward to letters from prison and on through those recording high hopes, great promise, and a passionate courtship of and marriage to Betty Wahl. Then comes the black comedy of children, five all told, great poverty, bad luck, and balked creativity. Central to this progression is the matter of where and how to live. Jim's married life was dominated by the search for "suitable accommodations," for a house that would reflect and foster the high calling of the artist. In the course of their married life, which lasted from 1946 until Betty's death in 1988, the couple moved more than twenty times. This included eight times across the Atlantic: four tenures in Ireland and four returns. "I vacillate," Jim wrote to a friend, "between wishing I had the wings of an angel—one whose wings would know where to take him, however—and a large brick house in which to hide myself, with books, music, etc."

Jim—James Farl Powers—was born in Jacksonville, Illinois, on July 8, 1917. His father, James (1883–1985), was the son of a man, also called James, who came from county Waterford, Ireland, and worked at a gasworks. He died when James, his son, was around seventeen. This James, which is to say Jim's father, aspired to be a pianist, was called a prodigy, and was offered a chance to study in Paris—or so Jim maintained. Instead, the young man sacrificed that future in order to provide for his sisters and widowed mother. "She was the woman who ruined my father's life, I hold," Jim wrote in describing his background to Betty, his wife-to-be, two weeks after they had met. It is a glimpse of his view of family obligations that should, perhaps, have given her pause. Stuck in southern Illinois, James ran dance bands, played sheet music for customers in a music shop, and operated an unsuccessful butter-and-egg store before finally becoming a middle manager for Swift and Company. He was laid off during the Depression and was out of work for some years until he was hired back by Swift as an accountant, a lower position. Jim considered both jobs demeaning and sad, all the more so as his father did not see them that way and was a conscientious worker and devoted provider.

Jim's mother, Zella (1892–1973), was the daughter of Matilda née Zilberstorff by her first husband, Farl Routzong, a farmer, painter and "grainer," balloonist, and semiprofessional baseball player who died of TB before he was thirty. Matilda's second husband (of at least three) was a rich and kindly farmer who put Zella through college, a rare thing for a woman in the early part of the twentieth century.

Jim grew up in Illinois, in Rockford and, later, Quincy, where he made lifelong friends, among them George Garrelts, later a priest. Gregarious, ambitious, high-handed, and adept in Church politics, Garrelts was Jim's closest friend for years and exercised a formidable influence over him. Both eventually attended high school at the Franciscan-run Quincy College Academy. After graduating in 1935, Jim moved to Chicago, taking various jobs, his first at Marshall Field's selling books. Later he found a position as chauffeur or, as he put it, driving "a big Packard for a bastard through the South and Southwest."

Eventually, he found work on the WPA Illinois Historical Records Survey in Chicago, where he met a number of writers from the WPA's Federal Writers' Project, among them Nelson Algren, Richard Wright, Jack Conroy, and Arna Bontemps. After that he sold books again, this time at Brentano's, from which job he was fired for refusing to buy war bonds. He spent a couple of semesters at Northwestern, where he took at least one writing seminar with Bergen Evans (afterward best known as the master of ceremonies on the TV quiz show *The $64,000 Question*). Meanwhile, Jim began to write stories, had a couple of love affairs, became a committed pacifist, and contributed pieces to Dorothy Day's newspaper, *The Catholic Worker*.

In the early 1940s, Jim became acquainted with Father Harvey Egan, a fellow assistant of George Garrelts's at St. Olaf's in Minneapolis. Within a few years, Egan had taken on the role of Jim's literary patron, bailing him out with loans and gifts over the decades. Possessed of a humorous, sardonic streak, Egan was also one of Jim's most important correspondents and a thoroughly appreciative foil for his dry wit and self-deprecating fancy.

When Jim met him, Egan was a rigorous "Detacher," as, indeed, was Garrelts at the time. Detachment is possibly the most forgotten strain in the nearly forgotten American Catholic countercultural religious and social ferment of the mid-twentieth century. (This also included Catholic Action, the Catholic Worker movement, the Catholic rural life movement, the liturgical movement, the Christian Family Movement, and the retreat movement.) The Detachment movement was inaugurated by the Canadian Jesuit Onesimus Lacouture with the aim of shaking the clergy out of its "comfortable paganism" and waking in it "heroic holiness."[1] It held as its first principle that a single-minded devotion to God is the true Christian goal and, further, that this state cannot be achieved without detaching oneself from unnecessary material things and earthly desire.

1 From an unpublished manuscript in the hands of Rosemary Hugo Fielding.

"Take pleasure in nothing," Garrelts advised Jim in a letter, "and you find pleasure in all things is the rule."

The American Church hierarchy viewed Detachment's rejection of the world as dangerous, as verging on heresy (Jansenism, in fact), and also opposed its insistence on pacifism. Nonetheless—and in part as a consequence—the movement had a powerful appeal to the contrarian Jim, not on its terms altogether, but on his own. He approved of its nay-saying, its criticism of American materialism and militarism, and its re-buke to complacent middle-class Catholics, who, for all their manifest religiosity, put "business sense" first.

At the prompting of the recently ordained Garrelts, Jim attended a retreat in Oakmont, Pennsylvania, led by Father Louis Farina, a pacifist and Detacher, that affected him deeply and strengthened his resolve to refuse military service. His chief concern was the effect this decision would have on his parents, whose friends and neighbors were sure to pil-lory them for their son's anti-Americanism and supposed cowardice. As a Catholic, Jim was denied the status of conscientious objector on the grounds that the teachings of the Church permit killing in a "just war." He was arrested after failing to appear for induction into the army in April 1943 and spent three days in the Cook County Jail before being re-leased on a thousand-dollar bond. He was later indicted by a grand jury and sentenced to three years in prison.

Before beginning his sentence, Jim attended another retreat, this for priests (where he passed as a seminarian), at St. John's Abbey in College-ville, Minnesota. It was led by the powerful preacher Father John Hugo, another influential Detacher, pacifist, and pioneer in reforming the lit-urgy and religious practices. Thus began the association with St. John's Abbey and University that influenced the rest of his life.

Jim served thirteen months in the federal penitentiary at Sandstone, Minnesota, before being paroled. In years to come, he covered up his prison sentence because of the pain it had caused his parents and his wife's relatives. Indeed, we, his children, only learned about it in 1959 when my sister Mary was mocked by a schoolmate for having a "jailbird" as a father.

While he was inside, Jim's first story, "He Don't Plant Cotton," was published in *Accent*, a literary magazine of high standing. It was also in prison that Jim's obsession with the relationship between the artist and his house appears to have begun, for among his fellow prisoners were two of Frank Lloyd Wright's apprentices, both incarcerated for refusing military service. One of them, Jack Howe, drew up a plan for a farm that Jim seemed to consider the answer to life on earth. His letter to his sister extolling it makes curious reading to one who knew him in later life. The farm would not only be a communal endeavor but also involve animal husbandry and a good deal of manual labor, none of which were much in Jim's line. It never advanced beyond drawings and talk.

After his parole in late 1944, and as a condition of his release from prison, Jim was assigned a job as a hospital orderly in St. Paul, Minnesota, living first at the hospital itself and later in a St. Paul residential hotel, the Marlborough, "an old red stone dump creaking with age and old women." Some months later, in November 1945, he met Betty Wahl, whose manuscript of a novel had been sent to him for his views by her teacher, a nun who considered Betty her star student. Jim and Betty became engaged within two days and were married less than six months later, having visited each other only five times after the first meeting. Instead, they corresponded almost every day before they were married.

Jim's letters to Betty touch on many things, though above all on his love for her and on how and where they will live. They are filled with optimism for the most part—and foreshadow doom, especially on the housing front, the matter of making a living, and Jim's denunciation of "business sense." Though there is already talk of Ireland, the couple decided they would live in rural Minnesota near St. John's. To that end, Betty's father gave them money to buy land in Avon, a few miles from Collegeville, where his work crew built the beginnings of a house, a barely habitable dugout that lacked running water. There, out in the woods, the couple, and eventually one baby, lived from early 1947 until mid-1948.

The region was a hotbed of Catholic reform movements, of people returning to the land and speaking ecstatically about big families, community, liturgical reform, and Catholic art. Thus, in a bantering way, Jim called the circle of friends who lived in the geographical and spiritual environs of St. John's "the Movement" and, on occasion, "the rural lifers," and the area itself, "Big Missal Country." Later, when the Powerses went away (only to return again and again), these friends became key correspondents. Confident that they would appreciate his subtle, undermining wit, Jim wrote some of his funniest letters to them, much of the humor drawing on how the lofty ideals of the Movement were so flattened by reality. His appetite for storytelling is everywhere evident, and as he wrote these letters, the members of the Movement became not only correspondents but literary creations—as did Jim himself and his family. That family was, in the end, Jim and Betty and their children: Katherine (myself), Mary, then yet another James, whom we called Boz, Hugh, and Jane.

In his letters to his friends, Jim dwelled on the failure of his own life to pan out as he thought it would and should. He presented himself as a man struggling—though not always terribly hard—in a world that didn't understand or appreciate him. His disappointment and discontent are notes that sound throughout the correspondence, often enough with a comic timbre, as he worked up the theme of life mowing him down. He often adopted a tone of macabre relish for the hopelessness of his situation: the absence of a house, the presence of many children and a desperate wife, the amount of time he had to spend on the mechanics of life, the piddling nature of his daily doings, and his longing for and lack of camaraderie.

"We have here no lasting home" was his constant refrain, drawing, with feigned smugness, on Christian teaching and, perhaps with irony, on the title of the first novel of his onetime friend the Catholic writer Joe Dever (*No Lasting Home*, 1947). In any case, the phrase always had the torque of a joke, for the Powerses were forever on the move, leaving some houses out of the urge to quit the country (whichever one it happened to be at the time), leaving other houses because they were taken by eminent domain or sold out from under them. But Jim also meant the statement as a summary of his essential belief: that life on earth doesn't make sense and that when you understood that, you understood reality. Still, for a person who held that the world is an obstacle-strewn journey toward one's proper home (heaven), he was more than ordinarily affronted by hardship and adversity, to say nothing of mediocrity and dullness. He was no stoic, and he took it all personally.

Of the handful of Jim's published stories that were not about priests, two were based on misfortunes in housing his family: "Look How the Fish Live" and "Tinkers." The problem of finding "suitable accommodations" for the Powers family was always with us and always impossible to solve, but not only because of bad breaks and no money. While Jim prided himself on having a clear, unillusioned perception of how things really worked, when it came to adapting to reality, he was not one for making suitable accommodations himself.

The world outside the house, whichever one he happened to be living in, became increasingly untenable to him, and his vision of the ideal house became ever more one of an asylum, a place safe from the contagion of the world and the line of complacency it peddled. As he retreated, the family he had once seen as having thwarted his calling as an artist became his model society—all the more so after most of its members had left and the idea could flourish unchecked by reality. In 1979 he wrote to me, then thirty-one and living, as were his other children, far away: "You referred to Boz's plan for me to make a lot of money so we can move back to Ireland. He may be right. I see it as idealism, but what else would work for our family? A big house not too far from Dublin, Jane weaving and dyeing in one room, Hugh philosophizing and botanizing in another, Boz and family in one wing, Mary etching in one tower, Katherine reading in another, Mama in the garden, Daddy with *The Irish Times* and *The Daily Telegraph* in his study."

To which scheme I say to myself now, as I did then: Oh, dear.

Jim's letters are assertions of comic might against the absurdity, as he saw it, of his existence. He wrote them in part to stave off chaos, to give reality a shape of his own creation, however dark. As it happens, the last communication between my parents was conducted—in a manner of speaking—in writing and was another attempt to fend off the unbearable. On the morning Betty died (at home, wasted by cancer, unstintingly cared for by Jim), he asked her what she would like for breakfast. She just shook her head. He went off and returned with a pencil and checklist with entries for "Eggs" and "Liver." He left; came back; no checkmark. He took the list away and returned with it, having added "Kisses." She smiled faintly and again shook her head. He left it with her, and when he returned again, she had marked "Liver." This struck him, as I have no doubt it was meant to by Betty, partner and butt of his dark sense of humor, as perfect in its intransigence and bleak comedy.

Betty died a couple hours later. Jim said he spent that time telling her how sorry he was for having given her such a hard life and no home. He never really recovered from her death, though he lived for another eleven years, alone, and long enough to be forced to leave another house slated for destruction.

A Note on the Text

I have selected the letters and journal extracts that make up the text of this book from thousands of letters and several personal journals with the aim of keeping the focus on JFP's life. I have cut letters and passages that are not necessary to the story, including a large number concerning JFP's deliberations and negotiations with editors and publishers.

Passages cut from the letters are indicated by this: [. . .]. Passages cut from the italicized interstitial material are indicated by ellipses alone.

I have created consistency in such matters as capitalization and corrected the very few spelling mistakes. I have added some additional paragraph breaks as JFP often sacrificed format to postage economy. I have also retained JFP's preference for the British custom of using no period after an abbreviation if the last letter of the abbreviation is the same as the last letter of the word being abbreviated—for example, "Mr," "Mrs," "Fr," "Sr," and "Dr."

Fortunately, I am under no obligation to earn a living wage

September 8, 1942–November 6, 1945

Letter from prison

In 1942, when this story begins, Jim was twenty-five years old and living in Chicago with his parents in their apartment at 4453 North Paulina Street. He had a job at the wholesale book company A. C. McClurg and was also writing. His story "He Don't Plant Cotton" (whose characters were based on the jazz musicians Baby Dodds, Jimmie Noone, and Lonnie Johnson) was accepted by Accent: A Quarterly of New Literature. The magazine had been founded in 1940 by Kerker Quinn in concert with six other editors, including Charles Shattuck, who became Jim's most helpful editor and critic.

CHARLES SHATTUCK

4453 North Paulina Street
Chicago
September 8, 1942

Dear Mr Shattuck,

Naturally, I'm very pleased that the editors of *Accent* like "He Don't Plant Cotton" well enough to publish it.[1] [. . .]

Concerning the who's who data, this will be my first published story. Aside from the fact that I am 25 and live in Chicago, there is nothing I wish mentioned about me: because those facts, paltry and insignificant, are at least accomplished.

Off the record, I work for a wholesale book company. In fact I might even be what the *Publishers Weekly* and booksellers refer fondly to as "a bookman," but the bestseller wars have left me, in spite of my tender years, battered and scarred beyond finding much solace in that hallowed term, smacking of crafts and guilds though it does.

In italics, I want to get away and, yes, you guessed it, Write. I am *not* working on a novel now.

---

1 Published in *Accent* (Winter 1943).

I do not think my years are tender. Time passing haunts me even more than Space intervening.

Thanks once more. I am hoping you will be able to publish the story soon.

Sincerely,

J. F. Powers

Jim applied for the status of conscientious objector in November 1940 but was classified 1-A in September 1942. His great friend from his Quincy College Academy days, George Garrelts, ordained a priest in September 1942, was a strong supporter of Jim's decision to resist military service. After a failed appeal, Jim did not present himself for induction on April 3, 1943. Arrested two weeks later, he spent three days in the Cook County Jail before being released on a thousand-dollar bond. He was indicted by a grand jury on May 6, 1943, and on September 30, 1943, was sentenced to three years at Sandstone Federal Penitentiary in Minnesota. He served thirteen months before being paroled.

While inside, Jim was allowed to write two letters a week. He worked in the hospital and, to some extent, on his own writing. Unlikely though it was, and thanks to the friends he made there, prison gave Jim a sense of what life might be for an artist. Among his fellow inmates were a number of cultivated, idealistic men who were also conscientious objectors. Among them were John Marshall, with whom he wrote and produced a play, and two of Frank Lloyd Wright's apprentices, Jack Howe and Davy Davison. Howe drew up a plan of a farm for Jim that represented to him a more intellectual and cultivated expression of the ideals of the Catholic Worker movement.

CHARLOTTE AND BILL KRAFT

Sandstone
May 22, 1944

Dear Charlotte and Bill,

[. . .] You make your life in New England[1] sound attractive—even to me. At times I've thought my place to be there. But most of the time I've wondered if there is any place for me except in some branch of the govern-

---

1 Bill was attending the Harvard Business School.

ment service. There is a justice, hardly poetic, in the way I find myself tied up in destiny with millions of people when what I want most is to be separated from them. [. . .]

The weather is nice and I'm tempted to get out of the dormitory, but when I do, there's only a sandy lot surrounded by concrete walls—and so monotony has the upper hand always. There is no grass. A while ago I saw somebody playing with a small snake. There it was lying in the sand, pushed about by prison shoes, and I guess it will die eventually. It can't get out either. [. . .]

Write when you feel like it—and love.

James (Powers) 1939

CHARLOTTE AND BILL KRAFT

Sandstone
June 11, 1944

Dear Charlotte and Bill,

[. . .] This is Sunday in Sandstone, and it has rained intermittently all day. [. . .] The letters from Mother and Daddy brought sad news also—Eric Swenson is dead and Russ Alonzo's brother, whom I hardly remember . . . Well, I don't know what to say about these things. I can only hope these boys thought they were engaged in good work. If so, it's not so bad, as we must all die sooner or later and it is a privilege to die for something meaningful—however funny that sounds. As Father George says, it is very strange how such fuss is made about certain saints who died for the love of God, the hardships and martyrdom they thrust upon themselves, and yet when millions die for—they don't know what, most of them—it is not wondered at, except secretly by many afraid to speak out. [. . .]

Wm Fifield,[1] [. . .] who wrote to me several weeks ago, mentioning that a nun plans to use "Lions"[2] in an anthology she's editing,[3] writes again that he is a CO and understands my situation. I had written to him, explaining my inability to write a long letter. [. . .]

Love,

James (Powers) 1939

1 William Fifield (1916–1987), the writer and editor.
2 Published in *Accent* (Autumn 1943).
3 Sister Mariella Gable was compiling an anthology of Catholic fiction, *Our Father's House* (1945), in which she included "The Trouble" and "Lions, Harts, Leaping Does."

Sandstone
June 25, 1944

Dear Charlotte and Bill,

This is Sunday again, and it's hot. [. . .] Despite the play and story I've done since coming here, it is impossible to work. Absolute absence of privacy and solitude and silence—makes James a disgusted boy. And then when a day like this comes along, I can't even escape my own body, which sweats and twists under the heat. That is why I hate summer and why I am happy whenever it is raining and grey. I look out the window now, see across the dusty yards, and there on benches the inmates sit and talk and doze. For all my indolence, I have no talent for that sort of thing. I guess it is the equivalent in my mind of the way Mother and Daddy used to sit out on the back porch. How to spend a lifetime in an evening. [. . .]

Fr George writes of the nice lady parishioner who came to see him about her soul and, more immediately, her finances. She wanted him to recommend a good investment. He recommended the poor. She appealed to common sense. Fr George told her she'd better come back and see the pastor. I'm rather dazed to hear the sermons at your church are strange and different and literate. What a relief it must be for you not to hear about picnics and carnivals. [. . .]

Love,
James (Powers) 1939

Sandstone
July 21, 1944

Dear Charlotte and Bill,

[. . .] I just finished a letter to Mother and Daddy in which I told them my ideas about political conventions and farms for the future. The farm is more than usually on my mind because I saw the complete plans the night before last. About six or seven cottages, a twin building joined by a walk: place to eat in one (including a fireplace, huge and "roaring") and a little theatre in the other (including projection room for movies, mostly "foreign"). Finally, a barn. A barn such as I cd not have imagined and which even now I can hardly understand, for the architect (one of Frank Lloyd

Wright's young geniuses)[1] understands the needs and whims of chickens, hogs, horses, cows, and all the rest. The entire project would cost between $50 and $60,000. Which I am told is less than the same number of buildings wd cost if they were (which they aren't) ugly and cheap. I know of course you are wondering what we get to drink here that makes me talk loosely about that much money. It is not so much, considering my literary prospects (not what I'll make from books, but the people I'll meet). Anyway, that's the setup. Something beyond a pension to work for. I'm wheeling and dealing where I can. [. . .]

The sky is beautiful today—peace, it's wonderful—and I can't remember the sky being like this anywhere else. A different feature daily. I was thinking today (while watching the clouds) how far I've traveled from the canoe trips I took with Ramona[2] around the Chain of Lakes. I told you she got married January 1943, but did I tell you that she expected a baby in November? Well, she's all taken care of, and it's a good thing, I'm thinking, for me. She never meant what she said about being different. It took Fr George to detect that a long time ago: the first time he met her.[3] [. . .] Listened to the convention tonight and lost a bag of cookies on Wallace.[4]

Love,

Jim (Powers)

MARIELLA GABLE

Sandstone

August 1, 1944

Dear Sister Mariella,

The authorities have graciously permitted me to write a special purpose letter to you.

I was very happy to hear that you wish to use my work and feel indebted to William Fifield and Harry Sylvester for bringing it to your attention. [. . .]

1 Jack Howe.
2 Ramona Rawson (1920–1999), former girlfriend, who did not show deference to George Garrelts.
3 Garrelts wrote to Jim (November 17, 1942), "A stand is about to be taken in re Ramona Rawson . . . You are not in love, are not likely to be, and cannot ever abidingly or successfully be. My evidence is detailed. She would not darn your socks. She would not accompany us to Mass. She sat sullenly by in the presence. She found no ways during our stay in Waupaca [Wisconsin]."
4 Henry Wallace was replaced by Harry Truman as Roosevelt's running mate at the Democratic convention in Chicago.

Since leaving Chicago, escorted by a U.S. marshal, I have been doing time at Sandstone prison in Minnesota. The "rap": failure to report for induction, or conscientious objection to war. For me, the project and prison have been gifts from heaven, periodically bewildering as such, but essentially blessings. I have had the honor of living among men of goodwill in these places, a few of the uncelebrated, if not unknown, victims of peace and war in our age "of moderate virtue and of moderate vice."[1]

[. . .]

In Christ,

    J. F. Powers

CHARLOTTE AND BILL KRAFT

Sandstone

August 4, 1944

Dear Charlotte and Bill,

[. . .] I have hopes for a merrier Xmas this year than last: I'm assured on all sides the war will be over and it is very probable I'll be out on parole and settled, as it were, by then. As a matter of fact, if Washington okays my parole, I may make it by September. [. . .]

Fr George is (or recently was) in Oakmont for a retreat, and a fellow here is going to Oakmont next week to work for Fr Farina.[2] Took a lot of accounting at Creighton University and came here as a Catholic CO and now knows accounting is as far from his heart as murder, and will donate his life to such work as Fr Farina and the CW movement entails.

You ask about the farm of the future. You are right: there will be no advertising or insurance men about (unless of course they have mended their ways). You are wrong: there will be no arty people passing through in the summer as though it were Wisconsin Dells. Who lives there lives there. No part time. It will not be a tourist camp. We will get our living from the earth. A living is not so much as the light companies and grocers try to make city people think. It will be a risk of course. I'm dead sure "risk" is the magic word. The condition of the cities is due to the fact that people will not risk anything to live. They would rather die for not living—it is a slow process like an all-day sucker.[3] A slow process, even if it isn't any

---

1 T. S. Eliot, *The Rock*.
2 St. Anthony Village, Oakmont, an orphanage under the direction of Father Louis Farina where famous retreats were given, especially those led by Father John Hugo.
3 Lollipop.

good. If you'll watch the forthcoming *Life* magazines, you'll see some specimens of F. L. Wright's work. It will be an article on "Broadacre City," Mr Wright's dream city. My farm is the work of a fellow whom Mr Wright called "the finest draughtsman he ever met."[1] [. . .] And now, once more, my love to both of you.

James (Powers) 1939

CHARLOTTE AND BILL KRAFT

Sandstone

August 18, 1944

Dear Charlotte and Bill,

[. . .] The weather here is cool again, and the trees in the distant bluffs are changing color, just beginning to, and I am told the summer has practically spent itself. I am glad. [. . .] I read "Renner,"[2] and it doesn't sound as bad as I was afraid it might—I've changed here: am not so quick to see tragedy where I did. I used to give the businessmen a rough go, and the mistake was in limiting such treatment too much to them. The innocents I find are ever harder to find than before. I am thinking of alleged pacifist societies and related groups. More than before I realize that pacifism alone is no use. It is an essential part of Christianity: there is the root—not in pacifism or labor unions or education. This means, then, I was somewhat taken in by "do-good" organizations; it does not mean the business boys, the common sensers, get off any easier. Being here has matured me. There are people and types of endeavor—architecture, for instance, which I was hardly conscious of. And they all have their way out for humanity. [. . .]

Love,

James (Powers) 1939

CHARLOTTE AND BILL KRAFT

Sandstone

September 1, 1944

Dear Charlotte and Bill,

[. . .] I'm writing this letter from the barbershop, where I'm waiting my turn. There are three chairs, and tonight the library and hospital workers

---

1 Jack Howe.
2 Jim's short story published in *New Mexico Quarterly Review* (Spring 1944).

get theirs. [. . .] Sometimes I feel I must have checked my brain and responsibility (to myself) at the front gate when I came in and they were mailed home with my clothes. I won't ask again about Bill's deferment, but only hope he stays unmolested where he is. There are train tracks within whistling distance, and when they sound in the night, and the dogs bark, you know you're in jail. [. . .]

Love,

James (Powers) 1939

CHARLOTTE AND BILL KRAFT

Sandstone

October 8, 1944

Dear Charlotte and Bill,

Sunday, about 9:00 in the morning, and I'm sitting at a big long table in the dayroom, listening to some wonderful Negro spiritual singing. [. . .]

We must pray that Dick survives and that Mother and Daddy are spared further sorrows.[1] I feel my parole will take a weight off their minds, despite my assurances that I was and am all right here, which is the truth. They were never able to believe that, I always suspected. When you were home, did you feel that they worried about my being here much? Did the neighbors make them feel embarrassed? Now the spirituals have stopped and it is white hymn singing, which, as far as I'm concerned, is something else. This is a chill bleak day, the trees in the distance are many colors and I should very much like to walk through them. [. . .]

All at once, with a date set for my departure, I find myself engaged in counting the days—an old practice among jailbirds. I have, of this writing, 23 days and a "get," which means "get up." I'll leave on the 9:39 train on the morning of November 1—All Saints' Day—a Wednesday. I'll be paid $50 a month at St Joseph's[2] and furnished with a room and meals. That isn't bad—especially the room. Not waking up in the morning in the midst of a multitude. Pray for Dick.

Love,

James (Powers) 1939

1 Jim's brother, who was running wild at the time.
2 St. Joseph's Hospital, St. Paul, Minnesota.

Sandstone
October 19, 1944

Dear Charlotte and Bill,

[. . .] This is the best time of the year for me, and I'm glad to think I'll see and smell some of it this year. I'm writing this on my lunch hour, birch trees stick up in the distance like white whiskers. The sky is dull grey and blue. [. . .] How I wish I had my typewriter, or the right to use one, when I look at my handwriting. Now a train is whistling across the frozen plains, and of course I'm put in mind of November. Till I hear from you again—Happy Days.

James (Powers) 1939

Jim was paroled on November 1, 1944, and, as a condition of his release, was assigned a job as an orderly at St. Joseph's Hospital, St. Paul, Minnesota. At first his duties included work in the morgue, an assignment he found unbearable; later he was given the job of sterilizing instruments on the night shift.

CHARLES SHATTUCK

St Joseph's Hospital
St Paul, Minnesota
November 3, 1944

Dear Mr Shattuck,

This will be a note, no more, to let you know I am out in the world again. I was paroled to this hospital November 1, All Saints' Day. You wouldn't think the government had such a feel for the liturgy. I am in my room in an adjoining building known as the Boys' Dormitory. So far the majority of the Boys are still in the throes of having solemnized Pay Day. That's the way one nun explained it to me. They are maintenance men and so forth and like the Middle Ages, the strange, maimed flock that always attaches itself to Catholic institutions. Civil Service wd never stand for them. When they find out I am a conscientious objector, they will either canonize or slaughter me . . .

[. . .]

Had to move a still sweaty stiff, fat too, around in the autopsy room yesterday. Wish T. S. Eliot might have been there. I will probably settle down to work in the operating rooms and orderly. Today I worked from seven to three, which leaves a good hunk of the day to me. Marred today by necessity to report to Police (as I'm one convicted of a felony), and it's funny to see them trying to take the questions and fingerprinting and photography seriously, all the rigmarole designed to keep society safe. [. . .]

Will send you something if I can write something. I may have ossified under censorship and indolence. [. . .]

Jim Powers

JOHN MARSHALL

St Joseph's Hospital
St Paul, Minnesota
[Late 1944 or early 1945]

Dear Marsh,

Friday evening and I have just received your card. [. . .] I have just been lying here on my bed, waiting for a certain bug to bite me again (presently, I don't know where he is on my person) and considering the nature of the religious who run places like this hospital: the latter train of thought precipitated by what we had, or didn't have for supper tonight. I ate a piece of bread and a glass of milk and left the scene of the crime. Fortunately, I am under no obligation to earn a living wage and can go out and eat a meal when this happens (this week, four times). [. . .] Write to me again, especially when you run out of postcards. And God—not the God of institutions—may He bless you.

Jim

JOHN MARSHALL

St Joseph's Hospital
St Paul, Minnesota
April 9, 1945

Dear Marsh,

I rec'd yours this morning and derive some consolation from your misery, as it seemed to take the edge off mine. You at least are a young man and have your life before you. Me, I am growing old and fast. I am moreover like a fish thrown up on a sandbank and left to lie there in the sun. I am speaking of the jolly hospital and, as Private Carr wd say, the fucking medical profession. Don't say a word against the fucking medical profession! All of which means things are beginning to catch up with me. The sunniness is gone out of my mien (remember?). Last Thursday and again Saturday (supposed to be my "day off") I worked till nigh on midnight cleaning up the morgue after the fucking medical profession. My sands are running out. I am not writing.

More and more I am considering the uselessness of trying to sandwich in a little sense in all this nonsense. There is no room for writing in my days and nights. The only extracurricular vocation open to me is that of the alcoholic. One could be drunk fairly regularly and get by. There are provisions for that. But when one is trying to set down something in writing and it grieves one's soul to see how it comes out, and then just when some of the awfulness, through work and revision, is going out of it, there comes the call to the post room.[1] What then? I am in love with the idea of nihilism and tolerable of unions. The first settles this hash for good, and the other comes to hard terms with it. I have thought of working a transfer somewhere, not that I'm sure it isn't this way everywhere and always, but I know it's a forlorn project. I have only my reasons. I can't think of a single one of *theirs*—and them's the ones that count. [. . .]

I have letters from editors wanting things, and I can't get time to produce them. The time I get is hardly enough to type them. I am becoming a has-been without ever having really *been*. Now, I don't want to mislead you into thinking I actually think my chips are all cashed in, but I do want you to know, as I'm beginning to, this spare-time creation ain't what I cracked it up to be in jail. Peace. Write.

     Jim

JOHN MARSHALL

St Joseph's Hospital
St Paul, Minnesota
April 27, 1945

Dear Marsh,

A line from the hospital. No enemas, etc., at the moment. [. . .] I am simply moldering. I am constantly tired. I walked down to the river after supper tonight. It is good down there. Things can be seen for miles: trains, limestone cliffs, the river losing and finding itself in the sun. But I

---

1 Postmortem room.

haven't the power to do more than fall on a bench and listen and look in a daze not of my own making. I wonder if I am physically deficient—or whether indolence has reached the tertiary state with me. [. . .]

I think if I had nothing to do—no work—I'd be all right. But I must say that it seems strange that I am not up to sweating for my daily bread like the others. God, it is often said, gives what he intends to take away, and only enough of whatever it is to go around. It seems now that I am only getting enough—to the last drop—to get me through the days. I find, on rereading this, I'm pouring out my heart to you. It all comes, probably, from the fact that I'm not writing anything these days. I don't feel quite the cad I did a few months ago; then, it seemed, I had a *little* time. Now I have none which doesn't suffer from the effect of rising and retiring. In and out of bed. A bug in a glass. [. . .]

Pax,

Jim

Jim found a girlfriend in a young woman, just out of high school, who also worked at the hospital. "Hugs and kisses, nothing else," she reported in a letter after Jim's death. "He coaxed me into giving him my high-school ring—I had just graduated. I left for nurses' training in September. [. . .] He never returned the ring."

JOHN MARSHALL

St Joseph's Hospital
St Paul, Minnesota
June 18, 1945

Dear Marsh,

Rec'd your letter today and was very happy to have it. I should have answered your previous one before this, but it was so full of things hard to write about and I kept thinking there'd come a day. There didn't, so I must simply say, as we say in the Men's Dining Room here, It's rough and tough and hard to stay with. You are indeed a very sensitive and complicated person, as even somebody like Domrese[1] could see, and the world is made to smash you if you are that and not some more things besides.

---

1 Walter J. Domrese, warden's assistant at Sandstone Federal Penitentiary.

Since you are some more things, you will be all right, I think. In fact I think I should be in the same boat if I were so fortunate, or unfortunate, as to be knee-deep in quail, the way you are.

I had my first chance, the first that was really right from all angles and especially the physical, in the last two or three weeks, but I put my foot down, thus hamstringing the moment for the comforts of the long view. I see myself a little better now and do not sally forth with quite the abandon, with only a heavy cargo of fine expressions which usually came to something else in the minds of my loved ones, but that was all right then as I kept hammering away at what I meant, which was usually something about beauty or life's tough and why not make the most of it, and all the time I was getting my carnal share. But my problems are not over by any means in that respect. I page through *Harper's Bazaar* and see several women each month I'd seriously consider settling down with if they weren't just in *Harper's Bazaar*,[1] so you can see I am still entertaining the idea of crossing over.

But now to other things. Quite a few people like the *CW*[2] stuff, and quite a few don't; it splits up into those who think of me as the fine young writer of fine short stories and those who welcome a little propaganda from any quarter and don't know much about the other. But I, as you suspect, know what I'm doing. Watch the *CW* as I have another coming and it's got its boots laced way up to here. After all I am, as I always maintained, a simple soul and simply don't want my sons (if I can get my wife out of *Harper's Bazaar*) to be a fuckin' soldier.

I am moving into other quarters. To the Marlborough. That is an old red stone dump creaking with age and old women where I will have two rooms, so to speak, by the grace of God and a piece of molding bisecting them, and a toilet I can call my own as well as a bathtub that sits out in one of the rooms with a lid on it. Sounds like (that letter) a fine setup for an old deflowerer of Quaker womanhood like yourself, the one-balled fury. It is a block from the cathedral, but truth to tell I don't intend to do much about that. The view is the thing, looking out over the City of St Paul and farther over the river and into the distant sun-swept hills. When I told Weinstein[3] this, he said ah ha at last you are set up in the approved *Esquire* style. Then—sound of

1 A conceit of E. B. White's in "Dusk in Fierce Pajamas," *The New Yorker*, January 27, 1934.
2 Jim had written some edifying pieces for *The Catholic Worker*.
3 Harold Weinstein, fellow inmate at Sandstone.

distant trumpets—I begin to write. [. . .] See you around. Let me hear from you.

    Jim

For a few months, Jim shared his place at the Marlborough on Summit Avenue in St. Paul with Ted LeBerthon, a newspaperman, critic, and writer who was involved with the Catholic Worker movement.

JOHN MARSHALL

150 Summit Avenue
St Paul, Minnesota
July 9, 1945

Dear Marsh,

    [. . .]

Your schedule literally knocks me out, just to scan through. How can you do it? I do not mean to express only amazement but curiosity. I want to know for my own sake. I find myself constantly weary, dropping in and out of bed in a way I never did before. I mean before the Stone. I was talking to a fellow who was hot on B Complex, but you know how luke-warm I am about anything in packages or via machinery, like your short-wave set. If I get some of this B Complex, it will be like going in to buy some condoms, that painful—which by the way I managed to do only once, in Juarez, and I was not moving only under my own power at the time. So you might, from what you know of my case, put a couple of dogs on it and let me know how it turns out. I have a lot of work to do and will never make it in my present condition. [. . .]

Now it is 10:30 in the evening, and I must go down the hill to the hospital. My American Sterilizer is waiting on a park bench for me. I work nights now, you know. 11–7. Get a couple of hours sitting or reading in. No posts.[1] Few people. Little food. Some heat. Also deliver ice at sunup. I am a familiar figure with my ice and tongs. I can't recall whether I told you I had moved: two rooms with a view.

    Jim

1 Postmortems.

Father Harvey Egan became Jim's greatest correspondent and an extraordinarily generous literary patron. He was also an industrious writer and sender of pamphlets, the subjects of which changed with his own galloping enthusiasms. Like Garrelts, Egan was, at this time, a zealous Detacher; that is to say, both priests were adherents of the rigorously ascetic movement known as Detachment.[1] Still, Egan's embrace of this persuasion did not affect his passion for baseball, horse racing, boxing, and hockey.

HARVEY EGAN

The Marlborough
Just off Leicester Square
Old St Paul's
July 25, 1945

Dear Reverend,

I'm going to give you one more chance before taking my cause to a higher authority. I am not ignorant of the sender of a series of cryptic missives received by me or my servants. The single, dread word "Detacher" is enough. I will not pretend to be unaffected. I am, as it would be foolish to deny, a man with a past. But I have paid my debt to society once, nay, a hundredfold, for I was in the beginning, as I am now, and ever shall be, an innocent man. I was, in fine, a Jansenist, a great follower of Baius,[2] Quesnel,[3] and the Saints[4] (Lanahan Blanks Blues, 3–0), yes, I guess I had my fun and there's still the piper to pay. But you are not the piper, Reverend Sir, and if it is not clear that I wish to put all that you and your ill-starred ilk represent behind me, then, forsooth, as I say, I shall seek out justice from the highest authority in the land. I have already sought action from a prelate I imagined to be your superior (he lives up the street from me), but my letter has been returned, initialed it is true, but saying only, "No longer with us. Try the Methodists or Presbyterians. Sorry." If you are, as His Excellency seems to believe, now with these other sects, the next threatening note or sign I have from you or any other practitioner of Detachismus will send me scurrying after protection, peace,

---

1 See Introduction.
2 Michael Baius (1513–1589), Belgian theologian.
3 Pasquier Quesnel (1634–1719), French Jansenist theologian.
4 St. Paul Saints, American Association baseball team. Farm team of the Brooklyn Dodgers at this time.

and justice (else this war be mockery!), yes, I'll not stop short of Harry[1] himself. I have spoken. Take heed.

J.a.S.S.W.F.O.I.T.

Just a Simple Soul Who Found Out in Time.

P.S. To think I once thought butter sinful!

JOHN MARSHALL

150 Summit Avenue
(the home of happy feet)
September 13, 1945

Dear Marsh,

I am tearing this off in the wee hours of the morning. You came to mind as I entered the realm of X-ray, cystoscopy, diathermy. [. . .] As for your private life, in some lamentable respects, it resembles my own, and I think I'll just skip that. I can go to confession. I don't know what you can do . . . wait it out, I suppose. I use that sometimes myself, instead of confession, as confession in some circumstances strikes me as the easy way out (a way to miss the meaning, destroy the chance of changing through experience); too much so. I do not believe I'll get married, ever. If so, it will be like lightning. I do not expect to be hit by that either. And I will not even go so far as to say, on the other hand, you never know . . . I see too much too soon in women to get very far along.

Recently, I've had glimmers of what a challenge it would be honestly to try to be a saint; glimmers in all the darkness, one or two or three. I am not much tempted, in what I imagine to be the classical sense (St Anthony), but all it comes to is "something to do" instead of cheering or barking, a chance to wag my tail over something one degree more than nothing. Sometimes I enjoy music more (do you know Ravel, *La Valse*?), but music is a sometimes thing. Sex, on the other hand, always affords that minor lift—or the idea at bottom does, if not it itself. The small pleasure of pulling one's fingers out of the dike; the sorrow soon after; the struggle to get the dike in shape again. Tick, tock, night, day, night . . . if the square root of death is one hour, you know it is not so long, life, and every hour in between is, if you could only let yourself see it, you would get up and

1 Harry Truman.

leave this interminable double feature after the thousandth time you saw it. Write.

     Jim

Elizabeth "Betty" Wahl had graduated that spring from the College of St. Benedict in St. Joseph, four miles from St. John's in Collegeville, Minnesota. She had been Sister Mariella Gable's prize student and was now living at home with her parents in nearby St. Cloud, working as a bookkeeper for her father Art Wahl's construction company. She was also writing a novel under the tutelage of Sister Mariella, who eventually asked Jim to read the manuscript and come up to St. Benedict's to discuss it. One cannot help seeing matchmaking on Gable's part and starry-eyed aspiration on Betty's. Twenty-one years old, romantic, and worshipful, Betty considered the ideal marriage to be union with the mind, body, and soul of a great artist. As for Jim, he was clearly in the mood to be hit by lightning.

MARIELLA GABLE

150 Summit Avenue
October 15, 1945

Dear Sister Mariella,

    [. . .] I shall be pleased to read Miss Wahl's book, only asking that you send it on and give me until, say, sometime in early November to get it read and up there to talk about it, as you suggest. [. . .] I am conscious of the possible irony in my criticizing the work of someone who has turned out 70,000 words at 21, words which you must not think badly of. But we shall see. I guess I might have more to my credit if I'd been born a girl or as I am with money enough so I wouldn't have to work at the nonsense I always have had to, or if the call to the colors hadn't gone out when I was ripe for them, or, as Ted LeBerthon says, if my aunt had whiskers she'd be my uncle. I am amused that you found me a "stripling." I wish I were five years younger at least. [. . .] Ted LeBerthon, who now lives with me on the sixth floor of this old brownstone ghost of a building, is 53, and most of the time it seems to be the other way around. We can still lie awake at night (Sundays, when I don't work, anyway) and talk. It is something I used to do as a child and again in high school (the chances of our team in the state tournament) and also when I graduated and hit Chicago (Pater, Huysmans,

Baudelaire, Symons). But I don't think I'll want to talk in bed when I'm 53. [. . .]

JFP

150 Summit Avenue
October 23, 1945

Dear Sister Mariella,

A line to let you know I rec'd your letter and the MS today. I have just finished the first chapter and without going any further would be willing to bet on the book and with more certainty on future books from Miss Wahl. The title, I think, is very bad: the first paragraph likewise. But after that it rides right along. [. . .] There is a very rare honesty, it seems to me, about the first chapter. I am even a little awestruck by it. [. . .] I like especially the *ease* with which Miss Wahl writes. Shattuck (of *Accent*) would love it. I have a private opinion ease comes easier with women. [. . .] A woman I know, the mother of a close friend, works as a saleslady in a department store. She used to run out and rub the back of a hunchback, calling him "old huncher," for good luck. I was fascinated with the idea of it, or not only the idea (the cruelty of it lurking at several removes) but this particular woman involved in it, but the more I said it in various ways to myself the further I got away from the art of the thing. [. . .]

Best,

Jim

MARIELLA GABLE

150 Summit Avenue
November 1, 1945

Dear Sister Mariella,

I think I ought to tell you the weekend of the 11th looks likely. [. . .] I will say I think the book ought and—which is more—will be published. I would offer the services of my agents[1] if Miss Wahl would care to have them. [. . .] But we can talk about that too. I should want (if my criticism is to be abided by, and I am not sure I wish it so) to go through every chapter. Such things as the candle making, the Sister who presides there,

1 Henry Volkening.

should be the case more often in this book. I feel something about the place (St Benedict's) is very wonderful and unique and deserves more going into than it gets. But, as before, more anon.

Best. Pax.

MARIELLA GABLE

150 Summit Avenue
November 6, 1945

Dear Sister Mariella,

[. . .] I have been negotiating with buses and trains and nuns. [. . .] It might be easier for all of us for you to leave the convent and for Miss Wahl to run away from home. [. . .]

Pax.

Jim finally met Betty Wahl on Saturday, November 10, 1945, and proposed marriage to her two days later. She accepted.

2

With you it will be like being ten years old again

November 12, 1945—November 29, 1945

Betty Wahl (left) *and Jim* (below)

Jim and Betty's engagement produced hundreds of letters. Jim's were filled with love and yearning, even Betty's way of saying grace before meals stirred him: "You say it with more beauty than anyone I've ever seen. It is perfect when you say it, like a dog digging a hole with his muzzle." The engagement also brought Jim more frequently to the environs of St. John's Abbey and University in Collegeville, Minnesota, a place awash with Catholic reform. Jim called the region "Big Missal Country," a witty reference to the prayer book whose use was ardently promoted by liturgical reformers. Jim already had an association with the place through his radical and reforming Catholic friends whom he called "the Movement." Chief among them was Emerson Hynes, who taught sociology at St John's and was, with his wife, Arleen, a fervent practitioner and leader in the Catholic rural- and family-life movements. Though Jim was fond of these people, he took an increasingly dyspeptic view of most of their causes, especially the emphasis on the family, which made him shudder, and the movement to increase the liturgical role of the laity, which he liked to call anticlericalism.

HARVEY EGAN

St Paul, California[1]
November 12, 1945

Dear Pere,

[. . .] I spent the weekend with Sister Mariella at St Benedict's. I am filled with what I choose to call Benedictinism. I saw Emerson Hynes and wife one night (Sunday), and my faith was shaken. T. à Kempis[2] is now no longer with us. I had thought he enjoyed an irremovable position. Much to talk about with you.

1 Joke.
2 Thomas à Kempis (ca. 1380–1471), author of *The Imitation of Christ*. He was revered by Detachers: a contemplative in contrast to the highly *active* Hyneses.

I have the road more or less prepared for you to enter into their midst.

I met the girl whose novel I was reading for Sister Mariella. I think I will marry her. That, too, to discuss. [. . .]

Pax,

JF

Don Humphrey, another member of the Movement, now enters the letters. An artist, sculptor, and chalice maker, he had also participated in the Catholic Worker movement. At this time he was living in poverty and precarious circumstances with his large family in the Twin Cities area. Jim found the best sort of camaraderie in Humphrey and was appalled by his predicament as a man of great artistic talent whose life was blighted, as Jim saw it, by too many children and no money.

BETTY WAHL

150 Summit Avenue
November 15, 1945

Dear Betty,

This is Thursday, and as I compute it, I should have had a letter from you today. Anyway, I got up at eleven this morning, in case it should be in the morning mail, and again at 2:30 this afternoon in case . . . and so already I am beginning to worry about you. I am standing on this corner, and you do not come. I do not think you are sick, and of course what I really know is that perhaps I could not reasonably expect to hear from you until tomorrow, even if you wrote on Wednesday, as you said you would. I have already had two dreams of you, not what you might think, but along Zane Greyish lines: someone is always getting in the way who has to be destroyed, and what happens then, when the happy ending should begin, I never know.

I also test you in this way: I think at all hours of the day do I want to marry you now. I do this when you might (or I might from my past experience) think the answer would be no, as in the morning, when many of my best-laid plans have stacked up to nothing, ideas and lines for stories written the night before. But the answer is always Yes. It is a little surprising to me each time it is, though a little less each time, of my having taken such a hard view of myself and the idea of holy matrimony for so long. So that is the way it is . . . if you are as you were and have not changed your mind or come to your senses—having seen through me and what a stinker I am, which happened to be one thing I admitted to, as then it always means the opposite. I am not sure of you. I remember looking at you and feeling that I could almost see you making and unmaking up your mind. I don't know why, in either case, granting the other. I ask myself what I would do if you did change your mind, and I know that it would probably not be disastrous, unless you call living one's life out as I have so far, a bachelor, disastrous. In this event I am glad I did not get to know you any better than I did, which incidentally required a deal of restraint on my part, which restraint you may not appreciate in the nature of things. But which you would have if it had been missing and one of those little nuns had come upon the scene with her head full of wholesomeness.

I have been out buying oysters and milk and rolls, and now, with the warmed-up coffee from Ted's lunch, I will eat. It would be good to raise oysters, mushrooms, and cranberries on a farm. Ted and Harrigan (editor, *Catholic Digest*) have just gone to Harrigan's for a farewell dinner. Ted is leaving tomorrow night. Our relationship has been blissful since my return. I think he was actually glad to see me. I told him about you, and he was glad about that (he read the first chapter of your novel and your piece on Catholic education which the *Digest* considered for republication and maybe still does) in a way I find curious. He is of the opinion I need someone like you, believing I will go wacky otherwise, meaning what he regards as "perfectionism" in writing leading to that. But now I think I'll leave this letter where it is for today, hoping for tomorrow.

Saturday. I am up again this morning, and how very, very glad I was to get your letter (and how could I write to you when I hadn't your address; but I did write to you, as see the foregoing, only not mailing it). [. . .] But now there is your letter, and you say you love me, once directly and once, at the end, glancingly, and I am very happy about that. No, it is twice directly. That is better. I have read your letter four times already. HG, I am given the light to understand now, is Holy Ghost. At first it puzzled me. I am, descending to the level of important things which really don't matter, but are better the way you say they are, happy your family is losing its peculiar antagonism to me.[1]

I love you, Betty. It is the first time, I know now, I ever loved anybody. But even if I'd never met you, this I know: I had never loved anybody the

---

1 This would have been based on Jim's stint in prison, his pacifism, and, above all, his not having what the Wahls considered a job.

way one is supposed to. So you are the first one. Do not catch pneumonia and die. God is against these things; for some reason really known to him and the cause for much dull absurdity on the part of the theologians, he does not want them to last. But, God, I say, this is different—and not just different in the ridiculous way I knew people thought their affairs, because theirs, were different. This is different, I feel, in an absolute sense. [. . .]

I want you to do two things in this letter: (a) send me your telephone number; (b) send me a dime store ring which fits you. I am going to get Don Humphrey to make a ring. I am going to Robbinsdale[1] tomorrow to see him and Fr Garrelts. I will tell them, as I know I've told too many already, Sylvester in Guatemala among them, that we are to be married. When, at the very earliest, could you come to St Paul? Ma mere is coming next week. I was thinking last night, providing you still loved me, we could go to Chicago maybe in Jan. or Feb. Tell me.

I love you, Betty.

Jim

MARIELLA GABLE

150 Summit Avenue
November 17, 1945

Dear Sister Mariella,

I have put off thanking you for everything in writing because I remember you were to be in two or three places and very busy this week or the one coming or both. I had my first letter from Betty today—after meeting the mailman for two or three days. It was a very nice letter, and I have read it too often already. [. . .] I have told everyone I've seen or written to since my return how you do things at St Benedict's. I use the poetic method. For instance, I tell my mother you scrub the kitchen three times a day and two nuns went blind making St George and the Dragon. [. . .]

Fr Egan has invited me over for Thanksgiving: it will be interesting to see what kind of table Detachismus sets on that day. I must tell him about St Benedict's and Betty. I called Fr Garrelts (tomorrow I'm going to Robbinsdale), and I actually felt sorry for him, as I do for myself, as I was . . . before Betty. [. . .] Pax —Jim

1 Church of the Sacred Heart, Robbinsdale, where Garrelts was assistant.

150 Summit Avenue
November 20, 1945

My dear Betty,

[. . .] Summer is terrible here, and my job is worse (I sweat lakes), but with you it will be like being ten years old again. And we can plot our getaway for the months we'll have to stay here. It is two blocks to the cathedral. There is Summit Avenue to take walks on. I have no friends in St Paul, but in Robbinsdale is Fr Garrelts (Fr Egan is in St Paul; you will like him) and Mr Chapman (who shuddered the other night when I saw him at the way the Irish are talking up Spellman for pope—"a terrible farce"). Fr Garrelts wants to see you, and so does Don Humphrey and his wife. Don will make the rings. It may be a funny engagement ring, as I do not think I can buy a stone and wouldn't if I could at a jeweler's. [. . .]

November 20. 8:00 p.m. I was supposed to be taking a nap for the last hour. I find it easier to be up with the lights on. I see things around the room to pick up, records, pipes, the typewriter. In the dark I see you. But you are not there. So it is very discouraging and in the long run promises to be an ordeal. I am glad that you suggested an earlier marriage. It will be like getting out of jail sooner. [. . .]

November 21, [. . .]

9:30 in the evening. I have just finished the rough draft of the story I mentioned yesterday. It will be short, 3,000 words; I had the basic idea from Sr Mariella. I will dedicate it to her, but only as SM, as it would probably fix her for good. I call it "The Lord's Day," and it is about nuns who have to count the collections on Sunday afternoon in the priest's house.[1] Do not say anything about it to Sr Mariella. I promised her I would write it, but I did not think I'd get at it so soon. I am thinking of you all the time. I do not know whether I'd get more done if you were here or not here. In either case you are an obstacle to work. [. . .]

Tomorrow Thanksgiving dinner at Madge Egan's (Fr Egan's mother); Fr Garrelts and others to be present. We will all be in our truest American manner. I intend to make heavy references to the Pilgrim fathers (I'm sure Fr Egan has never thought of them as anything but heretics). [. . .]

I have a story in process about an old man who thinks that it is too bad, feeling the way he does about his wife, who has died. If we were married, I would better know how he really feels. I will have to follow my

1 First published in *Cross Section*, 1947.

instincts, as it is. I hope my mother comes this week, so that you can come next or next or both. She is interested to know about you. She has a better perspective than perhaps you do on what it means when I say I intend to marry a girl. She knows I have never said it before. I am sure you will love her—I do not say that loosely or hopefully—I know you will. What is best in me I have from my mother, not that my father is second-rate. No, I mean that what faculty—admittedly underdeveloped—I have for listening and keeping my mouth shut I have from her. That is one of the very big things I see in you that I love and realize the absolute unique beauty of. [. . .] Now it is almost time to put on my silly white suit and leave. I love you and am sorry if I am getting tiresome with that line. [. . .]

Jim

BETTY WAHL

November 25, 1945

Dear Elizabeth Alice of the Sea Green Eyes,

I am taking my Royal (on loan from Egan Enterprises) in hand and endeavoring a reply to your wonderful letter rec'd this day. My mother is just to my left, on the davenport, mending things and sewing on buttons. She says, quote: "You certainly have been neglected." We are running out of buttons (myself, I am a plain dealer and use safety pins). [. . .]

It was most encouraging to hear that your father has been all those things. It is the first time I've felt good about him. You see, I know from experience I never have trouble with people who have been hoboes and so forth. Now I am watching out for your mother: a schoolteacher, whoa. [. . .]

Now, because you have asked for it, I will tell you about me. I was born of poor *and* honest parents, Irish on my father's side (County Waterford, the southernmost part of Ireland, where the name Powers, if you look it up in the *Ecclesiastical Directory*, is still the biggest one there, bishops, college presidents, bartenders, all have it), but his mother's name was Ansberry and she came from Liverpool, and I do not know if that means there's some English, but I think not, as Liverpool, a slummy place, is highly Irish and she was most definitely Catholic.

She was the woman who ruined my father's life, I hold. He supported her instead of accepting offers he had to go to Europe and study piano (he was considered a prodigy about Jacksonville—where I was born, in Illinois—practicing the piano nine and ten hours a day, working in a music store as a player of any and all music sold there at the age of twelve. We have some of his old exercises yet; they are pages more black than white with notes). It is another curse of the Irish to throw themselves away on an aging mother or not to marry because there isn't enough money coming in and brother John, who should undertake his share, is a first-class bastard. I am not making it up: my father had a brother John. I remember him as a tall, dark man with button shoes, gold teeth, and a large brown handful of silver from which he would select a quarter, say, and give it to you. Ten days later you would hear that he was in Boston or Spokane. He wore serge, and sometimes I think I have some of him in me.

My dad's father came here from Ireland, the land of saints and scholars, and worked in the gashouse in Jacksonville. I know very little of him, except that he was probably taken in as my father was after him. Many children, seven or eight, and a large dog who would bite the wrong people by the name of "Guess." What's his name? I remember my father telling me as a child, people would ask. "Guess," they would reply. Joke. So much for my father's side: many unmarried children on that side, maiden literary aunts like my aunt Kate, who read to me as a child; my aunt Mame, still alive, who is being forced out of the house she did huge washings in for fifty years; my aunt Annie, dead, a Catherine of Russia type, a real dictator and organizer, who ran a grocery store with an iron hand and who would give her customers hell every morning if they didn't order enough over the telephone. She liked me. In fact, they all liked me, because I liked them. My sister never did: she thought they were kind of crude. They were.

Turning to my mother's side, we leave the Holy Roman Catholic Church and enter the Old Time Religion, the Methodists.[1] Her mother is now living in Chicago with my father and mother and is now senile, the widow of three or four husbands, a dear old lady who should never have left the small town. She tries to go to the Methodist church in our neighborhood in Chicago, and everyone is nice, the minister shakes her hand after services, but they don't sing right. She wants everybody to join in, and they let one woman do most of it. My mother's father was a farmer

---

1 Jim's mother converted to Catholicism ten years after her marriage.

and painter; we have some of his work, which isn't bad at all (I'll show it to you when we go to Chicago together). He, her father, had nice hair, just like mine, my grandmother thinks. My mother went to college, a rare thing in our families, and did a little gentle sketching. She is a gentle woman.

My father had dance bands before they were married (he had them to make money; I think he hated that kind of music) and worked for Swift and Company. He became a manager and got the idea he was a sure-enough business genius. It was dispelled in 1934. Since that time, until the war and he got this paper-shuffling job, times were tough. Now he takes pride in this job which must go the way of all war efforts. It is too bad he becomes engrossed in secondary things. I subscribed him to *Time*. He likes it. If he sits down at the piano now (which is all out of tune), he fumbles around, and it hurts him worse than anyone. So he gets up and sits down to *Time* [magazine]. The American Tragedy. I think I see what happened. I am determined it shall not happen to me. Help me.

I went to the public schools first, had my first fights for girls, which I won incidentally, and in the third grade transferred to Catholic schools when we moved to Rockford. So on to the seventh grade, when I went back to the public school—it was the day of the purple and green felt hats and "Did you ever hear Pete go tweet, tweet, tweet on his piccolo?" You were six years old then, I was thirteen, smoking cigarettes and kissing girls after school. A year later I found out about masturbation. A year later a Franciscan came to the Catholic school, where I was making my first retreat, and made us all as clean as a hound's tooth. I submerged myself in the athletic life of the place. I had a fight and got my nose broke. I became a basketball star. I also played football. At the end of the year we decided to have a yearbook (my senior year), and I was not chosen to be editor. I did not want to be and, if I had, could not have been. Already I was beginning rather to want to be the dark horse in any enterprise, someone with no office or commitments who would do something daring or impossible and save the day. It is funny now.

I graduated and went to Chicago, where my family had been living for a year. It was hell after Quincy, after leisurely beers (we drank a lot of beer for high-school boys in Quincy), and nothing more serious than typing class or Washington Irving, the only writer I liked then that I could like now, I think. A couple of times I was almost a success. I always wasn't, though, when they finally hired somebody. I went to a public school (college) and quit at the half year to drive a big Packard for a bastard through the South and Southwest. I stayed in dollar hotels, a different one nightly, except for weeks in San Antonio and El Paso, when I would drink too much. I was put in jail in San Antonio, picked up one morning when I was returning from taking the car to be washed. They held me for a half hour when they found out I was from Chicago. The bastard I worked for was at the St Anthony Hotel, the biggest and best, but they preferred to call Chicago. When they decided to let me go, I told them I might be about on the next day and if they didn't have anything to do then—again—they could pick me up again. For this I got the rest of the morning in jail. It was my first jail: scrawlings on the wall, two race-track touts not telling the truth about themselves when I was so naive as to ask, cold white macaroni on a sallow tin plate. Across the border from El Paso is Juarez. Here I lost my virginity. I was nineteen.

I came back to Chicago in the spring. It was terrible still. I worked for Marshall Field's in the book section and met my first homosexuals. I enjoy their company today, so long as the situation is clear to them. I began to read, though while traveling I would look for my material on Sinclair Lewis in every town I'd pass through, and discovered Huxley, Aldington, and then, moving backward, Huysmans, Symons, Verlaine, Baudelaire. I took French lessons privately for two years because I wanted particularly to read Baudelaire. I got a job as an editor on Historical Records, WPA. I fell in love, or roughly speaking, did, with a Romanian girl. She taught me some things. It was the first time I felt that it might be good to know a woman who would worry about whether it was raining or missing a class (I was going to Northwestern at nights). But I spurned such pedestrian stuff. I wanted wine, women, and song—but not domestic wine, married women (married to me), and the best songs, I felt, had been made up at the time of Villon. I was a nice case of nonsense, I suppose. We parted. I met another girl who was more a woman. But I don't think I'll follow this any further . . . it is not good, I see, to go into these deals until we know each other better and perhaps never at all. I know I don't care to know about your affairs or whatever you call them.

Presently I am in love with you, as I have been with nobody else, as indeed I thought not possible for me, and as for other people being in love, I knew what they were all about. I love you, Betty. Please love me accordingly. It has taken me a long time to come to you. I have taken the long way around, and I have missed several turns. I am glad I missed them. I believe there is no one else in the world but you for me. I do not care what Uncle Em or the Catholic Church knows about mating males and females.

You are for me. I hope I am for you. There is no other way. You could kill someone if you told me now you no longer loved me. That is the way it is. Je t'adore is not wrong when I say it to you. I do. [. . .]

Love,
    Jim

JOHN MARSHALL

150 Summit Avenue
November 26, 1945

Dear Marsh,

Your letter rec'd, filed, and now in process of being preserved for posterity. Enjoyed your sample of the professor of anatomy, a dull business, methinks. How can I keep from looking down on doctors? I see little of them now that I work at night, but when I do, I think how meek and humble and poor fare for satire are priests compared to them. Doctors have the world by the balls as priests must have had it in the Middle Ages. A priest asked me why the St Joseph's nuns were so cold toward priests. I had to pretend incredulity and ignorance. I could not tell them that their priests wear white, have plenty of jack, and roll into the place in tweeds in the morning. I am trusting that you will rise above all this. What I mean, I guess, is that they make such an individual deal out of being a doctor (as though they were artists) when they are popped out of the medical factories like horseflies in August. You know all this, and I am not talking to you. I am just a little irritated, I suppose, to have to carry beer in a saloon the sign out front of which I don't care for. September, let us pray, I'll be a free man. [. . .]

I have met a girl I intend to marry in May or June. She is a writer, unpublished except for the college magazine, contests—Americanism, what I like about it—and *Atlantic Monthly* essay contests. She has written a beautiful novel. She is as fine as, say, you are, and I hope I won't be too crude for her. Catholic, of course, my priestly connections would never permit me to entertain heresy on such a permanent basis as marriage. [. . .]

Harry Sylvester is coming back from Guatemala in the spring to teach a seminar at St Benedict's (where Sister Mariella is head of the English department); Emerson Hynes, a rural lifer and a fine fellow despite all that, and a couple of other interesting people are bedded down in the vicinity (Back to Benedict). I expect my wife to be more popular than I'll ever be. That may sound like murder at a distance, but she is also a UChristian of the sort I've never come against before. I mean she *is* without being ugly, and so isn't of necessity. Likes Dante. Me, I like Grain Belt, a friendly beer.

Pax. Write.

Jim

BETTY WAHL

150 Summit Avenue
November 28, 1945

My dear Betty,

[. . .] Well, when I got up today, I found the toilet lying on its side like a wounded horse and the floor up in chunks all over the bathroom. It seems something broke, or has been broke for quite a while, causing water to drip down below. But since, as the plumber put it, I am not home much, the former occupants didn't mind a minimum of dripping, but now someone new lives downstairs, and they don't like dripping, even a minimum of it. I guess they're stuck up. [. . .]

I love you.

Jim

BETTY WAHL

150 Summit Avenue
November 29, 1945

My dear Elizabeth Alice,

[. . .] I have a large case of whiskers presently but can't get into the bathroom for the plumber and his toys, which are all over the place. No, Betty, we will "never have our first fight." I am counting on you to prevent that by seeing the ultimate truth in whatever opinion I hold on anything—such as pajamas. Why are you so stuck on pajamas? It makes me uncomfortable to think of you sleeping in pajamas and whatever else you wear, as implied. I think of LeBerthon in his ski suit. I am open to persuasion, however, but you will have to prove it to me along approved debating lines. Think of the poets, probably even Dante, I can summon to my side of the question. You will have only Edgar Guest and Longfellow (who slept in his beard, which is not the same thing) on your side. The angels—do you think they use pajamas?

I am sorry you prefer Fuzzwick to my middle name. I do not know what that means. I wonder if you could be contemplating violence where my dignity is concerned. Do you intend to make of me one of those hapless American males with a funny name, such as Blondie's husband, Dagwood? Beware, young woman, if so. It will go hard with you, and Mother Church will back me up, you know that, where discipline is involved, she is on the man's side (that is what Don Humphrey likes about it and what Mary Humphrey doesn't like). Now I am going to cut this off. I enclose a key to the apartment instead of putting it under the door. You keep it until you need it in May or June. Also some more mail—to show you what a big demand there is for authentic JFP on the market. (Actually, I am worried, but hope to lay up a few stories this winter, like squirrels bury nuts.)

I love you.

Jim

3

Should a giraffe have to dig dandelions?

December 4, 1945—January 26, 1946

*Father Harvey Egan ("Dear Pere . . . you can get your
checkbook out any day now.")*

Betty paid her first visit to Jim in St. Paul. She came by train from St. Cloud and spent a couple of days with him in relative chastity. In his letters, Jim began his campaign to drive home to her that he really did not intend to take a job. At the same time, he was becoming increasingly concerned about Don Humphrey's situation of near homelessness and ever more disgusted by the failure of those who had the wherewithal to support him to come through with the goods.

BETTY WAHL

150 Summit Avenue
December 4, 1945
A few minutes before seven the next morning.

Dear Betty,

A line to let you know I love you. I am feeling terrible this morning, and a couple of times last night I wondered if I would make it. I was deadly tired when you left. I guess I was tired when you were here but didn't know it with you to be near. In a few minutes I'll take a bath and go to bed. I will take this, and Fr Egan's letters, which I forgot to mail, downstairs first, though. I hope when we're married and living here you won't have such a tremendous effect on me, that it won't seem too much like hell to leave you and go through the motions I have to at the hospital. I know you must be worn out too today and hope you will sleep. You did look pale when I left you or you left me last night. You must be healthy if you are going to carry your cross, which is me, successfully.

I love you this morning.

Jim

150 Summit Avenue
December 5, 1945

My dear Betty,

I am up—it's almost two—and have read your little letter and am very glad to find there's nothing wrong. Sometimes it takes people two or three days to think things over, and I had been wondering if there'd been any cause for regrets. Had I done something all wrong? I've also been down for a quart of milk and six sweet rolls; the coffee is cooking now. In a few minutes I'll sit down to one of my famous home-cooked meals—which I hope you didn't find too rugged. I guess not, if you've not lost any weight. I am virtually recovered today. Yesterday I was still groggy from Monday night.

About the stars—why is it I'm a butterfly, and what does that mean? I am afraid it means the same old thing—fly-by-night, which is getting to be my middle name, and I had always thought, and thought others thought, I was fairly stable and all that. I can't put my finger on just what it is, whether it's because I don't intend to sell insurance or work in a bank or because I wouldn't dress up and play war with the rest of the fellows, or because I am a writer (if I am a writer) or what the hell it is. Anyway, I am getting touchy on the subject. Perhaps there is this much truth in it: I am worried about making a living, as I confessed to you again and again, because I won't go about it in the ordinary way—eight hours out of my life daily so that the system may prosper and the crapshooters running it.

But I don't think you want me to do that. If you do, it would be well to say so now. It is not something you can bring me around to in the name of "reform." I have no intention of letting you go, but if you have that idea (and I can't believe you have), I want you to get rid of it—else it will be worse than the War of Roses. My mother strove for years and years, with all things in her favor (five-day notices fluttering on the door), and she never won. I got little jobs, but she never won, and now she knows it. And, furthermore, I think it's indecent of Sister Mariella, and whoever else thinks so, that you should marry some dumb farmer who'll "make you a good husband"—for which I read "bull." It is because of such arrangements that we have war and strife: people getting the barn painted and letting the living room moulder away with a vase of wax flowers and the Sears, Roebuck catalog. There is much truth in the line about if you have a loaf of bread, sell it and buy hyacinths for your soul. I am not really talking to you when I write this, I think and hope I'm not. I am only if in my nearsightedness I have missed the little signs that my regeneration includes prostitution on a job masking itself as "honest labor." The jobs I had, in bookstores and the rest, were never honest. Not for me. Should a giraffe have to dig dandelions or a worm fly a kite? Now I see I've run into a corner I never meant to get into and the whole idea here is one I know you and I don't disagree on. I think I must just be threatening myself. [. . .]

I got a fine letter from that unpredictable lady La Mariella (she does so many good things and says so many bad things—yes, the farmer business again). She sent a photo of a house, a long description of it, and even posed as a possibility that Don might teach a little at St B.'s, as the Reverend M. has been wanting to enlarge the art dept. I sent all this data on to Fr G., and I know he'll go over to Don's tonight and make him very happy with it.

It doesn't take much of an opportunity to give Don all he needs (he caught deer with barbed wire fence when his family was living on the Catholic Worker Farm, Aitkin, Minn., and not just for fun, for they were hungry). I told you how he caught that chicken, remember? Sister M. mentions the possibility of Don finding work with an antique repairer in St Cloud (there's only one, evidently, and it takes months to get things repaired). That's what Don is doing now, for money. If he could live in this house (it's owned by the postmistress, a Miss Uhte) and teach a little and work a little and paint a lot—that would be wonderful. He is the greatest Catholic painter since El Greco. He is a wood-carver, sculptor, and chalice maker (and ring maker). For money he has repaired antiques, worked in a foundry as a molder, carpentry, and in fact anything that has the vaguest connection with the plastic arts and crafts. His wife is a churchgoer in the worst Irish sense. She is very fine also, not much on housecleaning, however; she'd rather go to church. She looms rugs. And now I come to the part in this letter where I want to tell you:

I love you. [. . .] Pax,
    Jim

BETTY WAHL

150 Summit Avenue
December 7, 1945

Dear Betty,
    Friday, noon [. . .]
    And, returning to your letter of yesterday, don't go telling Sr Mariella stuff, even in jest, like you're going to be a stenographer and let me be

great. We have to watch ourselves, else I am never going to be able to redeem myself in their eyes and stop being . . . a butterfly. I will, as you
suggest, watch my greens. I ate an apple this morning, which is a green,
isn't it? I do not have time to be lugging lettuce and stuff like that up here
and getting it combed down on a plate. I will wait for you to do that. By
the way, since I've just thought it, I'll mention it: I will make you a suit of
lettuce underwear, cool, succulent, to match your skin. Your aunt seems
to know all.[1] All my worries about properly impressing your family are
beginning to center on her. If I can get past her, I think, I'm in. [. . .]

    I love you.

    Jim

CHARLES SHATTUCK

150 Summit Avenue
Saint Paul, Minnesota
December 7, 1945

Dear Chuck,

    [. . .] I am living on the sixth floor of the Marlborough, once the show-
piece of St Paul, on Fitzgerald's famous Summit Avenue—which he calls
Crest in his notes—and it is falling to pieces, but I like it that way, high
ceilings, wide doors, everywhere space being wasted, and my window
gives me a look at the city, the countryside beyond on a clear day, and I
like that too, as I believe I contracted a slight case of claustrophobia that
year or so I was out of circulation. I have a phonograph and a coffeepot. I go
from Ravel to Respighi to Rimski-Korsakov and back again. I get up when
I feel like it, and sometimes when I don't feel like it, and eat what I care
to cook, which means usually coffee, rolls, hamburger, or soup.

    I am within walking distance (easy) to the library and post office; spit-
ting distance to the cathedral, the most formidable one I've seen; and
equally close to the ghosty houses that Fitzgerald was so impressed by
and me too. It is a funny thing: 599 Summit, where he wrote *This Side of
Paradise*, is solid smoky vermilion stone like so many of the other old places
along Summit, but—and a Freudian could do a thesis here—it is the first
place which is cut into several apartments, a hard man would even call
them "flats," and so he was right up against what he couldn't penetrate,
the one colored kid in the schoolroom, and I guess that's why he was

---

1 Bertha "Birdie" Seberger Strobel.

always so acutely aware of the society he was never an integral part of and could write about it as though he were, but which he'd have to have been decayed inside to have been and hence would have lacked the energy to do anything about except yawn. (Take that sentence to the cleaners next time you go.)

Continuing with my report on myself, which nobody asked to hear, including you, I am also in love. I met a girl at St Benedict's when I was up there a few weeks ago, a girl whose novel in manuscript Sr Mariella had sent me to read. She is a beautiful, simple writer, and I think you would like her writing. [. . .] I expect we will be married in May. In September we expect to retire into the woods in the vicinity of St John's and St Benedict's. [. . .]

Pax,

Jim

BETTY WAHL

150 Summit Avenue
Tuesday morning, 4:30 a.m., December 11, 1945

Dear Betty,

I am thinking of you now, so much as in my grogginess I am capable of thinking of anything, I am not thinking of my work, that I know. [. . .] Over the weekend, between Surgery and OB, they get out everything, and I have to sterilize it. I hope I do not die too early a death, or that you will ever have to work at the kind of job most people do. You will lose the nice sense of justice you possess now (which does not seem to be justice to me sometimes when it comes out in you), and you will not be so impressed by order, but will be more intent in stirring up a little chaos of your own. Somebody, Maritain, I guess, says too many people in the church and high places want justice based on order, instead of order based on justice.

So it is here. The hospital runs along pleasantly to the outside eye. But if you know the truth, it is that the floors get mopped and the garbage gets taken out because a sufficient number of men and women have made a mess of their lives and upon that broken rock the hospital runs; likewise the nurses who must go through three years of training in order to be able to earn six or seven dollars a day, and there is nothing they do that might not be acquired in a year easily. [. . .] I love you and want you to love me. [. . .]

Jim

Don Humphrey's plight was the specter before Jim of a future he feared for himself. He believed his friend was being sacrificed to the "business sense" of those whose privilege it should have been to assist him.

BETTY WAHL

150 Summit Avenue
December 11, 1945

My dear Betty,

I've been rushing around today ever since I got up, and I got up late—3:00, which is because I was tired from last night. It is seven or so in the evening. I've just written a letter to Harry Sylvester that I hated to write, asking him to buy the house for Don, at least until he comes in the spring. [. . .]

Your distraction,
Jim

BETTY WAHL

150 Summit Avenue
December 12, 1945

My dear Betty, and heavy on the "my":

Well, since I got up two hours ago (it's now 2:30 in the afternoon), I've been writing letters (Fr Garrelts, my friend Haskins[1] in Washington—all about you—and Abigail McCarthy). About "business": I think I told you that I'd written to Harry Sylvester asking him to let Don live in the house until spring if he bought it. I think, on the strength of Emerson's recommendation, which must precede my letter three or four days to Guatemala, that he will buy the house and that Don will be permitted to live there until his, Harry's, return. Which will amount to what you so kindly outline, a temporary shelter, but closer to things than the cottages you mention. [. . .] I am trusting then that Harry will buy the house; that Don will be able to move in, say, by the first of January; and that, until spring, he'll be able to impress the nuns at the college with his work and that finally he'll be able to find a place, or, better, build one such as he wants.

I find the extant houses around St Joseph's very undesirable, too high, terrible cracker boxes. Whenever I start hitting *Collier's* at $1,700 per, I

1 John Haskins.

will have my friend Jack Howe, who slept next to me in the clink (and Frank Lloyd Wright's right-hand man), draw a house just for us (he will not put a basement in it, however; they abhor basements). And that, I hope, takes care of houses until we hear from Harry and until we have to begin thinking of one for ourselves. (Won't that be a business?) I am getting confused by the situation. No money, a real need, and distance between us and the field of operations. I have attempted, in today's letter, to involve Fr Garrelts more . . . [. . .]

I love you.

Jim

BETTY WAHL

150 Summit Avenue

December 27, 1945

Dear Betty,

[. . .] Yesterday I went to Robbinsdale, and there were the Humphreys filled with the new life. Today a letter from Harry Sylvester saying he will not buy the house. He believes he is being robbed, among other things, and is looking for someone to blame. I have written to him, offering myself. I hope that I'll never have any money if it makes me that wary. I tried to call Fr Garrelts, but got Mr Chapman "Hello, AC. This Is JF." I'll call again tomorrow. There is no hurry about letting Don know. Harry wrote to Emerson and Sister Mariella too. I hope something turns up.

It is too bad Harry makes it sound as bad for himself as he does, or maybe he doesn't in the other letters. He talks about being "finished" with me and St Ben's; that is, he thinks his decision not to buy will finish him. That is silly. But just goes to show you how utterly normal supposedly enlightened people can be. I hope Sr Mariella will be able to cool him off and save his self-esteem. It will not be easy, considering the way he's got things twisted around. [. . .] Harry says: "Neither you nor Sister Mariella have a so-called business sense, and you are even proud of the lack; I wish I could afford to be without one." Hmmmmm. How does one get a business sense? I think it is nine-tenths talking dull and acting as though you have one. Do you have a business sense? I wonder if he means I don't write stories for *Collier's*. Suppose I sold a story there. What would he think then? I do not think he'd like it. [. . .]

Best to all and love to you.

Jim

St Joseph's Hospital
St Paul, Minnesota
Friday morning, 3:00 a.m., December 28, 1945

Dear Betty,

[. . .] I've been thinking we ought to go to Ireland as soon as we can when married. I am beginning to wonder if we can afford to settle down. Every time I think of the Humphreys, I feel rotten. I still haven't got Fr Garrelts yet, so suppose they are blissfully ignorant that they're out in the cold again. Confidentially, I do not want to see too much of the Sylvesters, after this. It must be very convenient to be able to assess one's dreams— for I assume that's what living at St Joe was for them, the prospect—at so many hundred dollars and if they come too high to abandon them. I'll be at the station to meet you Sunday. I love you, as ever.

Jim

Sister Mariella came up with a house for the Humphreys, one owned by the Benedictines.

150 Summit Avenue
January 13, 1946
[. . .] Sunday, 3 in the afternoon

Dear Betty,

It is that time. I'm just up. I went to 5 o'clock Mass (and Communion) this morning. That was because I had a helluva lot more stuff to sterilize than ordinarily on Saturday night. If it is like that next week, I'm afraid I won't be in such fine fettle for the party. As it was, I think, I was tottering on the edge of the state of grace. I won't go into it all. Only say I pray God I'll never forget these years and that if I'm ever asked to say a few words, anywhere, I'll remember the people who scrubbed the banquet hall, who will wash the dishes, and who will hope those present will use the ashtrays. [. . .]

There was something wonderful about the words ". . . when we leave St Paul" in your letter. The idea of leaving and leaving with you, having you as indeed I've never had anyone or anything unless it be my portable typewriter, which I used to travel with. If you would only consent to traveling a little. This country will never be the same. But you don't want to hear that, do you? [. . .]

I love you deeply.

Jim [. . .]

BETTY WAHL

150 Summit Avenue
January 16, Feast of St Marcellus, Martyr, St Honoratus,
Confessor, St Elizabeth Alice, Virgin Beautiful

Dear Betty,

It is your birthday. I have just come from the city, where I was hard put to find something for your birthday. I had put off thinking about it until today, hoping to stroll into something. I didn't, so I sent you books. I am sorry I could not get you something more essential or intimate. You were not much help, however, if you recall. I wish very much that the ring were ready. At times I regret that I didn't buy one at a jewelry store. [. . .] You are twenty-two. You are beginning to bloom. I thought of sending you the book *Lovely Is the Lee*, which is all about Ireland, but thought on second thought you would not enjoy it.[1] There is a line in it, but I find I don't have it now. Anyway, it says Ireland is like the heart of a woman: she will give all for love, nothing by force. That is good. It is too bad all women aren't like that. You are. Do not change. [. . .]

I love you.

Jim

Jim rejoiced when his obligation to work at the hospital was lifted. He arrived at the "great idea" of giving up the job and devoting himself to his own work with the financial assistance of Father Egan. This, two months into their engagement, was Betty's first experience of Jim's intransigence on the matter of work.

1 By Robert Gibbings (1945).

150 Summit Avenue
January 19, 1946

Dear Marsh,

A note I'd like you to answer at once. George Barnhart[1] called me from New York last night and said that it is now official, that it was "authorized," that we are now free to accept such employment as we wish at such wages as we can get, meaning the hospital stuff is no more. [. . .] I'd like to know what the word is in Chicago and assume you've had a better opportunity than I have here to find out. [. . .] I don't want a job, of course. Only the freedom to write and, it may be, starve. For I intend to make it like that, have had my mind made up for some time; and might as well begin to find out now if it's possible. [. . .]

Jim

BETTY WAHL

150 Summit Avenue
January 23, 1946

My dear Betty,

Your letter rec'd and read and reread. Also one from Fr Garrelts, with more ideas for the play;[2] from a friend in Chicago who gives me the lowdown on parole there, and it looks like I am a free man, but I am not rushing down to demand it, am giving them a few days; a card from Fr Egan in which he says "Prince of Darkness"[3] will only make the literati smirk, says it's a balloon in fancy dress, but he is glad it's over and now I can get down to work (I've got a notion to go over and confront him with my freedom, ask to be supported—he's always talking about he'll do it if I ever want him to); and that's the mail. [. . .]

And now . . . amen.

Pax,

Jim

---

1 George Barnett (joke).
2 Garrelts and Jim were going to write a play together.
3 Published in *Accent* (Winter 1946).

150 Summit Avenue
January 1946

Dear Pere,

I have just rec'd your bill of disapproval. I wish that you'd try to be more approving. After all, where would the NY *Times* Book Section be today if they'd *not* liked as many masterpieces as you are on record for not liking. You'll never be popular with that old critical attitude, finding everything wrong and poking fun. Did you ever stop to think that you and not the world may be wrong! Well, I am mostly curious about where you saw the story. More and more I am thinking you should have been a Jesuit, with your fabulous connections and interests, and all of them leading right smack into Rome. [. . .]

Incidentally, turning to a subject dear to you, you can get your checkbook out any day now. There is a report that old JF will go free (my agents in Chicago and New York both tell me that's the way it is now), and [. . .] of course I am going on the HFXE[1] payroll immediately. It was good of Fr Egan to offer to help me, and I was sure he meant it because he was always urging me to forsake my material concerns and fly to him. Pax.

Jim

JF "I can live on $100 a m." P

St Joseph's Hospital
January 24, 1946

Dear Betty,

It's a little past four in the morning, Thursday, and a few minutes ago, as I was removing the third "load" from the sterilizer, a great idea came to me. It does not directly concern you, so it is not absolutely great. But it is fairly great. I immediately thought of telling it to you, as I'm about to do, and then a few moments later it occurred to me that I ought to ask your advice, even permission. Here it is. I will quit this job and go live with Don and Mary, upstairs in one of those side rooms, the lightest one and warmest (though I will depend on an electric heater of some sort for heat), and

1 Egan.

write the stories I have in mind for the book, only two or three more, and will begin either my novel about priests (*The Green Revolution*) or the one about jail (*The Hotel*). By the time we get married, I will have a lot done. I work pretty damned well when I don't do anything but write, I know from experience. I will pay Mary and Don at least seven dollars a week, more if I sell some stories for very much. Now tell me what you think of that, what you really think. [. . .]

I hope this letter doesn't upset you in any way. I don't see why it should, but a couple of times I felt that you thought $80 a month, even if I had to work 48 hours to get it and you had to sleep alone nights, was the best we could hope for. I think a clean break is necessary. The pills must go, and we must have some surgery (powerful imagery). I will not go into this any further. It is very simple. More than anything, I want your honest and intimate opinion. I don't want you giving way if you think the idea is all wrong. It would seem to me to be a chance to get a head start on our future, so much of it as entails my writing for our living. And now, turning to the center of things, I love you.

Jim

BETTY WAHL

150 Summit Avenue
January 26, 1946

Dear Betty,

I looked for a letter very much from you today, but none came. It is three in the afternoon, Saturday. I got up at ten this morning and went to Fr Patrick Kelly's funeral, solemnized by the archbishop, at the cathedral. He was a wonderful old priest at the hospital, actually loved by everybody. He is a subject of mine, and I have only put off writing about him and Sr Eugene Marie,[1] who looked after him until she was transferred to North Dakota, because he was still living. I knew that when she left, he would die. He did five months later. I then stopped off at the parole office to see the man. It is all set: I am a free man whenever I wish to go, only have to let the hospital know and teach someone the job I have. I think it'll be the 9th, my last night. I had hoped to have your letter today so as to know what you thought of the idea I broached the

---

1 Sister Eugene Marie Earley (1901–1993), surgical nurse; involved with the Catholic Worker movement; worked at St. Joseph's Hospital; good friend of Father Egan's.

other night (and also to have your reaction to "Prince of Darkness").
[. . .]

I also bought a ticket for *Here Is Ireland* this morning and will go all by myself—the only one I know who takes me seriously on the subject of Ireland—tomorrow afternoon. I expect to enjoy myself. I made some coffee two days ago but forgot to drink it. I am drinking it now. It tastes flat. Does coffee get flat? Then, after buying the ticket, I bought a pecan roll. Then I went to see Fr Egan about the good news. To discuss us. He would like an early marriage. The dog (the Pastor's) tried to bite him while I was there. Very funny. I must write it. [. . .]

Fr Kelly lay in his coffin with his biretta on, dapper to the last. I am quite tired from not sleeping. To bed then. I love you but would like to hear oftener and at more length from you. It is a scheme to make me love you more. You can't.

Jim

4

It would seem you have the well-known *business sense*

January 29, 1946—February 14, 1946

Jim, ca. 1928, "a member of the Blackfoot tribe"

Betty, who had the Teuton's boundless appetite for drawing up schedules, budgets, inventories, instructions, and rules, embarked on a lifelong, utterly hopeless crusade to convert Jim to the joys of time management.

BETTY WAHL

150 Summit Avenue
January 29, 1946

Dear Betty,

It is Tuesday. I think you ought to know that, and I've been waiting since last Friday or Saturday for a letter. This morning two of them arrived. Yesterday, when no letter came, I was thinking of altering my future, or rather that it had been altered for me: you had decided I was too this or that, and you'd heard from Elmo again. Well, getting into your letter, I am sorry it caused you so much grief, my big idea. I know you are as anxious as I am to have me amount to something, as they say. I doubt that I will at this rate. When you split up the day and proved I had plenty of time for writing if I'd only stop fuming . . . shades of my mother. It would seem, though, when the smoke has cleared away, that I ought to stay here and continue what I've been doing. All right, we'll see.

Fandel's[1] is absolutely out. I won't go into why. If you knew anything about bookstores or department stores, you'd know why. It would be even worse in a hick town, selling *Your Income Tax* and Lloyd Douglas. In some ways whoever it was that wanted you to go to Chicago and get a job and see the world was right. I mean, working isn't what it's cracked up to be by people who don't do it and by those who do but haven't desire or imagination enough to know the difference. As for going to the Humphreys', you have killed that prospect dead. I had not thought that it would be like

1 St. Cloud department store that included a bookshop.

that. I would go to Sandstone again before I'd go there. I am glad to know it is that way. I would have perished in the snow getting away if I'd gone there first and then found out.

I ought to write a happy letter, I suppose. I am awfully glad you love me enough to cry over letters for fear you'll run against my grain. I respect that and love you for it. It is true, though, that you have nothing, just as Sr Mariella has nothing when it comes to a solution. It is always the same. I had thought this the time for me to get a head start. When we are married, the screws will be much tighter; then considering a plan to write would amount to nonsupport and desertion and six or seven other things that the state and church sit on you for. I ought to wind this letter up cheerily. I can't. (My mother sent a clipping showing me where somebody got $125,000 from Hollywood.) I don't want to live in your grandmother's house. We'll live here. I love you.

  Jim

Let me say, Betty, I was sorry I put the issue up to you, especially the housing part. It was my responsibility. I don't know how to meet it except to say we'll live here. So we'll live here.

BETTY WAHL

150 Summit Avenue
January 30, 1946

Dear Betty,

Wednesday. Your letter came, and I have read it. I trust you rec'd my letter of yesterday today. I did not feel like writing Monday, and that is why you didn't get one yesterday. A card from Sr Mariella in which she tells me it is not necessary to come and see her as you would have told me everything she had in mind, which of course you have, and she concludes, however, with the thought that one must live one's own life and it is my neck if I wish to risk it. In a little while I'll be eating with Fr Egan. I called him a while ago and told him I was snowed under again (the last time I saw him, I was young and gay with the good news), and he said he'd pay me $80 to clean his pipes before he'd counsel sticking with the system. I do not plan to keep the hospital job if I can get anything else. If I can't, I'll try to get it down to five hours a day, but they won't like it, and of course I'll have to take less money, all of which seems like a damned nuisance to me. But, let it be clear so your heart can be at rest, I plan to get something, and I will keep the apartment, I am not going to do anything drastic, etc. Enough of that. I guess we are both tired of it. [. . .]

It is snowing. I am not going on the retreat this weekend. I will need what money I have, I imagine, if my brother comes. Anyway, I am in no mood for it. As a matter of fact, I am not in the mood for anything good. I hope you didn't dislike what I said in my letter about Fandel's and so on. You must try to understand, Betty, that I have been through the old bookstore mill and it has left its mark on me. And about continuing work—for twenty-seven months, in jail, out of jail, carrying bedpans, sewing up corpses, sweating a lake of sweat with the sterilizer, and hauling a mountain of ice, all this time I have been looking forward to freedom. Or what I thought was freedom. Anyway, it is not easy, especially when you are as short on virtue as I am and long-suffering, to accept someone's gentle counsel, even when you love that someone and perhaps recognize some truth in what she says, to continue the same old grind. I am lazy too. I hate regular hours. I like to walk when I want to. Sleep when I want to. Listen to music. I will go pretty far to get in a position to do these things. I love you, you know, and I'll try to find some way.

Love,
Jim

Jim and Betty's plans for the future included leaving St. Paul in September and renting or buying (with the assistance of others) a farm near St. John's. This would take them away from the world of getters and spenders and bring them into the company of such friends in the Movement as Emerson Hynes and Don Humphrey. One possible farm would have made them neighbors of some committed Detachers—whose views Betty loathed.

BETTY WAHL

150 Summit Avenue
January 31, 1946

Dear Betty,

I just got up. It's hotter than hell in the apartment. I have the windows open. But no cool air comes in. Your letter, one from my mother, one from Fr Garrelts. About the things in your letter. It will be a sad day old JF writes a letter to the abbot[1] about a job. As any old pitchman will tell you . . . never give a sucker an even break. That is what asking for a job is like . . . anywhere and especially at St John's. I have seen the abbot operate. He is a good man, but his last name is Deutsch, and if he's like a lot of other Germans, and I think he is, he expects to get to heaven for not having made any impractical moves during his stay on earth. I have often wondered why they didn't try to prove, somewhere along the line, that Jesus Christ received a gold watch for 33 years of service. I think, in short, you had better worry about your novel and stop thinking about me and a job. I love you for your interest. On the other hand you are quite young and innocent.

Present plans call for me to visit Stearns County on the 10th, all right, with Fr Egan. Our special end will be to see the Koppy farm.[2] Whenever you find out about it, or your father does, just write the details quick. You don't have to phone.

I see, on rereading your letter, that it was Mariella's idea to write to the abbot. Please tell her to say the rosary 1,000 times for my special intention. Yes, I found the missal. Who would steal it? We had a good talk last night, Fr Egan and I, and I told him all about everybody's plans. He had the phrase for the Fandel's deal. "Fandel's . . . Brentano's," he said. "Your life is a game of Monopoly. Pay the bank and go back to the start." I think that takes care of that, except to say I'd have been ashamed to have you working there in the morning, as you suggested. I have always found these man-and-wife, work-and-win, and don't-forget-to-say-thank-you-to-the-customer combinations very depressing. All right, all right, that's enough talk about jobs. Please don't mention them anymore and I won't. The important things are: I love you; I wish you were here; I wish I were there; I wish we were both somewhere. [. . .]

Love,
Jim

Betty Wahl to Sister Mariella Gable, ca. February 1, 1946
This is to stop you worrying about a number of things. In the first place, the farm was unfit for human occupation, so we have lost that future connection with the Detachers . . . Anyway, there is a 10-acre plot 2½ miles from St.

1 Alcuin Deutsch, abbot of St. John's Abbey from 1921 to 1950.
2 A possible future dwelling for Jim and Betty—to be purchased with the assistance of others.

Ben's and ½ mile from the St. John's gate . . . There, surrounded by Benedictines, and with Emerson only ½ mile off through the woods, all seeds
of heresy ought to fall away effortlessly. Jim is only slightly touched by the
Detachers. His writing is considerably more influenced by it than his life
is. He is much more of an epicurean than a Detacher. He is a sucker for
the viewpoint of the Detacher as far as making destructive comments
goes . . .

I agree that Jim needs a conversion, to the positive side of the Church.
Dante, Giotto, Gregorian chant, Augustine (used sparingly), Chesterton
(large doses, for optimism), Benedictinism, . . . and the Hynes family.
(Dennis gets butter and honey, all over the bread, and down the sides a
little.) The plan is still indefinite. He and Father Egan are coming up
Monday, but with Father E. listening to every word, I probably can't do
much then, unless I want to convert him too.

BETTY WAHL

150 Summit Avenue
February 1, 1946

My dear Betty,

I love you. Your letter of today was very good. The best I've had in
some time. There were two things I especially liked, that we could live on
$40 a month (whether true or not, I liked it) and that we could put shut-
ters up when we go to Ireland. Because we are going to Ireland sooner or
later, if only for a month, and I would prefer to go with you willingly. I went
over to see Fr Egan immediately. He agrees that the farm we had in mind
is out if it's the way you say it is. [. . .] Now about the other two spots. I
wish you would draw a map of them. [. . .] You say nothing about how
much you would expect would be wanted. If they are together and could
be bought as a unit, Fr Egan would be interested and would have some
cash. [. . .] I am interested. It would seem you have the well-known *business sense*. Now try to answer all these questions like a good girl.

A good letter from Sr Eugene Marie today with many memories of Fr
Kelly. My story about them, I think, will be the best thing I've done. It will
be as long as Fr Burner, I believe. I guess that's all I have to say tonight. It's
seven-thirty Friday evening, February 1, 1946, the year I married my wife,
Elizabeth Alice. [. . .]

I loves youse.

Jim

150 Summit Avenue
February 5, 1946

Dear Betty,

[. . .] I am going to sign with Doubleday for two books, the stories and a novel. I will get a "small" advance on the stories and monthly payments on the novel. That is not so bad, is it? [. . .]

I love you.
Jim

150 Summit Avenue
February 6, 1946

Dear Betty,

Wednesday, 11:00 a.m. [. . .]

I was talking with Mother St Ignatius the other day about her nephew and Evie, having mentioned that I was interested in a five-hour night and that I was marrying a St Cloud author (you). Then we talked about a conversion, or rather reconversion, she made with one of the boys working at the hospital, a colleague of mine. He turned Jehovah's Witness during the war, only, as Ig explained, it was a woman that led him astray. She evidently believes most bad things happen through the offices of women. I agreed with her. I said, however, that you were different and very spiritual and that we didn't even expect to have carnal intercourse as it's so carnal we think and mostly live by the spirit. She said that was fine and that she didn't have time for much c.i. herself. I refer to her as Ig because Fr Kelly used to do so (he is my source and justification).

Well, Keefe[1] is in Robbinsdale today. He and Fr Garrelts were erstwhile friends and enemies. He is from Quincy too. We all played on the Quincy College Academy teams—the Little Hawks we were called. That is because the college was the Hawks proper, but we were bigger than the Hawks, us Little Hawks. So you are marrying a Little Hawk, please tell everybody. You must send me your old girdle, now that you have a new one. I will venerate it as a first-class relic. [. . .] Now I must end this. I love you, Betty, and expect to love you more in a couple of weeks. Right now I have 18 or 19 projects knocking around in my head.

1 Dick Keefe.

Send me a kiss the next time. You have never done that. I don't just want an *x* either.

 Jim

CHARLES SHATTUCK

February 1946

Dear Chuck,

 The lid is off on the parole business. I am free to starve again. The state is losing its memory. I am shedding my number and assuming a name again. I expect to be in Chicago next week, where good government combines with good living, and it may be that I will make a pilgrimage to Urbana, my literary birthplace. [. . .]

 I am coming back to St Paul about the 21st and am going to finish some stories. Just write. I have already made arrangements to quit the job, perhaps effective tomorrow night or at the latest Saturday.

 Naturally, I feel pretty good about all this. [. . .]

 Pax,

 Jim

Betty Wahl to Sister Mariella Gable, February 14, 1946

I was, of course, shocked when I heard that he had quit his job. After I said no once, he just didn't mention it again. Perhaps it is best that he did. We will get this period over before we get married. It will give him about three months' time. If he really can work, and can work in big enough quantities to bring in about 80 dollars a month, there is no point in his going back to work. If he fails, he agrees to get a job of some kind. There is no danger of starving immediately. Father Egan is being his patron. (I don't know if he told you, or even if he wants you to know, but you should know.) I'm not too afraid of being indebted to F. Egan, because we spent (Jim and I, I mean) about three hours thoroughly hashing out all the questions about the Detachers and I am satisfied.

5

I am like Daniel Boone cutting my way through that bourgeois wilderness

February 14, 1946—April 26, 1946

April 22, 1946: (left to right) Zella, Art, Money, John Haskins, Pat Wahl, Betty, Jim, Jim

After quitting his job at the hospital, Jim paid a week's visit to his parents in Chicago. Living with them were Michael, the dog, Jim's grandmother Tilda, and his brother, Dick, who was something of a rogue at the time.

BETTY WAHL
4453 North Paulina Street, Chicago, the I Will City
St Valentine's Day, February 14, 1946

Dear Valentine,

I am at home, sitting in our living room. It is a wonderful room, very dear to me, scene of many a long night and early morning of writing My books are all here. The phonograph. My family. My dog, Michael, who is sitting in the window now watching the janitor shovel snow away from the Fourteenth Church of Christ Scientist. It snowed like hell for the last miles into Chicago and must have been going here quite a while. I [. . .] sat in the smoker for most of trip as the windows open better to the country. Very memory provoking, looking at the Wisconsin hills, the frozen streams, the farmhouses, with each it seemed sporting a dog who would break into a run when we went by, but at a great distance so that it was like an old print. I wish that you had been with me, except that you would have been tired. I read a paper edition of *The Grapes of Wrath*. And smoked until the pipe got bad-tasting. A letter from Shattuck waiting for me. He expects to see the crime wave rise now that I am free. [. . .] My folks were disappointed that you didn't come. I have promised you to them now. So keep that in your head. And this in your heart: I love you.

Your

Jim

4453 North Paulina Street, Chicago

February 14, 1946

Dear Chuck,

I'm in Chicago now and have your note. Evidently, you are looking for the new Bluebeard in me. I think I'll disappoint you. I am a simple citizen only, made in the image and likeness of Harry Truman, which is plenty for me, and if you weren't one of them stuck up professors, it would be plenty for you. You may count on me Monday next. I'll take the 9:05 a.m. out of Chicago. It will be a nice alibi as, if everything works out right, my draft board will perish mysteriously that afternoon. I may bring George Barnett with me. He is returning to Chicago to eke out. He has been in New York doing basal metabolism. He wants to outlaw the atomic bomb. I know a priest who wants to popularize it; he says look what small arms did for Ireland. Pax. How is Falstaff these days?

Jim

4453 North Paulina Street, Chicago

February 20, 1946

Dear Betty,

Here I am still in Chicago. Wednesday afternoon. I am leaving either tonight or tomorrow. I am staying by special request of my folks. I am anxious to be back in St Paul, to read letters I expect to find there from you and to begin writing. Sunday night—to give you an account of my stewardship—I met Nelson Algren, whose two novels I like very much but which are probably too rough for someone as nice as you. Then Monday morning I went to Urbana and stayed with the Shattucks. That meant a lot of beer, more beer than good conversation, as a matter of fact. Some of the erstwhile editors of *Accent*, back from the wars, came over, and I met them for the first time—the Carrs and Hills. [. . .] I am loving you.

Your

Jim

150 Summit Avenue
February 25, 1946

Dear Betty,

Monday, 4:30 in the afternoon, Fr Garrelts here for lunch and now out for a walk with Fr Egan. Fr Egan brings bad tidings about Fr Burner.[1] It seems St Paul and Minneapolis are boiling on account of it. I can't determine why exactly. Fr Egan says it doesn't do any good and probably does a lot of harm. He holds it isn't a purely parochial reaction, but I am still inclined to think that is what it is, nothing else coming to light on it. Newsstands are asked for *Accent*. Copies are at a premium. I should be happy about it, I suppose, but I'm not. It will blow over, I suppose. [. . .]

When are you coming to see me? When am I coming to see you? I won't feel like it until I turn out a couple of these stories. I think that's all for now. I love you of course. Do not get upset about the wedding. I seem to detect the beginnings of hysteria already. Stop trying to finish your book on a weekend. No good comes of that.

I love you.
    Jim

BETTY WAHL

150 Summit Avenue
February 26, 1946

Dearest Betty,

Tuesday morning before I get into the day's work. Did I tell you, I think not, that the barber suspected you when I told him the other day that I wanted it left rather long? He took special pains after that, he said, as he was cutting it for two people now. I thought at the time, what will I ever do in Stearns County for haircuts? You will have to learn how to cut my hair. I would not trust one of the agrarians (farmers) with it, not that I am particularly vainglorious. [. . .]

The maid says the beer bottles must go and she hopes I won't be mad at her for telling me, like they got downstairs (Dr Ruona). The exterminator man says it's the bottles that draw cockroaches. I have a small fortune in bottles, beer and milk, which I intend to expend for a wedding gift for

---

1 Father Burner is the main character in "Prince of Darkness." The story was condemned by many members of the Catholic clergy.

you. Well, today you have moved the date up to the 22nd of April. Why don't you concentrate a little harder and make it the day after tomorrow? Then we can both settle down to our work, you calm in the knowledge that I married you for your literacy virtues and business sense, me calm in the knowledge that I married a "cold" woman who thought a husband was something every growing girl ought to have. [. . .]

I must write Harry Sylvester and tell him I am now a public enemy myself. I am referring to the clerical forces now allied against me on account of Father Burner. I suppose it's a healthy sign. Joyce had the same trouble in Dublin with his stories. Fortunately, I don't think they can touch me. I am very glad that Sr Mariella approved of the Doubleday deal, but wonder what she means when she says that's the only way I'd ever be able to make it, as though it were not all right that way. As for living off money I haven't earned, that's silly. When I write the stories, it's earned then and there, and when they're published is something else. Someday I'll gather all you Teutons into a single classroom and lecture you a little on True Economics, a course I'm famous for. [. . .]

I love you, Betty.

Jim

Jim's aunt Margaret came from Chicago to stay with him for a few days.

150 Summit Avenue
March 9, 1946

Dearest Betty,

[. . .] My Aunt Mgt has gone to a morning movie downtown—*Leave Her to Heaven*—oh, God! I might have gone to see *The Lost Weekend* with her, but oh no . . . she could see enough drunks in the streets without going to a movie about one. So it is. How right Hollywood and the *Ladies' Home Journal* and the rest of them all are. They aren't negative, not them. I think I'll be negative to the day I die, I think, when I sound someone like Aunt Mgt on things. What a damn terrible thing this system has done in the years to people. Everybody she ever knew "had a good position" with Armour, with the Pullman Company, with Field's, with National Biscuit, or was "in business for himself" with a dandy line of mops and ironing boards. And they all, every damn last one of them, had—"nice homes."

I am like Daniel Boone cutting my way through that bourgeois wilderness, the first one who ever didn't lose himself in a corporation or go into business for himself. I hope—I sincerely pray—you are not making a mistake about me. If you think I'd go along just because you were my wife and asked it, or because we had twelve children who needed milk and bread. You said something last Sunday about how I'd cook with the rest of them. I am not saying I'd poison the children, but you'd better take another reading if you think I can be domesticated and made to like it. All the king's horses and all the king's men will not make JF do some things. It gives me a pain to have to say all these things, but sometimes I get to thinking you don't know me at all, don't know what you're getting into, and if you do, you think changes can be made which, as a matter of fact, won't be made. [. . .]

I trust you can see I am not kidding about all this. I love you.

Jim

BETTY WAHL

150 Summit Avenue
March 17, 1946

Mavourneen,

Sunday, Feast of Patrick, bishop, confessor, patron of Ireland . . . and I love you. I have just had breakfast: pancakes, bacon, eggs, pecan rolls, tea (tay). It is a good thing, quoth Aunt Mgt, that Betty can cook. I told her you could. I get up in the morning, feeling in an Olympic frame of mind, and the first thing I have to do is argue about whether I want cereal or not, whether we are to have pancakes or not, etc. I trust you will cook our meals and not create problems of that order for me. I don't care one way or the other, but it is customary, evidently, among Aunt Mgt's friends for people to talk as though they don't care when they really do and are being polite and resigned, feeling very strongly on the question of jelly roll and pecan roll and you know the rest.

Now I am getting the menu for tomorrow morning—tomorrow morning and it is not afternoon yet of today. The root of all this planning seems to be: not to throw anything away. To hell with what you want, how you feel, munch away on that dead hunk of cake until it is all gone. Quoth

Aunt Mgt: "I never throw anything away." It is as though, comes the Last Judgment, there will be but one question: Did you ever throw anything away? I hope you don't read this as spleen. I enjoy having her here very much. I can't forgo analyzing her, however, the prerogative of a writer, or of a man where a woman is concerned and vice versa. We have been up since nine this morning (Aunt Mgt since eight) and are now patiently waiting for the last drop of rain to fall out of the sky. We will probably go to 12:30 Mass. Amen. [. . .]

Well, Betty, I see I've said nothing at length again. I love you. I think of you. I want to take you in my arms, to possess you body and soul, to be possessed by you. But this isn't the time or place for that. It seems as far away as ever to me, the time and place, and you in your letters farther.

Jim

BETTY WAHL

150 Summit Avenue
March 18, 1946

Dear Betty,

I am writing this in flight at Robbinsdale. I rec'd your letter mailed Saturday this morning before leaving for Minneapolis. I was pleased to see that it went three lines over a page. You should not mind that I scold you about your brevity. It is my prerogative. It seems I am always mentioning my prerogative these days. Look out. [. . .] You know I love you, and so I will not go into that. I am not excited, but that doesn't mean I am any less happy. I am too old inside to get excited even about the most important thing in the world, which is you and our marriage. You will find me very young outside, however, and by that I mean physically. And perhaps I will become that way inside with you, loving you until we are one and we will not know ourselves apart from each other, at least a certain large beautiful part of our life. Strong words to come out of the rectory, aren't they? [. . .] And now I think that's it. I have already said it. Say it to yourself and know I am saying it to you.

Jim

150 Summit Avenue
March 27, 1946

Dear Betty,

[. . .] I looked at cars from the window of the streetcar today, cars in lots, and they looked terribly expensive, except one or two that said $125 and they didn't look very mobile. I had a horrible dream last night, not about you, but about me. I woke up thinking I was surely in hell. I tried the lights (I thought), and they would not work, and I understood that to mean I had died and switches had another function wherever I was, hell, I guess. A man had me by the wrists and was on my back, looking over my shoulder, but I could not get the lights on to see who he was. Finally, I did stumble out into the light, a hospital it was, and found a mirror. I was afraid he would be gone before I could see who he was, but he was still there, looking over my shoulder at me as I was looking at him. It was me, an older, tireder me, and he would not let go. Then he went away, and I guess I was awake then, though I was certain I was awake before that, that it was no dream, that I was dead. Very interesting, the most interesting dream I've ever had. I also had clam chowder last night about 1:00 a.m. I think that is enough substance for one letter. [. . .]

Jim

150 Summit Avenue
April 2, 1946

Dear Betty,

[. . .] Do not be too hasty about picking up old furniture from atticks. We do not, as I see it, need very much beyond a table, the bed you have, and chairs. And we can buy what we want, rather than have the place loaded down with monstrosities from an earlier age. But of course I am really stepping out of my province, I suppose, in having ideas about furniture. I do have them, however—having been in very few places in my time which looked livable, unless your taste was governed by *Better Homes and So Forth*, which mine ain't so much as by organic need (F. L. Wright). Well, that will be all for today—rather a businessy letter, not? I love you, but I can't do anything about it and won't go into it here.

I have asked Fr Garrelts to perform the ceremony. He will. So would have Fr Casey, but it seems I had been wrong in thinking that Fr G. did not want to do it. He does and will. I wish you'd try to iron out whether it is going to be a low or high mass. I think it ought to be high, not just because the local priests want it that way, as they obviously do, but for other reasons. However, if your dad can't see it that way, it is all right. Just you be around and explain to all 75 people why we always get married at a low mass.

    Jim

BETTY WAHL

150 Summit Avenue
April 5, 1946

Dear Betty,

    [. . .] You said nothing about the ring in your letters yesterday, and so I suppose it is still on the way. Well, there won't be anything like that again, Betty. Old JF may not have this business sense, but he knows what happens to letters that come in the three-cent mail, how they are put aside and forgotten, and likewise orders which don't come airmail. Are you still wearing your gloves to cover up your finger? I am sorry. It is in part my fault for waiting on Don so long. But of course the system, the good old system you don't know about yet, is mostly to blame. I am closing now. I love you. Write.

    Jim

By the way—whenever you want me to come, you'd better enclose train fare. I will need it then.

Father George Garrelts exerted a strange power over Jim. It sprang from his gargantuan personality, from his having been a member of Jim's inner circle in their halcyon high-school days, and, not least, from his being a priest. He had nixed Jim's other great love, Ramona Rawson; he pressed for writing collaborations with Jim; and, in time to come, he would push Betty to the side, most gallingly in a trip to Scotland that he, Jim, and Betty made together. Even before her marriage, Betty felt vaguely hostile toward Garrelts, beginning, perhaps, with a feeling that his initial disinclination to perform the marriage ceremony meant he disapproved of Jim's marrying. She came to believe that Garrelts intended to intrude on their life as a couple—as, indeed, he had with the Humphreys.

150 Summit Avenue
April 17, 1946

Dear Betty,

Wednesday, and your letter. Very nice letter, except one paragraph which is probably the worst thing I've ever heard from you, causing me to think back to the time a similar sentiment was expressed by a true love of mine and it was the last time I ever saw her. I quote it so you will know what I mean:

> Who said Father Garrelts was going to come and spend his vacation with us? I hope it's not you. We have absolutely no place for him anywhere, either at the lake[1] or in our house when we have it.

Now, so far as I know, Fr Garrelts has no intention of spending his vacation with us, and I am damned sure he would not care to spend even a little time with us ever if he knew about this. I am sorry if you did not mean to sound the way these words sound. They do sound, however, and I won't be able to forget.

When I think of how well I know Fr Garrelts, what a wonderful friend he has always been to me, and I think of what Mary Humphrey and her enemies (also Christian), between them, are doing to Fr Garrelts, I am afraid I can think of nothing but a lot of people who had a lot to say about one man none of them knew a long time ago, and it was Holy Week too. As yet Fr Garrelts has had nothing to say. And the comparison is not as strained as you might like to think. Now, you can either accept my evaluation of Fr Garrelts, and enjoy peace, or spend the rest of your life sharpshooting to make an impossible point.

I assure you the Blondie-Dagwood myth, which is held in such deep esteem generally, will never be true of us. I think it better to let you know this now—though I had thought it was pretty clear—before we are married, for afterward such a hard paragraph as this one and yours might easily qualify as the reality and our love as the illusion. Both are real, and one does not exclude the other, although either one, in this case, could kill the other if the truth were not told. Now I shall try to pick up the pieces and get to work. [. . .]

---

1 They were going to begin their married life living in Betty's parents' summer cottage on a lake.

You did not ask if I loved you, but in case you doubt it after reading the above, let me say I do, very much, I do.

Jim

Fr G. did ask me several weeks ago to find him a cottage near St Ben's for a couple weeks in June, but I had never considered renting yours to him, or moving him in there, hard as that may be for you to believe. He had wanted to work with Don at carving, etc. I will now make it plain that Wisconsin is preferable. He was getting the cottage primarily for his mother and his stepfather, both of whom incidentally would be accepted where he never would be, both of them having done the right things all their lives and amounted to nothing unless you call 40 or 50 years switching trains something.

BETTY WAHL

150 Summit Avenue
April 19, 1946

Dear Betty,

[. . .] It is Friday morning, Haskins is here (shaving now), and in a few minutes we'll eat breakfast and then out to Calvary Cemetery, I think, to see Fr Kelly's grave. I want to get a look at it; there may be something significant. Last night I, or we, got a cable from Osaka, Japan, from my friend Weinstein, to the effect that the Japanese love us, that the cherry blossoms are in bloom, that we should be happy, and he signs it Lafcadio Hearn, whom I daresay you never heard of. He was an American writer who went to Japan to live about fifty years ago and died there, a good writer. It is not clear from the paragraph you write about Fr Garrelts how you came to say what you did, but it is all over now and perhaps ought to be a lesson to both of us. I think that is all. I am not very happy about things in general, outside of you. I mean my folks not coming according to schedule and so far as I can see the general failure of my relatives to remember the occasion tangibly. I would not mind if I did not know that even if you are above making comparisons, the others are not. I love you.

Jim

Jim and Betty were married on April 22, 1946.

KERKER QUINN

150 Summit Avenue
April 26, 1946

Dear Kerker,

[. . .] I was married last Monday. Please tell Chuck in case he wants to offer up a litany or two for my wife and me. It will be rough and tough on both of us, no doubt.

Pax,
Jim

6

Something seems to be missing, and you say it's me

Memorial Day 1946—April 3, 1947

Jim, the 1931 Chevrolet, and Stearns County

Upon his marriage, Jim left the Marlborough and St. Paul and moved with Betty into her parents' summer cottage on Big Spunk Lake in the little town of Avon, Minnesota (population approximately 880). The Wahls—Art, Money, Pat, John, and Tom—took up summer residence on Memorial Day weekend. Jim and Betty decamped to a small boathouse, an outbuilding of the cottage. The situation, with its constant family activity and common meals, was not a happy one. Betty and Jim were waiting for a house that was being built for them — by Art's workmen—on land bought by the Wahls for the couple as a wedding present. It was in the Avon woods, some three miles from St. John's.

CHARLES SHATTUCK

Avon
Memorial Day 1946

Dear Chuck,

Very glad to hear from you and that the stories are all right.[1] [. . .] I am sorry to be so reticent about my wife, about getting married, if I have been. I automatically figure it's unimportant to other people. [. . .] Well, we are living in a cottage owned by my wife's folks. They are moving out here in a few days, however, and we will move 20 steps nearer to the lake, to this little 10 x 15 house I'm writing in now. It has a big window on the lake, which is called, amusingly enough for any reader of Joyce, "Big Spunk." Now, Big Spunk, it seems, was an Indian chief, but I never think of him so much as of Molly Bloom when I hear a native pronounce the name. I get out on the dock and cast for large fish, using one of those plugs which always struck me as spectacular and incredible in Illinois. To date I have

---

1 Asking for his editorial comments, Jim had sent Shattuck stories for what became the collection *Prince of Darkness, and Other Stories.*

caught one fish, not counting bullheads (that I call catfish, after the fashion in Morgan County, Ill.) and two perch, a four-pound black bass. He was out of season, so I had to toss him back, thus creating the illusion that I am now a law-abiding citizen. The truth of it was I thought him too beautiful to cut up and eat. I guess that takes care of my private life and the local color. [. . .]

Gratefully,

Jim

CHARLES SHATTUCK

Avon, Minnesota
July 15, 1946

Dear Chuck,

A note to let you know I am still here, did not come to Chicago after all. It will be later, I think. My reason for deserting this seeming paradise was that days go by and I get nothing written, being too occupied with the little body politic, the trials and tribulations of living too close to too many people. [. . .] I do not fit into the pattern of life I find here. There is too much to deal with all the time: meals, dishes, company, humor, all the product of another unit, my wife's family, on whose good graces we seem to presume, and their time is not my time, nor their ways my ways. We have no open difficulty. It is just that I constantly fail to come up to their idea of a son-in-law. And inside me there is a constant dialogue that never gets spoken aloud. Once I would have tried to cut a path through them. Now, no more. I retire. They think I am *physically* ill. I say, going along, I feel a little better now, each time I'm asked. [. . .]

Pax,

Jim

Jim and Betty (who was expecting a child in March) traveled to Brewster, on Cape Cod, and lived in a house belonging to friends of Harry Sylvester's. They intended to remain there until January 1947.

CHARLES SHATTUCK

Brewster, Massachusetts
October 8, 1946

Dear Chuck,

[. . .] So far Brewster has been very much to our liking. We have had clams, mussels, and oysters from the bay, and I like all those. The worst thing is not having a car, making us dependent on the Sylvesters, even for milk (nobody will bother to come down here where we are). The next worst thing, now more under control, is the fleas. The people who own the house have a dog, and the dog has fleas. The people and dog are gone, but the fleas are always with us.

[. . .] Pax,
Jim

HARVEY EGAN

Brewster by the Shore
Tuesday, November 19, 1946

Dear Father Egan,

Rec'd your letter some time ago and very happy to have it, to know we are missed, and not in the usual way, in Minnesota [   ] Betty is fine. You knew, I think, from reading a letter from Harry last summer, in which it came up, that she is to have a baby in March. Should we call it Harvey or Savonarola? I guess with the war over, and Russia the bête noire again, Dr B. is having a field day with his pamphlets and addresses to the dear ladies. I hope you are still on his list. I see from *The New York Times Book Review* (which we read avidly here, being authors, all of us) that "*Our Sunday Visitor* described *The Scarlet Lily* as 'a bang-up, gripping word picture of Mary Magdalene.'"[1] Bruce is also publishing a "thought provoking book for everyone interested in the future of America"—*After Hitler Stalin?* Or Blessed are the ~~Peacemakers~~ Defenseworkers and Those with Deferments. That's what I like about us Catholics, books like that, coming like now. Enough for now. Pax.

Jim

Any rumors about who's taking over Ray's job with the Saints?[2]

---

1 Novel by Edward F. Murphy, SJ (Bruce, 1944).
2 Ray Blades had been manager of the St. Paul Saints.

Betty suffered a miscarriage on December 12 and returned to Minnesota by air to stay with her parents at their home in St. Cloud. Jim spent a few days in New York, then traveled to Washington, D.C., to visit his friend John Haskins before going to Chicago to stay with his parents. He spent a couple of weeks, including Christmas, there.

BETTY POWERS

4453 North Paulina Street, Chicago

Christmas Eve 1946

Dear Betty,

It is about ten o'clock, and all through the house not a creature is stirring except me, Mickey, and my grandmother. The tree is lit up and going; there is a red candle burning in the window; the presents have been opened; and my brother is out and also my parents. I have written two notes to people. Now you, after much sitting and staring into the tree, wondering how it's going with you, if the presents are opened there, if you are having refreshments (eggnogs and toddies unlikely, on consideration, probably coffee). It is another sad Christmas for me, the third or fourth in a row, and I no longer know why, only think I've seen my last merry one. Oh, yes, my grandmother insists that I tell you she has not forgotten you but can't get out and shop, a fact which is manifest but which puzzles her nonetheless. [. . .]

So glad you like the house. So sorry the water and electricity aren't coming around. Don't get yourself frustrated over that. I don't have any idea how much money we have—though it's safe to say not much—but again I think we ought to pay people, I mean the plumber, for services rendered. I thought so after other occasions of charity, and so did you, if I remember. I miss you very much, Betty. You must know that. I am hoping, but despairing, that our life in the future will not be aggravated as it has been in the past. I trust you got my wire, Merry Christmas, Betty, this afternoon and knew it meant more than that. You know how you have to put it in a wire and will realize it was that which kept me from saying more. I say it now. I love you. Do not be downhearted. Remember some of the things we have learned together about us.

Jim

Chicago
December 31, 1946

Dear Betty,

Tuesday morning. Rec'd your letter written Sunday night, the sad one, and was glad to get it, but sorry to hear you feel so low. I don't know what to say—and am sending this special so you'll have it about as soon as the one I wrote yesterday, the bad one. I don't understand what you feel so bad about. Aside from my not being there, that is, and even that is not too clear. We have no place to live. We should have all our strife over again if I were there now, living with your relatives. You know that. I am pretty much the same. Hemmed in and haunted here, yes, but not landlocked. I can get out of the house and go somewhere, see somebody, though not many anymore. I saw *Colonel Blimp*, an English movie, last night, alone. Then went over on North Clark in a couple of joints and watched some stripteasers while I had three bottles of beer. Then I got on the streetcar and came home. [. . .]

And now, my love, I leave you . . . loving you.

Jim

Chicago
January 2, 1947

Dear Betty,

Your brief letter written last Monday night arrived this morning. I was glad to get it, though it was a very dismal account of your life there. Something seems to be missing, and you say it's me—but I am not so sure it wouldn't be that way if I were there. Well, we'll see. I have more or less decided to do a certain story and would like to finish it before leaving Chicago. It should not take so long. It would seem that we need some money. I don't feel I can begin the novel with so much poverty lurking about us. I hear nothing about "The Valiant Woman,"[1] and you say nothing about your stuff. I wrote a note to Cunningham at *Collier's* and mentioned your story. If I can write this story, and write it right, it might go

---

1 Eventually published in *Accent* (Spring 1947).

somewhere. Then we could get a car and have a few bucks, say, enough to carry us into March or April. [. . .]

Much love,

Jim

Chicago

January 4, 1947

Dear Betty,

Two letters from you today, none yesterday. Very glad to have them both. I am sorry I caused you so much concern by not writing. I only stopped writing, as you ought to know now, when I didn't hear from you for several days. If I had not heard from you today, I would not have written either. I am in the dark on your sorrow, why you should go about weeping, and hope you aren't going to fulfill all of Harry's worst warnings. I do know it was many, many times worse for you, losing the baby, to say nothing of the pain you suffered. I do not feel so bad. I would feel shakier than I do, about money, if we had a baby. In that respect I am relieved. If that makes me a pagan or something, that's too bad. [. . .]

Is it my ice skates you want me to send? If the word in your letter is "skates," it is a new form—but I intended to bring them or send them. I am a very fine skater, both plain and fancy, and daresay there is no one quite like me. But surely you suspected that. I should very much like to whang Emerson Hynes, that eminent rural lifer, across the shins with a hockey stick. Enjoyed your account of Harry in the eyes of Sr Remberta[1] and others. You must not, and I suppose you are the last one who would, contribute any little facts on Harry that we picked up in our stay at Brewster. [. . .]

Tell me more about the Stearns County scene. Does it seem the same? Does it seem worse? Better? Tell me, for a change where this subject is concerned, the truth. Can we actually live there? What do we burn in our stove in Avon? Wood? Coal—if so, do you have any ordered? I mention it now, knowing how slow everything and everybody moves. Also, I love you very much. Would like to be near you, very near. Would like to call you some names. There is nobody here like that but Mickey, and he is sometimes a cross patch. Are you gaining, losing, weight? Are your breasts

1 One of Betty's teachers at St. Benedict's.

swollen yet? Are you going around in bobby socks, with your knees sticking out, like Elsie Dinsmore or the Bobbsey girls? Or are you a big girl now? Now, you just sit down and answer all the questions in this letter, and I ought to have a good one. Thanks for the special of this morning. How did you bring yourself to do it? You might have hoped, as last week, that somehow, someway, I would get it without sending it special, and I would be mad, the letter would arrive Monday, and you would be wide-eyed and wondering when I didn't write. Much love. Hold tight.

    Your

    Jim

BETTY POWERS

Chicago
Tuesday morning, 10:00 a.m.,
January 7, 1947

Dear Betty,

    Your long letter rec'd today. [. . .] Well, you get into quite a few things in this letter. It gives me a good picture at last of the Avon situation. I am especially pleased to note your enthusiasm for carrying water, coal, excrement, etc., and hope I can keep up with you. You even put a Catholic Worker interpretation on it. Obviously, in Brewster, we were not under that illusion, for things certainly did pile up there and we had none of the carrying to do that we both look forward to in Avon. Surely you don't mind if I amuse myself with this, do you? I am not surprised. I had expected to have to do worse things, and still do. [. . .]

    I love you.

    Jim

THANKS FOR THE CHOCOLATE BARS! They were enjoyed by one and all. Better get some for Avon. I prefer them over Hershey's. I don't know what to do with the $10 you sent. My libido is very high, but you would not want me to use it for that, would you?

Jim and Betty moved into the newly constructed house in the Avon woods in January 1947. Betty, at least, had high hopes for the rural life, intending, among other things, to keep bees, going so far as to acquire a bee veil and smoker.

The house was a rudimentary dwelling, a one-story structure built into the earth with a tar-paper "roof" and no running water. Jim and Betty—and, eventually, I, Katherine—lived in it for periods in 1947 and 1948. The couple also bought a car. "My cross grows heavier," Jim wrote to Kerker Quinn. "We have taken unto ourselves a 1931 Chevrolet."

CHARLES SHATTUCK

Avon, Minnesota

The Wee Hours, April 3, 1947

Dear Chuck,

[. . .] Haven't done much since getting back in Minnesota. I weigh a theory now and then which goes like this: this country is not housebroken (perhaps St Paul is the only place in Minnesota which is), and the savage spirits still lurk in the trees and lakes and they do not like this writing going on, and so it is harder than usual to get things on paper right, the spirits always getting in the way. Who will tame the wilderness with prose? [. . .]

Pax,

Jim

Now I am going to drink a bottle of bock in your honor.

7

Camaraderie

July 9, 1947—October 14, 1947

Robert Lowell, Yaddo, 1947

Jim's first book, the short-story collection Prince of Darkness, *was published by Doubleday in the spring of 1947. Jim and Betty (who was expecting a child at the end of October) went to Yaddo, the artists' retreat at Saratoga Springs, New York, arriving on July 1. The weeks that followed approached an idyll for Jim as he made friends with a number of men who shared his taste for male camaraderie, literature, and high-wire conversation. Chief among them were the poets Robert Lowell, known as Cal and, at times, Rattleass (from Boston, Mass.); and Theodore Roethke, "a big long fat man who needs a lot of stoking," sometimes called Champ or Beast (of Bennington); Harvey C. Webster, from the University of Louisville, sometimes called Clocker because he, like Jim, was a devotee of the track; Bucklin Moon, Jim's editor at Doubleday, and the writer Arna Bontemps.*

HARVEY EGAN

Yaddo
July 9, 1947

Mon pere,

Your letter and two spot rec'd. Saratoga does not open until August, and so I'll try to keep your deposit until then. I like your system: an 8–1 bet in the fourth, then a 3–1 in the fifth. If that does not produce results, I do not know what will. Well, we arrived here without a bit of trouble, not even a flat, and our merry Chev rolled all the way without a cough. Chevrolet builds great cars! Since coming here, we've not done a lot of work, though some, and there are no excuses for not working. It is not an amusement center; everybody is working on a book or painting a picture or chiseling a bust, and production means survival once we leave this haven of rest, and so there isn't much loafing—at least if there is, everyone is careful to do it in private. We have a couple of big rooms and a bath but use just one. It's two or three times as big as our house in Avon. We have breakfast from 8:15 to 9:15, lunch in our rooms (they pack it) at any time, and dinner at 6:30. Food is very good, about the best I've had, except in certain rectories. Among the notables are JF, his wife, Marguerite Young, Robert Lowell, Owen Dodson, Bucklin Moon, Arna Bontemps, Michael Seide. Others, but I doubt that they'd mean much to you. I see mostly Moon and Theodore Roethke: we form the non-intellectual center. But do some fishing with Lowell. The little lakes are full of bass. Went to Mass Sunday and heard an intelligible sermon.

Emerson sent me Riley Hughes's review from *Columbia*; it was quite flattering to me; not so to Harry Sylvester.[1] Emerson wonders if it will make for strife between the authors. No doubt, but then Harry is selling, and I am not, and there should be some consolation for him in that. There are 25,000 copies of his book in print now. Mine, Moon tells me, is doing much better than expected but is still under 2,000, I think. Book business is very bad, and of course short stories always go to the post with two strikes against them. Thanks for sending the *Best Sellers* review. I thought it rather spotty for them. Favorable enough, but not very well done. For instance, there is no character in my book guilty, so far as I'm concerned, of gluttony; certainly not Fr Burner, or the priest in "The Lord's Day."

I've been thinking a lot of places since coming here and have just about decided that St Paul is the place for me. It is about right, it's old, it's not too big, I have what friends I have there, and perhaps I could make it my Dublin. As Dick Keefe told me, "Jim, you're a city man." So, if there's any chance for peace in the future, I think I'll concentrate on insinuating myself into St Paul. The bomb is the big but. No one here seems to have much hope. Lowell (he's a convert, you know, an ex-con like me, for being a CO) says it's pacifism or nothing, says we must become pacifists. I say I don't know, maybe we should become travelers. But where is the big question then. Geographically, I prefer the East to the Middle West. The country doesn't go on and on forever; there are more trees and hills. Well, well, I know you don't hold still for much of that kind of talk. This is a huge old pile, in the Summit Avenue manner, only bigger, and is crammed with junk: statues, bishops' chairs, ugly pictures, miniatures, fountains, books, etc., possibly the biggest heap of its sort for many miles. I rather like it, though. Enough for this time . . . pax.

Jim [. . .]

1 *Columbia*, July 1947. Review of Jim's *Prince of Darkness* and Sylvester's *Moon Gaffney*.

See Monty Woolley, the actor with the beard, all the time in one bar, waiting for a live one or somebody he can insult. They say he's queer as a crutch.

CHARLES SHATTUCK

Yaddo
July ?, 1947

Dear Chuck,

A line to let you know how things are in these parts. We've been here since the first of July, drove it all the way with no trouble with my runabout, which I believe you have a picture of. And now that we have it here, the runabout, I am quite the most popular person; Yaddo lies more than a mile out of town, and the bars, of course, are in the town. My most regular passengers are Buck Moon, Theodore Roethke ("The Beast of Bennington"), Robert Lowell. The first two are most regular, sometimes go without me, and Lowell is usually likewise broke, though it's more oversight with him; he forgets to cash checks. [. . .] There are some Brooklyn painters, and they are awful. Also a few analysts posing as writers, also awful. We play croquet evenings, quite the bloodiest thing I've been mixed up in since I gave up Pollyanna, the Glad Game.[1] [. . .] Ruth Domino[2] is sort of a fixture here—at least she puts out the mail and has charge of library books—but I do not know much about her, except her accent is German. Lowell says she was investigated by the FBI last spring for being a Communist, but then so many of us have been investigated by the FBI, even you. [. . .]

Pax,
Jim

HARVEY EGAN

Yaddo
July 23, 1947

Dear Father Egan,

[. . .] Lowell apparently is having his dark days. He says he is "not a practicing Catholic," but I will not give him the satisfaction of asking why

---

1 A version of Parcheesi.
2 Berlin-born poet and Quaker.

not. Something to do with his marriage. His wife is Jean Stafford, author of *Boston Adventure* and *The Mountain Lion* (Harcourt, Brace), but she is or was a Catholic before him. I figure characters like Lowell and myself flourish without direct apostolic work. The bark is always there. He knows it. He can climb on whenever he gets tired enough. Pamphlets and all that are out with his kind. He is a very nice guy. It's just a matter of time. Enough. Pax.

Jim

HARVEY EGAN

Yaddo
August 20, 1947

Dear Fr Egan,

Yes, there you are, lounging around, living the good life, and here I am up to my neck in handicapping and creative labors. I am grateful to you for all the reviews. [. . .] Who is Rev. E. J. Drummond, SJ, PhD? Is he the dean of the graduate school, Marquette University? Is it true that perhaps my hand is not as yet sure in the handling of complex symbols? What are complex symbols? Can I find them in the *Racing Form*? I am at sea. Should I look up Fortunata Caliri[1] in New York and get taken around? What would Betty say? All in all it's very funny, and I only wish there were more such reviews. I would not like to be panned, the way Harry is being, at least not for the same reasons, but I do enjoy being dissected by these English teachers. [. . .]

Haven't been to the track. Last time over saw Stymie beaten by outsider, Rico Monte, the Argentine beetle. This town, when we enter it, is full of New York touts and torpedoes and their women. Go in for a beer now and then, Michelob; "Glass a Mick, Jack." Seldom see or recognize the better classes, though we did see Elizabeth Arden, the cosmetics lady, and Harry Warner, of Warner Bros Pictures, the other night at the horse auction. Harry paid $44,000 for a yearling filly by War Admiral out of Betsy Ross II (please pass that info on to Fr Casey). [. . .]

They postponed the drawing on the Buick at St Clement's here. We have a ticket. The lady who "does" our rooms says Father said everything was going so well he thought they'd extend the carnival a few days, post-

1 Caliri reviewed the book for *Sign*, August 1947 ("One would like to take Mr. Powers around and introduce him to some of the truly admirable priests that one has met").

pone the drawing, and besides it rained Saturday night. You should have his job. He sits out on the sidewalk downtown with the Buick and helps the eighth-grade girls make change. I hope we win, not that we need a new car.

Pax,

Jim

Jim and Betty left Yaddo for New York City on September 2. Betty took the train for Minnesota on September 4. Jim returned to Yaddo on September 5.

BETTY POWERS

Yaddo
September 5, 1947, Friday afternoon,
a few minutes after returning

Dear Betty,

I don't quite know where you must be now, probably in Chicago, or coming into Chicago, or about to leave Chicago. It is around 2:30 here. I had an egg sandwich, clam chowder, and a piece of pie downtown before getting a cab and coming out; all at remarkable low prices. It was raining this morning when I went to Grand Central, as it was yesterday evening when we went, and so I took a cab, though I'd thought of walking. Well, after I came back from taking you to the train last night, I was pretty sad and tired. I took a bath and napped until Buck came, which was almost ten. Then we talked for a while, went out for a beer, only one, at Jimmy Ryan's, a jive joint on 52nd Street, and walked up Broadway, which was truly awful in the heat, though I wish I'd thought of taking you there—just for the horror of it. [. . .]

The effect of your things on the clothesline over the bathtub in the closet is . . . not good, little memories of the summer gone by. So, along with the now comparatively mild ghosts of Buck and Champ and Lowell, there is you. I am living in a haunted house. I do not expect to see anyone I want to see here in September. I expect to work. I feel that I must. I also won't be able to find the distractions I did when you were here. [. . .] And now, before I take my bath, let me tell you—you always forget—I love you. Do not be sad. Get to work. Take it easy. I hope you'll be staying at Bertie's but am addressing this otherwise because I don't know B.'s address.

Jim

Yaddo
Saturday, September 6, 1947

Mon pere,

[. . .] I expect to leave here around the last of September. It was possible for me to stay, and I began to wonder why I should return to Stearns County. As you see, I found no good reason for it. It has thinned out here, though, the old crowd I ran with no longer here: Buck Moon; Theodore Roethke; Rattleass Lowell . . . We were wined and dined in the grand manner this time in New York. Cocktail party, the *Saturday Review, Life* magazine, *New Republic, NY Times* Book Section people all there; yes, they all asked about you. Luncheon at 21 and Giovanni's; dinner at Cherio's. We stayed at the Algonquin at Doubleday's expense. "Red" Lewis[1] was there, another Stearns County boy.

The big thing, though, was landing $1,000 from my publishers without showing them a thing, no chapters, no outline. So now we are planning on having a well and probably will if they will come and drill it before we run out of dough again. I wanted to get a toilet too; J. L. Benvenisti,[2] when he comes to lecture, can stay at our house if he wants to. I thought I'd try to sell him to the Avon Commercial Club. He is my favorite *Commonweal* writer. He is the only one not so fair-minded that it makes you tired. I am thinking seriously now of doing that piece on Bishop Sheil for *The New Republic*.[3] I talked it over with them. They seem to want to be very favorable about him. I do not know if I can do a piece like that. Somebody told me once that he was a grandstander. Of course I could not do that either, a piece making that point. (In fiction, yes; naming names, no.) We'll see. It will be something to do when I'm in Chicago. Any leads?

Jim

BETTY POWERS
Yaddo
Thursday morning, September 11, 1947

Dear Betty,

Your letter written Tuesday came this morning, my only piece of mail,

---

1 Sinclair Lewis was born in Sauk Centre, Minnesota.
2 British economist.
3 Bishop Bernard James Sheil (1888–1969), auxiliary bishop of Chicago and celebrated advocate of social justice.

and I was glad to hear from you, marveling at the picture you painted of Stearns County and its denizens—horrified really to remember in detail and depth what I'd rather forgotten. I mean the people in the doctor's office and their language. [. . .]

I dreamed off and on last night of jail. Guess it was brought on by a letter from home, about my brother not working, narrowly escaping trouble all the time. I met Agnes Smedley last night in Clocker's studio.[1] She is not very much fun, I think, though that is the wrong idea, I guess. Other people find her inspiring, such faith, love of people, etc. Joe[2] and Steve, I hear, went on record this morning at the breakfast table as saying Bob Taft[3] was a fascist and a stinker—all sentiments culled from Agnes Smedley—and Mary Townsend[4] was there. Mary was very bitter about it indeed, even said something about Agnes ought to be kicked out of Yaddo. I think that's about it. Mary's husband was a speed demon, one of the boys out of Waugh's *Vile Bodies*, I guess, and she is filled with the conservatism of the unthinking, well-off; Agnes is filled with radicalism of the opposite. Somehow, though, it comes to about the same thing in them. Their personalities render their beliefs negligible. The funny thing, I guess, is that Joe and Steve don't know what happened, though they were there to see and hear it. They are a couple of beauts. To my knowledge I have never heard either one say anything I do not remember reading many times in the newspaper. And now I leave you, having analyzed the local scene for you. As you can see, it's pretty much the same. Clocker is about the only one left I can stand at all.

Love,
Jim

What about the well?

1 Agnes Smedley (1892–1950), writer, journalist, Communist sympathizer, chronicler of the Chinese revolution. She was at the center of a divisive campaign launched by Lowell to eject Elizabeth Ames from Yaddo in 1948.
2 Joe Lasker (1919–), artist.
3 Robert A. Taft, conservative senator from Ohio, who wrote the Taft-Hartley Act.
4 Assistant at Yaddo; violently anti-Communist; resigned in 1948 during the Agnes Smedley imbroglio.

Yaddo

Friday afternoon, September 12, 1947

Dear Betty,

Your last letter rec'd last night. This is one hell of a hot day, altogether as bad as we had in early August. I envy you if it's getting cool there. [. . .] I am hoping that in one of your letters pretty soon you'll finally get around to giving me a picture of things as they really are. So far you've skipped around as though you haven't had time to sit down and think; in your subject matter, that is. I am wondering: Do we have electricity? Do we or are we going to have a well? When? How are the Hyneses? The Humphreys? I am not very interested in the sermons at church or weddings. Now, praise the Lord, it is raining. I'm afraid, however, it won't last. Very glad to hear you are so healthy and that we aren't going to have twins. I think a week in Chicago will be plenty, and if I leave here on the 27th, I should arrive in St Cloud in plenty of time for event. What do I do at it? I promise to cut the first person dead who expects me to act like Dagwood or Carlos Cotton[1] with the cigars. [. . .]

Much love,

Jim

Yaddo

Friday afternoon, September 19, 1947

Dear Betty,

Rec'd your good, long letter this morning and felt right away that it was too bad I had to write such a bad one, like yours that preceded it, yesterday. [. . .] I was very glad to have so much information on Don. That is the sort of reporting I'd been hoping for. Now, if you could do as well on Sr Mariella and the Hyneses, I think I'd be satisfied. Do not count on it, however. I had a long letter from Fr Garrelts this morning, and so I really started the day off well, with two good letters. Yes, it is rather scarifying, the way things are going up in price, and we will have to devise other ways of eating, as you suggest. I still doubt that very much can be done about our menus, though, without spending money. Those silly damned menus you get in the paper are no help at all. It is even insulting to read

1 Artist, member of the Movement.

them. I see where the Calvert Distillery people are using actual photos of the people who have changed to Calvert's now. Imagine that. Imagine the people who let themselves be used in that way. It is the proof of our degeneracy. [. . .]

I've decided that Joe isn't so bad. He told us the other night about how he sketched a nude model in the Artists' Village in the World's Fair but couldn't take more than an hour of it. He had to wear a smock and flowing tie. The man was sorry to see him go, the manager, but Joe had to go. It was too much. "And now we black in the head" is the sort of thing he had to say to the carnal mob which was supposed to be made up of people interested in sketching. [. . .] I hope this letter makes up for my last, bad one. I miss you all the time.

LOVE,
Jim

I guess I might as well do another page, since you did so well by me. [. . .] Fr Egan, did I tell you, sent the review from the *Catholic World* of my book. One of the worst ones, on the *Sign* order, but worse: "With a few deft strokes he limns a character . . . There is an economy of incident and word . . . Simplicity of style and language does not conceal the telling phrase . . . Interest is sustained and suspense is not lacking . . . A priest will rightfully be moved to irritation instead of meditation by the ineptness of the surgery that hacks rather than cuts cleanly"—in short the whole Catholic works, or why we will never have a legitimate literary criticism. And who is the reviewer assigned to my book? He is the author of the forthcoming *Judicial Philosophy of Justice Cardozo*.[1] God save us. I am seriously considering never appearing in a Catholic publication again. This is an extreme case of it, of course, but *The Commonweal* is only different in a degree. It is all contained in the evaluation of fiction. It is for women. Nonfiction, now, that is for men. Fiction is not taken seriously. We are still tied to the apron strings of all the old bores. Then too we are still in a ghetto, Catholics who write, or even read . . .

I am hoping we'll be able to keep warmer this winter than last. This winter will probably be worse, too . . . Everybody remarked last night how wonderful you were, pregnant, so bouncy, so glow in the eye, so bloom on the cheek. And I had to say I had not noticed it, but I guess I had without putting it in words. I do remember how pretty and sad you looked in that

1 The Reverend Walter T. Gouch.

restaurant where we had our last supper . . . It seemed a terrible shame to leave you, to remember the things, some of them, I'd said to you, and worse, the nice things I'd only thought and not said to you . . . Enough. I'm getting out of hand . . . I love you . . . Betty.

Jim

BETTY POWERS

Yaddo

Saturday, 6:00 p.m., September 20, 1947

Dear Betty,

[. . .] I had a great long talk about doctors and analysts and the world condition today at lunch with Clocker and O'Connor Barrett. I found that Barrett and I have the same outlook, the rather unmentionable one which says that about all an artist can do is his work; that the goals of the cooperators, communists, and other reformers are not new goals at all; that it would be a lot better use of the language if they would state that they are bent on a petty, stuffy little crusade and not the great soul-stirring one their literature seems to describe, patching, not creating. Last night Elizabeth[1] sat in the main room after dinner and went into Yaddo history, including a great ice storm, and it was fairly interesting. [. . .]

Still no word about our well, or any real news about the rural lifers, in your letters, which are good but omit these things as though it were almost a conspiracy to keep me breathless, waiting. Why don't you go to the telephone and call somebody up? Or won't your dad take you out to Hyneses some Sunday? Or won't the Meades talk over the phone? I hear the gong. I love you. Write.

Jim

BETTY POWERS

Yaddo

September 22, 1947

Dear Betty,

Dullish short letter from you yesterday, Sunday, and nothing this morning, but I guess I must love you just the same, consider it with your other faults as nothing against your virtues. [. . .]

1 Elizabeth Ames.

Yesterday *The NY Times* ran that stuff about me in People Who Read and Write and Fornicate, getting my initials wrong and, it would seem, cutting out a vital message about priests and doctors. At least the paragraph on me is headed "Priests and Doctors," but there's nothing about either one. I imagine it was my famous thesis about doctors nowadays having the eminence that priests had in the past that was cut. [. . .]

Do try to get to Hyneses soon. I am anxious to know if Zahn and Leonard[1] will be around to temper the monotony this winter. [. . .]

I must prepare to meet the Stearnsers. With the prospect of more expense on the car, I am almost absolutely resigned to not going to Washington.[2] You do see the dilemma for me, though, don't you? When I hear from you that Pat is spending a thousand dollars for furniture and you are trying to get a cabinet for our baby for five . . . if we are two in one flesh, we are not yet two in one spirit. It is not your fault at this point . . . you are a woman in a world you never made, and not to be blamed for wanting things you ought to have, for being brave . . . about things I guess I'd hoped you wd not feel you'd have to be brave about to do without . . . I don't know what you can do now. I suppose I thought I'd made it clear there'd be times like these. Maybe you can make a lot of money. Perhaps you'd counted on that, and that's where the trouble is. Is it so bad, though, that you have to be brave? You have said many times that you didn't want to marry Elmer or the dentist . . . Excuse this reverie. I'm really sorry I wrote this last bit I don't believe in it. It is the same thing Buck's wife gets him saying. I think the thing in women that gets men feeling guilty in this way is bad. I think such women have married the wrong men. I think it's their own fault.

Love . . . . . .
Jim

ROBERT LOWELL

Yaddo
Thursday [September 25, 1947]

Dear Cal,

Glad to hear from you, only wishing I might have seen you two "leftists" (Harry S.[3] and you) together in New York, or anywhere for that matter. [. . .]

1 Gordon Zahn and Leonard Doyle.
2 He planned to visit John Haskins and Robert Lowell.
3 Harry Sylvester.

The car—you would want to know how the car is, wouldn't you? The car was given six new spark plugs, fresh oil, and air in the tires. For almost a week it ran like a dream. Then it rebelled. [. . .] I had counted, until then, on driving through the Alleghenies, down from Elmira, where I am paying a call, and on into the nation's capital, there to see a friend and you—I am doing a paper on the percentage of Latin words, rather of English words of Latin origin, to be found in the work of Theodore Roethke, as against Walter Savage Landor, and I understand that you are very helpful in such matters. But, no, alas, I must needs take the shortest road home (Chicago). Now that I have your schedule, I see it might have been possible to drive you to the Middle West. You would have liked that? In any case it would have been nice driving you about the nation's capital, letting it be seen right away that you were not without friends of substance . . . I thought the limerick (Powers, sours, races, paces, hours) unkind . . .[1]

I heard from [Robert] Fitzgerald (not Fitsgerald, or do you mean it that way?). He enclosed the review he wrote which might have been if I'd been newsworthy or whatever it is they look for in a writer . . . [. . .] Just Agnes Hart, Edw. Maisel, and Joe and me left—and Agnes Smedley, but she doesn't seem to be my type and vice versa. These are tough times for a clerical fascist. Agnes is writing the life of a one-eyed Chinese general; he is what she calls "an amazing man." God bless you.

Pax,
Jim

BETTY POWERS

Yaddo
Friday morning, September 26, 1947

Dear Betty,
[. . .] Well, today is my last here, and I'm afraid I hadn't anticipated the feeling I have about leaving. I don't want to. I can't think very straight either. I'd expected to work right through until the time I left, but my state of mind won't allow it today. I guess you must have felt that way . . . about working, I mean, on the last day. Nice old place here, I've enjoyed it so

1 "There was a [illegible] writer named Powers; / Got stinking on 3 whiskey sours, / And entered his car at the races; / But after he'd gone fifty paces / The horses had finished for hours." Robert Lowell to J. F. Powers, September 24, 1947.

much, even now, though summer was better when everybody was here, and I hate to leave. I do leave, however, tomorrow morning: Mary Townsend is having my sandwiches put in a bag. So much for leave-taking . . . [. . .]

I guess the St John's games are something, as you say, and I hope we'll get to one together since you like that. Maybe the last one in October if the baby comes around the middle and we can get someone to take care of the baby . . . oh, God, with that statement I realize again that we are moving into another category. Do not talk about not wanting the baby. You will have it; you will want it; so will I. [. . .]

Now, my last letter from Yaddo, with love. Keep happy. If you have any cravings which can be satisfied under ten dollars, let me know, or go ahead and get it yourself.

     Jim

Jim left Yaddo and drove to Elmira, New York, to visit Ted LeBerthon, who was in the midst of a nervous breakdown. He then drove to Washington, visiting John Haskins and Robert Lowell. He drove Lowell to Gambier, Ohio, to Kenyon College, after which the two traveled on to Chicago.

BETTY POWERS

2115 F Street, N.W.
Washington 7, D.C.
September 29, 1947

Dear Betty,

First chance I've had to write to you on the way—and I will have wired you my whereabouts by the time this arrives. As I mean to say in the wire, the car was running so well, and the situation in Elmira looked so bad, so unpropitious to camaraderie, I decided to go to Washington. I studied the roads in that tour book and found the hills or mountains are not so much, as in fact they aren't. The thing that was bad, which they did not mention, was the condition of much of the road. Good stretches, then bad stretches. However, the car is doing wonderfully, and I know you will understand my decision to make the trip after all—after deciding I wouldn't. I intend to see Lowell while here, perhaps this morning, and may get a little more information on the Guggenheim—let that, I think, be justification for my coming if you can't feel good about camaraderie—and I know I'm making you hate that word, if you don't already. [. . .] It is Monday morning. I love you.

Jim

Washington
Wednesday, October 1, 1947

Dear Betty,

Just a note to let you know nothing in particular. We are leaving tomorrow early—7:30—for Gambier, Ohio, Kenyon College, and should leave for Chicago Friday or Saturday, arriving Saturday evening. I am again in no very collected state of mind, much wrangling here over bookcases, food, etc., things on which Hask and Mrs Hask differ and which I am expected to take sides on. Yesterday had lunch with Lowell and Hask, and then Lowell and I went out to St Elizabeth's Hospital to see Ezra Pound. I wonder, alas, if you ever heard of him. He was the "discoverer" of Eliot, Cummings, Joyce, and others, a great figure in literary history, who spoke on the radio for Mussolini during the war and now is supposed to be out of his mind and is supposed to be tried for treason if he ever recovers. [. . .]

Love,

Jim

Paulina Street, Chicago
October 5, 1947

Dear Betty,

Well, sir, I know you'll think this letter is too long coming, but we arrived here only today. We had no trouble, none at all, all the way—and you can tell that to E. Hynes, C. Cotton, and D. Humphrey. We left Washington, as you ought to know, Thursday morning and arrived at Gambier, O., that night around nine-thirty. It was definitely the longest, hardest day of all. It was almost 400 miles and much of it over winding roads after dark, and there was also those awful towns around and including Pittsburgh to go through. For the time I was passing through them, I was all for the rural life.

Yesterday we set sail for Chicago, after a good evening with John Crowe Ransom, editor of *The Kenyon Review,* and some of his cronies: a very literary evening during which hundreds of names came up and I hardly knew them at all, the Elizabethans and Pope and Dryden and Juvenal and Petrarch—in fact, I guess, many of the people your education prepared you to talk about. Very good, though.

After traveling sixty miles or so yesterday morning, I got gas and discovered Chicago was still over 300 miles. We had been told by the classicists that it was 275 from Gambier; it would seem to be almost 400. So, though we might have made it, we decided to take it easy and come into Chicago this morning, which we did. We spent last night in one of those "cabins" you rent. We went to bed at 10:30, trying vainly all evening to have a good time. No use, though; it was one of those noisy little towns pierced every few minutes by a train going to Chicago and coming out of Chicago. We had thought originally to get a cabin on the shore of Lake Michigan, but that can't be done, evidently.

We went to one place, inquired, were told to wait a minute, but by then we began to notice it was inhabited almost entirely by old ladies sitting tight in rocking chairs. So I decided we ought to move on. We managed this, or I did, by asking the woman who'd told us to wait: Have you got a bar? She stuttered and asked to have the question repeated. I repeated it, or Lowell did, for he was enjoying himself; it was almost like Boston with all the old ladies reading through magnifying glasses. She said: I should say not! So we left, meeting a man in the yard wearing a brown shirt, wearing binoculars, and looking like a scout master. He got his map for us; his map was more detailed. We left. We end, as I said, having our beer and dinner in this noisy little town. It was the only place you could get anything but beer; so I guess I ought to add that we had martinis too. It was called Chesterton. So maybe there's something to be said for the Catholic revival, or wasn't he in it? [. . .]

Lowell and I had good fun all the trip. We left better friends than ever. He paid for most of the gas, meals, etc. He ended by imitating the car's voice all the time, always thinking, what was it thinking now? This morning we talked for hours about what if New York and Chicago had a war. [. . .]

Henry[1] lectures me in one letter: says I've got more fame than anybody ever had from one book of stories, including Joyce, Porter, and Welty. Wants me to relax and stop agitating. It's a good letter, much sense in it; I

1 Henry Volkening.

do think, though, he had seven old-fashioneds for lunch that day. [. . .]
Take good care of yourself. I love you, Betty.

    Jim

BETTY POWERS

Chicago
October 6, 1947

Dear Betty,

    No letter from you today, but then I suppose you didn't get mine today either, the one mailed yesterday. It is quite warm, even warmer than warm, here, and that doesn't do much for me and Chicago. [. . .]

    I was wondering if you were being so lenient about my return—you said not before the 29th—on account of you are so sweet or on account of we still don't have a well, with the prospects about the same. Which? Both, you say. Well, I'll be back before the 29th, never fear. I may leave here around the 13th, stay a day or two with Jack Howe at Taliesin, a day or two in St Paul, and then, triumphantly, to Stearns County. Doesn't seem much of a drive, Mpls to St Cloud, after my travels. Do wish my folks would get out of this animated ghost town. If they were somewhere near me, somewhere within easy distance, say a hundred miles or so, I think my greatest emotional worry would be over. I guess they would move all right if it weren't for Grandma. She doesn't want to leave her friends, the only trouble being that no one has ever seen one of them. Her money is in the bank here too. She probably can't get it through her head that it could be transferred, or perhaps she just wants to make it miserable for my mother as long as she can. You get the situation. I think my mother could be your second friend—until me, you said, you never had a real friend—as she is a beautiful soul, always fixing up something, making something, for you. She is my mother. I am prejudiced. It is also all true. Well, I've come to the end of the page. No more. I love you. That's all.

    Jim

ROBERT LOWELL

Taliesin
October 14, 1947

Dear Cal,

    Just a line to tell you that Katherine Anne Porter and Dudley Fitts said yes, KA wiring me "by all means go ahead," and writing a fine letter which makes me feel good.[1] I heard from Kerker Quinn that she is doing the *Sewanee* review of my book; Zabel[2] is doing the *Accent* one; and that is certainly flattering, for how many books do they review? You are the fourth one on my Guggenheim application, the three aforementioned [*sic*] and you. [. . .]

Don't think I'll do the Sheil piece. It'd be rather ironic, the way I'd have to do it, now that I know what I know—too many microphones and cameras in the bishop's life—and so I'm skipping it, though the Lord knows, and Betty knows even better, that we could use the money.

Staying here a day or two with two friends from the prison days.[3] I saw a plan yesterday for raising the face of Pittsburgh. About all that remains of the riverfront is the cathedral of learning, and it's dwarfed by other things. This is another monastery, devoted to another god. I seem to spend my life in other people's monasteries, listening to talk of other gods. [. . .]

My address now: Avon, Minn. Let me hear from you.

Jim

---

1 Recommending Jim for a Guggenheim grant.
2 Morton Dauwen Zabel (1901–1964).
3 Jack Howe and Davy Davison, Frank Lloyd Wright's two "young geniuses" from Sandstone prison.

8

I've a few stipulations to read into the rural-life-family-life jive

November 6, 1947—April 5, 1948

The "house" in the Avon woods, 1947

Jim and Betty were living again out in the woods with inadequate heat, no
water, and plenty of dampness. Betty's baby was overdue.

HARVEY EGAN

Avon

November 6, 1947

Dear Fr Egan,

I haven't heard from you in some time, hope you are still in good standing. It is snowing here today, the first snow of the season, which makes it
seem like old times, and our roof is leaking, which really makes it seem
like old times, and still we do not have a well. Already, however, Betty has
filled a bucket with snow, thinking it will melt and give us water, but she
does not reckon on our stove, which always stays cool, no matter what we
do to it. In short the rural life is about the same. Betty is still very much
with child, the event being over a week delayed now, and I must say I am
getting tired of it. It holds up my trip to the Cities. [. . .] There doesn't appear to be any real prospect of our getting water—all we get are promises,
the same ones we got this time last year—and we've been thinking we
ought to postpone our life here. Do you suppose you could find a place in
St Paul, cheap, roomy, private? Soon? I suppose not. I know what I'm asking. Still, it's the only thing I can see. We might, probably will, stick it out
here with baby and no water and damn little camaraderie, but I think
we'd be happier this winter in St Paul. Or Mpls, I would say, though I
prefer St Paul, as does Betty. I told Fr G. about this in a letter yesterday.
Please let me know, only don't strain yourself, I know it's a long-shot bet
at best.

   Pax,

      Jim

I was born on November 11, 1947. Jim and Betty stayed in St. Cloud for a while, Betty with her parents and Jim with the Strobels, Betty's aunt, Birdie, and her husband, Al.

GEORGE GARRELTS

St Cloud

Martinmas, November 11, 1947

George,

It's a girl . . . nine lbs and fourteen ounces. Very damned grueling, the whole business, really too much for a man to take. Slogan of the day, bandied from nun to nurse, and back again: she'll never remember this when it's all over. I guess the idea is not to discourage the male, lest the race die out. Tell Fr Egan, will you? I think he ought to know, and I don't feel up to even a note like this. Katherine Anne will be the name, I think.

Pax,

James

HARVEY EGAN

St Cloud

Sunday morning, November 16, 1947

Dear Father Egan,

[. . .] I wrote Fr G. the other day, the day the baby was born, and asked him to relay the news to you. I trust he did. If he didn't, it was a girl. So we can't call it Harvey very well. We are calling it Katherine Anne, after Miss Porter and my dead aunt Kate. The baby was born on St Martin's Day. "Martinmas" is the title of Betty's story in the November 15 *New Yorker*, in case you want to look it up at the library. Tomorrow, I believe, Betty is coming home—home to the Wahls'. I am staying here, at the Strobels'—their house is bigger, more luxurious, my style—but not for long. I expect to visit the Cities any day. Research is calling me. [. . .]

I am being felt out by St John's to teach creative writing. Can't make up my mind. Don't go much for the teaching part, but do feel it'd give me a chance to use the library and meet the boys (not the students). [. . .]

Jim

Jim took over a creative writing class at St. John's for an instructor who had left mid-semester.

HARVEY EGAN

St Cloud

November 1947

Mon pere,

Rec'd yours yesterday on one of my jaunts up-country—you know of course that I keep a place in the country, a sort of hunting and fishing and praying retreat—and am happy that you thought to suggest the name Catherine Ann. The only thing is we are going to call it Katherine Anne. I have just come from the upper regions of the Wahl house, it is early in the morning, but already they are working on it, giving it a bath, etc. Add to all this the past week and I have had a snootful. Are you sure I am too old to get in at Nazareth Hall?[1] I don't know a lot of Latin, but always got good marks in English and with the vernacular on XXXX (no XXXXXXX eraser in the whole damned house; it was never blessed, I'm sure) the way, maybe I'd be just what they'd be looking for. I am also a close friend of R. M. Keefe, who did a lot of time at Mundelein,[2] so may be said to know the ropes. I realize that I would have to give up "my writing," as they say in panel discussions, but then that seems to be outmoded no matter how you look at it. Here, if I stay here, it is just a matter of time before I am clerking at the Schmid General Store in Avon or, if I would prefer the city, at Linneman's in St Joe.[3]

I see that it snowed again last night. Well, it'll have to do worse than that to keep me off the highway this week. I think it'll be Thursday now. I am driving Don in too. I am going out to Avon and live by myself, beginning today. I've got the oil burner to keep me warm . . . and privacy. I may stay a week in St Paul and Mpls, so figure out where I can stay cheap and be able to work. I don't mean the rectory. I intend to be around longer than that. A man's got to breathe, don't I?

Jim

---

1 Preparatory seminary at the College (as it was called then) of St. Thomas, St. Paul.
2 Chicago seminary.
3 Avon's population was around 880; St. Joe's (St. Joseph's) around 1,200.

Rural Life

Avon

Thursday evening, November 1947

Dear Fr Egan,

Al Jolson is singing on the radio now, and naturally my thoughts turn to you. Very glad to have your note and the enclosure . . . but why is it that the *Sign* keeps picking on me? Why is it that Mrs Lamb doesn't like me? (Al says at his time of life he likes beautiful music.) Very cool here in Stearns County, around 50 in our house, degrees, not people. I am still meeting my class. It is pretty much of a snap, though I do have to watch myself that I don't take them too seriously and get them sore at the stuff they turn in. [. . .]

We like to go to St John's [Abbey Church] because there is no lay participation, or I do. I am only slowly getting the idea that I am surrounded by people who are working night and day for things like the dialogue Mass. Imagine my dismay at the discrepancy between the party line and my own feelings in these matters. However, it's only feelings with me, not theory. Big party last Sunday night at the Cottons': Zahn, Hyneses, Gene McCarthy, Nugents (Canadians come to live the good life in Stearns County), Gills (she's the former Rosemary Jensen), L. Doyle (he's the translator of the forthcoming *Rule of St Benedict* done in Easy Essays form) and Betty Finegan (she's going to be L. Doyle's wife, and that *is* news), and the Powerses (she's the Dante scholar; he's the former track man at Saratoga).

I am certainly considering your invitation to Laurel Avenue but will let you know for sure, and when, if. Fr G. was here last week, staying overnight, seeing us all, enjoying the winter sports (spitting at the stove), and I wish you'd find the time and enthusiasm to visit us, anytime. Dick Keefe will be the godfather by proxy.

Buck Moon at Doubleday announces from Florida, where he is resting up with his folks, that there's a new Fr Murphy[1] in the house and it makes *Forever Amber* sound like "The Three Bears." I hope so. It ought to rip the book-reviewing boys and girls wide open in certain pious places. Buck is sending me a first-edition copy when published bound in the hide of a Black Protestant, so he says. He says all the Doubleday hands were wondering where they'd take Fr M. the last time he hit the big town, and

1 Edward F. Murphy, SJ, *Père Antoine* (1947), published by Doubleday.

Buck finally said, 21 of course. The others thought 21 might be too worldly. When they all arrived there, risking it, it turned out that all the waiters in the place knew Fr M., his favorite food. Enough for now. You'll be hearing from me. You might send me a hockey schedule so I'll know when to come.

    Pax,

      Jim

ROBERT LOWELL

Wednesday, November 26 [1947]

Dear Cal,

[. . .] Well, we had a baby, a girl, on November 11, Armistice Day, but even more significantly St Martin's Day, or Martinmas, which is the title of Betty's story in *The New Yorker* for November 15. She's heard from a few publishers already. Is it all right, since they are looking for novels, to mention yours?

Got a kick out of your description of goings-on in Davenport, especially likening the priests to Buck and Champ. That struck me as exactly right; they are that way, the Roman clergy—the only clergy today that is, perhaps accounting for the vitality of the Church, to say nothing of its blindness, its honest blindness.

Do not hear from Champ, indeed did not expect to, but I guess Buck would like a word. Be sure and see him if you're in New York. There were a couple of days here, hell and high water days, when I was virtually off for the East. I had an offer of a job as editor at *Commonweal*, the one Broderick gave up for *The New Yorker*, but I saw it would take me away from my book, the St Paul book, and withstood the temptation. Then, too, it was not clear what I could do there, beyond seeing that a few books got properly reviewed. I didn't want to get away from St Paul, find myself like Marguerite and Elizabeth Hardwick adrift in the great city at the mercy of it all.

The baby is crying like hell now. I am not liking it one bit and do not expect to grow used to it. What a foul fiend I am to have for a father.

I enjoy Ezra's little messages. The last one: See here Darkness, don't tell me you're just a blue eye'd boy who sold one to a mag . . . I guess he's right about that lowbrow stuff. But then I've come quite a way. It was the sort of thing I'd been given to believe in the Thirties, when I came of age, that stories were made of. And of course it's the kind of thing Ezra set his sails against at the beginning.

We are calling the baby Katherine Anne, after you know who. Outside of that I haven't had much to do with it. [. . .]

You ask me how it feels to be a father. About the same, I think. Except I've a few stipulations to read into the rural-life-family-life jive that circulates in these liturgical parts. If you must get married, I say to young people, be sure you can afford a fifteen-room house and servants. That comes as a blow to them. They read *The Catholic Worker* and all the rest and are accustomed to thinking in terms of Mary and Joseph and the manger. We have the manger, but we are not Mary and Joseph. Anyway, we are not Joseph.

A monk got tired of teaching creative writing at St John's, so I took the job for the rest of the semester. They are paying me $250, or about $20 an hour. It's only an hour on Tuesday and an hour on Thursday, about my limit.

I had to write *The New Republic* and tell them I wasn't the man to do the piece on Bishop Sheil. It would not have been very inspiring if I did it, and I don't care to have a controversy with *The NR* or Catholics on those grounds. Harry Sylvester thought I was being precious in my objections. I say Bishop S. went into labor and race the way Notre Dame went into football under Rockne. Nobody would enjoy that, save perhaps my friends, if I wrote it that way.

Let me hear from you.

Jim

HARVEY EGAN

Avon

Monday night, December 1947

Dear Fr Egan,

[. . .] Well, the child is baptized, and it is good, as you say, to have a little Christian among us. It gives Betty some company too. I have been weighing the future and believe, since you predict plenty of blood around the nets that night, I'll journey St Paul–ward on Christmas Day, right after one of those family gatherings in St Cloud. It will serve as a beautiful excuse to leave early. So get those ducats for the 25th. Is there some concordance or Lives of the Saints I could read in the meantime so I'll be as hep as you are? All I know is the blue line. [. . .]

Peace,

Jim

Avon

December 12 [1947]

Dear Cal,

[. . .] My days are so active here that I don't get much work done. Now it's storm windows. Betty is painting them in the kitchen. The temperature in our house, so called, is always around 50. That doesn't make for much relaxation. I bought a bottle of whiskey and a bottle of rum, a little cheer, but there is no one really to drink it with. Your plan which has us all teaching at one school is charming, but not teaching much. How about Buck and Ted? Can't you work them into this perfect society? I had a letter today from the president of Bennington offering me a job for the spring quarter, I think it is. I asked Betty if she'd like to go to Vermont. She said she would like to. I like the idea, not settling down there, which isn't indicated in the letter, I believe, but getting away from here for a while. You know I've been here in Stearns County two months now, fighting the elements every minute of it. [. . .] I enclose a new picture of car. Guess what it was saying when I went out and found it like this one morning: Some shit!

Write.

Jim

ROBERT LOWELL

Avon

February 13, 1948

Dear Cal,

[. . .] I heard from Buck today, and he has recommended me, at Ted's instigation, to Bennington, but I do not hear. Do not worry so much about that, though. St John's here owe me $250 but cannot bring themselves to remember, or perhaps I am getting it in prayers. Says Buck: "Champ was here and took New York, Doubleday, and the chickies like Grant took Richmond. He had steak, white wine, and truffles for lunch (thank God I'm not his editor) and was seldom found with a straight elbow during the cocktail hour." Dear Champ, I knew him well, well, fairly well.

Glad to hear Caroline [Gordon][1] likes my stories. I enjoyed Tate's piece

1 Caroline Gordon (1895–1981), novelist and critic. Recent convert to Catholicism and married to Allen Tate at the time.

on the bishop in the current *Western Review,* having reread *The Crack-Up* the night before and scenes from *Gatsby.* For some reason I can't penetrate into *Tender Is the Night.* And got through first James the other night, "Lesson of the Master," and think it quite wonderful, the main problem of the writer always.

Yes, it is too bad about the Living Gallery.[1] I've seen pictures of the foundress, a thin little sister wasting away under the decisions she must make and the attack of un-housebroken authors like Harry Sylvester, and now you come along with perhaps the worst blow of all.[2] So far as I know the only other living author not primarily a librarian she had was Waugh. I don't know what I'd say if asked. [. . .]

Pax,

Jim

Regards to Ezra and Mrs Pound. (I sent the list of names for advance copies, the Italian translation, of my book to my agent, asking counsel, and he replied for God's sake let's stay clear of Pound's old fascist colleagues— Ezra had sent me a list of Italians who'd be able to "introduce" my book properly over there.)

ROBERT LOWELL

Bad Avon[3]
February 18, 1948

Dear Cal,

[. . .] I ought to tell you that work was completed today on our drainage system. I have been digging a trench, in which I have been hoping to put sewer pipe, building fires to melt the ice, chopping the ice, looking at the ice, and now it is all over, and the mud is drying on my galoshes. I see that the foregoing gives the wrong impression, the impression of achievement. What I meant to say was that I gave the damned thing up. The pipe is stacked outside our door. We await the thaws of spring . . .

1 The Gallery of Living Catholic Authors, a literary hall of fame for contemporary Catholic authors founded in 1932 by Sister Mary Joseph Scherer, an English teacher and librarian at Webster College in Missouri.
2 Invited to join the gallery, Lowell, a Catholic convert (for a time), told them that he had fallen away. ("I had to break the bad news to them, and now masses are being said for me—God rest my soul; you seem to be the only one that doesn't go in for that sort of thing." Lowell to J. F. Powers, February 5, 1948.)
3 "Bad" as in German "spa." Joke.

Thanks for the James list; I appreciate not having to wade into his collected stories cold turkey. I am more skeptical than ever of Faulkner. Several weeks ago I read his story "Spotted Horses," described as one of the funniest in the language by Cowley in the *Portable* I have,[1] and though I liked spots very much, the whole thing is not for me.* I get tired trying to put his sentences together, not just for sense and transition, but to get some idea of the effect he had in mind . . . I read Conrad's *Heart of Darkness* the other night—my first Conrad, incidentally, having been killed off in previous attempts—and I was reminded, especially in the action scenes on the steamboat, of Faulkner, the confusion of the language. I have a secret theory, not that, just a feeling, that action is better and easier when described not in chronological, realistic terms but as impression, with here and there a realistic effect. Faulkner does that. So does Conrad. It enables the prose writer to use poetry. I don't feel it's legitimate, though—at least now I don't—and I don't want to try it for fear I'd find it easy, the sloppy way, and I don't intend to try it. I see, on rereading this, I am trying to make it all sound reasonable. The truth is I feel it is not a matter I can be reasonable about. I do not care for Faulkner—spots, yes, the story "A Rose for Emily," for instance—as I don't care for Hemingway. In these apostolic parts I am always meeting people who think Graham Greene wonderful. It is the same thing, only I do not mind so much being in disagreement with the Greene-ites . . . Enough for now.

Pax,

Jim

*The thing I remember and remember is where that fat kid is caught eating out of the candy case. Shades of Uncle Bud!

Weary of the rigors of living without running water in a damp half cellar in the woods, Jim and Betty started looking for an apartment in St. Paul—which is to say, they put out the call to their various friends.

1 *The Portable Faulkner*, edited by Malcolm Cowley.

Avon, Minnesota
1948

Wish to rent apt in Cathedral district. Writers, smoke, drink, have baby, but no narcotics. Consider exchanging same for uninhabitable woodland retreat near monastery. Fairly desperate.

Catholic couple wishes to rent apt in Cathedral dist. Have baby, own furniture, Mixmaster. Best ecclesiastical reference. Reasonable.

Hockey fan and wife need roomy apt suitable for salon. Baby but . . .

Have you an apt to rent to famous author, critic, lecturer and wife and offspring? Could coach basketball or baseball.

Friend of Rev. R. Bandas[1] desires living quarters in or near Cathedral. Homeless today. Is this tomorrow?

Will the Saints get out of the cellar in '48? Will young author, wife, child? What have you?

Ex–second baseman needs a home near Cathedral and Lex. Has batted against Fritz Ostermueller's brother.

Homeless horseplayer, wife, and child seek living quarters and floor space adjoining suitable for handbook in exchange for reliable turf information.

Dear Fr Egan,

I have been mulling over the housing situation, as you can see from the above, but can't quite settle on the best angle. Fr G. was here for a few days during which Betty was in St Cloud and we lived the full life out here. Now he has gone to Quincy. He wanted me to go, but I was just

1 Father Rudolph G. Bandas (1896–1969), a particular bugbear of Egan and Jim. Rector of St. Paul Seminary at the time; theologian; author of many religious books.

strong enough to refuse. He threatens to run ad like #2 above in Mpls paper, but Betty says we do not want to live there, only St Paul, only near the cathedral, so I must head him off before he returns this week Thursday. Things are not too bad here, at least not for me (very hard on Betty with no water and diapers all the time), and I was thinking for a time at Mass this morning that it might work out. I get little flashes like that, though this one might have been due to the fact that I worked until 5:00 a.m. last night. I think it was Bp Schenk[1] kneeling up in front this morning, but couldn't be sure, he wouldn't turn his head. Had a lot of trouble with his skullcap, though, kept falling off.

Thanks for the clip on Harry and Msgr Smith. I don't know which one is wilder. I kept wondering who the good Catholic publications were that Msgr Smith had in mind. *The Register*, I suppose, for one; the *Visitor* for two; and *Sign, Extension*, and the *Catholic World*. Spare us, O Lord. Why don't we start a magazine called *Puck*, with you doing a column called In the Sin Bin? Wish I could be there for the Winter Carnival. Looks awfully good in today's paper.[2]

Pax,

Jim

A possible four-room apartment in St. Paul found by Father Egan fell through.

HARVEY EGAN

Avon, Minnesota

1948

Dear Father Egan,

[. . .] I rec'd a note from Fr Judge[3] (remember him, healthy-looking fellow in a black suit?) with a ten spot enclosed & I would not have thought a few months ago watching them saddle up under the trees of Saratoga that $10 could mean so much. [. . .]

Letter from Sr Eugene Marie, still flourishing, and her brother's wife or somebody in St Paul will look for a place for us and let you know if anything ensues. I'm afraid, though, we won't get the vision of four rooms

1 Francis Joseph Schenk (1901–1969), bishop of Crookston, Minnesota, at the time.
2 Joke.
3 Associated with *The Catholic Worker* and rural lifers.

again, which I liked the sound of, thinking I could have my mother and father visit sometime. When I took my solemn vows, I did not understand that I would have to forgo the sight of my father and mother, rather dear to me, but that's the way it turns out; I do get to see Art and Money, however. We were in today, always a struggle, lugging the wash around and water cans and baby.

I do take advantage of the occasion, though, to pick up a *Pioneer Press* and *Chicago Trib*, and the latter has the complete morning lines and results, and that keeps me handicapping far into the night. I am thinking of inserting a little ad in *The Commonweal*, asking that readers who have subscriptions send me their old copies of the *Racing Form*. A world of good reading. I am disgusted with the Saints. Every time I tune in Halsey Hall,[1] they have dropped another. Yes, I am dust . . . but some of my best friends are clergymen.

  Jim

ROBERT LOWELL

Avon

April 1, 1948

Dear Cal,

Glad to get your letter today. Please tell Jarrell[2] at once that I am grateful he thought of me, but it doesn't seem like my kind of place, just as Bennington doesn't, from whom I've heard again. I told you, or did I, that they hired somebody else for the spring quarter but would pay my expenses there for an interview with an eye to next fall. I must write to Burkhardt, the president, right away and tell him I'm not coming. I think I'm going to Marquette. I had a talk with them a month ago in Milwaukee: good, Champish characters, and I'd have only six hours a week—4:30 to 6:00 at that, the lost part of the day anyway for me—and they'll pay $3,000. The big thing would be being around the clergy, for I'll be in the middle of my St Paul novel, and incidentally St Paul, where we can't locate, is only six hours from Milwaukee on good trains. Not being close enough to my material would be the trouble with Bennington—and I expect I'd have to put in a full schedule there too—and North Carolina . . . but again please thank Jarrell.

1 Sports announcer and sports program host.
2 Randall Jarrell (1914–1965), poet, critic, novelist.

About this summer, now that is something I look forward to. I am thinking of Ireland; perhaps I'll go in May so as to get back in time for Marquette. How can I afford it? I can't even with this break I got last week. I rec'd one of those American Arts and Letters things that you got last year; through K. A. Porter, I know for sure, and perhaps through you, for all I know. If so, thanks. It is supposed to be a secret till they announce it officially, I'm told, so please keep it to yourself; I told Buck, but nobody else (I felt I had to tell Buck: I know he worries I'll try to knock them down for more advance money). [. . .]

Well, it's bock beer time here, the best time of the year, simply because of that. They could close up the place if it weren't for that. If I go to Ireland in May, I'll meet the two friends who may also go, in Ireland: one is a priest, the other an unfrocked seminarian,[1] both of whom are in my novel. It would be good if you could be along. Your kind of fun. Both big men over 200 lbs, inclined to cigars and thirst. You see I am trying to interest you, but I know you can't be in Ireland and Washington at once, or can you? [. . .]

Sorry you've had so much to do; it is a little hard to imagine . . . do *you* get things done? I'll say a prayer for your father. I am partial to fathers and mothers when they get old. One of the good things about Champ; he loved his mother, didn't care what it looked like in the eyes of the analysts at Yaddo. [. . .]

Jim

ROBERT LOWELL

Avon, Minnesota
April 5, 1948

Dear Cal,

Late Thursday night, heavy with bock, Betty in town with her folks, my good friends and bad company gone lurching off to their homes and rectories, and I want to tell you, first opportunity I've had, I am a Guggenheim fellow. Got the good word Saturday last and want to thank you now for the backing up you gave me. I might have written sooner, but I went to Mpls–St Paul to decide what I ought to do. Finally decided I'm not going to teach, am going to use this year right. Not that I couldn't write and teach if it meant only six hours a week, but I'll go better this

1 Garrelts and Keefe.

way, and I need all the time I can plus the best breaks to get this book in hand. [. . .]

We might get a place in St Paul for six weeks. That will enable us to explore the possibilities for a permanent place. Maybe we'll get a place big enough to hold you and Champ and Buck and all your mallets and balls and bottles. Ireland looks dimmer now, too much money, too much trouble with boats, etc. I think I can get a passport. I found out in Chicago that I got amnesty, but I never heard from the gov't; it was in the paper there around Christmas.

All for now. My regards to Mr Ransom if he's there. How did Ezra and Randall fare together? Don't know Randall, of course, but think it might have been good to see. Guess it would be good to see anybody with a few opinions of his own having an afternoon with Pound. Sorry about the Maine mess, postponement, etc.[1] It seems a funny, public business for you to be mixed up in, but you can't have everything, all that peace and quiet and singleness without paying somehow.

So long.

Jim

We have founded this day a Third Order of St Bock. There are two divisions, lay and clerical, devoted to cockery and bockery, respectively, though both are united under Bockery in the larger sense. We wear a bottle opener on a string around our waist, beneath our underwear of course.

1 Lowell's divorce from Jean Stafford.

9

The truth about me is that I just don't qualify as the ideal husband

July 1948 — Christmas 1948

Mary Farl Powers, 1952

Jim and Betty moved with the baby to St. Paul in mid-April, bringing to an end their adventure in rural living. They lived first in an apartment at 414 North Lexington Avenue while looking for a more permanent place. In the end, they moved back into the old Murlborough at 150 Summit Avenue around the end of May. Betty was expecting another baby in November.

ROBERT LOWELL

150 Summit Avenue, St Paul

July 1948

Dear Cal,

We're all Americans. It is very damned hot in the land of the sky-blue water, . . . and I look forward to the summer encampment of the Order of St Bock. In the meantime I've placed gin in my aspergillum.[1] That was nice of you to invite me and the family to Yaddo. I'd like to be there, but in August, for the races. Instead, though, I'll be here and for two weeks on an island in Lake Superior.

I broke down, and I do not mean that lightly, and bought *The Kenyon Review* with your nun poem in it. I think it is very fine, which is what I told you, I think, at the time you were putting it together. I do have some doubts on Rabelais. I've been rereading him lately, and though I can see why Mother should have been reading him, would she? Wish I could come upon a few nuns reading Rabelais. I particularly like the brisk dialogue which takes place between Panurge and the Semiquaver Friar.

Do not lament your singleness. You are well-off, and I rather think you know it. Let that be taken as a word to the wise from the . . . and no commentary on me and mine. I wrote a review of Waugh's new book[2] for *The*

---

1 An instrument used for sprinkling holy water.
2 Review of *The Loved One*, by Evelyn Waugh, *Commonweal*, July 16, 1948.

Commonweal, my last venture in that field for some time to come. I hope if Taylor saw my review of his book, he liked it.[1] I know I meant well, and if that didn't come through, it is because I don't know the forks of reviewing, for which thanks be to God. Meantime, as I say, we're all Americans.

ROBERT LOWELL

150 Summit Avenue
St Paul, Minnesota
September 29, 1948

Dear Cal,

It's night, and I'm just back from the Temple Baptist Church, where I heard an "ex-priest" tell them all about it. He is evidently one of the crowd which advertises all the time in *The Nation*. I came prepared to pity the man, I suppose, and indeed I did before he spoke, all during the time the various deacons gave thanks for his salvation, said deacons reminding me of the Jehovah's Witnesses I've known; but when he began to speak, I could tell, or thought I could, that he was quite serious about it; and as the fates would have it, there were two Catholics sitting in front of me who giggled and sneered and sighed, "Oh, the lies!" So I came away, curiosity fairly well sated, and will have news for the brethren the next time we bend an elbow together. One very hot item is the plan to open up a home or seminary, it wasn't quite clear, for those of them who want to pull out but can't figure out where to go, and this to be established in St Paul or Mpls. [. . .]

I'd like to take you up on Yaddo, but it is utterly impossible. Betty will have another baby in November, and even if that weren't in the offing, my book keeps me here, also the rent we have to pay, and I might even mention that I'd need an invitation from Elizabeth,[2] to whom extend my best wishes. I'll admit the prospect of your putting my book into a sonnet interests me. Are you sure a couplet wouldn't do it? After all, it's just prose. [. . .]

And you? Will you attend the World Series in Boston and throw out the first bottle? Things are pretty furious here on the apostolic-athletic level. The Saints (our team) are in the play-off, and if they win that, we'll play Montreal in the Little World Series. If so, the box seats, more than

1 Review of *A Long Fourth, and Other Stories*, by Peter Taylor, *Commonweal*, July 16, 1948. Taylor (1917–1994) was a short-story writer, novelist, and playwright.
2 Elizabeth Ames.

ever, will be a sea of black suits. I have already rec'd orders and money from Rome to buy up a section. Did I tell you I now smoke cigars? I have to, if I don't want to stand out in our crowd. Enjoy the Saratoga autumn. I imagine it's very good.

    Pax,

      Jim

P.S. I sold the car; sold, I said. Ora for it.

Betty went to St. Cloud to stay with her parents to await the baby's birth.

ROBERT LOWELL

150 Summit Avenue, St Paul
All Saints' 1948 [November 1]

Dear Cal,

    [. . .] Now an ironic thing is happening on the radio. My friend and candidate[1] (the first time anything like this ever happened to me or anyone I've known) has just thanked us one and all for all we've done, while in the bathroom, stashed away, are the circulars I was supposed to circulate in this building, about sixty apartments. I'd postponed it till tonight, but now that he's thanking us, I wonder if it isn't too late. The candidate is really a nice fellow who never amounted to anything like all my friends, but he has deserted our ranks, and I still can't believe it.

    I drove Betty to St Cloud yesterday, and now she awaits the coming. At that time I'll journey hence. Two babies is a lot. I have no idea how we'll manage; it was enough with one. I may have to rent an office in the Pioneer or Guardian building. They look sufficiently broken-down to support literature. That's an idea for a foundation. Given a billion dollars, I'd establish a trust to set up everybody in one old building, each with an office, with the name on the frosted glass: Theo. Roethke . . . Rob't Lowell . . . Wm Barrett . . . B. Moon . . . The Pig . . . E. Pound . . . Mrs Chas Seide . . . Horace Cayton . . . Marg. Young . . . Card. Spellman . . . all the literary lights of this century and regular hours with lunch from 12:00 to 1:00. I forgot Clocker Webster. And myself, of course.

    My book goes slowly. [. . .] I am living here alone, doing my own cook-

---

1 Eugene McCarthy (1916–2005), elected to the U.S. House of Representatives the next day.

ing. Today it was breakfast: a glass of milk; lunch: T-bone steak, bread, milk; dinner: a malted milk; tonight: beer, olives, swiss cheese. All for now, Cal. Wish I were there. I saw a movie this afternoon which showed the Saratoga racetrack. I yearned to be there, making my selections.

Pax,
Jim

Drink my health in Sperry's. Have you forgotten it . . . on Caroline Street, I believe.

Have you read Gogarty? *Sackville Street? Tumbling in the Hay?*

BETTY POWERS

150 Summit Avenue
November 5, 1948

Dear Betty,

[. . .] That is very interesting about your father sitting down with pencil and paper awaiting the returns after sixteen long years.[1] I imagine my father did likewise. Fr Garrelts, I guess, is the only one who forecast the turn of events, except Harry himself. Fr G. has the best theory, I think: there just aren't enough Republicans to go around; it is like the soft jobs and big money; just not enough of it to go around. Fr Murphy was left at the post too, hoping for a Rep victory. So far as anybody could tell, however, he was against the Dems because Barkley[2] is "too old." "Yes," Fr G. agreed, "he's about old enough for the cardinalate," which put things in a stronger light, I guess. [. . .]

You are wrong about my not missing you until the sheets need changing tomorrow. I miss you daily and at odd hours and minutes during the day. It is raining now, very grey and dull-grey, streets black under the wet. [. . .] Well, I miss you, love you, and will be seeing you . . . and remember what I said about too soon rather than too late. Where will I stay? I will try to work, as ever, try, that is.

Jim

1 Hoping for a Republican victory in the presidential election—which the Democrat Harry Truman won.
2 Alben W. Barkley (1877–1956), who was Truman's running mate.

150 Summit Avenue
November 15, 1948

Dear Betty,

[. . .] A note from Buck saying something called *Thinker's Digest* wants to run excerpts from my stories, at their leisure, I guess, they want blanket permission and say they never pay for anything because they publicize books so well: need I tell you it's a Catholic outfit? [. . .] And now, once more, much love.

Jim

150 Summit Avenue
November 22, 1948

Dear Betty,

[. . .] Feel pretty good today. I ate the last of the strawberry preserves and am into the cherry now, which isn't so good. We had an interesting trip back,[1] no dangerous accidents, or even narrow escapes, eating something at Elk River. Fr G. was on the famished side. I guess he'd hoped for a little something among our rural friends. [. . .]

I picked up a yesterday paper from the basket by the elevator. I enjoy it more that way, I find, with no investment in it, just the loss of time. I did up the dishes and cleaned the ashtrays before I left yesterday, so the house is in good shape. You looked very sweet and pretty yesterday, and I was glad you are my wife. I know I repeat myself, but do try to anticipate the time, so I can be there in time. I realize too how weary you must get of someone asking you when you're going to have the baby, but I can't get it out of my head that you should know more about it than you do, or could know. [. . .]

Much love,

Jim

---

1 From Collegeville and St. Cloud.

St Cloud, Minnesota
November 29, 1948

Dear Katherine Anne,

[. . .] I am here in St Cloud, known rightly as Granite City, awaiting the birth of another baby. I hope it doesn't come as the blow to you as it did to us (I might lift that line for my headstone, containing as it does much of my "thought" and more of my "style"). Betty is 18 days late in having this baby, and the strain is beginning to tell. We are set down here with her family, who are filled with all the expectation families seem to have at such a time; but even they, at this late date, find their joy a heavy thing. It is like a party that everyone's tired of but won't leave. And the truth about me is that I just don't qualify as the ideal husband. The doctor with a big, knowing smile predicts a big bouncing boy, and I'm damned if he has my number there. Betty and I decided that having children is not the same thing for a writer. There is no room in our economy, in the largest sense; the old rowboat leaks already. [. . .]

Your Katherine Anne here is a flourishing fatty. She has one flaw, an eye that doesn't focus quite right, and one virtue that I take to be art: she dances to music, though she doesn't yet walk.

Very best,
Jim

Mary Farl Powers was born on November 29, 1948. As they were to do in the case of all the babies, Betty's parents paid the hospital bill.

BETTY POWERS

150 Summit Avenue
December 4, 1948

Dear Betty,

[. . .] I did a job on the house yesterday, cleaning. I scrubbed the bathroom with my own little hands, including the toilet bowl, and mopped the floor in here, including the hall, and *including* behind the davenport, where it was about an inch deep, the dust. I washed the windows on the inside, swept the kitchen, and thought how nice it would be if I could vacuum this rug, but I can't take ours seriously, our vacuum cleaner. I must study it. [. . .]

Do you need money? I don't suppose you'd have enough sense (I mean this lovingly) to make your hospital check out big enough to get some. Tell me. Much love. Katherine Anne gave me some nice kisses when I left the other day.

    Jim

BETTY POWERS

150 Summit Avenue
December 11, 1948

Dear Betty,

Saturday afternoon. Fr G. has been here for lunch, so to speak, beer, swiss cheese, pepperoni (a new food I've found, kind of bologna), and Black Forest bread. [. . .] I won't deny I've had a little too much beer, as you can tell from this typing, but it is wearing off. [. . .]

I went to the Alvin[1] last night. An old comedian from Chicago days, pretty good, but the girls weren't much. I meant to speak to the manager, but didn't. Do you think *A History of Burlesque* would go? Thomas More Bookshop Selection. I'm considering it. All for now. Much love. I vacuumed the rug yesterday. Very tough going, but I find the nozzle is good for sucking the dust out of corners, furniture, and picture frames.

    Jim

I'm going to get some pepperoni for Ezra Pound. It will make a nice gift for him, something to go with the crackers.

Jim went to Chicago, to his parents', for Christmas. His sister, Charlotte, was also there with her first child, Dennis, a toddler. Betty, Katherine, and Mary stayed in St. Cloud with Betty's parents.

BETTY POWERS

Chicago
1948
J. F. Powers, His Christmas Letter

Dear Betty,

Here it is Christmas 1948, and another year has gone by. I am sitting

---

1 Burlesque theatre in Minneapolis.

here in my steamer robes writing to you, thinking of the years gone by, the years to come, thinking of our heritage of freedom, of the Minnesota centenary, of rural life, of rural fun, of Life . . .

Now, the truth is I have not heard from you for three days. Maybe I should have called you last night, or today, and maybe I will (there is some agitation here that I should), but I remember how unsatisfactory our phone calls have always been, and I hold back (there is also the matter of the cost, and I don't know you well enough yet to determine whether you'd be happier to have me call or not to call: mystery of matrimony, inscrutability of woman). Anyway, as you can tell, I am irritated that I haven't heard from you, but I realize you are probably very busy with our off-spring, that and the confusion of the holidays, the dinner at your house today, or is it the Strobels' on Christmas? I do hope you are not getting nervous and run-down, and I fear you are.

My one big plan now, aside from the novel, which is always with me, is to get a big house and someone to help you, and I don't know how I can do it. I want to buy a house on Summit, big enough for my mother and dad to live upstairs or somewhere, and I fear you are not with me in this. It is the saddest thing in my life, however, to see my mother worked the way she is here, to say nothing of my father. I think, is it too much to ask of you, and really, all things considered, I think not. I think it would be good for you; I know it would be good for me. I think my mother might become the friend you've never had (and as I say that, I feel you draw away), but I believe that, Betty. With two other women I might have married, I know it would have worked out, and you are better than either one of them; no comparison, otherwise. However, I am not trying to be cunning about this, it is the simple truth, and I wish I could believe that you might see it. In any event, I feel I must work much, much harder, and I fully intend to, and I do not kid myself about schedules, etc., not since the one I made out before I married you, the one that used to hang on the wall. There is a little too much activity here (the child) for me to collect my thoughts very well, but you have the fragments.

I want to tell you, too (what I feel is unnecessary), that I love you very much, that I wish I might make your life easier, and that gets back to the house and help again. Will you try to go along with me on this? I almost say, If you love me . . . but that would be wrong; I know you love me. Perhaps you should listen to me in a few things, though, such as you did in having your hair cut, and they will be better for you than you can imagine. You are inclined to think along traditional lines; I mean, if we haven't done things, it is a good reason not to do them; but we must make a few swift surgical moves and departures: after all that is how we got married in the first place, and to my mind that is the best way; at least it is good to think that we fell in love all at once and were not cautious then and we haven't been, except at intervals, since then. We have won a lot that way; we have lost too; but I think I'd rather have what we've won . . . and I know exactly what I mean, though you might think me vague. [. . .]

I love you, then. [. . .]

Jim

10

If you can't win with me, stop playing the horses!

January 18, 1949—September 6, 1949

Evelyn Waugh and Jim, 1949

ROBERT LOWELL

150 Summit Avenue
St Paul, Minnesota
January 18, 1949

Dear Cal,

[. . .] What word of 'Ted?[1] I always said, remember, we'd mean nothing to him if he ever married that money he talked about, but I did not think we'd be cut off until then.

This month is my "hard time." I am trying to get a MS together for Mr Moe, with an eye to a renewal,[2] but what I thought was going to be just a typing job has turned into a worse job than the original. Just imagine a doctor with the patient all apart on the table, or a mechanic with my car, and add the time element, the February deadline, and you have my predicament. I've had it from my agent that renewals are hard to get anyway. I've been flirting with the idea of buying a house (with the money I haven't got but might get if I took a job with something called the Catechetical Guild here: they are dealers in all kinds of religious junk and are thinking of opening up a new department publishing, with Doubleday, Catholic "classics" in the Permabooks format. If that doesn't develop, I don't know what I could do there; even if it does develop, the least that would happen to me would be the loss of my faith, I think, just seeing all the junk they have to convert the heathen—games like Pollyanna or Monopoly, for instance, except they deal with the sacraments or dogma. Waugh would love it. Me too, but I wonder, buying a house on it, if I could do the novel about it that would inevitably accumulate).

The truth is I've got to buy a house, with these three girls of mine (I count Betty among them). And I think I'd try to buy some awful big

1 Roethke.
2 Renewal of the Guggenheim.

damned place up the street, from 12 to 40 rooms, the kind nobody else wants anymore because they cost too much to heat and are gloomy; rather in the direction of Yaddo style, architecturally. But I haven't really looked into it; don't know what they cost. And also, I haven't got the job I'd need. I couldn't do it on the Guggenheim, though. Ah, well, let me be a lesson to you. Stay single. That way you can afford to be yourself. [. . .] All for now and best.

Jim

Journal, February 14, 1949
Betty told me that the priests had been up to see Sister Mariella . . . and in the talk this came out about me: He's lookin' for a job, didja know that? And that because I was foolish enough to go out and see them at the Catechetical Guild. I thought I made it seem disinterested enough, but I guess not . . . I think it gave them joy to think I was around begging for work—from them, too, whom I'd hurt so much in the past. Oh, God. Impossible not to think of Joyce and all he had to say about the Church—or is it just the Irish? . . . That "He's lookin' for a job" is a terrible reminder of my own father and all the time he spent looking for a job . . . And the world is waiting for me as it waited for my father—he's lookin' for a job! Sister M. said the priests referred to me as to the devil incarnate—but that is probably exaggerated—a little.

Father Egan had run afoul of someone big in the St. Paul diocesan hierarchy, most likely because of his radical Christian views, and was assigned to a parish in Beardsley, Minnesota, a parched little town on the border of South Dakota. In the summer, it was one of the hottest places in the state. "Whenever the wind blows a particle of dust in my eye," wrote Jim, "I think of you out there on the lunatic fringe of the world." Egan threw himself into the duties of the parish and maintaining the rectory.

HARVEY EGAN

150 Summit Avenue
April 2, 1949

Dear Father Egan,
Friday night and I trust you are back in Beardsley by now. I enclose

some clippings. I'll try to keep sending these to you, only the best ones. You know I didn't get a chance to send stuff to the boys in the last war (due to a little mix-up), and so I intend to make up for them with you. After all, it is like that, what you are going into. And I want you to know, speaking for our block, that we think of you often and will try to make it up to you if you ever return to the States. We are also holding forum meetings in which we discuss the problems of the day, and this, we humbly hope, will make St Paul a better place to live in, for us and for you when and if, as I say, you return. It shouldn't have happened to a dog, what happened to you, but then we can't have everything our own way all the time, can we? (I'm not so sure about that, but a certain Fr B.[1] is said to hold with that doctrine, and so I go along, knowing what happened to some that set themselves, however secretly they thought, against him.) All for now. (Jamaica opened today: weather clear, track fast . . .)

    jf

St. Paul, "Home of the Saints," was much better suited to Jim's temperament than rural Minnesota. The city provided the company of Saul Bellow, Robert Penn Warren, and other writers with whom he enjoyed the conversation and sense of fellow feeling for which he longed. Evelyn Waugh, who was writing a piece on American Catholicism for Life *magazine, arrived in St. Paul. He and his wife came for dinner at the Marlborough, where Betty served them lobster Newburg.*

HARVEY EGAN

150 Summit Avenue
May 2, 1949

Dear Fr Egan,

Your letter and enclosure rec'd this morning. You are very free with your funds, and kind as always. I would not hesitate to cash the check, and perhaps that's what I'll do. But I got $189.57 from England (advance on my book[2] over there, just now arriving) last week, and that should take us through May. (We've already paid the rent with the usual flourish.) I've not had any luck with the two stories yet, but have not despaired entirely,

1 Father Bandas.
2 *Prince of Darkness.*

and Betty mailed off a new one yesterday. I did get the shakes two days after I saw you last, however, and wrote to Marquette to say I was ready to deal again. That may end in nothing. I require certain things: housing, short hours, big pay—something to compensate me for leaving St Paul (though the attractions are fewer as time goes on; Fr G. is the only one left), and they may not see fit to provide.

Things are rather rough here with the babies. Don't expect much peace during the day, but when they take over the night too, that's bad. What's the Church's stand on desertion? Very rough on Betty, body and soul; only my soul suffers. (She, B., was down to have some of her hair cut today, a triumph for me.) So I'm going to keep your check, in readiness—please don't change banks. Since you won't mind, I think I ought to tell you, though, that I wouldn't give the check much of a chance to pull through uncashed. Thanks. I wonder if you can get Marty O'Neill[1] way out there but doubt that they make radios that good or that you'd have one. Anyway, the Saints won their 11th game tonight. That's 11 and 0. I haven't been out yet. Somebody said there's now a plaque at Lex. where you used to sit.[2] [. . .]

I mentioned your slate roof to Art. He seems to think there's nothing to it. He explained it all to me, how you replace them, using a certain kind of hammer to peck out a hole for the nails (they are nailed), and shove a piece of copper in, and . . . well, I'll tell you, Father, I went through all this once, and it won't do you any good coming from me. Anyway, it's not much of a job, according to Art (come to think of it, nothing ever was). On another page I've prepared a scratch sheet for next Saturday.[3] I called the Chancery, and it's official you don't have to hear confessions during the race. In fact, it might be laudable and meritorious if you listened to the broadcast and·smoked a cigar. You see there's nothing wrong with these things in . . .

Jim [. . .]

Do you suppose from all the Latin Joe H. Palmer uses he's an old assistant that went south?[4]

"If you can't win with me, stop playing the horses!" —Clocker Jim

1 Play-by-play announcer for the St. Paul Saints baseball and hockey teams.
2 Lexington Park, St. Paul.
3 Kentucky Derby.
4 Joe H. Palmer, racing correspondent for the *New York Herald Tribune*. "Assistant," meaning parish assistant (a priest).

150 Summit Avenue
St Paul, Minnesota
May 25, 1949

Dear Cal,

Are you mad at me or just in a tunnel? I haven't even seen your name mentioned in *Time* or *Life*. The last I heard was some time before I applied for a renewal of the Guggenheim that I didn't get. A few weeks back I wrote to Mrs Ames about coming to Yaddo for August, Betty and me, and she said it would be all right. I wonder if I can hope to see you there. Or will you be going to Europe with everybody else, or can't you go? I hope you're working well.

I took a new grip on myself when the Guggenheim failed me and wrote a couple of stories for publication. To date nothing has happened to them that would lead me to think my plan to live by writing was a good one. So recently I signed up to teach creative writing at Marquette come September. I'll have six hours only, and they say they'll find us a place to live. Not the way I'd like it, but it does beat depending on the whims of editors of the magazines that pay a living wage. I remember you told me that in the beginning or what now seems like the beginning. So barring the unforeseen, I'll be in Milwaukee for at least a year.

I signed up for a writers' conference at Kansas last winter, and now that it's almost upon me, I wish I hadn't: mostly I mean I have to write a speech, and it is gradually dawning that I have nothing to say. I don't know the truth about any writer, about literature, about culture, and so what my thesis will be is still a mystery. You don't have an old college essay lying around that I might read, do you? As my own, of course. Perhaps I could say a few words about the eating and drinking habits of poets, with particular reference to Roethke. That is more in my line. Allen Tate and his wife[1] will be at the conference. I don't know them, though, and suppose I can't look for much help there. They were here a couple of weeks ago—he gave a reading at the university—but I was out of town, on some kind of a trip with a clerical friend who was trying to get away from it all. We went fishing up on the Canadian border. Didn't catch anything. Seems you have to have a pack of guides and an airplane to do it right. Some people from Chicago, two couples with two Cadillac convertibles, twins, did it right. It was good to see them

1 Caroline Gordon.

going off in the morning and returning at night with all their army and equipment.

Waugh was here in March. Said he came to Minnesota to see me and the Indian reservations. He is also interested in Father Divine. He was all right, and his wife, but it wasn't anything like the bout I'd anticipated from his books. Suppose that's life. Drank wine. Still don't think I care for it, not dago red at ten in the morning. He wanted to know how old you were when I asked if you'd met yet. He wanted to know how old I was too. Seemed relieved to know he'd been younger when he pub'd his first book. I may be wrong about that, but that was all I could make out of it. The other day I rec'd a beautiful edition "edited" by him of Msgr Knox's sermons.

I met R. P. Warren at a party in January or February, very fine, up to what you and everybody always said about him, though we didn't see a lot of each other. It was a party for John Dos Passos given by the descendants of the Washburns, the flour people, and I was there, I know, as a prop, as were all the others who might conceivably qualify as writers. How about a catering service for such parties that would fly out some writers from New York, like seafood? Just an idea. I learned one thing that night (many of the other "writers" were off to Mexico or somewhere): a writer ought to own a chain of drugstores.

Pax,

Jim

P.S.—I ought to tell you that in a piece on St Paul I did for *Partisan Review*, I made use of your prophecy concerning the war between New York and Chicago. I thought of giving you your due in a footnote, but it seemed a little gauche to do so in print, not knowing your mind, so I didn't. I had to use the idea, needing substance sorely. I hope you don't mind.

Jim and Betty went to Yaddo at the end of July, leaving Katherine and Mary in St. Cloud with Betty's sister, Pat.

Saratoga
Track Good
August 1, 1949

Dear Fr Egan,

Just a few lines to warm up on. We arrived here two days ago. The place is unchanged. We have the same rooms as last time. Today the races begin. It is also Monty Woolley day here. After Mass yesterday I got a *Form*. It's going to be a hard day, tough, and I may not bet a race: two two-year-old races and a steeplechase. I was over at the track yesterday morning. Very pretty, the rose and green grandstand, and the men dragging the track to dry it out. [. . .]

Jim

Yaddo
Wednesday night, August 18, 1949

Dear Fr Egan,

Your letter and five spot rec'd. I am happy to report that you are still breaking even, i.e., beating the game, for I have not risked it yet. I have been three times, losing a little each time. I know you won't believe that, but there it is anyway. The way it is, so many two-year-old races and the daily hurdles, eliminates opportunity to get ahead. I have to concentrate on the remaining races, and haven't done badly, but am a lot away from that $90,000 I set for myself. [. . .]

The absolutely big news I have for you is that I dropped Joe H. Palmer a line, and this evening he phoned, and we have an evening planned for here Friday night. I saw him at the yearling sales one night, with his wife, at a distance, and got to thinking I just had to see him. So I risked a note. He sounds on the phone something like he looks: "Hallo, this is Joe Palmer." Wish you were going to be here. I am not telling the other inmates. They would not know about him anyway and also might not have enough sense to honor him as I intend to. It means I'll have to get a bottle of bourbon in. He's from Kentucky. I'd like to ask Jack Conroy (a writer) down (he lives above us), but I don't want to set him off. He's been on one toot since coming about a week ago. He is from Moberly, Missouri, originally, but for many years was considered the white hope of the proletarian novel. Nice fellow. Lot of stories. I have not seen a radio since coming here and might be said to be taking the cure.

I see where the Holy Father is routing us contemplatives out of our tunnels, says we've got to mix more. How do you feel about that? (I have had two good ones, one paying $33.00, one $27.50, but I had them to show, and those are the win prices.) A fellow selling tip sheets in the grandstand said: "Some days it doesn't pay to get out of bed." I plan to attend the morning works tomorrow. I sit behind the clockers. There are two sets. Those who work for the track handicapper, and they are Negroes; those who work for the *Racing Form* and *Daily Telegraph*, all white. The former are better for dialogue, though the others have their points. They have big binoculars, notebooks, handbooks, encyclopedias, and typewriters. When a horse comes on the track a quarter of a mile away at the gate, up go the binoculars, and that is all they need, just a glance, to tell which one of thousands it is. Would that I were one of them, but, no, I had to be what I am.

We have a place in Milwaukee lined up. Three bedrooms, so we'll expect you now and then. I'll tell Joe he is your favorite arthur. ("Arthur" is one of Conroy's words. When he was famous, after the success of his first book, he sent for all his old friends in Missouri, and they came like a plague of locusts, eating and drinking all before them. It was the habit of their leader to ask at literary parties: Sir, are you a published arthur?)

Fit and ready.

Jim

HARVEY EGAN

Yaddo
[late August–early September 1949]

Dear Father Egan,

[. . .] Saratoga meeting no great success; no great loss (about 12 or 15 dollars, I'd say). Your five went the hardest. I send you the chart. The horse was Greek Song: the bet, as ordered, to place. You can see what he did. I blame the boy for not breaking him right. A cousin of Skoronski, who, you may recall, rides like a Chinaman. The meeting a great success in every other way, though. Had Joe Palmer over here two or three times and his friend Jim Roach, who does the same thing, but not so well, for *The NY Times*. Joe took us to the track for breakfast one morning, picking up the tab for $7.90 (that was for us three) and also sending us six passes to the clubhouse. You would have liked him. [. . .]

Breezing.

Jim

HARVEY EGAN

150 Summit Avenue
September 6, 1949

Dear Fr Egan,

[. . .] We plan to leave the babies in St Cloud, move them from there to Milwaukee. I have my family's car, a 1940 convertible, for the trip. We drove up in it, Betty and I, after looking over the place in Milwaukee. It is out in the country. I'm going to need a car to escape it, I fear; the country, that is. It is brand-new, you know, upstairs from the people who're building it. It is better than we deserve. Things will be tough at first, since we must buy a new gas stove, washing machine, etc. I don't believe I was led to believe in the necessity for such things in *The CW*.[1] But then there wasn't much about your housekeeper either, was there? [. . .]

Do you have movies in Beardsley, or lantern slides? We'll expect to see you on Sunday the 11th. I'm sorry about Greek Song, but that's the way it goes: some days it doesn't pay to get out of bed.

Pax . . .

Jim

1 *Catholic Worker.*

I'm beyond the point where I think the world is waiting for me as for the sunrise

September 19, 1949—October 7, 1951

Art and Money's "little rambler house" on the Mississippi, 1951—Mary and Katherine with cousin Michael Bitzan

The Powers family left St. Paul for Milwaukee, where, for two school years,
Jim taught creative writing at the Jesuit-run Marquette University. "Betty and
I feel sad about leaving St Paul," Jim wrote to the exiled Egan in Beardsley.
"Perhaps, though, we can have a triumphal return someday. Perhaps about
the time you have yours." The family lived on the second floor of a house in
a new, treeless neighborhood far from the heart of the city.

HARVEY EGAN

Milwaukee
September 19, 1949

Dear Father Egan,

Monday morning. We have a semblance of order here now. The books are still in boxes. We await another baby bed before the "den" can be cleared out for me. I am in no mood for work yet, however. Yesterday I journeyed—three transfers on the bus—to Borchert Field, where I saw the Saints go down to defeat, Roy, the Brewer pitcher, giving one hit, Naylor, who would have been the last man to face him. So that means they go to St Paul to finish off the series. I went with Gordon's old friends, the Hollanders. They are very cynical about the Brewers and Nick Cullop, whose scalp they seek.[1] I teach my first class tomorrow afternoon. Do you suppose they would understand if I called it off on account of having to follow the team back to St Paul?

Which reminds me that *Life* arrived the other night at 11:15 p.m., special delivery: the Waugh story on American Catholics with a picture of JF and Harry in it. My picture is one that *Time* took two years ago at Yaddo for that review they never ran. I think I look like a queer in it, but perhaps that will boost my sales in that important quarter. The Waugh piece has

1 Manager of the Brewers.

some good things in it but is cloudy at the end, I think. It is the Sept. 19 number in case you want to pick up a copy—on second thought where in Beardsley will you be able to do that? Fry's?

Katherine Anne is here buzzing around the typewriter. She is a good girl, as is Mary. Both behaved themselves all the way from St Cloud. We have a secondhand stove, a good bargain. We expect you to stay here whenever you come this way—on your way to and from conventions, the track, etc. I am going to get a special bed for the "den," where I intend to stock such visitors as yourself. We won't have it in time for Fr Garrelts next Friday, and there may be some trouble about who sleeps on that lounge we have. He has kicked against that goad in the past. All for now. Let us hear from you.

Jim

This place very bright and, let's face it, soulless. Deadly nice little houses nearby peopled by souls taken up with new cars and lawn mowers. [. . .]

Two years previously, Jim had written to Betty in a spate of pique: "I should study the mind of the Church which knows the one thing to be got out of marriage is children. The which we are getting. Now, if we only had some veneer furniture and a Studebaker." The specter of veneer furniture never materialized, but Jim now found himself with a Studebaker, the first of two he was to acquire from the Strobels after they retired them.

HARVEY EGAN

Milwaukee
Monday in the desert, October 11, 1949

Bone pastor,[1]

[. . .] There is a monsoon blowing at our little blockhouse today too. We are situated on a prairie. Today is my day for reading MSS—tomorrow being a class day. I've just finished one, probably by an ex-seminarian, about a fellow who decides to leave the seminary. My comment, in effect: "Does this character have holes in his head?" Then there was one about a gambler who stole gold from a prospecting Chinaman; my comment: "Whence this materialism?" And so on. It is really, so far, an easy way to

---

1 Good shepherd (Latin).

earn one's daily bread. Not what I've been used to in recent years, but better than the years before, and I hope I'll not have to do worse in years to come. Hold that sexton's job open.

After much financial strife, the reward. I sold a story to *The New Yorker*. So I am going to buy Strobels' 1942 Studebaker. I hope to get it at the end of this month—Mr S. should have his new one then—and if so, I might pick up that crackpot[1] in St Joe and come see you. Like to see you among your platters.[2] We are hard put for a church here. I try to plan it so I'm downtown on Sundays. Out here, well, out here . . . it's not the cathedral, just as it isn't Summit Avenue; raw country, raw people. Between the virgin land and the neon signs, nothing; no history; nothing.

I don't see anybody at Marquette. I come and go. Very good that way, though I did hope to get in with the chancery crowd here too. They're freezing me out, though, or else they don't know I'm alive. Have had the usual invitations to say a few words, though, and turn them down. [. . .]

I went to Chicago Saturday for the day and bought a sport coat at Jerrems—I felt I owed it to my students, always appearing in the same sack; they might think there isn't money in writing. If I do get to Beardsley, I trust I'll get to see your friend Popeye. Did you leave him some literature? What is the approach in the country, with no streetcars to leave Catholic publications on? Suppose you thrust it under the hens and the farmers get it when they come for the eggs [ ] Write and pray

Jim

I have a Chinese fellow in one class. He was a general in the last war under Chiang. About the nicest general I ever hope to meet. Only on English for two years, so there are problems, literary problems.

Jim took an increasing interest in the career of Del Flanagan (1928–2003), a middleweight prizefighter born in St. Paul. Del and his brother Glen were known as the Fighting Flanagan Brothers. In his letters to Father Egan, Jim worked up the idea that Del's woes were akin to his own, eventually calling him "the J. F. Powers of boxing." The racehorse Greek Song came in for the same treatment.

1 Don Humphrey.
2 For collections at Mass.

Milwaukee

ca. December 8, 1949

Dear Betty,

[. . .] Del Flanagan of St Paul won a big fight in Detroit last night, over Sandy Saddler, the featherweight champion, but as fate would have it, Flanagan was announced from the ring as "from Minneapolis." Such, you see, are my considerations. [. . .]

Love

Jim

HARVEY EGAN

Milwaukee

March 29, 1950

Dear Father Egan,

[. . .] I trust you saw where the Irish race[1] was won by Freebooter, the favorite, ridden by Jimmy Power, a Waterford boy—which is where we, and all Powerses, presumably hail from. A barkeep in Chicago won $70,000. The state gets more than half of it, though, so maybe it's just as well.

Katherine Anne has taken to sitting in my chair here in the study. I have to sit on the edge of it. It is symbolic, I think, of the years ahead. I've had a good, satisfying life, however, strong on purpose, and so I am not reluctant to step down and let the younger ones take over. How is that old grey head of yours? Easter promises to be an ordeal. I have only six days off—is there something wrong with Easter in the Jesuit view? [. . .] Write.

Jim

HARVEY EGAN

Milwaukee

June 12, 1950

Dear Fr Egan,

Your letters and *The Priest* came today, and glad to hear from you. Thanks for *The Priest*, but it's just pathetic (such ignorance no longer

---

1 The Grand National at Aintree, the race upon which the Irish Hospitals' Sweepstakes was based.

gives me a moment's pause; I expect it), not as regards Harry[1] and me, for we seem to be running as an entry at all the tracks, but just that a man could wade through *The Cardinal* and not know it was fake from the first page on.[2] I tell you, Father, there is much work to be done—but I for one am not going to do it. I'm busy with my handicapping and radio programs every day, yes, and even with what I call my writing.

I had to call Chicago Saturday morning, seeing that Greek Song was going in the Belmont. Placed an across-the-board wager with my father, who in turn placed it with my brother, who in turn placed it with the Syndicate. The inevitable happened, or would seem to be the inevitable with Greek Song. He came with a rush in the stretch but was too late. [. . .] He was fourth by a head; at 35 to one, if I'd collected the show bet, I would be ahead. The jockey rode him like a Chinaman, that's all I can say. Really do think he got a poor ride. I thought of calling you Saturday morning to find out if you wanted in, but now I'm glad I didn't. You evidently have little faith in me anyway, as a writer, and if you despaired of me as a handicapper, there wouldn't be much left, would there?

Father, I am not worried about getting a book out. I would like to have one ready, yes, but I'm beyond the point where I think the world is waiting for me as for the sunrise. I gather you think short stories a preparation for novel writing. That is not true. I'm not trying to exonerate myself. The truth is I'm lazy, and after that, a family man, a teacher of creative writing, and finally I don't care to get a book out just to get a book out; I'd rather make each one count—and in order to do that, the way I nuts around, it takes time. I know too that there's no demand for a book such as I can write. I am outside the system, the economics of writing, in that sense. Do you know that I've cleared more on the one story for *The New Yorker* (over $1,500) than on my book, which did better than any book of stories in its year except Somerset Maugham's? [. . .] And now, goodbye.

Jim

---

1 Harry Sylvester.
2 Robert Paul Mohan, review of *The Cardinal*, by Henry Morton Robinson, *Priest*, June 1950: "Mr. Robinson . . . has none of the depressing negativity of Powers or Sylvester, who have also given pictures of the clerical scene."

Milwaukee
Monday, July 24, 1950

Dear Fr Egan,

Your letter and *The Herald Sun* publicity rec'd.[1] I may subscribe to *The H-S* for a month and renew if it's any good. I *am* in the market for a good paper. I wonder if *The H-S* is it. The prospectus is well written. [. . .] I see no mention of racing news in the table of contents. That's the acid test. They'll have that old family-life corn, Somebody Winks who has five children and a sense of humor, and they'll have Health and Books and the rest; but what of the Sport of Kings? Did you know that in the Albany[2] Diocese, during August, the paper has a racing supplement, à la the Yoot Section[3] in the *Visitor*? Racing is a Christian sport if Ireland is Christian. The Irish are a strange race, fools and wise men at the same time (I suggest you send that to the *Catholic Digest* for This Struck Me). [. . .]

I played a little golf last week with my brother-in-law[4] (he's employed at the bomb works in New Mexico) and enjoyed that. I may get some clubs again. There's a course up the road from here. We played with a manufacturer of toilet seats who happened along and made a nice three-some. I had been shooting an Acushnet Titleist, under the impression that the big pros used them, but the kindly manufacturer, friend of Sam Snead and Gene Sarazen, said they're all using the Dunlop Maxfli now and had been doing so since Bobby Locke came over a few years ago and burned up the fairways. I know this won't alter your life much, but it does show you that I'm living.

Jim [. . .]

Greek Song took down $50,000 first money at Arlington a week ago last Saturday. My brother, who subscribes to my service, had him across the board. He (GS) goes in the Arlington Handicap next Saturday. Listen at 3:30, NBC.

---

1 *The Sun Herald*. (Jim has the name wrong here.) A national Catholic daily newspaper (with an antiwar position) founded in 1950 in Kansas City, Missouri, it lasted six months.
2 Albany, New York.
3 "Youth" section in the St. Cloud diocesan newspaper (Stearns County pronunciation).
4 Bill Kraft.

JACK CONROY

Milwaukee

August 9, 1950

Dear Jack,

[. . .] Very warm and dull in Milwaukee. I was in Chicago last week for a day. I was on North Clark but only in a streetcar. I find I'm getting a little old for the good life. I toured the Near North Side in daytime, alone, and meditated on the vanished splendor. I doubt that it's vanished from anywhere but me. I heard Nelson Algren on the *Chez Show*, a radio program emanating from the Sapphire Bar of the Chez Paree—you see I've sunk to the lower depths—and he got off a line about Hollywood being a con man's paradise, which wasn't a very nice thing to say in that setting. The following week I heard this fellow Stuart Brent,[1] and he seems to be in charge of culture in Chicago. He's sore at New York, apparently, for thinking it's so smart. [. . .] Drop me a line, let me know who's there[2] this year, and thanks for the leaflets—do you have one on narcotics? I'm trying to kick my habit.

Jim

HARVEY EGAN

November 1, 1950

Dear Fr Egan,

[. . .] Just six years ago, about this time of day, I was being measured for my whites at St Joseph's Hospital; I had already been shown my room; and I had a great hunger for coffee and cake, which I satisfied at Mother Merrill's and Mickey's Diner, alternating so as not to seem an addict. It was the start of an era which closed with matrimony; then there was another era; and now, I think, I am somewhere in the middle of the one after that. [. . .] If there were some way of becoming writer in residence at, say, Belmont, I do think that may be the field for me. I'll never know, though, this way, deprived of even a *Form*.

Waugh sent me a signed copy of *Helena*, "with warm regards," and I'm grateful for that. Joe Dever messed up the review in *The Commonweal*. I don't see why they don't remove him from the reviewing staff. I think Joe can write some, but he's no reviewer. His mentor, Fr John Louis Bonn,[3]

1 Bookseller and outspoken advocate of good literature who had a radio show called *Books and Brent*.
2 Yaddo.
3 John Louis Bonn, SJ, novelist and teacher.

was here some weeks ago, from Boston College—he has a new novel, the Catholic Book Club selection—and I could see where Joe picked up part of his act, the worst part. I met Bonn at Pick's one night and found him fairly interesting. Then the lecture . . . it was as rough as anything I've ever heard. All he needed was an electric cane and a rubber nose. I mean it was pure ham, and to top it off, he ended on that Fulton Sheen pitch, whispering and groaning about our Lord Jesus Christ in the Tabernacle, which has nothing to do with anything he'd said. Shades of our old retreat master at QCA, Fr Peter Crumbley, OFM. [. . .] Please write.

Jim

HARVEY EGAN

Milwaukee

Washington's Birthday [February 22, 1951]

Dear Fr Egan,

[. . .] Suppose you've been mulling over the big basketball scandals in New York.[1] I hope they don't dig into things to the point where they discover what really happened to us Little Hawks in the State Tournament in '35 at Decatur. I don't know what Dick Keefe got, but I do know that George and I were living mighty high when it was all over. You may remember that we downed the home team, St Theresa, in the first round, and the talk was that I'd be All-State. But in the next round, going against a clumsy but determined St Bede's five, I fouled out early (so as to be able to go through the lockers in peace), Dick dropped his cup and just wasn't himself after that, and George complained of an old ailment with him, shin splints. They said we went down fighting, but I wonder what they would've said if they could've seen us being paid off later in Ott Quintenz's tavern[2] (Ott had been a Hawk himself at one time). I could tell you some tales. All I wanted was to set myself up in business. All for now. Write.

Jim

---

1 Huge college basketball scandal involving point-shaving and payoffs from bookies.
2 Joke.

Milwaukee
March 30, 1951

Dear Chuck,

[. . .] I had hopes of a summer near the ocean, I'd sent for a directory of cottages in Maine, but when I got the rejection,[1] I knew I'd been kidding myself, thinking I was Irwin Shaw or somebody. It'll probably be Big Spunk Lake at Avon—leaky roof, outdoor toilet, mosquitoes, the salty breeze off North Dakota. [. . .] Just goes to show heaven is our destination.

Jim

HARVEY EGAN

May 2, 1951

Dear Fr Egan,

Thanks for sending the McManus book and piece about Ireland. McM. is pretty rich for my blood; Betty is reading it. The piece about Ireland is informative but lame in spots—not enough about *why* the good Irish writers are "anticlerical"—I think it's just a natural reaction, and I wouldn't call Frank O'Connor that. Sean O'Faolain gives a depressing picture of Dublin—the Sacred Heart picture in the hallway, all the young men belonging (at one time) to the IRA, their female equivalent to the Legion of Mary—both organizations, he says, bore him. Much moviegoing, as here, among all classes. I mention these things so you'll think I know about these things even now. I would not expect anything better . . . and I am not going to Ireland (if I'm going to Ireland) to get material, etc. I'm going for the change, to work on my book about characters over here. So many people make that mistake about me. Rectors and seminaries, I understand, are closed to me because it is believed that I'm looking for material! Incredible but true! You know better. It's true I'm not above taking away a little, if it's good, but I never go anywhere to *explore*. That kills whatever it touches, that spirit, like a conducted tour. [. . .]

I had a letter from Sr Eugene Marie, with an enclosure—your church bulletin. I don't see how you do it sober. I think you're growing gage (marihuana) in your back yard, and incidentally that would be an ideal

---

1 From *The New Yorker*.

crop, terrain, weather considered, and the church would be a perfect blind. [. . .]

I'm grateful for your invitation and plan to come. Will let you know when. One thing, however: make that discipline tough. I had the impression you were being soft. We move out of here on May 31. Write. Come.

Jim

No baseball for me, second base my spot, but I can no longer make the double play. Legs gone.

At some point around this time, much of the land attached to the house in Avon was taken by eminent domain for the construction of a highway. Though they didn't especially want to live there, the couple was incensed by the state's high-handedness. Jim left Marquette with the idea of moving with Betty and the children to Ireland that coming fall. After leaving Milwaukee, he made an extended visit to Father Egan in Beardsley, Minnesota, while Betty and the two girls stayed with the Wahls in their new house on the Mississippi, four miles up the river from St. Cloud.

BETTY POWERS

Beardsley, Minnesota

June 1951

Dear Betty,

Saturday afternoon—3:30. After I left you yesterday, I stopped at the place in Avon (our place). The grass is high. Some trees have been uprooted near the Achman road, which has been widened, and that may be why the trees were leveled. Except that along the old road (the one we used for a driveway) there is one tree cut down and lying partly across that road; an ax was used, and I can't make anything out of that, any reason for it, I mean. The house itself is the same. Except the storm window on the window near the door is out, several panes broken (it was leaning against the remains of that old icebox, but I moved it), and possibly someone has been snooping around inside, though there are no signs of vandalism, no more than we left, I mean. The place is wet inside and shows some evidence of things like gophers. I didn't go in, however; all this seen through the window I slid open. I looked for highway department stakes and saw two: one in the old driveway and one just on the house side of the bank that goes down to the old driveway. Not very far in, I thought, but they are very insubstantial-looking stakes, just lathes, and perhaps don't mean very much. It's sad, going back there, as you might imagine. But it's sad because of what we did there, all the work and inconvenience; not sad when one thinks, as I did, that we don't have to make anything out of it. [. . .] Much love to you.

    Jim

BETTY POWERS

Beardsley, Minnesota
July 1951

Dear Betty,

This is Thursday afternoon. I look out the window and see Fr Egan working some kind of gasoline agricultural instrument. I'm using his big wide-carriage typewriter, the one he probably uses for his mimeographing. I've been working in the church basement but thought of knocking out this letter to you here in the house. I just took a bath, having done some carpentry work for Fr Egan this morning, cutting three inches off a chest he has by the refrigerator for brooms, jars, etc. Now the chest and refrigerator—reefer, as you and Mr Chopp say—fit snug, and Fr Egan, possibly even the housekeeper, is happy. [. . .] Much love.

    Jim

I was compelled to buy a can of Velvet, America's Smoothest Smoke. Pretty tough, after Brindley's, but I suppose I'll harden to it.

On his return from Beardsley, Jim joined the rest of the family, living with the Wahls. In October, he visited his own parents, who had moved from Chicago to Albuquerque, New Mexico, where Charlotte and her family now lived.

HARVEY EGAN

3509 East Smith Avenue
Albuquerque, New Mexico
October 7, 1951

Dear Fr Egan,

As you can see from my address, I am visiting my folks—and that

means that the story was sold, after all, to *The New Yorker*, after rewriting.[1]
[. . .] I expect to leave in about ten days. We have made preparations to
leave for Ireland on October 25: applications for passport, passage, etc. It
is going to run into more money than we hoped (for instance, no tourist
accommodations available, have to go cabin class, because of our last-
minute arrangements), but then, as you always say, what is money? Standard Oil gasoline down here is known as Chevron. Great need for grass
and trees. Drop me a line if there's anything you want me to look into,
Penitentes,[2] etc. All for now.

    Jim

---

1 "Defection of a Favorite," *The New Yorker*, November 10, 1951.
2 A society of Spanish-inspired flagellants in New Mexico and Colorado.

12

The water, the green, the vines, stone walls, the pace, all to my taste

November 7, 1951—November 3, 1952

Leopardstown Racecourse, 1952

The Powers family boarded the SS America *on October 25, 1951, bound for Ireland, and arrived in Cobh on October 31, 1951. Jim was smitten by the look of the country on the train from Cobh to Cork: "Most beautiful vegetation . . . hundreds of plants growing together and many kinds of trees. Gulls and many varieties . . . of fishing birds trekking in the mud of tideland. Stone fences which would be worth a fortune to a millionaire in U.S. Moss growing in cracks in slate roofs. Green and grey the color of the day." In Cork he found, as was his wont, the plight of humanity reflected in the animal world: "Gulls crying, swans moored, it seemed, against the other bank, not to associate with gulls. But fresh sewage pouring into river—the Lee—brings them together at intervals. Commentary on reality, on gaining one's daily bread, what you have to do."*

HARVEY EGAN

Standard Hotel
Harcourt Street
Dublin
November 7, 1951

Dear Fr Egan,

I've just told the girls a story about a dirty old grey rat that used to eat mice and baby seagulls, and now the questions are flying concerning the whole rotten business. We arrived in Ireland one week ago, went up to Cork, stayed there until last Saturday, then came here. We're staying at the Standard Hotel on Harcourt Street, famous for Oscar Wilde and Bernard Shaw, a high school up the street they both attended. The street is beautiful in my opinion, solid Georgian stone and brick, immense windows, lots of brass plates, oversize doorknobs. The big business in Dublin or in Cork, for that matter, is candy, sweets of all kind, tobacco, and stout. The big business on Harcourt Street is "Dental Surgery"; door after door with brass plate, So and So, Dental Surgeon. Needless to say, I'm telling them what's wrong with them. Every day I grab a candy bar—Cadbury's milk chocolate is the favorite—out of people's hands. Naturally, until I explain why, this strikes them as odd. My theory, derived from you doubtless, is that they eat all this junk, have tea all the time too, because they don't eat a square meal all day. It must be a great place for the tapeworms.

We've discovered that the meat here is good, the tea, eggs, but look out for the vegetables—if cold, like the remains you see in the sink after the dishes are done, a sprig of sad lettuce, a tomato skin with one seed hanging on it; if hot, just mush. They should bring in the Chinese to teach them about vegetables. Instead, there's a big deal about African missions, tag day, etc., Negro dolls dressed up like Martin de Porres. After seeing Santa Fe, hearing McKeon on the need for money there—to work with people who are already presumably Catholic—I am cold to African missions.

There's something rotten about religion here, I think, and something great, both to an extent, I suspect, that we don't have in America.[1] Little boys and girls, all patches and hobnailed shoes or rubber boots without stockings, kneeling for half an hour at a time, apparently praying. I don't remember anything like that where I come from. Of course the gigglers and punchers are here too, but the others stay with me. On the other side, there are many hard-faced women, some in black shawls, and I'm not so pleased by the look of them. Perhaps they all had drunks for husbands, or perhaps they didn't have husbands to avoid the inevitable, I don't know. [. . .]

The poverty here is tremendous. It's a Dickens world. Lots of talk about the duty Irishmen have to stay here, not to emigrate, and yet it's a dog's life if one stays, I think, in too many cases. Betty was at an employment bureau, went down to "interview" someone to look after the girls when we go looking at houses tomorrow and Friday. Women all herded together in a common room. The woman who runs the employment agency shouts at one—like scooping out a minnow—and she comes. Name: Mary Ryan. Wage: 10 shillings ($1.40) a day; the employment agency's charge (of us): 10 shillings. A maid is supposed to be lucky to get $5.00 a week, but there's also a shortage. Many contradictions. For instance, a worn copy of *Prince of Darkness* in the rental library of Eason's, the biggest bookstore in Dub-

1 "I don't feel right about the Church here. Even thought the poor Protestants might be holding back the deluge, one finger in the dike." Journal, November 4, 1951.

lin. Naturally, I picked it up and demanded that it be banned. [. . .] All for now. (I realize I've overstepped my limits, set by you, in writing such a long letter, but ask forgiveness) . . .

Jim

Jim and Betty rented Dysart, a house in Greystones, county Wicklow, and took up residence on November 15, 1951. Betty hired a sixteen-year-old girl, B——, to look after Mary and me while she wrote. B—— was good fun, taking us on walks during which she would meet her best friend. This girl, also sixteen, was already equipped with a complete set of false teeth and earned our horrified admiration on one occasion by taking them out to remove a piece of toffee.

HARVEY EGAN

Dysart, Kimberley Road
Greystones, County Wicklow
Heaven on Earth
November 21, 1951

Dear Fr Egan,

I picked up your letter and enclosures when in Dublin yesterday and now hasten to reply so you'll have our permanent address—I mean as permanent as an address can be when heaven's our destination. [. . .] Art slipped me a twenty when we left that morning for New York, and that just about completed my drive. I now owe everyone something—you the most—and I'd suffer more than I do—I do suffer considerably, by the way—if it weren't that the thing I do is priceless. At the moment the thing I'm doing is lighting a pipeful of Carroll's Donegal (Aromatic) Sliced Plug, and a little later on I'll open a bottle of Guinness—run by the Freemasons, by the way. Then I'll maybe jot down a few pages of my memoirs. I've given up stories and the novel I used to talk about—when I'd talk, that is, for I've not forgotten your complaint about my silence, my unwillingness just to sit and talk for days on end, your comparing me with one other friend. I'm calling the new book *My Turn to Make the Tea*. There's another one out by that title, by Monica Dickens, [. . .] but by the time mine is out, I daresay the title will sound fresh again. [. . .]

Yesterday we started having a maid. She asked for 25 shillings, or bob, a week, and so we are magnanimously paying her 30—I wonder how are things down below for those who defraud the workers. Still, it's that way all over. She's just a kid, 16, [. . .] about ten kids in her family, went through the eighth grade—to get to this position in the world. [. . .] Life is real, earnest, tough, for most people in Ireland who have to work, I think.

A paperhanger told me that only 10 percent of the people in Greystones have to work; all retired, ex–army men, pensions, coupon clippers, and 95 percent pro-British, he said. He was himself, it turned out, told me Guinness was run by the Freemasons, as indeed everything really big is, to which I showed no feelings one way or the other—fortunately, I guess, because he ultimately showed that he believed that to be the way things ought to be. He thought I must be Protestant—because American, I guess—and spoke for a while about "us," how we have incentive, "they" don't, hence the situation he described. Irish, he said, the victim of large families. If they'd just use their heads, lay in a little contraceptive jelly, well, they might have a chance. I pointed out it would go hard with "us" then, nobody to wait on us, no poverty-stricken large families condemned to carry our water, hew our wood, for what we'd be willing and able to pay. When I confessed to being a Catholic, the conversation tapered off, and a good thing, for I was weary of homely wisdom. I gather, in little ways, that the Catholic government is the opposite side of the coin that has tails on both sides. Nobody can win for losing. I send you the latest list of censored books. But it's a beautiful place, everything I dreamed it might be, a lot draftier in the house—I didn't dream of that—but the water, the green, the vines, stone walls, the pace, all to my taste, and the meat and drink, likewise, mea culpa. [. . .]

I'm glad you sold the DeSoto, I never liked it, now I can tell you. [. . .] Yours, fondly.
    Jim

HARVEY EGAN

Dysart, Kimberley Road
Greystones, County Wicklow
December 22, 1951

Dear Fr Egan,
    You are the first one (outside the family) to see our new stationery. Please let me know what you think, if favorable. I felt I ought to have it to answer numerous inquiries that come my way, mostly regarding literary

matters, but unfortunately none has arrived since the stationery did. Maybe something Monday.

Glad you now approve move to Ireland. I'd like to have a house like this in U.S. Eight rooms, laid out longwise, rather than squarewise, so one puts some distance between himself and, say, the children. I will also need a fireplace in my permanent home, preferably a small coal-burning one such as the Marlborough, I suspect, had originally. I like to stand in front of it with pipe or glass. Back to Thackeray!

Fr Fennelly, our PP,[1] dropped in this afternoon. He must be sixty, or close to it, and his conversation seemed to say that he'd just been given a parish, Holy Rosary, Greystones (the church on the postcard I sent), last summer. He's got a heating problem, and over that the problem of getting people to contribute in general. Says they don't realize times have changed and they—"the ordinary man," one of his phrases—have to do what their betters did in palmier days. Offhand, I'd say he's asking for it (just like a young pastor in the U.S.), trying to get people to use a missal and do their part, and he refuses to use a form (in which parishioners' past performances would be published for all to see and handicap). He's not a victim, however, not a softy full of theory. He seems to admire Spain (before Franco), has no time for America or Britain, speaks of the old families with their sense of noblesse oblige, and is an author (a book of prayer for children and some other stuff, not clear what, written as a curate and therefore, he said, "anonymously"). I think he's lonesome, but doubt that I'm the one to fill his evenings. [. . .]

You'll be gratified, I hope, to know that in the past week I've been shown how right you can be sometimes when you sound pretty far gone. We have had bad cases of the crabs, or lice, both girls and Betty (only mildly). I favor capital punishment in this matter for the disseminators. Mr Power, the local chemist, hopes we don't blame Ireland for our trouble. It's touching to see people like him, so hopeful that we'll like Ireland, won't think it too slow, etc. I think most opinion of the U.S. here is reached through listening to returned stage performers tell about it, about Broadway, Times Square. I told Mr Power he doesn't know the meaning of slow and would be glad to give him the name of a PP who does. [. . .]

My turn to make the tea. Guinness has gone up 1 d., but they're increasing the specific gravity. Can't get Smucker's here. We have to settle

---

1 Parish priest (the pastor).

for Fruitfield. They're a good house but no Smucker's. Fairly Happy New Year!

     Jim

HARVEY EGAN

Dysart

March 8, 1952

Dear Father Egan,

[. . .] I haven't seen *Commonweal* for a while. It comes in spurts. Here I read *The Irish Times*, *The Times* (London), *Time*, the *Wicklow People*, the *Standard*, the *Catholic Herald*, *The Observer* (Sunday, London), the *Sunday Times* (London, not the aforementioned). I think there's room for another paper, preferably one with the word "Times" in it, say, *The Catholic Times*, here. Except for *The Irish Times*, the Irish papers are awful; *Sunday Visitor* stuff, cutouts for children, a dress pattern for mother, sports for dad. As the new nuncio (O'Hara) said, Ireland is one country that works hand in glove with Rome. The press shows it—except *The Irish Times*, which is Anglo-Irish literate. The *Standard* is good for a diocesan paper but full of the usual junk too, enroll in the Golden Book of Our Lady of Something, Liverpool, only ₤.

I had dinner at the Bailey—a restaurant in Dublin—with Sean O'Faolain and Frank O'Connor the other night. Liked them both. O'C. is going to the U.S., hopes to settle there, can't live or write here, he says, because of "personal troubles," meaning his marital troubles, I guess. He now has an English wife, an Irish one here, numerous children, etc. O'F. is riding it—being happily married, it appears—riding it out on purer lines, the problem with being a writer in Ireland, I mean. O'C. said it would be impossible for him or O'F. to live anywhere but in Dublin, in Ireland; O'F. seemed to agree they'd be in physical danger in Cork, where they both come from. They were stunned to discover that I'd been employed by Marquette. O'F. is very calm, cool, and, I suspect, long-suffering . . . O'C. great admirer of A. E. Coppard and Saroyan. O'F. might have been a Dublin businessman, from his dress, dark suit, white shirt; O'C. raffish, orange wool shirt, wool tie, blue tam. O'F. in good health. O'C. has trouble with his liver, his wife tells him what he can eat, drinks light wines and lime juice. He paid the bill. That sums up the evening, my impressions. "Urbs Intacta" was the only Latin used—by Mrs O'F.—referring to Waterford, which she belittled, and fortunately I picked up on "Urbs." "Inter alia," I said, urbanely, "wasn't that a long time ago?" I was smoking some small black cigars—Wills's Whiffs—and probably made a very good impression, seen from the tables around us. We had Vichy water at the very end. Trying to cap that, I called for a jar of Smucker's, but they couldn't provide it. "What! No Smucker's!" I cried, which got over the idea that the management, and indeed everyone, including parties all around us, had a lot to learn. "1943 is the best year," I said. " '45 is acceptable." Then I went on to tell them about that little place in Chicago that I took you to, not much to look at and all that, but what food, what service! [. . .]

My PP came by and took me for a drive around his parish. Very interesting he is, once the sun goes down, and he loses his way, not the man then that brought us *You Can Change the World*.[1] He conscripted Betty to come and utter an opinion at St Kilian's Hall, where he was throwing a parish debate. Subject: The Hand That Rocks the Cradle Controls the World. He outlined what Betty ought to say, leaving a pamphlet about this little Italian girl (Goretti) who's up for canonization. I hadn't heard about it—at least didn't recognize the name when he was here—and that was somehow in my favor, made me out to be a good, healthy male preoccupied with my pipe. "Oh, he thinks he's running the show, but it's the little woman every time. She's the one who keeps him straight. He just tags along, if he only knew it"—ha, ha. I said I knew it only too well, that I knew the torture of marriage, had dreamt of the beauties of celibacy. He hadn't been prepared for such an ad-lib, was silent, lips twitching—and I could see that, though I'd spoiled his act, he was pleased to hear what he too regarded as the truth. [. . .]

O'C. and O'F. spoke of Waugh as though he'd lost his mind. Said he had his servants wearing livery, the latest development. I must get something for my man, a cap anyway, who brings me wood, takes away my ashes, works around my demesne. He doesn't work very hard, brings me green wood. Betty says he knows I'm a fool—her exact words. "Fool for God?" I ask eagerly, but I gather she doesn't mean that kind. [. . .]

Clark[2]

1 One of Father Fennelly's pamphlets.
2 Clark Bars—Jim's favorite.

Dysart

Easter 1952

Dear Fr Egan,

[. . .] The first blood was drawn at Leopardstown[1] a week ago. Two winners (8–1; 6–1), and I guess it's going to be nip and tuck from now on between the track and me. Unfortunately, there are those two-bob[2] (28c) machines, and I go with Betty, so even when I win, it's moderately. A wonderful way to spend an afternoon, though. When I'm there, I always know what you and Thoreau mean. [. . .]

Let me know what the sales were for your book.[3] (That's what writers talk about, incidentally, and you asked.) Got another in the works? Same publisher? Any nibbles from others? Who's your agent? Any personal troubles? Have to drink to write? I haven't had a Guinness for a week. Just a little John Jameson. Write.

Jameson

Greystones

May 11, 1952

Dear Fr Egan,

I enclose an advance complimentary copy of *The Children's Mass Book*. I hope that after you have had the opportunity to read it, you will write to me. I value your opinion and look forward to hearing from you. The editor is my PP. Perhaps we could work out an exchange plan: you buy his book and he'll buy yours. By the way, how *are* sales?

Haven't heard from you in some time but suppose you are busy with your yellow slips.[4] Did you ever think of getting linen ones, to stand up better under the constant shuffling? I could get you a fair discount on linen. [. . .]

Do you like the new *Commonweal* format? I object to that arrow ending up at 15c. All for now. You owe me one, so I won't try to make this more impressive.

Seamus

1 Racecourse south of Dublin.
2 Two shillings.
3 A book of prayers.
4 Egan's to-do lists.

That May, aside from receiving an exhausting visit from Garrelts and an-
other priest, Jim saved a boy from drowning and was awarded a "certificate
of bravery." Betty described the incident in a letter home: "Some little boys
ran up carrying a life preserver and said, 'A boy's after falling in the ocean.' . . .
So Jim found himself standing half in the water on a ledge of rock, holding
on to the boy in the life preserver and the waves trying to splash them both
out into the ocean. And he had to keep his teeth shut tight because he had
his pipe in his mouth and no hand to take it out . . . There were no end of
women and retired men and boys around but no one strong enough to pull
them out until the guards came, and also the milkman. (There is nothing that
can happen in Greystones without the milkman being there with the first of
them.)"

HARVEY EGAN

Greystones
June 3, 1952

Dear Fr Egan,

[. . .] The Irish—here and everywhere—worry too much about what is written about them. Their favorite reading is writing about them, any chance reference, anything that doesn't please. It's all in Joyce, the petty chauvinism, the chemist who wants us to buy Irish soap (which is not very good soap), the piercing look following the question, how do you like Ireland? I like Ireland, but I don't like these little boosters. Tell them that.

Well, George and Fr Dillon arrived, and we had a fast three days in a hired car, Limerick, Galway, Mullingar races, evening at Sean O'Faolain's. Our guests left for the Continent . . . and we went to bed for three days to recover from the rush. George, it turns out, is a tourist with a vengeance, picks up with everybody, and finds out more in three days than we have in six months. They went to the races in civvies, though priests were everywhere in black and white, and the touts called George "the Yank." [. . .]

Fr Fennelly will be glad to hear you approve his book. He should be back from Barcelona any day. Before he left, he made it clear to the congregation that he was going there to "suffer," in case, I guess, anyone should get the idea that he was going off on a holiday. Said he couldn't stand the heat, had no accommodations, would just have to take his chances. I was amused but not impressed by this, remembering his remark last fall that he'd always wanted to go to Spain, having been everywhere else he'd wanted to go—no desire to see the U.S.—but then that's the Irish way, isn't it? I do the same thing myself.

Hump[1] is still putting out that Lenin-Tolstoi jive. I think he fell on his head sometime in the Thirties. And something stopped inside, turning him into an LP record. Ah, well. When I think of going back, I have to think of going back to Hump—I do think *he* misses me, is perhaps the only one who does—and I just don't know if that's what I want. We are pilgrims only, but since the trip's quite long, I tend to look around for suitable accommodations. I am desireless. There's no place anymore that strikes me as the place for me. This is no reflection on Ireland, since I never meant to make this my permanent abode, but on my condition, which is not the condition of most: most can still dream of somewhere else, you of your next year's garden or a parish in St Paul—I'm just speaking in a manner of speaking, I don't want to hear of your contentment in Beardsley. You won't deny, however, that you have a passion for farming equipment, manure, your yellow slips. Me, I have no desires. There's nothing to give up. Is this perfection?

[. . .]

Please write.

Jim

HARVEY EGAN

Greystones
July 5, 1952

Dear Fr Egan,

Well, here it is Saturday noon, and your gift has come—three days early for my birthday—and already I'm three sheets to the wind. Betty has her hands full keeping the kids out of the room, for they sense something is up, and I guess she's right, not wanting them to see their old man in such a condition, having Smucker's taken.

Father Fennelly was overwhelmed by your acceptance and approval of his prayer book. I let him see your letter, and where you say it's fortunate we are to have a literate PP, he says: "He must mean literary." No, I say, he means literate. "Why, that means to be able to read, surely he doesn't mean that. No, he must mean literary. I can understand that. Ha, ha," he laughs, at your reference to Sunday as the day on which you count the

---

1 Don Humphrey.

money. "These Americans! He must mean literary." No, I think he means what he says—literate. "Oh, not at all. Literary is what he means. Just a slip of the typewriter. He *must* mean literary." I don't think so. "Oh, no doubt of it." I say nothing. This is the man just back from Barcelona, the Eucharistic Congress, where he met the Spanish people, stayed right with them, in fact, in the same house with some, and they found him so different from their own clergy. "Yes, he means literary. The *e* should be a *y*, that's all." You know, Father, I think he meant to write literary where he wrote literate. "Oh, no doubt of it. Well, that's pretty good, getting to see a letter like this. You have a typewriter. Make me a copy." Just keep it. And so, after a while, I got him to keep your letter, and yesterday Betty met him in the street, and his printer hadn't understood all you said—"Here, take a look at this if you think you understand the English language"— but he got the general idea, the *e* in that one word should be a *y*, of course, and there's no doubt that you've made Fr Fennelly happy—happy as any other author would be at being well received by the critics. I gave him a copy of your pamphlet, and perhaps you'll be hearing about it from him. I can't help thinking of other great literary friendships, Flaubert and George Sand, Knox and Waugh, the Brownings. [. . .]

We saw the Ardagh chalice—pretty uninspiring, I thought—and the Book of Kells, also disappointing. It's at Trinity, the university founded by the first Elizabeth and now off-limits to Catholic students except by special permission, which is part of the present archbishop's policy—just when the Catholics were beginning to dominate it, according to Sean O'Faolain. He told us—this when George was here, when we visited him at his home—of a priest, an old man who, speaking of the Book of Kells and where, alas, it had come to rest, said to the congregation, "If there was a *man* among you, you'd go down there and—have a look at it." [. . .]

I have no advice for you, with regard to getting the people to come up with it. Hy Weber, in Quincy, used to take 50c bets, and since I was just a lad then, with little to lose, I was glad that he did. [. . .]

Always remember that I feel indebted to you, that on top of being indebted to you, and that I intend to make it up to you someday—if we both manage to live so long.

By "yellow slips" I meant those slips of paper, yellow in color, on which you write various tasks to be done and then play solitaire with in the mornings. No offense?

Believe it or not, it doesn't rain here, and the grass in the backyard is brown. I carry water out to it in pans.

Lost at the Curragh (the headquarters of Irish racing), and didn't like the place either: cement, gravel. Leopardstown is my place. Horses for courses, as you always say. [. . .]

All for now. And thanks for the Smucker's—it's given me quite a nice edge.

    Jim

Jim traveled with Father George Garrelts to England, where they visited Evelyn Waugh at Piers Court. Waugh was fascinated by the soles of Jim's shoes, which he asked to examine more than once. They had been repaired, in a manner of speaking, by an Irish cobbler who had simply nailed ridges of rubber onto the original soles, giving Jim a rocking gait.

Jim and George went on to Scotland, where Betty joined them in Glasgow, leaving the girls at home looked after by an older Greystones woman. It was a disappointing trip for Betty, whose paternal grandmother had given her a hundred dollars to spend on visiting the Highlands, where she had longed to go. It was not to be. Leaving Betty in hotels, Jim and Garrelts went off together, sometimes to pubs, spending her money. In the end they visited only Glasgow, Edinburgh, Galashiels, Dumfries, and Stranraer, all crowded and tourist-ridden in Betty's opinion.

HARVEY EGAN

Greystones

August 22, 1952

Dear Fr Egan,

Yours rec'd and enjoyed as usual and in fact read by George, who was here when it came, all of us—add Betty—having just returned from Scotland. I don't recall whether you got into the British Isles (I know you weren't here), and without being sure, I wouldn't want to give you my impressions, which will be coming out in book form anyway (the Wanderer Press, 10 deutsche marks). Needless to say, I had enough to make a full-size book, had to, according to my contract. I'm taking a respite to write to you, having been very busy for some days with a chapter of my novel (the Wanderer Press, 5 deutsche marks), trying to get it into shape as a story. You know we have to do that, sometimes, to keep our names before the public who soon forget (but not soon enough, in my case).

We had a visitor this evening, our first since George disappeared

(I don't say "left," because you know the melody lingers on, as does the Drambuie he gave us). But enough parentheses; I remember being cautioned about them; five on a page and you're out. The visitor was Hep; W. D. Hepenstall, the playwright of Greystones. He's an elderly gentleman (non-Catholic); had a play, *Dark Rosaleen*, on Broadway, way back, killed by hot weather—I report the news, no editing—and we hadn't been favored with a visit since last winter. I think he found us damn little fun, expected a little more from Americans, not to find them as he found us, however that is.

I can't say that we have a roaring time either. Every now and then he looks at you—usually, Betty—and says, "Well, what did you think of Eva Perón?" or "Well, how're the family?" Seems Eva was just a peasant girl, before she met Perón. Weather in America—he's been there, was out west in Buffalo—pretty tropical. Yes, we bathe in the river and irrigate the plantation (sometimes it's the ranch), and you can really hear dem banjos ringin'. Takes soda in his Drambuie, thinks it's regular scotch, I think. But all right. Brought us some incdible apples in a briefcase, much appreciated by Betty. When someone brings me watermelon, I'll sit up. Or Smucker's. I confessed Smucker's last time, got the works; wants me to cut it out or at least—the confessor was on the *in se* himself—to cut down. How can I? I'm human.

In England, Geo. and I saw Fr D'Arcy (who has since written to the Earl of Wicklow,[1] who has now written to me, and I have to him; we'll have a meal: he wanted us to join him on a pilgrimage to Lourdes, if you're wondering how well we know each other). Fr D'Arcy fine, no ball of fire as we understand the term, but seems to have a way with people who read. Saw his room on Farm Street, lots of pre-Reformation junk, statues, chalices, plaques, big chair before fireplace, electric fire also nearby— someone said he's waiting (and wants) to die—and I could see him there. Confessed desire for subscription to *Time*. Must see if George arranged for that, though it seems criminal to increase the circulation.

Saw Msgr Knox, briefly, after sermon at Clifton, Bristol Diocese. He's a healthy man. I hadn't thought that from his pictures, where his head looks like it's making a basket—two points—in his collar. I'm afraid he didn't know who I was. Do you know? I told him about the Irish customs wanting to take his book (*Enthusiasm*) away from us, as banned. Only memorable thing I said on the whole trip; I'm not much anymore.

---

1 William Howard, 8th Earl of Wicklow (1902–1978), converted to Roman Catholicism in 1932.

Saw Waugh at Piers Court. All a lie about liveried servants. Carried out his dishes himself. Very nice, but no fun for me. Gave me his new book, not published, *Men at Arms*, which I haven't had time to read, and that should tell you I'm working. Feel guilty about that, about not being able to write and tell him that I like it, as I think I will. George and Betty read it. They say it has a wonderful chapter on a chemical toilet, which George seemed to think was my baby, if it was ever to become literature. It may not be what some would consider sex, but it still isn't my sort of thing. I'm waiting for someone to point out that whatever else old JF may be, he's never dealt in sex. But, no, there's no one saying it, and America's cleanest writer goes his lonely way. I may duck out and come into the church again, in time for my novel's publication, to get the full convert treatment if the market holds. You can see I'm brooding, can't you? All for now. Thanks for the clippings. My blessing upon you and all your lawn mowers.

Jim [. . .]

HARVEY EGAN

Greystones

September 9, 1952

Dear Fr Egan,

[. . .] Betty and I have been working in my office for over a week, a ten-by-ten room, radio, map of Minnesota, electric fire, a stack of unread London *Times*, four numbers of *Time*, and so on. They've been repairing our chimney and papering the walls—this in our good room, with the view—and we go back in there this evening, with roaring fire, gale raging outside, sea crashing on rocks. Perfect site for a bestselling author, but again something comes between one and sales. Incidentally, about *Prince*[1] being on that bargain list in Springfield, I suppose they bought too many copies (out of personal admiration) and just couldn't sell them. I was never very strong in Sangamon County. Horses for courses. George used to make good money at the state fair, barking up the Unborn Baby show.

Was there any truth in what you said about yourself, your health, in a previous letter? Do you actually suffer from something—physical, I mean? Wouldn't make much sense, if you did. I'm afraid I'd be tempted to

---

1 *Prince of Darkness.*

peel and eat a Clark Bar right in front of you. Give me a little more information on that. Remember I was once very close to medicine. [. . .]

We did meet the Earl of Wicklow and Saturday had dinner with him at the Bailey. Like him a lot. According to his friend, a young barrister (former European 147 lb champ), Lord Wicklow is holy, not pious, which is a distinction I've heard made over here once before. The earl's favorite phrase is "Don't you know!" Another friend of his—young man working for the transportation bureau—sounded positively American, when, oh, when would we start living according to Christ in this most Christian of countries (he and the champ both drank club orange, by the way), to which I made no immediate reply, to which Lord Wicklow said, "Don't you know!! Don't you know!" The apostle in transportation, unmarried like the champ (who also drinks club orange), takes his pleasure in letters to *The Evening Mail*, some of which I've sent you in the past and a few snatches this time, never knows when he's coming out in print. He writes mostly under the *nom de course* "Pro Publico Bono" and hits pretty hard, I understand, and they also say he is easy to read. But I do want you to understand that I found the earl and his two friends great sport, the best people I've seen in Ireland for my purposes, which admittedly are not everyone's. We hope to have them out.

Here's the payoff on Fr Fennelly. You know he usually talks about the need to use a missal. Whatever he talks about, though, there is one rather dirty bastard whom he keeps referring to as "the ordinary man," and it is this fellow who is running the world today, outvoting men like Fr Fennelly, crossing him at every turn, and unlike the landed gentry in the old days the ordinary man just doesn't pick up the check, wants his union wage, his newfound position, without the responsibilities. And so on. The payoff is that while getting my hair cut the other day, the barber (an usher at the nine o'clock), who speaks fondly of former pastors, how nice they were, etc., referred to Fr Fennelly as "the ordinary man." I guess that's what the natives call him. He had it coming, I guess, but I am still one of his supporters, preferring excitement on Sunday. I admitted to the barber, however, that it might be because I was just passing through. To which he said, "Well, for that matter, we all are." So there is a certain quickness, aptitude for the verities, among the common people here. [. . .] All for now. Write.

Jim

Greystones

September 25, 1952

Dear Leonard and Betty,

Can't remember whether I owe you a letter or not, but feel a desire to renew communications with someone in the Big Missal Country. Here, incidentally, it's enough that we use Fr Stedman's little number. Betty (my wife), always one to be more Catholic than the Church, now uses a rosary during Mass.[1] [. . .]

We've had Fr Petrek (former seminarian at St John's) for a couple of days and enjoyed having him. He's very young, as we older men say; not even Rome seems to have slowed him up, apostolically, I mean. He's going to Louvain now for a few years. Talks of taking rooms with a family, so as to be close to it all, and there was nothing I could do to dissuade him, and I used both precept and example. [. . .]

I was beginning to take heart about American politics until reading about Mr Nixon's speech this morning, about his wife, his dog, his love for his country, etc. Apparently, since the speech went over, things haven't changed a lot. Fortunately—so I'm informed—he won't make it, even with all that to offer. Is Gene McCarthy going to the post again? I heard him nominate Humphrey over the American Forces Radio from Germany, kept tuned all the way, enjoying Gene's voice, hoping he'd mention some of us in passing. [. . .]

Jim

HARVEY EGAN

J. F. Powers
America's Cleanest Lay Author
Greystones
September 26, 1952

Dear Fr Egan,

Yours rec'd, with enclosure, much enjoyed. I must say *Catholic Action News* fills a long-felt need here. But why quarterly? Surely we ought to get it oftener than that. Unless I miss my guess, they'll have to put it out monthly, then weekly, and ultimately it will be the Catholic daily we've all

---

1 Joke.

been wanting. If they want my recommendation for publicity purposes, here it is, and you may quote me without changing a word: "Good, good, good!"

It will be nice for you—it will, it really will, if I remember rightly—to be able to catch Bp Sheen on TV when you go in for your treatments, which I trust you'll arrange accordingly. Now for a word from the ignorant. Get rid of that fluorescent light in your office. You sit in the dark, except for it, and that's bad for the eyes. I don't say your trouble doesn't go deeper than that, but I do say sitting in the dark, with only a fluorescent light, is bad. I do not have this advice from science but from my own observation of myself in like conditions. Call it spot glare, which is what Betty calls it. Of all the manifestations of Standard Oil, in the broad sense, as we used to employ it, the fluorescent light is the worst. [. . .]

Betty is sore at Nixon, doesn't go for that mother and dog line he puts out. (Dick Nixon is the candidate for the vice presidency on the Republican ticket.) Letter from Dick Keefe indicates he may go political if Stevenson wins. Hopes for the commissariat of education and hopes to make scholastic philosophy for first graders a required subject. One of Dick's brothers (Tom) has been on the Stevenson bandwagon for years. But I think he's all right, if we want an educated man for such an important job.

I wrote to Leonard Doyle last night and now hope for word on my friends, or should I say acquaintances, in the Big Missal Country. I enjoy a little gossip, you know, see nothing wrong in it, in itself. What I don't like is to sit around for hours and even days just talking, but I don't have to tell you that.

Humphaus wrote one letter, something of a record for him, but not very rewarding. Dear Jim, How are you? Everybody same here. Don.

Winter on here. We have our fireplace going. Tourists gone. Seafront vacant. Flat races running out; the hunt season, steeplechases, beginning. We may return by Christmas, if things work out. [. . .]

Jim

Give me a ten-day trial on the light. The idea is to have more than one light in the room—and real lights. [. . .] No heart, no food value, in fluorescent light.

November 3, 1952

Dear Fr Egan,

[. . .] Fr Fennelly over last night for a few minutes. No believer in democracy, he, he says. It is a hard thing to take when you've lived under a king. But I'll take democracy, since it's closer to reality, as I see it; closer, its idea, to Christianity. Waugh and others want noblesse oblige, but after the fact that those who should have had it, didn't, hence the deluge. As near as I can make out, listening to Fr Fennelly, Waugh, others, something just happened; the great did their best. Did you read the Rhys Davies story, though, in a recent *New Yorker*? ("A Visit to Eggeswick Castle.") A good argument for the other side, the monarchists. The right way lies somewhere in between. Hey, how about *that*?

We went to the Phoenix Park races one day, a lovely course, one nearest Dublin but we'd never been there. No winners but rewarding. We have so much to learn from the Old World. Como[1] could be like that. [. . .]

The election tomorrow. Betty's gone over to Stevenson—to the dismay of her folks, who are part of that tight little band who expect the miracle of the loaves and fishes every four years, the miracle in reverse, I mean.[2] Ever since George was here and assured me Stevenson would win, I've been convinced of it, except for a few days there when Nixon resorted to soap opera; I was not so sure then. As Stagg[3] feared Purdue, I feared that.

1:00 a.m., listening to a German station, as usual; my favorite language. Tomorrow night, the unholy family goes to see *The Pirates of Penzance* in Dublin, at the special request of the girls. Mary gets tired sitting around the house every night. Looks accusingly at me and says, "Why never don't we see a show?" They went to *Pinafore* only last November, but that's youth for you, always on the go. All for now.

Jim

1 Como Park, St. Paul.
2 They hoped for a Republican president.
3 A. A. Stagg, University of Chicago football coach for forty-one years.

13

In Ireland, I am an American. Here, I'm nothing

Christmas 1952—June 3, 1953

Betty and Mary and Don Humphrey. Summer 1953, living with Art and Money, up the river

The family returned to the United States on the SS America, arriving at the beginning of December 1952, and once again moved in with Betty's parents. It was not a happy arrangement from anyone's point of view except that of the children, who loved being with their grandparents in the clean, modern "rambler" on the banks of the Mississippi. Jim quickly set off for Albuquerque to visit his parents. He returned mid-January.

HARVEY EGAN

Albuquerque
Christmas 1952

Dear Fr Egan,

[. . .] I am now in Albuquerque. Spending the Christmas and days to follow with my folks. [. . .] Betty and children on the Mississippi. We'll be there, officially, when the Wahls—in another providential break—leave for Florida for three months. After that—who knows? It's too early to care, when you have put yourself, as we have, beyond mortal cares. (It says here.) Betty had a piece in *The New Yorker* two weeks ago.[1] I have a story coming, a long one, certain to bring me orchids and other things from one and all.[2] It is My Answer. I hope you'll like it but suspect you won't, which is where we both came in. I have another at *The New Yorker*, of another sort, as indeed I ought to have, having come to the end of my moneys from Doubleday, having turned down a job at Marquette for next fall; one at Univ. of Washington, for a semester; a writers' conference next July in Bloomington, Indiana. So hold that sexton's job open. I understand Bp Bartholome[3] is going to hire a chauffeur—or at least a man

1 "Tide Rips in the Teacups," *The New Yorker*, December 13, 1952.
2 "The Devil Was the Joker," *The New Yorker*, March 21, 1953.
3 Peter W. Bartholome (1893–1982), coadjutor bishop of the Diocese of St. Cloud, 1942–1953. He became bishop of the Diocese of St. Cloud in 1953 and retired in 1968.

to drive him around—and I was wondering . . . [. . .] I saw George, passing through Mpls, and had a good evening with him. He drove me to St Cloud, for my triumphal return—not so triumphal, by the way, though Don did throw a party at which people who hadn't ventured out for camaraderie for some time (Emerson, for instance) were present. They tell me I've not changed. Little do they know. I've aged; my perspective on my own, my native land, is sharper. [. . .] I'll be returning and will let you know when. We'll have room and bath for you on the Mississippi. I do even less drinking than I used to, and so am not the dangerous companion I used to be.

I am, sir, Yr Obed. Servant,
Jim

BETTY POWERS

Albuquerque
December 29, 1952

Dear Betty,

[. . .] Yesterday with my father and mother I went to see *The Quiet Man*,[1] and it was all right—very melancholy making, however, seeing the trains, the houses, the scenery. I think it was the trains and the CIE men that made me think most of Ireland; it was Technicolor, and the green of the train carriages—the white 1s and 3s for first and third class—was authentic. There were little authentic touches along the way: the retired English officer reading the *London Illustrated* during all the commotion of a riot; the C of I clergyman and his wife—Eileen Crowe of the Abbey. Too many of the actors were American, I'm afraid; they didn't sound rightly Irish, but suppose they'd been difficult to understand if they had; even Barry Fitzgerald sounded American to me, except in those flourishes of language. Perhaps the best thing was when the American arrived on the train and everyone began to tell him how to get to where he was going; I remember that happening to me. Anyway, you should see it if you get a chance; the story itself is silly. [. . .]

Well, I think that's all for now. I think of you often, pray you periodically pull yourself together and try to look and walk like a lady—which you're getting to be, you know.
Jim

1 A 1952 movie, directed by John Ford, starring John Wayne, Maureen O'Hara, and Barry Fitzgerald.

BETTY POWERS

Albuquerque

Tuesday afternoon [January 1953]

Dear Betty,

The bad news—*The New Yorker* rejecting the story. I enclose Henry's letter.[1] It came yesterday. I've been low ever since. And rather expect I'll be that way for some time, unless, by some miracle, *Collier's* should take the story. The immediate future is now jeopardized, as I see it, for the novel, I mean—which is where I came in last October. I don't know just how we stand, economically, though my overall feeling is one of despair, what with taxes, the cost of living we'll soon be bearing, to say nothing of setting up housekeeping if we should find a place. I find myself vacillating between stories and the novel again, but I think it folly to think of the latter—until I get to thinking now I'd like to have another book published. And then I think the next book I publish will probably be short stories, and so on. You know how it goes. [. . .]

I've not heard from *The New Yorker* since mailing off the working proof. I suppose I will, soon, and there'll be a lot more work on the story. I don't know what to think about the rejection. I'm just full of nothing; numb and void. I wonder where you're living by now. You don't say where I should direct this letter; in fact you didn't even sign your name. I understand, though. [. . .]

I'm very glad the girls are better. Would they want cowboy boots? No, I wouldn't want them to have them; I would, if Hopalong Cassidy and all that hadn't come along. I've seen television here a couple of times. It's not worth it, I think. They have only one outlet here, a combination of NBC and CBS and other programs, but I doubt that that makes the difference everyone says: if we just had more outlets! I'm right up to here—meaning my gills—with advertising, supermarkets, etc. This was evidently a deep-fry Christmas among the young married set. Remember the pressure-cooker Christmas when we were first married? Those were the days. It's time for Betty Crocker, and here she is—America's first lady of food. Fr Egan's friends (the Regans) live according to the stiff observance, wheat bread, etc. They tell me brown sugar is actually refined, then colored brown. The only good sugar is raw sugar, which you get at those vegetarian stores. One would do well to sell one's soul to Betty Crocker, at an early age, for invincible ignorance. How's the lemon bisque? My mother's suit

---

1 Jim's agent, Henry Volkening.

(as I indicate earlier here) did come, and in good condition, and you did very well with the pressing. You are a good girl, and I'm sorry I can't do more for you, can't settle you somewhere with maid, etc. But I can't, I guess, and that's your cross. All for now, except try to relax, and much love.

Jim

HARVEY EGAN

Albuquerque

Saturday, January 10, 1953

Dear Fr Egan,

[. . .] Very sorry to hear about Fr Nolan, but found his last words rewarding. I like that tone—see you in heaven. Now and then, from something like that, I get the idea that Catholics really do believe what they hold. It is an idea, that idea of death, that I'd like to see stressed more. As my friends and parents grow older, I think more along those lines; have to, I guess, not able to accept the tragedy it would be if it ended here as it does, this life. [. . .]

Juarez, I'm told, has been cleaned up, not what it used to be when I was a boy; much private enterprise then, every girl her hut and fire; now all spick-and-span, five houses run by a syndicate.

Don Humphrey threw a party for us in St Cloud, with food and drink; not the customary coffee and cake; and I guess he hopes I'll settle there. Will I? Truth to tell, I don't know what I'm doing.

My mother has dug out a pair of Indian moccasins I made as a boy, and they lie here at my feet—is there a clue in them, to the future? You know, I believe, that my desire at one time was to be an Indian, a member of the Blackfoot tribe. Then it was baseball, a member of the Brooklyn Robins (under Robbie, remember?). Then it was leader of a dance band; I had the baton and often directed, standing before the radio. Then. Then. Until now. Ireland again, yes, but I'm afraid you can't go home again— which probably won't keep me from trying, if I can ever work it out, the financial side, I mean. In Ireland, I am an American. Here, I'm nothing. And you, Father?

Pax,

Jim

The moccasins, I notice, point NNE.

BETTY POWERS

Albuquerque
Your birthday, January 16, 1953

Dear Betty,

[. . .] Downtown today with my mother. She got the girls some brace-
lets; I got them little cross necklaces the other day. I'm sorry to hear things
are so bad there, your father not feeling well, etc. I hope the girls (and you)
don't make it worse. I've been thinking a lot about you; often, in detail. It's
a sad state of affairs when a man's most carnal thoughts are all about his
wife. See that you are worthy of them. Kiss the girls for me. Don't upset
your life too much—to come to Mpls; I'll understand if you aren't there.

Much love,
Jim

*Jim returned to Minnesota, taking up residence again with his family, still
living up the river at Betty's parents' house. The Wahls left for Florida, intending to return north in April.*

ROBERT LOWELL

c/o A. Wahl
North River Road, Route 2
St Cloud, Minnesota
February 5, 1953

Dear Cal,

Glad to hear from you, after so long. [. . .] I went to Ted Roethke's
reading and afterward saw Ted in a saloon. I was with Buck Moon. It was
a little like old times—except that I wasn't in condition and suffered too
much the next day and day after. Ted looks pretty good. I thought he'd
have gone downhill (physically, I mean), but I was wrong. Buck is working
at *Collier's*, as a fiction editor. Ted is on a Ford. He wavered on street corners, clutching at his coat collar, and said he didn't know whether he
should go to Florida or Saginaw. I advised him on his delivery, suggesting
that he not try to be mindful of the audience, that he forget his tendency
to seem lovable, which just doesn't become him.

We arrived back from Ireland in December. [. . .] I managed to work
more than I have in years. I enjoyed the papers, the fireplace, the sea, the

theatre in Dublin, and racing. Now we're supposed to be looking for a house. There aren't any for us. You're lucky to come from New England. I think there must be houses there. I have to be a big success and build, to make out in this locality. I understand writers like Eliot and James better, why they left, I mean, but I don't feel up to doing it myself, going whole hog, becoming a subject of the queen or a citizen in Ireland. In short, be thankful that you want to be somewhere that is also where you belong. My family (now in New Mexico) just moved around too much. [. . .]

Our children are both anemic; as is Betty; but we are all happy together. Presently we're living in Betty's family house, on the Mississippi, while her folks are in Florida. [. . .] Best to you both.

Jim

HARVEY EGAN

North River Road
St Cloud, Minnesota
March 27, 1953

Dear Fr Egan,

I was wondering what ever happened to you, when your letter came today. Offhand, I'd go along with that doctor who says you're only anemic. Guinness for you. A pint of plain is your only man. You've got good stuff in you, and though moderation is a good thing, you don't want to go off the deep end. Myself, I have no need for stimulation, being numb to the world, but you, you're different. So much for that.

Now for the things which really matter. I have made some *flats*—one of my favorite words now—and have planted ten varieties of tomatoes (seeds), some Savoy cabbage. That was a week ago. Well, already the little bastards are beginning to rear their little shoots, first the cabbage, today the first of the tomatoes—the Fargo Yellow Pear, I believe, not having time to refer to my master key. As I understand it, we'll need some land pretty soon for these plants, if they continue to prosper. We can't use Art's, I think, because he's a gardener in the local manner, gets his tomato plants from a greenhouse—John Baer, I believe they're called—and sets them out. You'd be surprised how resentful people are (I think of Mary Humphrey, for whom all tomatoes are equal and John Baers are the most equal) when one approaches gardening with imagination. It all goes together, as Eric Gill said.

A man who reads *The Saturday Evening Post* will plant John Baer tomatoes. [. . .] Betty says robins stop, look, and listen, as they do, for the voices of worms, which they can hear. Is that true? I don't know what to believe nowadays.

Pax,
Jim

The Wahls returned from Florida, and with the prospect of a family Easter gathering before him Jim went, once more, to stay with Father Egan in Beardsley. He instructed Betty on the care of his beloved tomato seedlings. Alas, under the crowded conditions in which the family was living, the "crop" failed. "Rain. Rain. Rain," Betty wrote to him. "About a dozen of the seedlings folded over one nice day. Others should be brought in for this cold weather, but nowhere to bring them except basement."

BETTY POWERS

Beardsley
April 1953

Dear Betty,

Just a note. I felt bad about leaving you as I did —the hassle over tomatoes, I mean—and hope you didn't brood over it. Since coming here, I've been having plenty of food and music and conversation. [. . .] I don't know when I'll return, in a day or two or maybe next week. I mean to discuss that with Fr Egan but don't, somehow. [. . .] I hope you're feeling all right, that the girls are well, that things aren't too difficult for everybody. I also hope that something is happening about our future habitat but suppose that's not to be, yet. Now I must close, having nothing else to say. [. . .]

Much love,
Jim

Jim returned from Beardsley. Art Wahl told Betty he would contribute ten thousand dollars toward a house for the Powers family.

North River Road
St Cloud, Minnesota
April 30, 1953

Dear Fr Egan,

[. . .] Art has offered to put up cash to buy an old house here. But we've not found one we like or can afford; the former, particularly. There was one, five bedrooms, two and a half baths, but in poor condition, ready for burning, I think, some dark winter night. The real estate man was interesting, like my character Mac. Bow tie, mustache, chewing gum, smile, station wagon, and line. "Boy, when I see a cash customer, I move right in with him." "That's right. Tell the truth and you never have to remember what you said." Lots of small talk that you would've loved, which I didn't respond to properly, which caused him to ask presently: "You folks from around here?" as if he seriously doubted it. Nice fellow, though, really on our side, and if there's ever a black-market economy here, I mean to look him up for some square deals. Good idea for a fiction character, if I knew more about the realtor's life. His driving around, as he does, looking at other people's houses, some not for sale, and saying: "You like that one. I might get you that." I think he will live, in the American grain. [. . .]

And now Betty comes in with the mail and a book, a guide to recorded music, and I know you're the only one who would send me that. Thanks very much. If I ever get my Magnavox out of storage, I'll need it. I haven't heard any music (excepting Guy Lombardo and the Ink Spots) since I left Beardsley, seat of my cultural life.

Best to Brother.

Jim

North River Road
St Cloud, Minnesota
May 7, 1953

Dear Fr Egan,

[. . .] Everything very much the same here—nothing good in real estate coming our way. I vacillate between wishing I had the wings of an angel—one whose wings would know where to take him, however—and a large brick house in which to hide myself, with books, music, etc.

We watch the papers for new movies, and I rather think that's what a lot of people are doing here. Something good comes here, and for days afterward you might hear Don, the Petterses, the Palmquists, the Powerses, adverting to it, having been there on opening night, as it were. It's what you've got there in Beardsley, only not so you can see it so clearly. It is possible to divert the mind from time to time into thinking maybe things aren't so bad. Work, I say, in my lucid moments, that is the only thing. [. . .]

George and Dick[1] were here for lunch—at the Modern Bar—one day two weeks or so ago. Dick is quite a bit larger than life. Had a pocketful of El Productos and dreams of more education for everyone who can afford to go to St Louis U. [. . .]

Guerin on Native Dancer was bumped. Ireland, I find, has killed me for racing here. It's just not it anymore. Rather ungrateful of me to say that after all racing has done for me here. It may be that I need a two-bob ticket to feel right about the whole thing, the depression keeps coming back and spoiling the outlook at the track. I just don't know. Thanks again for all that research you did on Quebec. It doesn't look good, economically, and my intuition is also against it.

Jim

HARVEY EGAN

North River Road
St Cloud, Minnesota
June 3, 1953

Dear Fr Egan,

[. . .] Potato bugs, armyworms (now being sprayed by a man in a truck), and so on here. You'd think with so much DDT being used, we'd have fewer harmful insects, wouldn't you? (That is what is known as a leading question.)

Bp Busch's funeral today, but Don and I decided not to brave the clergy, hordes of whom are here for it.[2]

Guess that makes Mom Bartholome top dog.[3] Heard a good one about her lately. Seems she was at some big celebration or other, and feeling

---

1 Garrelts and Keefe.
2 Joseph F. Busch (1866–1953), bishop of the Diocese of St. Cloud, 1915–1953.
3 Mother of Peter Bartholome, now bishop of the Diocese of St. Cloud.

called to say something timely to her son (I guess it was not a speech, just something she felt compelled in the circumstances to say), she said: "Son, save your money." [. . .]

Best,

Jim

14

A place too good to believe we live in

October 5, 1953—April 14, 1954

James Ansbury Powers (Boz) and Jim, 1954

*In September, Jim and Betty finally found a solution to their housing prob-
lem in the "red house," the oldest house in St. Cloud. The arrangement was
that Jim and Betty would act as caretakers in lieu of rent and also share
residency for part of the year with the two women who owned the house.
Writing to Egan, Jim said, "I know you and know you'll not like the setup,
that we don't have the whole house; but that is where the facts of life come
in: we don't belong in a house like this, just as we didn't belong in Ireland—
both being beyond us, in this our time, in this our plight."*

*Built in 1856 as an office and storerooms and expanded into the house
it became in 1861, the place had served as a tea garden (Grandmother's Tea
Gardens) in the 1920s and 1930s. The grounds were set out with lilacs and
other flowering bushes and shaded by oak, elm, maple, black walnut, and
mulberry trees. Occupying half a block across the road from the Mississippi, it
was, as Jim wrote to Katherine Anne Porter, a "nice beat-up old house . . . with
probably the loveliest yard, all unkempt, in St. Cloud, crawling with railroad
lilies and mosquitoes. The sensation, walking through it, is one of buoyancy."*

HARVEY EGAN

509 First Avenue South
St Cloud, Minnesota
October 5, 1953

Dear Fr Egan,

Your letter rec'd this morning, the only piece of mail, which just shows
you what life has come down to for me, and a Monday morning at that.
Why, I remember the day when every mail brought invitations to write or
speak (for nothing). Now I might as well be in Barry.

I write so soon because I want to tell you the good news. I was up on
a ladder in a high wind mending a squirrel hole in the house—they bowl
nuts in the attic about two in the morning—when a wire came from Ken

McCormick of Doubleday saying I'd be getting $3,000 in the coming year from the Rockefeller Foundation. I'd applied, on his advice last winter, or spring, and had hoped to hear in July. I'd given up some time ago. Now, it would appear, we'll be able to live another year, eat and everything. To think you used to talk against Standard Oil! Well, I'm telling you, but don't tell anybody. I want to see how long society will cold-shoulder me. I refer to the fact that no one comes to see me, no one writes.

Naturally, I'll take up the novel again, providing I can get rid of the hammer and saw I carry about with me, night and day, and wallpaper brush. Send me some of your old yellow slips: squirrel hole, hole under my workroom, hole in shed, hole in attic, wiring in cellar, furnace, pad for my room, rug for my room, Hamm's, and so on.

[. . .] It is a run-down place but very beautiful in its way, and the grounds are the loveliest in St Cloud, I think. The owners, sisters of advanced age, both unmarried, name of Mitchell, Presbyterians, are descended from the original Yankee settlers; their father was author of the *History of Stearns County* and had a newspaper and holding company here. I like them, Ruth and Eleanor. They live in Mpls and St Paul, respectively; Hampshire Arms and Laurel Avenue. That's about it. [. . .]

Write. Come.

Jim

James Ansbury Powers was born on November 13, 1953. His name mutated from Bother Brown to Bozzer to Boz.

HARVEY EGAN

509 First Avenue South
St Cloud, Minnesota
November 14, 1953

Dear Fr Egan,

[. . .] I am alone here, Betty in the hospital. We had a boy yesterday morning (6:09 a.m.) and will call him James, I guess, making him the fourth one. The girls, who wanted another girl, are staying at Wahls. They consider boys selfish, "miners"—someone who grabs things and says, "That's mine!" Hump says now I'm really in business, in the family-life sense, and I guess expects my life to become more of a shambles, but we'll see. [. . .]

Went to see *Martin Luther*, the movie, and found it interesting, but confirmed in my faith, which proves something, I guess. If you would shake my faith, let me see a movie made under Catholic auspices. When I saw Luther at home, with Mrs Luther rocking the cradle, sewing, and Dr Luther teaching nine-year-olds sitting all in a row, I saw that the appeal was primarily sentimental, and so I guess it must always be, here, in lieu of anything else, anything like theology. Letter this morning from the First Methodist Church, mimeographed, welcoming me to St Cloud, suggesting that I come around unless I have other affiliations—which is very often not the case. The curate is Japanese.

Les McCarthys[1] (French) were here Wednesday afternoon. Word from them on the Sylvesters. Guess Rita is in a state asylum. Harry teaching in N. Carolina and divorced from her, in love with another. There's comedy and tragedy for you. He never should've left the sport page, Gene McCarthy said, and that's about it, I think. [. . .]

Now I must close, pick up some food for Betty to eat in the hospital. She says she's never tasted any like it.

When are you coming to see us?

Jim

CHARLES SHATTUCK

509 First Avenue South
St Cloud, Minnesota
November 30, 1953

Dear Chuck,

[. . .] We have found this house, a place too good to believe we live in, run-down as it is, owned by these elderly sisters who come for a few days now and then and are easy to take: I see they have left me the *Saturday Review* with KAP's picture on it, knowing we named our Katherine Anne after her. And I got this grant, after giving up on it, having applied last spring and expected to hear in July, and got it in the nick of time, in October, with Betty about to have a baby, movers to pay (from Milwaukee, where our furniture was in storage), and though I didn't know it until four days later—there were four days of perfect bliss—with a rejection from *The New Yorker* in store for me: another cat story, one I would've bet on, and consider, with the usual revisions to be made, superior to the other

---

1 Eugene and Abigail McCarthy.

two. [. . .] For someone as unprolific, or lazy, as I am, it's a bitter blow, from which I'm just now recovering. I took it out on the red squirrels that have made the attic and the walls of this house their home; with trap, gun, and fence I fought them, as the character in Joyce's "Counterparts" made up for everything by beating his children.

Anyway, I'm damn happy to have the grant and to be eating, as is Betty. She had a baby November 13, a boy, and we're calling him James Ansbury, after my father. His father was also a James: the Ansbury was his mother's name (she came from York, he from Waterford [Ireland] where all the Powerses come from). [. . .]

    Jim

ROBERT LOWELL

509 First Avenue South
St Cloud, Minnesota
December 2, 1953

Dear Cal,

Glad to have your letter. I want to thank you for your efforts in my behalf, with regard to the $3,000 grant from Iowa. I wish I could do something for you, someday. [. . .]

I have looked up Duxbury on the Mass. map in my *Britannica* (1890), and I see it's on the sea and that the "Telegraph Cable to France" is close by on the coast. I think your idea of going there and living and reading is wonderful. I know those 1937 Packards. I think they were the last cars— the following years got more and more away from the Rolls-Royce front— made in this country. I was going to buy one in 1949, having sold *my car* which you remember so vividly. It was a dark Pullman green and had a trunk rack in back and a mohair steering wheel, which showed that the previous owner was the careful sort, but I didn't buy it. I hope to ride in yours and trust that Elizabeth does all the driving. I think you need a battery, a new one, if you're not getting out these mornings, or maybe the connecting wires are afflicted with verdigris. You've got to live with your car, Cal, and whatever you do, don't laugh at it, don't talk against it. [. . .]

    Do write.

    Jim

JACK CONROY

509 First Avenue South
St Cloud, Minnesota
March 17, 1954

Dear Jack,

[. . .] No, Jack, I'm not running a tavern here. I do keep a little Hamm's in the house, though. If you ask me, it's the best of the better beers. But I seldom drink anything. I mean that. I don't know why. No proper company, I guess. I go down to the bus station and get the *Chicago Tribune*, for kicks, and it always reassures me that I was right in leaving Chicago. The local paper reassures me that I'd do well to leave here too. The truth is, Jack, that my heart is often in the highlands a-chasing a deer. By that, I mean I don't see any future for me here. I think I'd do better in Ireland. Where I was happier—with the newspapers (London ones, which I subscribe to here), plays at the Abbey and Gate, which I could afford, and horse racing. Also, I didn't feel so different from most people there. Here I sometimes look askance at the life I lead, wonder how long it'll be before the system catches up with me. I find, too, as I grow older, I don't care for the writers-project way of life, if you know what I mean; going around taking what's left by my betters, the salesmen of this world, the food they won't eat, the houses or apartments they won't live in, the cars they won't drive. I don't want to get in and pitch with them, or against them. I just want to go away. I must say you would've enjoyed the sight of me in Ireland, having my morning coffee before the fire, unfolding my *Irish Times*, listening to music from the BBC and from my stomach, full of good bacon and toast and marmalade; or at Leopardstown Racecourse; or walking along the sea . . .

Meanwhile, we're happy with this house, the oldest one in St Cloud, run-down though it is. It is owned by two maiden ladies who let us live here rent-free. We keep it up, heated, lighted. But when I leave the house—there's quite a library upstairs—or turn on the radio, I don't think I'm long for this world, Jack. Sometimes I think I should maybe give up entirely and install television. In Ireland a voice seems to be calling, though, and I think I should prepare myself to answer it ultimately. But how to live? I've thought on historical novels, but there's nothing in my pedigree or early form to indicate I can go the distance, writing them; I can't even read them. Sexy novels? What then would happen to this reputation I've built up over the years as America's cleanest Lay Author—I wish somebody would do an article which would bring out that aspect of my work. You just may be the one, Jack, with your feeling for tracts, the eternal virtues so often sneered at in our modern day. Best to you and yours.

Jim

April 14, 1954

Dear Fr Egan,

[. . .] Nothing happens here. Well, two visitors. Ammon Hennacy[1] a couple of weeks ago, and Sean O'Faolain (with George) last weekend. Ammon was interesting, I thought, and more impressive than I expected him to be. He reminded me of Fr Roy,[2] his concern with sound doctrine (sound or not) and always counting the numbers who heard him and appeared to be very interested. He had a big meeting—Mary Humphrey's word for it—at St John's, thanks to Fr Emeric,[3] I think, who has an idea of a university. Sean was here overnight, with George, and we had a good night of it, and a day among friends here, on the run: Doyles, Hyneses, St John's. George brought Sean to Newman,[4] you know, and next in line are Fr Hughes (the historian)[5] and Fr John Courtney Murray.[6] It seems to me Newman, under Fr Cowley[7] and George, is doing more, is doing more to bring in worthwhile people than any of the colleges hereabouts. You know the creeps and Swiss bell ringers the Catholic colleges get. [. . .]

Take it easy.

Jim

1 Ammon Hennacy (1893–1970), pacifist, member of the Catholic Worker movement, Christian anarchist.
2 Father Pacifique Roy, who prepared a retreat at St. John's given by Father Hugo that Jim attended.
3 Father Emeric Lawrence, OSB.
4 Newman Club in Minneapolis.
5 Philip Hughes, SJ (1895–1967).
6 John Courtney Murray, SJ (1904–1967), moral and ecumenical theologian.
7 Leonard P. Cowley (1913–1973), pastor of St. Olaf's and head of the Newman Club at that time.

15

I had a very fine time—laughing as I hadn't in years

April 23, 1954—July 14, 1954

Theodore Roethke, Yaddo, 1947

Jim accepted an invitation to travel to the West Coast to speak at the University of Washington, the University of Oregon, and Reed College in Portland. He chose the topic "reality in fiction." ("The writer lowers himself into the pit of his experience and imagination, and for a time all is black and hopeless. Then the lines suggest themselves, just a little of themselves showing.") "For this I'm getting $1,500," he told Father Egan, "but I continue to doubt that it's enough." During the six-week trip he visited Theodore Roethke in Seattle and also traveled to Victoria, British Columbia; San Francisco; Fresno, where he saw Ted LeBerthon; Los Angeles; and finally Albuquerque to see his family.

BETTY, KATHERINE, MARY, AND BOZ POWERS

Hotel Edmond Meany
University District
Seattle 5
April 23, 1954

Dear Betty, Girls, and Boy,

[. . .] Seattle and the country around here remind me of nowhere else I've been. It is the sea, I guess, which makes for all flowers, vines, blooming trees. The grass is green as in Ireland. The homes, though this is a smaller place than Mpls, seem much better, and there seem to be more of them. It must be the sea. The sky has clouds; the green has depth. It is close to heaven, the look and feel of it, and I regret some that I wasn't born here. Then, despite all the rawness of buildings and signs and streets— what you see everywhere, in every city—it might be a place to think of as home. I read one perfectly wonderful story while here and am asking the author—a doctor's wife—to send it to Henry. I think she might very well be a real writer. I see *The Captain's Paradise* is down the street and may go to it tonight. [. . .] Love to you.

Jim

Aboard *Princess Marguerite*[1]
Sunday, 10:00 a.m. [April 25, 1954]

Dear Betty,

I am sitting in a smaller, grubbier version of the lounge of the *America*. I am surrounded by my compatriots—playing cards, reading the Sunday papers, sleeping upright. [. . .] I can't remember seeing so many bad neckties in the past. I had thought the worst was over, but the science and industry patterns are very evident here. Out on the deck looking at the water, it's easy to recall Ireland. [. . .]

I got up at 6:30 this morning. I had dinner and quite a bit to drink at Ted's[2] place last night. I was drinking Jameson's since he got it in for me (as I got it for Sean). His wife, Beatrice, cooked a very fine meal. Steak—the best I've ever tasted. It was very thick, but the steak sauce (Ted's) is what made it. Beatrice had a sauce on asparagus that was very good—what asparagus needs to offset its wateriness. It is made out of ham fat or drippings. I had a very fine time—laughing as I hadn't in years. [. . .]

Much love,

James

Jim

DA

Buckeye

Portland, Oregon
Sunday night, May 2, 1954

Dear Betty,

[. . .] The Pacific was really beautiful. I expected it to be inferior somehow. But the rocky coast reminded me of Ireland as you first (and last) see it. We saw the sea lions—at some distance and with a wind blowing, and still they stank like dogs—at 200 yards. I want to read about them sometime. They live 40–60 years. Most of them appear to be asleep, but there is a honking clamor just the same. Their only enemy—said a sign—is the killer whale. [. . .]

I was happy to hear that your father has turned against [Joseph]

---

1 On the way from Seattle to Victoria, British Columbia.
2 Roethke.

McCarthy. I heard a snatch of it the other night = disgusting. I'd hear every word of it, if I could—so you're lucky I'm not there. In these circles, everyone is convinced that homosexuality is at the bottom of it all. [. . .] All for now. *Much love to you*—and the other *people*. XXXX

   Jim

Portland

Monday p.m. [May 3, 1954]

Dear Betty,

   [. . .] I saw Portland from a high crest today. The country all around was shrouded in mist. It's like Ireland, the weather, and texture of the air (and grass); the viny-ness. English ivy everywhere. Things—the way people live—seem more bourgeois than Minnesota. Food is much better. You buy very good breakfast rolls everywhere—and they are always served warm. That's just one thing—but it's significant. Things cost more, but you don't get the atrocious stuff (rolls, hamburgers) I'm used to (in eating places, I mean). [. . .]

   Much love,

   Jim

Albuquerque

May 15, 1954

Dear Betty,

   [. . .] I was naturally sorry to hear of KA's falling in with the larger boys and trust you'll not let it happen again; not that it was your fault. I don't see why she has to play with boys anyway. I suspect it's those kids who live in the Atwood house, on the alley, where the yard looks like a country fair all the time. You are right about letting the girls get some experience of other children. But I wouldn't feel that we're monsters, in the way we've brought them up so far. In this matter, most parents are wrong, and the situation they create is wrong. We must use discretion. There will come a day when the girls will see the point in our prohibitions—which don't strike me as severe at all, not unless I consider them from a point of view which, in fact, I abhor, popular *now* and *here* though it is. And you know how many people are out to break down what order we have managed to establish in our house, where the children are concerned. They will not rest until they've made us like everyone else, you yelling pointlessly and me carrying a potty wherever we go.[1] I guess, secretly, I'm preparing for the day when we can leave this country for Ireland or England, where, it seems to me, if we continue as we have with the children, it will be possible for them to make the change without too much trouble. So much for that. [. . .]

Here the sky rumbles constantly with the noise of airplanes, mostly jets, like a sick stomach. All for now. Much love to you and the girls. XXXX

Jim

BETTY POWERS

Albuquerque

May 22, 1954

Dear Betty,

[. . .] I was glad to hear that you're battling off the red squirrels. That was my constant fear, while away, that they'd get back in again, maybe while you were up the river. [. . .] XXXX

Jim

I dreamed of Marilyn Monroe last night. Nothing serious, just amorous dalliance, when George and a couple of other people, males but not priests, came along and put a stop to it, using ridicule but insinuating that I was a family man. I ended up going down the street—seemed to be in London—with a faulty umbrella, in the rain. Interesting?

HARVEY EGAN

509 First Avenue South

St Cloud

June 5, 1954

Dear Fr Egan,

[. . .] George was here last weekend with Fr Philip Hughes, the historian. Good time. Refreshing to meet someone now and then, I mean, another *human* being.

Haircut today, and my barber (knowing my line of work) asked what

---

1 As in fact became the case.

was *the* bestseller now. Might have been the beginning of a stimulating discourse, but I had to tell him I don't keep up with things anymore. [. . .]

Jim

Jim gave a short creative writing seminar at the University of Indiana, stopping in Urbana, Illinois, to visit Charles Shattuck and Kerker Quinn. ("I had a good time," he told Betty, "not too much to drink in case you think so.")

BETTY POWERS

Indiana University
Monday, 1:00 p.m., July 12, 1954

Dear Betty,

[. . .] It is hot here. I had my first class this morning. It went all right. I have more MSS to read than I've ever had before. But have plenty of time, I guess. The big occasion today is an escorted tour through the Institute for Sex Research, with a good chance of hearing a few words from Dr Kinsey himself. If he looks my way, I'll expose myself. Keeping the welfare of Stearns Co.—and its problems—in mind, I'll inquire as to the work going on in the Bestiality Division. I get the impression we're lucky to be taken behind the walls. [. . .] Hope you are all well—and not fighting.

    Mama KA   M.   Bozzer

BETTY POWERS

Indiana University
Wednesday afternoon, July 14, 1954

Dear Betty,

[. . .] The visit to the Kinsey's domain was interesting, and I rather liked the man. I'll tell you (and everybody) more when I get home. I ought to be in some demand—even though most people don't care a lot for me. "I spent 2 hours with Dr Kinsey" will be my tentative title. [. . .] Love to you—the girls—Bozzer.

Jim

16

There have been times, though not recently, when it has seemed to me that I might escape the doom of man

September 2, 1954—January 10, 1956

Caricature of Jim by Jody O'Connell, mid-1950s

509 First Avenue South
St Cloud
September 2, 1954

Dear Fr Egan,

Thanks for the Orwell. Betty and I've been reading it. Amazing, I think, his power to be interesting. I'll have to discount a lot of what he says against England. I wonder what he would've thought of this country if he'd had any real experience of it. England, he says, is a family, with the power in the hands of doddering aunts and uncles. America is a supermarket, where you're at the mercy of the clerks and checkers, and just being in it is demoralizing.

I spoke to Don about your chalice, and evidently he has definite plans for it. More I'd like to do, but you know how it is. He doesn't respond to strong treatment —like grabbing a handful of water. I didn't understand him, or Mary, until I went to Ireland, which is full of such people. [. . .]

Jim

Jim once again ducked a family Thanksgiving, spending it in 1954 with Egan in Beardsley.

509 First Avenue South
St Cloud
March 19, 1955

Dear Fr Egan,

Glad to hear from you. Have been about to write to you several times, but was never sure where you were. I heard some weeks ago that you were very sick after I saw you—embolism, I think it was—but this was hearsay from Mary Humphrey, and by that time evidently you'd recovered. I've been wondering—let's face it—if I'm very high up in your will.

[. . .]

We're expecting a visitation tomorrow from George, Caroline Gordon, and an unspecified number of interesting people. They are bringing their lunch.

Yes, this vale of tears is just that. I got some money in the mail this morning, enough to keep us another month. I was just beginning to wonder how you'd like to have me for the rest of the Lent, fearful that you'd have some prejudice against me during that time. No, not really; I wasn't coming. We've had a hard winter of it. I keep seeing where Irwin Shaw, or Truman Capote, or James Michener, is doing this at Cannes, or that at London, and wonder if I haven't missed the boat. I am in the textbooks, and they aren't, but I'm not sure that's important. After all, I have just the one life to live. I am not by nature cut out for this life, as it's defined in these parts by the chamber of commerce and our bishop, who is devoted to Christian family living, as everyone knows.

The big thing is the new Cathedral High School development. A Mr Foley came to town, representing a fund-raising outfit, and made a sale. Gosh, he was edified at the spirit among us here in St Cloud. (Remember the old vaudeville characters who were always glad to get back to wherever they happened to be playing?) I explained the peculiarities of my income to a representative, and he was very understanding. Most people give on a weekly basis, so much out of the old paycheck, but there didn't seem to be a category for me. But fortunately the representative was in the same boat with me (he's a real estate man), and we worked out a plan whereby I would contribute as I got it, on an if-and-when basis. Sure, I feel okay. One of the communiqués from Mr Foley's outfit asked how much we spent on playing the horses in a year's time.

The girls are fine, show no effects of progressive education, nor do we.
Come and see us when you can. All for now.

Jim

509 First Avenue South
St Cloud
Ascension 1955 [ca. May 20]

Dear Fr Egan,

[. . .] Life goes on and on, and the mailman keeps doing me wrong. Last night, reading in Boswell's *Journal* of Dr Johnson's trip to the Hebrides, I came across this:

> *Yet hope not life from pain or danger free,*
> *Or think the doom of man revers'd for thee!*

There have been times, though not recently, when it has seemed to me that I might escape the doom of man. I think of those nice nights in Lexington Park, when I was on a Guggenheim, when Pat McGlothin and Phil Haugstad[1] were young.

But I begin to see that I am cut out to be another Don Humphrey, frustrated and flailing at the air, the system eating away at me, the old body taking in more water, sinking, sinking . . .

How would you like me to handle a fund-raising campaign for you at Beardsley? I only want a fair share.

No word, no visits, from George. Idly, I wonder where he'll go this summer. I have no trips, no lectures, scheduled. I am too heavy to ride on the flat, and the hunt season doesn't open until November. I wish I could count on being in Ireland then. I don't want much. Just a place on the rail at Leopardstown, a couple of bob down. Is that asking too much of life? Is it absolutely certain that one can't go home again? [. . .]

Ah, well.

Jim

What did you think of the Dodgers' victory skein under Walt?[2]

---

1 Both played baseball for the St. Paul Saints.
2 Walter Alston. Big year for the Dodgers, who finally won the World Series.

509 First Avenue South
Sunday a.m. [November] 1955

Dear Fr Egan,

I've been contemplating your invitation[1] hungrily but must not accept, I fear. Betty is with child, and it could come around Thanksgiving; probably not; but it could. I'm sorry I can't make it. I have nothing else (but Beardsley) to satisfy my yearnings for the higher things. Very dull here.

Last night, however, Mary Humphrey threw a big love feast (*see* Methodism, for my usage here). Fr Casey present with tape of Fr Hugo's sermon. Many laypeople. The sermon holds up very well, I thought. [. . .]

Accent (fall) not here yet.[2] *Commonweal* soon, I understand;[3] problem of story's length, so (say I) why not make it an all-JF number? Introduction to my work by you; television ads from the hierarchy; reproductions of MS pages; and a garland of quotations from People Who *Knew* Me, headed by GGG.[4] [. . .] All for now.

Jim

Think of me if you have Bridgeman's[5] on Thanksgiving.

Hugh Wahl Powers was born on November 25, 1955.

509 First Avenue South
November 30, 1955

Dear Fr Egan,

Baby born on Friday,[6] and so I'm glad I didn't go to Beardsley. We call him Hugh Wahl Powers. I held out for Harvey to the very end, put up with remarks about rabbits,[7] etc., but perhaps it's just as well. You never know how anyone's going to turn out, though I guess calling him Harvey would've paved the way for him.

1 To spend Thanksgiving in Beardsley—as he preferred.
2 With Jim's "Blue Island," *Accent* (Autumn 1955).
3 Not until the next year: "Zeal," *Commonweal*, February 10, 1956.
4 Garrelts.
5 Bridgeman's ice cream.
6 The day after Thanksgiving.
7 A pooka, in the shape of a large rabbit, played a part in the movie *Harvey* (1950).

I read your lines on how much better I am with each child with a jaundiced eye. Let's just say—from what I've seen so far—I'm not long for this world, to say nothing of the literary world. With each succeeding child, I see better the wisdom of H. Sylvester, a prophet of yesteryear, who, however, committed hari-kari.[1] You know he remarried—a woman with three or four kids of her own. It's hard not to get confused. Yesterday, enjoying an hour at Gopher Wrecking,[2] it occurred to me I really ought to speak to someone there about work.

I'm glad you liked "Blue Island,"[3] since good news hasn't come my way lately—hardly any response to "A Losing Game"[4]—and your approval has always been elusive when it comes to my work. I know you admire the man of family, but what of the artist, I sometimes think.

Latest on the local front is that the Bp[5] refused to consecrate one of Don's chalices—made for one of the Hovda-Fehrenbacher[6] school. Too big,* the Bp said. Well, keep it to yourself. I gather Fr F. shouldn't have told Don at all what happened, and came around later to undo what he'd said, to get Don to believe it in no way reflected upon him and his work. Of course Don is a great one for seeing the worst side in a matter like this. I counsel caution. Time, I say, cures all, and besides he hasn't got a leg to stand on. Few of us have.

All for now. I'm interested in a few days around Christmas at Beardsley, and will let you know later how matters shape up here.

Speed.

(I sign my name as it is in religion.)

*made to priest's specifications, and there are bigger ones at St John's, and there is no limit, evidently, on size; size being—hell, I don't know—I'm just trying to fill you in on details as I understand them.

---

1 Had been in favor of birth control and eventually left the Church.
2 Railroad salvage store, much frequented by Jim.
3 In *Accent* (Autumn 1955).
4 *The New Yorker*, November 5, 1955.
5 Bishop Bartholome.
6 Father Robert Hovda and Father Henry Fehrenbacher, liberal priests, associated with the Catholic Worker movement and liturgical reform.

509 First Avenue South
January 10, 1956

Dear Fr Egan,

[. . .] I went to St Paul last Saturday for a party at Gene McCarthy's house, at his invitation via long distance; down on train, back with Hyneses. Pretty good evening, lots of politicos, including the governor,[1] whom I missed on purpose, and Miles Lord, the attorney general, an ex–Golden Glover, Gene said, who is having sleepless nights (Miles, I mean) over the bingo issue.[2] Someone said if there's ever an American pope, he'll take the name Bingo I. Hey, what's wrong with bingo? May it not be laudable and meritorious? [. . .]

Yes, I have the D'Arcy and would like to keep it a while. I'm reading it now and would like to trap Hump into reading it (he has *Black Popes*[3] now). I don't think Don has ever entered the Church intellectually—and now the word is going around that he's left it because the Bp refused to consecrate that chalice (this rumor from St John's, some monk or other), due no doubt to Don's big mouth somewhere along the line. Then I think of what Joyce said, that he'd preserve his life as an artist through silence, exile, and cunning—and Don, in a place quite as stuffy as Ireland in 1900, unable to practice any of these things. Well, he's wide open. Emerson wants me to make a move, as Don's friend. But I am doing nothing. I have to see the whites of their eyes, and maybe even then I won't shoot. [. . .]

Jim

---

1 Orville Freeman (1918–2003).
2 Whether the game—so popular in Catholic parishes as a way of levying money—should be illegal under the antigambling laws.
3 Thomas d'Esterre Roberts, SJ, *Black Popes: Authority; Its Use and Abuse.*

17

Four children now, Jack. And this year, the man said, bock beer is not available in this area

February 29, 1956—August 24, 1956

Standing: Mary and Katherine; sitting: Hugh, Betty, Jim, and Boz

Jim's short-story collection, The Presence of Grace, *was published by Doubleday in March 1956.*

HARVEY EGAN
FROM THE DESK OF J. F. POWERS, AMERICA'S CLEANEST LAY AUTHOR, PUBLISHED BY DOUBLEDAY, THE HOUSE THAT MEANS BUSINESS

February 29, 1956

Dear Fr Egan,

So glad to hear from you, to hear that you enjoyed "Zeal"[1] at least until the end. [. . .] I am trying to shake down some British publisher for a decent advance. I have a contract (which I haven't signed) from perhaps the best one over there, Gollancz, but he won't go over a hundred pounds (and I've heard that that much changes hands in seconds in poker games). There is an error on the front of the jacket, but then the effects of original sin are always with us—ain't that right? But they've used better materials in the book than is commonly done nowadays. I am presently seeing no one much. (Fr Ong, SJ,[2] was here with George, briefly, a month or so ago.) Adlai Stevenson is coming to St John's on Saturday. I ought to call up the Hyneses and tell them Jacques Maritain[3] will be here at our house on Saturday and see where he really stands; Hynes, I mean. They do love a lion, Arlie and Em. [. . .]

Jim

---

1 Published in *Commonweal*, February 10, 1956.
2 Walter Ong, SJ (1912–2003), professor of English, historian, and philosopher.
3 Jacques Maritain (1882–1973), French Thomist philosopher and social thinker.

Thursday morning, 1956

Dear Fr Egan,

Your letter came just now, and I hasten to reply (not that it calls for that). I was writing to you the other night when despair overcame me and I tore up the letter and went to bed.

Yes, the Waugh review is good.[1] There is much to meditate in it, as I told him in a thank-you note I got off yesterday. I hadn't realized my diction was a difficulty; I had always thought I wrote without benefit of a private argot, not doing the sort of thing, say, that Algren, with his thieves' language, does. I suspect you're right in thinking with Waugh I don't have the gift of fantasy. I wish that I did, of course, but until I know what is meant by fantasy, I must pass. I mean I actually don't know. [. . .]

I have signed with Victor Gollancz in England, for £200 instead of £100. There was a note in a recent CW[2] that he'd visited Hospitality House in N.Y. He is a first-class publisher—Sean O'Faolain said he was the best in Britain—and lots more, as his visit to the CW might indicate. I have been difficult in my dealings—amazing my N.Y. and London agents, I'm sure—but in the end it was worth it. We will now get through June, or a good part of it.

I don't get enough mail, contrary to what you might think. No offers at all. Well, there was one to speak before some creative writing group in Mpls. The letter was written on Pillsbury Mills stationery, and for a long time I just gazed at the envelope, smelling a grant. Not a word about expense money even. I should come down there on a Sunday evening and listen to their manuscripts being read. I gave them the green Montini.[3]

I haven't got TV yet. Am waiting for the big break still. I crave it but can't bring it off. Lots of surgery coming up: Boz's eye (same kind of deal KA had) and KA's tonsils. And I haven't made good on my pledge to Cathedral High School. [. . .]

Did you know that Mickey Spillane is a Jehovah's Witness? I read it in an English paper. His publisher was in London and said Mickey has decided to mend his ways as an author. Won't *that* be awful? All for now.

Jim

---

1 Review of *The Presence of Grace*, *Commonweal*, March 30, 1956.
2 *Catholic Worker*.
3 Joke evocative of "the green banana" in Jim's short story of that title. To give "the green banana," meant roughly, in Jim's and his friends' parlance, to dismiss or reject, in this case linking it to the powerful Cardinal Giovanni Montini (who later became Pope Paul VI).

509 First Avenue South
St Cloud, Minnesota
April 4, 1956

Dear Daddy-O,

Thanks for that flattering review.[1] Whatever else you were, we'll say, he was good to his friends. I have had some good reviews, though nothing as far west as Chicago until yours; nothing at all in Minneapolis or St Paul; and I guess this is what comes of not playing the regional author game, of not seeing anybody who can read. [. . .] I don't recognize this colony you call the Huntington Hartford?[2] What kind of purses? I prefer to race on turf, you know. Actually, I am a victim to family life. Four children now, Jack. And this year, the man said, bock beer is not available in this area. This is one hell of an area, Jack. I am ordering Whey-Plus.[3] I hope it changes my life. I haven't been to Chicago for a couple of years, and the last time just passed through, from station to station at night. All for now, and again thanks for going to bat for me, Jack.

Jim

HARVEY EGAN

Saturday afternoon, 1956

Dear Fr Egan,

Has spring come to Beardsley? Has *any*thing? I am engaged in reading twelve MSS, about half of them book-length, for the Hopwood Awards, University of Michigan, for which I am to receive $200. It is *not* nice work, but I can get it. [. . .] We are going through our worst period, economically, in many years, but in two weeks, when I get these MSS read, and the money comes from England, and I come to another agreement with Doubleday, we'll be all right. I am not complaining, understand, but would welcome the chance—like the French and Italians—to register a protest vote. [. . .]

I can't think of anything you should be told. No TV here yet, to put it mildly. I don't know what I'm doing next, as a writer, I mean. Fr Kelly resists me. Enough of this raillery (which will hardly make the judicious grieve).

Jim

1 *Chicago Sun-Times*, April 1, 1956.
2 Huntington Hartford Foundation, a colony for artists and writers.
3 Food supplement.

There was no trouble about the girls and First Communion. They were examined for an hour and a half yesterday by our pastor, passed, and, as Betty found out later, had been given a half-dollar by him. The Polish in him, I guess.

JACK CONROY

509 First Avenue South
May 20, 1956

Dear Jack,

[. . .] Life is very dull here, Jack. My only friend, a silversmith who makes chalices, who had been doing that for a living for several years, has taken a job.[1] That leaves me St Cloud's last self-employed artist, and sometimes I think I can make out my name on the wall. Still I turn down jobs now and then, at good money, but teaching writing courses in remote places for a year or two. We have an old house here, the use of it, with a big yard, and get by on very little, and so I stay on. When I move, I want it to be abroad—but how, with taxation worse in Ireland and England than it is here, I'll make it isn't clear yet.

All for now, Jack.

Jim

ROBERT LOWELL

509 First Avenue South
St Cloud, Minnesota
Memorial Day 1956

Dear Cal,

Very happy to hear from you, after so long and after sending you a copy of my book—I'd begun to think it was a mistake. I sent Buck Moon a copy and have not heard from him; as a result, I can only deduce . . . I wasn't pleased to hear that you are driving a car still, even if you are getting better. Is it the Packard still? Elizabeth is right in criticizing you. To have great drivers, we must first have great critics. [. . .]

When Betty read of your coming blessed event, she said, "Poor Lowell." Which is no reflection on Elizabeth, who must bear it and, doubtless, take care of it single-handed. I guess we think of our contemporaries—

1 Don Humphrey.

those who are writers—who are childless as gods, sporting about the world and going out for dinner with no thoughts of babysitters. We go nowhere. Of course, here in St Cloud there isn't much temptation to go out.

Aren't you a little young to be writing your autobiography? I expect to bring out a book of verse before I do mine. That means I haven't given it a thought. When I do—and it first occurred to me when you mentioned yours—I realized that is one book I don't even have material for in my dreamiest moments. In those moments, it isn't hard to compile a long list of novels and plays I might write. Well, if you get to Yaddo in the first volume, and I realize you probably won't, I have several nice glossy prints of my old car with whom you were on such intimate terms. Also a nice snapshot of Ted Roethke in a rowboat smiling at a little bass he caught. And one of you not smiling at one you caught. This is from your wading and night-fishing period. All for now. Best to you both, and write again.

Jim

Jim took a vinegary pleasure in being attacked by Catholics who were scandalized by his portrayal of the clergy. He was especially taken with the review of The Presence of Grace *by a certain Father Ferdinand C. Falque in the Catholic newspaper* The Wanderer. *Falque wrote: "If you are interested in some literature that lays bare the studied affectations of a diseased and twisted mind, the book will prove invaluable . . . The stories are as unreal as the visions of an opium addict and even more vague, vapid and vain. Like the portrait of the author's feminine face behind a masculine pipe, they are soft and weak and in no sense literary. They reek with revelations of psychological frustrations in their creator. They are sordid . . . tedious and emotionally vicarious. They are as grotesque as his pitifully, almost clinical portrait on the inside flap of the jacket."*[1]

HARVEY EGAN

509 First Avenue South
June 11, 1956

Dear Fr Egan,

Glad to hear from you. I was wondering what ever happened to you. I see where Fr Dunphy is retiring at 82. I don't know why I mention that in

[1] *Wanderer*, May 1956.

this connection, except one of these Junes I hope to see where you've gone up in the world—and no one knows better than I how unrewarding that can be. I mean, life *is* a bowl of cherries. This letter may strike you as something less than crystal clear. It is because I'm listening to Halsey Hall broadcast the Minnesota-Mississippi game from Omaha. I went out for the St John's–Minnesota game, my first in years. The usual thing. St John's should have won, etc., and they would've if they hadn't let them drop unattended (the balls hit between two fielders) . . . I am trying to interest Doubleday in taking a piece of the fence (the spot between Bert Baston's Chevrolet and Gluek's Beer) to advertise my book, signed copy to any player who hits a home run over that spot, not a new idea, I know, but never before applied in the field of book advertising. I am speaking of the field here, Municipal Stadium, where the Rox[1] play. [. . .]

My attention was called to Fr Falque's review about a week ago. I arrived at Don Humphrey's one morning, and as is my custom, in person and over the telephone, I called out: "Any stirrings in the Movement?" This is a reference to the family-liturgico-rural-life movement which engages so many of us in this diocese, thanks, need I say, to an alert clergy (alert to the real dangers of the times), not the least of whom is our bishop, himself the product of family life and parents. "Yes," Don said, "and it's all about you." He had attended a gathering the night before, and there had been some discussion of the review in question. At least one person thought I should go see the bishop—why is it so many people counsel me to go see the bishop?—and seek permission to sue Fr Falque. It seems I, being one of the faithful, need to do this if everything is to be correct, as regards the Church and my lowly position in it. Well, needless to say, I didn't think much of that idea—and at this point hadn't even seen the review. So I went down to the public library and found the review in a back number. I must say I enjoyed it, only wishing I'd met Fr Falque sometime in my wanderings. Do you think he'd sit for a portrait? As someone said, he didn't like the book and he said so. The only thing I didn't care for was the reference to my "feminine face"—I hope that isn't accurate. I have never thought so, or been accused of having a feminine face, and it seems uncalled for when applied to the father of four, ungrateful, I might add, when you consider how much I've done for family life, at considerable trouble and expense.

Due to the length of the ball game, *Listen to the Classics* will not be heard tonight (WCCO).

1 Northern League baseball team, New York Giants–affiliated Class C team at the time.

So if I do go to the bishop, I think that point should be brought out. Meanwhile, I am working through Don, trying to arouse my dear friends, to get them to write letters of protest to *The Wanderer* and sign their names. Apparently, a much harder thing to bring off than, say, a visit by me to the bishop and suing Fr Falque. [. . .]

A note in the French edition of *Perspectives*, the Ford Foundation magazine pub'd in four languages, explaining the meaning of "les KC" in the first cat story: "Knights of Columbus, association catholique d'immigrants en majorité d'origine italienne." This is the translator's note. [. . .]

I took a bath tonight and put on a clean shirt and drove down to the Press Bar for a glass of beer. It was formal like that, and something I've never tried before. Bless me, Father, I was trying to give St Cloud a chance. I was in the mood, Father, and I was prepared to take a certain amount of pleasure in it. The choice was Cold Spring or Pfeiffer's (Schmidt's), because I wanted no bottle beer in my mood. I wanted it from the keg, or ex cathedra, if you understand my meaning here. Well, I drank the bitter draughts and departed after one glass, returned home, and that, I'm afraid, was, and is, it. The Press Bar was dark pink inside, and I was alone at the bar.

Alone.

Jim

[. . .] As it says about me in this edition of *Perspectives*: "Il vit aujourd'hui à Saint-Cloud, Minnesota, et s'est entièrement consacré à ses travaux littéraires."

HARVEY EGAN

509 First Avenue South
Sunday noon, June 1956

Dear Fr Egan,

[. . .] I saw the Miss America pageant from Atlantic City last night on TV, and I must say it has become a noble affair. It used to be girls in bathing suits, but now it's talent, personality, character, like a lodge induction. I hope they put it on film and that this will be shown in England—they think they're so smart in these matters, coronations, and the like. There was one rather close tie-in with Philco, when the new Miss America entered the sacristy after her coronation, but I think this will be eliminated in the years to come. [. . .]

Pictures of the new archbishop[1] reveal (to me) the possibility of pride and ambition. Of course he's young. [. . .]

Jim

HARVEY EGAN

509 First Avenue South
Monday morning, 1956

Dear Fr Egan,

I called my agent's hand, and he had me. I had expected he would reply at once, and that much was correct, but he didn't send the money; he still talks of . . . well, I enclose his letter rec'd this morning. So if you still have that little envelope, I'd love to see it.

Also heard from Michigan again, and they want me to reconsider.[2] At the moment, I am. Just one semester, and then we'll go home . . . [. . .]

I also heard from an MM[3] by the name of Cosgrove.* He is in Formosa and wants to know what makes me tick. He says I should move into other fields.

Jim

What I mean in the first paragraph is that if my agent had advanced from his own till what is on the way from England, and had also told me that he wouldn't expect his 10% on Doubleday advances, I would hold still. I was badly out in my calculations, but this certainly confirms me in wanting out.

*I have just recently given birth to a Big Catholic Layman by that name—and suppose he'll have to be renamed.[4]

HARVEY EGAN

509 First Avenue South
June 21, 1956

Dear Fr Egan,

Your note and check rec'd this morning, and the letter has found its

1 William Otterwell Ignatius Brady (1899–1961), appointed coadjutor bishop of the Archdiocese of St. Paul, June 16, 1956.
2 He was invited to teach at Ann Arbor.
3 Merchant marine.
4 He remained (Billy) Cosgrove in *Morte D'Urban*.

way downtown already. I have the lawn mower back, new tires and sharpened, all ready to roll, but now it's raining, and I can see the grass growing away. Tomorrow it'll be a battle between us, the grass and me, a battle I don't mind when better equipped than I've been this year. I love the smell of cut grass, and I imagine you do, too. [. . .]

I was relieved when I read in your note that you thought I'd do better to take Michigan's money before Doubleday's. Probably I'll take both—unless the story at *The New Yorker* succeeds there—but this morning I wrote to Michigan and said, with two qualifications, I'd be happy to take the job for the first semester: the two being (a) that I have nothing to do with poetry, (b) that the days come together so I could get home often and keep up my police work with the children. It will be for only a little over four months. We will hire a woman to work mornings here, which will give Betty some time to finish her book, and I will get some privacy in Michigan, I trust, to continue my gentle chronicles. The Mitchells will be here for a good part of the time, so Betty will have someone else in the house at night, a matter of some importance to her. And we will buy necessities we've been doing without, coasting then down another long hill, I imagine, into another teaching job, and so on. I can't believe I'll ever make much on my work. I see I am running 10th and last in America's book log for June; 9th in May. I guess the boy had to drop back a little and is taking me up on the outside. Slayer, needs goo.[1] He'd better go to the whip. Ridin' like a Chinaman, that Falque.

What do the beautiful changes among the hierarchy mean to you?[2] How can you lose, okay.

See you, then, on the Wolverine out of the LaSalle Street Station, or the Twilight out of the IC.[3] Here, I'll get this round. Well, the next one then.

Keep in touch.
Jim

---

1 Mud.
2 Bishop William Brady had been appointed coadjutor bishop to the Archdiocese of St. Paul and Minneapolis on June 16, 1956. He succeeded Archbishop John Gregory Murray on his death in October 1956.
3 Wolverine: train from Michigan; LaSalle Street Station: in Chicago; IC: Illinois Central.

509 First Avenue South
June 25, 1956

Dear Fr Egan,

Hope you're no longer here (at the hospital) but that this follows you back to Beardsley, or to the second week of the retreat if there is one. Don't forget, if you should miss out in your diocese, there is always New York state (and Saratoga in August).

Oh, yes. This is from the English advance.[1] It actually came.

I am on my way over to see Hump now. He went to a picnic yesterday out at Hyneses, and according to Mary, whom I've seen in the meantime, everything went all right except for one argument Tom had with Arleen, who maintained that our bishop is not as *bad* as were Stalin and Hitler in their day.

Again, thanks for the lift.

Jim

Thomas Merton, visiting St. John's, came to dinner at "the small ancient red wooden house," as he put it in his Journals. *He saw Jim as "a mixture of dryness and spontaneity, a thin, sensitive person whose vocation is to go through many unbearable experiences."*

509 First Avenue South
July 30, 1956

Dear Fr Egan,

[. . .] Now, this is top secret, though everyone knows about it. Father Louis, OCSO,[2] at the mental health institute at St John's, was here for dinner with companion (a doctor, also OCSO) and Betty's brother,[3] who was used as a go-between, rec'd permission to attend at last moment. He was the one who kept stressing, in telephone calls with Betty, need for secrecy; I suppose they fear the newspaper publicity. But who should ring me up from downtown on Friday, the day of the dinner here, but one

---

1 Jim paying back a loan.
2 Thomas Merton (1915–1968; Order of Cistercians of the Strict Observance—that is, Trappist).
3 Father Caedmon (later Father Thomas Wahl), a Benedictine at St. John's.

R. M. Keefe,[1] who now looks like two of the same. Well, Betty was worried that it would seem that I was protecting myself, and worried at the impression Dick would make, he being so fun loving, but in fact it was a good thing. He got along fine with the doctor, and it was a good evening. I liked Fr Louis quite a lot. He is now novice master and said he'd like to get someone like Dick now and then instead of what he's getting. You realize, I trust, that this whole affair was not my idea but his. I gather that he is still being tempted to turn Carthusian. He hadn't read *Grace*, though he's bought five copies of *Prince*, he said, and so I sent him a copy with a quotation from St Bernard, who, in my humble opinion, is the best writer among the saints, admittedly few, I've read. I gave it to him in the original Latin, which should be safe enough, providing I don't ever see him again. You know I've never been much of a Latinist; inter alia (there was a horse by that name in Ireland) was about as far as I got.

Tonight, after dark I am to attack a hive of wasps who have taken up residence in the wall of that bay window in the kitchen. I have devised a trap made of screen into which, providing I can get it over the hole in the house wall, I expect the wasps to fly. Then I will do them in with DDT and also shoot some into the wall where the hive presumably is. I wish you were here because I must dress in veil and padding to do the job, fearing stings. Whereas you, Father . . .

Boz will have his eye operated on Wednesday morning, August 8, and I'd be very grateful if you'd remember him then and on the days following. Please tell Sister Eugene Marie, who, I suspect, stands in well with heaven.

All for now.

Jim

Egan was finally released from exile in Beardsley and assigned to St. Mary's Hospital in Minneapolis as chaplain. Jim, unable to resist the tawdry spectacle of the summer's political conventions, bought a TV.

1 Dick Keefe.

509 First Avenue South
August 24, 1956

Dear Fr Egan,

Glad to hear from you, and think you're in your element: cancer, newspapers hot from the press, TV channels clear, and most of all freed from your maintenance work, heating, caulking, watering, etc. Allow me, then, in the light of all this, to congratulate you on your new assignment.

I visited Mpls last week on a buying trip: tea, clothing for Betty and children, typewriter for Betty, and so on. There wasn't time for what we did, and so I didn't call you, but I'll be seeing you at Schiek's or somewhere in the weeks to come. We have been buying everything in sight. A new refrigerator (the old one was still running, a 1936 model); a foam rubber mattress; and TV. Yes, the pressure built up to a terrific pitch for a few days before the Dems convened, and I went into a flurry of research—as usual CU[1] and the other outfit had nothing to say. So I went by hearsay and the look of the cabinet and bought a Spartan, a table model. It is doing well by us, with a thirty-foot antenna. We've seen some good movies, mostly English: *Pickwick Papers, The Man in the White Suit, Carrington V.C.*, and others. I enjoyed the Dems; their opponents, what a bore, and what a flop Stassen turned out to be. I thought Eisenhower's speech good, though, as those things go. Did you hear Clement's?[2] I see in *Newsweek* where Red Smith said the Democrats (using Clement) hit the Republicans with the jawbone of an ass.

Yes, as you would know from above, *The New Yorker* bought the story, and it should appear sometime this fall.[3] I was exhausted from revising it (and it still isn't ready) and haven't done any work for two weeks. Pretty soon Ken McCormick will be back from Europe and will be asking how's the novel coming. I am beginning to regret my decision to teach at Michigan and hope I can make it count as time in the desert, peace and quiet, and get some of my work done that I wouldn't find possible here. [. . .]

Write.

Jim

1 Consumers Union.
2 Frank G. Clement, governor of Tennessee, gave the keynote speech.
3 "The Green Banana," *The New Yorker*, November 10, 1956.

18

The Man Downstairs is entertaining tonight. Pansy and Dwight are quiet

September 25, 1956—January 12, 1957

Red house in winter

Jim left for Ann Arbor in September for a semester of teaching at the Univer-
sity of Michigan. He rented the apartment of the scholar and literary critic
Austin Warren, who was on leave from the university. The adjoining apart-
ment was occupied by a couple, Pansy and Dwight, whose goings-on—and
those of the metal hangers in their closet—were clearly audible to Jim, who
was as fascinated as he was annoyed by the situation.

BETTY POWERS

507 Church Street
Ann Arbor, Michigan
Tuesday, September 25, 1956

Dear Betty,

[. . .] The woman who cleans was here today, worked three hours, and
really worked. I haven't seen a woman clean like that for years and years.
She is colored. She will also do my laundry. She seems nice, very worried
about Austin, called him "a poor old man," and she's in her sixties, I'll bet;
Austin is 57, was born 1899 at Waltham, Mass., according to a note in one
of his books. [. . .]

I sent Boz a little book yesterday, one of those little Potter ones that he
should be able to understand and the girls can read it. It is about six in the
evening now, and I'll go out and mail this. I am hungry but can think of
nothing I want. Except you, of course.

Much love,
Jim

507 Church Street
Ann Arbor, Michigan
September 26, 1956

Dear Betty,

[. . .] The apartment is very nice. Its defects are that you can hear through the walls, and the bed in the same room with the kitchen. The living room is very nice, though crawling with books, ikons, pictures, which has a depressing effect on me, makes me feel anything but well-read. There is also a table with candlesticks, a piece of marble, a crucifix, a Roman breviary on it; it looks like an altar. Mr Rice[1] isn't sure what Mr Warren does with this, some kind of service, he thinks. Austin's name is on the mailbox downstairs, but up here, on the second floor, there is a little card on the door that says: "Oratory of SS Basil & Gregory." Apparently, Austin has been getting more and more . . . uh, ecclesiastical, as the landlord put it. He is Greek. Austin has joined the Greek Orthodox Church, I understand. [. . .]

Mr Rice is a nice man, making a study of science fiction because he hates its implications so much, he says. He grouses about all the new buildings—for social work, he says, and says he's only lately been able to accept the idea that the university in this country is—I forget his phrase, but he means what you might think. I haven't yet got around to inviting him to leave the country, but he seems a very promising prospect.

BETTY POWERS

507 Church Street
Ann Arbor, Michigan
Thursday morning, 11:00 a.m.,
September 27, 1956

Dear Betty,

[. . .] I attended a faculty meeting yesterday—just the men teaching English 31, 32, and 45, or something—and how like the one I once attended at Marquette. This time it was Mr Carr; there it was Chub Archer. It just takes forever, mince, mince, and hardly a word intelligible. [. . .] I have one MS to read, but more coming in, some to be dropped off here at the house. One fellow is coming to see me here for a conference,

---

1 Warner G. Rice, chairman of the English department.

since he works day and night, having three jobs: bass in a jazz band, injecting monkeys with narcotics at the university (they are trying to find a cure for drugs), and writing news for a local radio station. He also has one of those waterfall mustaches ("waterfall" is original with me—I think—and I hope you know what kind of mustache I mean). Some woman called last night and in a kind of hillbilly voice asked if she could get in one of my classes. I of course referred her to Mr Bader,[1] but in the course of the conversation she asked how I liked Ann Arbor, calling it "our fair city," and then proceeded to tell me where to drive, to see this and that, flowers and best view of "all Ann Arbor," and to all of this I feebly assented—except that she'll have to see Mr Bader. She sounds prolific, is doing a Civil War novel—spare us, O Lord. [. . .]

Much love,

Jim (Austin's ballpoint)

BETTY POWERS

507 Church Street
Ann Arbor, Michigan
October 10, 1956

Dear Betty,

Wednesday, no letter from you, one from K. A. Porter, and that was my mail. [. . .] K. A. Porter wonders why Austin didn't rent his place to her when she was here. She lived at the Union and sat on the side of her bed, she says, with a chair for her typewriter, and no one would bring her a cup of coffee in the morning. She stood in line with her tray for meals. I had heard, from Mr Rice, I believe, that she didn't want to do any housework and that was why she stayed there. [. . .]

I am listening to the World Series. Looks bad for the Brooks. Well, as you can see, I am brimming over with nothing to say today, but I trust you'll appreciate getting a letter, even this one. I write it with some effort. Much love—and kisses for the boys and girls.

Jim

---

1 A. L. Bader, head of the Hopwood Fellowship program.

507 Church Street
Ann Arbor, Michigan
Sunday evening, October 14, 1956

Dear Betty [. . .]

The people in the adjoining apartment are entertaining again tonight. Real slow, unscintillating dinners they give. It has been good for me to hear how people live, as I do living next to them. The other day—it was during the World Series—*he* came in with the paper and said: "Well, well, Yogi Berra got another home run—and Skowron too. Say." Which sounds like the beginning of a play for which no one is expected to be on time. Now I'll close, and hope there's a letter from you in the morning.

Monday morning. Dear Betty, he continued the next day. [. . .] As to your letter, it's a very wise one. I'm surprised how wise you are about the necessity of living in genteel poverty if one is a writer in these times. It is true, and I know it, but I don't think I have formulated it as you have, in a law. It is one, though, and people like KAP[1] try to go against it. And the worst thing is what they think is worth it, the junk they buy, or tell themselves when they are paying too much for something in a *good* store. [. . .] All for now. Much love. [. . .]

Jim

507 Church Street
Ann Arbor, Michigan
October 30, 1956

Dear Betty,

[. . .] I had from Victor[2] a transcript of the *Critics* program. Parts of it are snipped out by the BBC if they think such matter shouldn't be perpetuated: apparently, where someone gets too critical, or nasty. But I seem to do all right with all the critics except the one for films, a woman by the name of Lockhart.[3] She opposes the others, and in the end, after Walter Allen likens my work to Chaucer's, saying you have to go that far back to find something like it (which of course soothes my soul), the Lockhart woman cries out that she prefers the Father Brown stories or

1 Katherine Anne Porter.
2 Victor Gollancz.
3 Freda Bruce Lockhart.

Don Camillo! I will be surprised indeed if she isn't one of the Faithful. Her tone is the very one of the Catholic reviewers over here who, wounded, cry out righteously and then, thinking to hurt their persecutor, try to play down my achievement as a writer. I will send the transcript to you in a day or so; I am still studying it. [. . .]

I saw an item in *The Times* (London) to the effect that E. Waugh, the author, had sold his place Piers Court, where he had lived for 19 years; nothing else, except that it had been on the market from the first of the year. I dropped a line to Anne Fremantle thinking maybe she could tell me the meaning of this, worried that his hearing voices might be a factor in this strange removal.[1] I had regarded Waugh as established there till death did him and Piers Court part. It seems a rootless thing to do, for him. [. . .] I miss you all, and you most of all.

Love and kisses,
Jim

BETTY POWERS

507 Church Street
Ann Arbor, Michigan
Halloween, 11:00 p.m., 1956

Dear Betty,

[. . .] I have been listening to the lousy news from the Middle East.[2] I must say I am confused. I would not have believed such a thing of the British or French—and resent such blah-blah experts as Randolph Churchill, who cables Beaverbrook's press that Americans *really* admire the Anglo-French move but are waiting until the election is over to show it. The British do hatch a terrible kind of ass, it seems to me: people like R. Churchill and Nancy Mitford.

A card in my mailbox at the English office today—*The Michigan Daily* asking me to state my preference for president. I put down Stevenson, with some misgivings. Of course I wasn't asked to sign my name. I should've written in something funny, I guess: Card. Spellman. [. . .]

Much love,
Jim

1 As described in his novel *The Ordeal of Gilbert Pinfold*.
2 Suez Crisis.

507 Church Street
Ann Arbor, Michigan
November 2, 1956

Dear Betty,

[. . .] I came home and got the United Nations session[1] on a New Orleans station and listened to that until about 3:00 a.m. I am still shocked at the tactics of Great Britain. If, as seems likely today, Russia is marching back into Hungary—so what? I believe this is the end of the United Nations, even the theory of it. It seems incredible that Israel, Great Britain, and France should be the immediate causes; the executioners. I listened to the Israeli ambassador, and he was very convincing about the sabotage and violence along the borders, the constant raids, but . . . the *but* was still there when he was through. I don't see how, if the Egyptians are defeated militarily, as they presumably are already, the Israelis expect to survive in the Middle East. They are outnumbered, greatly, and this conflict should make everything, bad in the past, only worse. Of course the canal will be lost to Nasser, and that is the objective most likely to succeed: the Anglo-French objective. It seems to me the Israelis have made a terrible blunder and will pay and pay from now on. Ah, well, why go on about it? It only confirms me in my own attitude toward government and politics. It also makes Ireland look better than England as a place to settle. Of course England is split, but apparently only on political lines, or so we learn. I did hear that the Abp of Canterbury opposed the Eden government on this. [. . .]

A letter from a Miss Riordan, who wants the author of *The Presence of Grace* to write an 800-word story for her magazine for blind children. Is this not the woman who got me to write one before and then wanted me to change it after I did write it—to which request I never responded? For a long time I had her letter around in my study. Now I must close. [. . .]

Much love,
Jim

---

1 Emergency session of the UN General Assembly on the Suez Crisis.

507 Church Street
Ann Arbor, Michigan
November 10, 1956

Dear Fr Egan,

Long time no hear. I am established here in two rooms with a view, the radio is giving me the Michigan-Illinois game, *The New Yorker* is on the stands with my latest story,[1] the first chapter of my *new* novel, I am smoking "Erinmore Flake," a product of Northern Ireland, smoked on my arrival in Ireland and so full of sweet dreams for me. Tomorrow is Katherine Anne's birthday, Tuesday is Boz's, and I've just purchased a wristwatch for him: I want *him* to learn the value of time. He and Betty are arriving for a short visit on Tuesday. Except for the necessity to introduce Betty to the faculty, and probably have some people in, I am looking forward to the visit. [. . .]

It is now 1:30 Minnesota time, and I must try to get the Iowa-Minnesota game. I suppose the Hawkeyes will play dirty again, as they always do against our guys. Regards to Sr Eugene Marie.

Jim

Betty and Boz came for a visit; Jim gave a party; both ventures were surprisingly successful.

BETTY POWERS

507 Church Street
Ann Arbor, Michigan
November 17, 1956

Dear Betty,

Nine o'clock here, in an hour you'll be arriving in Chicago, and since I left you, I've been thinking about you, both of you, and hoping all goes well. [. . .]

I put the table back in the living room but otherwise have left everything untouched. It is cold here tonight, or can it be that you're gone. The Man Downstairs is entertaining tonight. Pansy and Dwight are quiet, even to the hangers. I regret that I must have seemed rather dim and

1 "The Green Banana," *The New Yorker*, November 10, 1956.

unresponsive in the station. All for now. Write when you can. And love to the girls, Hughlie, and to you and Boz.

    Jim

BETTY POWERS

507 Church Street
Ann Arbor, Michigan
November 23, 1956

Dear Betty,

    The morning after Thanksgiving, with George here reading a book. [. . .]

    I had a miserable night with George. He snores, spins rapidly in bed at intervals, and in general gives you a rough time. So I was tired all day yesterday. He may come and see us around Xmas time; I urged him to do so. [. . .] Much love to you all, and especially to you.

    Jim

Dwight: I don't know what's wrong with me.

Pansy: You don't take care of yourself. You're too proud to wear your sweatshirt.

Hangers: Clang, clang, cling.

BETTY POWERS

507 Church Street
Ann Arbor, Michigan
Wednesday, 6:30 p.m., December 5, 1956

Dear Betty,

    [. . .] I have just eaten one of my little dinners, quaint I guess you'd have to call them: spaghetti, half a can of corn, tea, and cookies. It was between that and pancakes, but I decided to hold off on them for a bit. I have MSS to read tonight because I have two appointments in the morning. [. . .]

    I went down for the mail this morning and met Mr Collins. He asked me to mention to Mr Rice that some apartment or other would be vacant on December 15. I looked at him, wondering if he'd said something that really concerned me. I was pretty sure he wasn't talking about this apartment. No, he meant the one at the head of the stairs. "They're going back to California. He doesn't like the climate here." I rocked and teetered at this news. Finally I said, with a winning smile: "Well, it's better than California." To which he nodded and smiled. So Dwight and Pansy are departing, and that little scene I conveyed to you was pregnant with meaning, as we say in creative writing. I feel I should give them some kind of going-away party, but the trouble with that is that I haven't yet met them. Maybe just a gift. Even that presents difficulties, for I heard Pansy, through their open front door as I was coming up the steps, telling someone that they were asking so much for this and so much for that. They are selling their furniture! How can they do it? They've lived with these things since last September.

Now I'll close. Mr Kennedy and Mr Whelan[1] are taking me out for dinner tomorrow night. I was surprised to learn from Mr K. that Mr W. has only just in the last week rec'd his master's. I told Mr K. that if I'd known that, I wouldn't have been quite so friendly with Mr W. We have to draw the line somewhere, after all.

Much love,
Jim

Jim and Betty planned a Boxing Day conversazione to be held at the red house.

HARVEY EGAN

GO BLUE![2]

507 Church Street
Ann Arbor, Michigan
December 6, 1956

Dear Fr Egan,

It was good hearing from you after so long. George, who at Thanksgiving trained in and planed out, said he'd seen little of you. I wonder who your friends are, now that you're cut off from janitor supplies and

---

1 X. J. "Joe" Kennedy and Robert E. Whelan Jr., both teaching fellows in the English department at the time.
2 University of Michigan football team.

hardware and merchandise in general. I passed through the Twins last week, not stopping except for a tasty breakfast in the Mpls station.

My calendar grows more and more interesting: only eight more classes to be held. I've been a regular con about marking off the days. Not that it hasn't been good. I am better for it, of course. I was getting a little shaggy, intellectually. With my basically brilliant mind, it wasn't long before I was making sallies with the best of them. Another thing I've been doing in collegiate gatherings is suddenly hitting someone on the arm, the idea being to leave a black-and-blue mark. We all do that. I tried ripping open a few flies—some, like Hask, majored in that at Quincy College Academy—but the zipper has done away with all that. Tripping, of course, is still done, and breaking wind. The more we change, the more we're the same, I always say. As I say, it's been good, not only for me, but for those I meet. I seem to be very popular. I have been asked to read from my work here and there, but of course I had to refuse, at the money offered.

I'm glad you thought the last story good. I never know what you'll think. The response has been light except from my immediate family. Actually, I think I'm outgrowing my public. I'm shooting for immortality.

About Yuletide cheer, we are planning a really big affair. You'll get an invitation, and in your case and George's we can offer overnight accommodations. We are flushing the woodwork for guests, and it should be plenty gala. I am going into Detroit on Saturday to look for a punch bowl. I saw a beauty in Chicago the other day, but it was priced a little high ($500) when you consider you don't use a punch bowl every day. In the end I may settle for a commode belonging to the Mitchells. I don't know Phil Silvers's work. I think Sid Caesar's skits good, though, and like to look at Jackie Gleason, who always reminds me of Dick Keefe.

I am glad to hear that *The Wanderer* is getting after Elvis. Somebody ought to, not that there isn't a lot of good in him, or in the way our merchants prepare us for Christmas, for that matter (vide L. Cowley). I don't know what can be done for Gordon.[1] I do think, and hope, he'll be spoiled for the grey life he was leading in Chicago, not that there isn't a lot of good in a grey life, and certainly Chicago is a good place for it, not that Chicago doesn't have its . . . Say, how do you like these apples? About that marriage course for student nurses, skip it. Not that such a

---

1 Gordon Zahn.

course isn't . . . Hey, I can't stop this! How would you like a rubber Santa Claus over three feet tall, more than thirty-two inches around, roly-poly, and best of all you just pull the tape and he actually talks, says, "Merry Christmas"??????

Jim

Please try to make it up for the fete, for which you'll soon have an invitation.

BETTY POWERS

507 Church Street
Ann Arbor, Michigan
Sunday, 2:30 p.m., December 9, 1956

Dear Betty,

I carried your letter to church. [. . .] They had the pledge,[1] after a long fatuous explanation, and I remained seated, conspicuously. I didn't have anything but exasperated thoughts all during Mass. To hear that awful apology for what the man himself knew better about, but making the most of it because it was demanded by the cardinal.[2] I think there is nothing drearier than that aspect of the Church in America and cast around in my mind for a way to act. In *Grace*, though, that story, I've said about all there is to say. I noticed a little more nervousness in the man about to ask the people to rise and join the Legion, but of course it will go on and on. So much for that. My Sunday Sickness is on me, and bad today.

Much love,
Jim

The payoff on my experience in church this morning was that I stumbled going up the steps on the way out (it was in the basement of the church proper) and was down for a moment. Pride goeth before a fall!

Did you see Mr K.'s poem in Dec. 8 *New Yorker*?[3]

Invitations look good.

1 Legion of Decency pledge administered on the Feast of the Immaculate Conception: "I condemn all indecent and immoral motion pictures . . ." and so on.
2 Spellman.
3 X. J. Kennedy, "Epitaph for a Postal Clerk," *The New Yorker*, December 8, 1956.

507 Church Street
Ann Arbor
Monday, 12:15 p.m., December 10, 1956

Dear Betty,

I've just finished a morning of heavy reading of MSS. The mail came a few minutes ago: two from you, one from Fr Egan, who wants to know what to wear and when it is and, if there is to be boxing, whether he should wear his aluminum cup. [. . .]

I was dismayed to hear about KA and Mary getting lost. I must reread it when I have time, your account, and see if it makes any more sense to me. Yes, that should be the end of such junkets unchaperoned. [. . .]

You can look for Fr Egan at the conversazione, and probably George, though maybe not. For he's sure to have something planned. I do hope Barnharts won't come. But if they do, I think it won't make much difference, considering how gala everything and everybody will be. [. . .]

Much love . . . and keep things under control, as you've been doing.

Jim

507 Church Street
Ann Arbor
December 11, 1956

Dear Fr Egan,

Your letter rec'd, and I hasten to fill you in. Boxing Day, as any dictionary will tell you, is the day after Xmas. You are to come at 8:30 p.m., though in your case we'd like it if you came earlier, since you are so handy. I have a lot of decanting to do at the last minute, and somebody will have to park cars—I am buying one of those batons they use to direct traffic at night. Can you see Snyder's Drugstore (or Fr Stelmes) about the use of klieg lights, or searchlights, or whatever you call them? I want this thing to be memorable, plenty gala. Yes, do wear your cup. It may get rough later on, with most of the guests (I daresay) only one short generation away from utter alcoholism: prim characters like Doyle and Hynes, I mean, their closets jam-packed with skeletons: it is these I hope to bring out. We are serving Xalapa Punch, and no substitutions. I am of the opinion that none of us is as bad as we seem to all the others. I am making one more effort to encompass us all with fellowship. [. . .]

I am also inviting, from St Cloud, Mr and Mrs Wormhoudt: *he* is the author of *The Demon Lover* and other books dealing with literature as a kind of wet dream (a Freudian).[1] Hyneses have been wanting to meet the Wormhoudts, regarding them with some alarm, I think, as perhaps representing a threat to Christian family life and *its* approach. Me, I say they're all, intellectually, very shady characters. If that Legion of Decency pledge came from the hand of your new archbishop, as I think it did, he is still suffering from the same thing as my own bishop, as you've noted on occasion, tautology. I say "still" because his statement on Abp Murray's death might have come from Amos and Andy, from the latter to be exact. However . . . it becomes more and more apparent to me that the function of the American hierarchy is to test the humility of those under their guidance. I thought this as I listened to the priest here Sunday explain the purpose of the Legion of Decency pledge. I am still unpledged. I wish the whole thing would get lost. I am sending you some Trollope, a paper edition, and suggest you read *Barchester Towers*; Mrs Proudie's reception is sort of what we have in mind for Boxing Day.

 Academically,
 Jim

BETTY POWERS

507 Church Street
Ann Arbor
December 12, 1956

Dear Betty,
 [. . .] Late last night I got to work on Fr Urban. I had my best night since coming here and also, I think, one of the best nights ever: it is Christmas Eve at Duesterhaus[2] and all through the house . . . only the noise of checkers. [. . .]
 Much love,
 Jim

The door to their apt stood open, the apt was bare, and obviously Dwight and Pansy had flown.

---

1 Arthur Wormhoudt, *The Demon Lover: A Psychoanalytical Approach to Literature.*
2 The fictional town near St. Clement's Hill, the retreat house to which Father Urban was exiled.

507 Church Street
Ann Arbor
December 13, 1956

Dear Betty,

[. . .] I'm worried about all the sickness, though the last things you said were hopeful. I wish we could find out why we have so much of what KA has now.[1] It is really a disagreeable habit for a family to get into, and we seem to have done that, for several years now. I am not blaming anybody, understand: it is a development I don't like to see, and that is all I have to say. [. . .]

I had a malted and hamburger at a drugstore where I came across an article by Leslie Fiedler in *The Reporter*.[2] I then went to work on a letter to the editor, a copy of which I enclose.[3] I don't know if they'll use it of course, or what the effect will be, but I think it's time someone made the points I do. Or think I do. [. . .]

A letter came yesterday, airmail from England, for a James Purdy. This morning I see it is still outside the mailboxes, now marked "not at this address." I went down, after thinking about it, and had another look, brought it up, compared the typing on the envelope with that on an envelope of Gollancz's. I decided to open it, remembering that Austin has some Scotch tape and the phrase "opened by mistake." It is a letter from Victor,[4] which I enclose. [. . .]

I was amused to hear of everyone having so much trouble with Boxing Day. I think they have more than we planned: I think of them, more than ever, as barnyard animals going their familiar paths from stall to pasture and back, day in and day out. Any kind of reading would have familiarized them not with the exact day but with the word. [. . .]

Jim

---

1 Sore throat, earache.
2 "Some Footnotes on the Fiction of '56," *Reporter*, December 13, 1956.
3 Published in *Reporter*, January 10, 1957.
4 Gollancz.

507 Church Street
Ann Arbor, Michigan
December 18, 1956

Dear Jack,

I'm sorry to say that I have joined the academy too, and so what you say about us two, degreeless and alone, isn't true for the moment. Yes, in fact, it is true. I am still degreeless, and I'm left pretty much alone. I came here in September and will finish up in mid-January. I thought I needed the money, Jack. We had been running down ever since 1953, my last good year, everything wearing out and machinery giving up. I see by my little calendar, which I keep amending, an old con doing time, that I have only five classes to go; one tomorrow and four in January. Then back to St Cloud and Ignorance!

Yes, I did see Leslie Fiedler's article. I have written to the editors about it. If they publish my letter, it will be worth reading. I concentrated on the dig about publishing in *The New Yorker*. I know Fiedler, and like him, but decided to return the frankness, if that's what you call it. It is a problem what to do about the books of one's friends, a problem I've tried to avoid. What I really dislike about the article, and this I don't mention at all, is that I and the others were invited to the ball, as it were, but in the end he's dancing every dance with Saul. I doubt that Saul's as good as he says in this book.[1] Someday I'll read the book and see. At the moment I'd rather not confirm my suspicions. Actually, as you must know, Jack, I don't have much heart for literary controversy. What I'd like to be is a horse trainer, or simply a man of great wealth, and go about doing good, not forgetting myself.

When I finish up in January, I intend to look you up for lunch. It'll be the 17th, I think; a Thursday. Could you hold that open? I'll let you know if it's to be another day.

Academically yours,

Jim

Very glad to hear Clocker[2] is abroad again and at Oxford. I have noticed that he's become an expert on British writers, have read his reviews here and there. Tell him I'd like to see him at Oxford, sunning himself at

1 Bellow's *Seize the Day*.
2 Harvey Webster.

Parson's Pleasure or bicycling on High. I often think of Clocker. He is, in fact, as we used to say in fun, a sweet guy. Would that we could go racing together in England!

BETTY POWERS

507 Church Street
Ann Arbor
Tuesday morning, December 18, 1956

Dear Betty,

[. . .] Who the hell sent the envelope addressed "Earl"?[1] Mrs Barnhart, I imagine, just to make it perfect, and you did say they'd accepted. The hand is what you'd have to call illiterate, and so I eliminate Mrs Wormhoudt. Ah, well, I'm glad the printer didn't make that mistake. [. . .]

Don't worry about the liquor. I'll just buy a case of everything. I may get the wine in St Cloud anyway. I expect to have a merry time of it on my way home, stopping people all along the way and wishing them "Many of 'em!" After all, all I'll be carrying is my canvas bag, a punch bowl, twenty-four cups, a half-dozen fifths of whiskey, gin, rum, etc. "Same to you!" [. . .]

Jim

The conversazione was a great success and remembered as such into the twenty-first century by survivors in the Movement.

HARVEY EGAN

The Cloisters
St Cloud
January 2, 1957

Dear Fr Egan,

[. . .] Nothing has happened here since the conversazione. The last few guests left this morning. No one stayed overnight, though we'd made up beds for four. I gather that it was a success, and if so I'm glad. That is all I hoped. I knew I wouldn't hear anything memorable at such a gathering.

1 Jim was incensed by people who, thinking that "Farl" was a typo, changed his middle name to "Earl."

There remains the problem of refusing invitations resulting from it, but we are comparatively safe with the children as alibis for staying home. [. . .]

We were very glad you could come and stayed as long as you did. Maybe in Ireland when we give a hunt ball, you'll stay all night. I have no plans for that, however. I'd like to finish a novel quick. That doesn't seem to be how I do things, though. [. . .]

Ace Brigade

Merton sent me his new book, but I haven't read it yet. Mary Humphrey got right to it. She does most of my spiritual reading, she who doesn't need it. But as you say Doris Day used to say, "That's life, I guess."

BETTY POWERS

507 Church Street
Ann Arbor
January 8, 1957

Dear Betty,

[. . .] It is now 11:00 a.m. Tuesday, and I've just had a call from Clyde Craine[1] of the University of Detroit. Apparently, he knows me better than I know him; he calls me "Jim." The whole affair grows. I am to be interviewed on WWJ, the NBC Detroit outlet, at 2:30 or 2:45, I guess it is; then I call Clyde; then we have dinner; then we put something on tape; then there is the reading itself; then we see some people afterward; and then I either stay overnight at Clyde's or return on the midnight train. In fact, it isn't as busy as it sounds, and Clyde isn't, actively, pushing me around, but the thing just builds up, of itself. And I keep wondering what it means. I am not that well-known. I wish I were. Boredom, I guess, on the part of everybody. Even I am looking forward to it, but tell myself to watch that I don't drink or talk too much; I must put the whole thing under the glass of analysis. Clyde was for my reading "The Valiant Woman," though the story always bothered his boss, he said; a Jesuit, evidently. I got the impression that there might be crusaders in the audience, book burners and the like. I hope so. I wish that I could purchase some pneumatic horns, attached to glasses, say, that I could blow up and put on for reading. I am to read "The Presence of Grace." Well, that's enough of

1 Clyde Craine, head of the English department, University of Detroit.

that. Having just spoken to Clyde, I am still full of it, you understand.
[. . .]

 Much love,
  Jim

I am wearing Austin's rubbers here.

BETTY POWERS

507 Church Street
Ann Arbor
Saturday, January 12, 1957

Dear Betty,

 [. . .] Now for my day in Detroit. I arrived by bus around 1:15, looked in the windows of a whole row of shoe stores, asked about a couple of pair—whether they came in black; they didn't—and forgot about that. I appeared at WWJ, waited a few minutes in the lobby, then Fran came in—a combination of Mrs Hancock, in "Blue Island," and Mrs Mathers—and up we rode in the elevator, we being the aforementioned and Lanny Ross[1] and his entourage, girlfriend, photographer, another man. In the fifteen seconds it took for us to go down the hall after leaving the elevator, before we entered the studio, Lanny questioned me. Obviously, he was annoyed that he was having to share the program with me. "Writer," I said, asked what I was, though Fran had told him as much when she introduced us. "What kind of writer?" "Short-story writer." "Something like this?" he said, pulling out a pocket-size pulp magazine—detectives, or something. "No," I said flatly. "Well?" he asked. "*The New Yorker,*" I said. "Oh," he said. "That's kind of whimsical, isn't it?" "I suppose," I said. Then I heard him saying to Fran, as I was removing my coat and putting it on the grand piano, "Is this going to be a round-robin?"

 Well, to make a long program short, Fran has heard of me through *Time* magazine, through having seen the best books of the year, and I am introduced as "James Powers." And at first she and Lanny sort of give way to me in the program, asking me questions, and I answer them as sweetly as I can, but there is a disturbing drift toward the negative, culminating in my saying a literary man could no longer associate himself with a newspaper. Fran wants to know right away if I know this station is owned by a

1 Lanny Ross (1906–1988), American singer, actor, and songwriter.

newspaper. I say, yes, and that I sometimes read the paper on Sundays but that I am not singling out Detroit papers, just all papers. I say I am able to read a few of the British papers, which are "written," and Lanny says, "Like *The Manchester Guardian?*" and I say yes and add *The Observer* and *Sunday Times.*

All the sudden we're off that and into Lanny's new project, which is singing in supermarkets, in behalf of a new series of records, Master-Something-or-Other Records, "lovely Strauss waltzes," and "My Fair Lady," very popular with teenagers in Fran's family. Well, I detested Fran, but I rather liked Lanny. You could see the nasty yellow hair dye, and he looked pretty burned-out around the eyes, but he was a man and he'd been somebody once and maybe he still was. He saw that I wasn't trying to hog the microphone; he saw, I think, I didn't give a damn. Toward the end of the 15-minute program he broke into folk song, rather a surprise to me, but I was glad to hear something else. I haven't seen anybody dressed like Lanny since Ken McCormick appeared in Milwaukee. Subtle grey herringbone topcoat, black shoes, grey and black tie, white shirt—sombre, crisp though, like the grey side of the dollar bill. I was walking out without a word, since the photographer was snapping Fran and Lanny together, when Lanny came over and said he'd been glad to meet me and was going to look up my work—the Gollancz edition was in my hand—and Fran too said she'd been glad to meet me. There you are, a short résumé of that part of the trip to Detroit.

I then called Mr Craine. We had two drinks at the Detroit Athletic Club, drove forever to the restaurant, where we dined with his wife, Fr Farrell, dean of the graduate school, and another couple. This was rushed, time being short, and before the reading I cut a tape with a fellow who asked me a typed-up question which I looked at before we started cutting. This ultimately took a negative turn too. Then came the reading, a much bigger crowd than they expected, about 200 people, I'd say, and they'd expected under 50. The reading seemed to take forever, and I didn't do as well as I'd hoped. The questions afterward, however, went on for over an hour. This was pretty stimulating, I was told. I won't go into it all—except to say that things took a negative turn. I did sense, however, that Mr Craine and others felt that it was quite an evening.

Then we went to one of the faculty's house and had one drink. It was rushed so I could catch the 11:59 train for Ann Arbor, which I did. I walked home, feeling I needed the air. Then I smoked a pipe here, thought I ought to set this sort of thing down in a journal but felt it was too much trouble, that I should say what I have to say in my work—and wondered, though, whether the journal, if I kept one, might not have a more lasting value even as literature. [. . .]

Before I close, I want to say that there were some wonderful faces among the clergy there last night. One wonderful old man whom I'd been conscious of during the reading and questions came up and said I was *too* kind to the clergy, we're worse than that, he said. This was nice but irrelevant to my real interest—which was in him himself, what a wonderful face, so round, the hair, so white, the eyes, so blue. I hated to think of him dying, as he would in a few years, all that perfection disappearing from the earth. All for now. It won't be long now. Time is working for me now.

Much love,

Jim

19

This room is like a dirty bottle, but inside is vintage solitude

January 23, 1957—August 1, 1957

The Vossberg Building, suite 7

ROBERT LOWELL

509 First Avenue South
St Cloud, Minnesota
January 23, 1957

Dear Cal,

Every now and then I wonder whether you are a father yet. I hope there has been no difficulty about it, or that there will be none. I don't see anyone who would be able to enlighten me. (Allen Tate, I heard, was in India, although last week there was a piece on him in a Mpls paper about the Bollingen prize.) I'd appreciate some word on this from you. Ordinarily, I take no interest in this sort of thing, which is so common hereabouts, but it's different with you.

I returned from Ann Arbor last week, having completed my semester there. Things are getting back to normal, with me up all night and the temperature 15 below.

No doubt you saw that I am to be one of the Kenyon Review Fellows in Fiction. This is hard to explain, the honor of it, especially since I've never published there, and though I haven't had it indicated to me in any way, I attribute this to Peter Taylor. It is a break, and it, with what I have contracted to extract from Doubleday in advance royalties when the need arises, assures me of two years of economic freedom. I'm hoping I'm old enough, finally, to make the most of it as a writer and not to fritter the time away as I have in the past.

I read Elizabeth's story in *The New Yorker* last night and greatly enjoyed it.[1] I hoped, when I finished it, that it was the beginning of a novel and wished—I always envy good work—I could command the academic scene, which does interest me as one of the few in which you can make some sense out of what happens in terms of the past and ideas and character.

---

1 Elizabeth Hardwick, "The Classless Society," *The New Yorker*, January 19, 1957.

I see Flannery O'Connor has won the O. Henry with her "Greenleaf" story. I dropped her a line from Michigan when I read the story last fall. I thought it was very fine, only regretted that she killed off Mrs May, such a waste and not necessary. I advised her to go on with those characters just as if Mrs May hadn't died. She said that death was the great temptation after she'd written thirty pages about any of her people. I've heard this called the Irish temptation or "out," and suppose she might've been referring to that. [. . .]

Best to you both.

Jim

KATHERINE ANNE PORTER

509 First Avenue South
St Cloud, Minnesota
January 25, 1957

Dear Katherine Anne,

Your letter received this morning, and I hasten to clarify a thing or two. I decided I'd be wise to take the Kenyon, which is worth $4,000 to a married man. [. . .] I am better off than I've been for a long time. Now I must watch myself: I have a great capacity for indolence, for lounging about. In Ireland you'll find me at Leopardstown about this time of day (3:00 p.m.), with as much as ten shillings riding on a race. That is another thing I liked about Ireland. I could go to the races, to the theatre, eat out, and even buy books without feeling profligate. I have a gaudy feeling I don't like whenever I do such things here. To do what comes naturally partakes of a spree here. [. . .]

Our success, survival rather, has been due to the fact that we did without things, and we know we'll do so again—and again. We know where we come in economically—that we don't really exist economically. What we did in Ireland was move up a caste, with our American money. [. . .] All for now.

Jim

509 First Avenue South
St Cloud, Minnesota
February 11, 1957

Dear Cal,

Your letter came this morning, and while it's fresh, the news about Harriet, let us congratulate you, Elizabeth as well as Cal, and hope you bear up under parenthood. I'm afraid it gets harder, or has for us, anyway. [. . .]

Your reference to Miss E. drew blood here. Betty hired a woman last fall, and she is still, more or less, with us. But she doesn't do anything well and, though a character, not enough of one to be useful as such to us. Betty says she (B.) is a coward, or she'd go out and fire the woman. Betty has threatened (over the phone) to mail the woman her apron several times. And so on. My comment on your Miss E.: you couldn't find a woman like that in a town like this. That's the last word on that, for the moment. My head feels like a vacant lot where children go to break bottles and swing dead cats. [. . .]

We are sending Harriet (not that she cares) a blanket and trust it will not be found wanting in some particular that Miss E. demands of a blanket. We have used them in our household, but more and more I see that we have made a lot of mistakes. It has been my pleasure to look about me and give thanks that I, that we, don't live like that. Now I find the contrast not so great. Ah, well, perhaps you'll write a book and tell us how to live though parents.

All for now. Best to you and the girls.

Jim

Finding no peace at home for work (or quiet ease), Jim rented an office, suite 7 in the Vossberg Building in downtown St. Cloud. It was decrepit and cheap and he loved it.

St Cloud
February 27, 1957

Dear Fr Egan,

To you I'm sending my first words written from my office in downtown
St Cloud. Your old Royal, fresh from the repair shop, is here. A chair,
which may or may not be a bargain at $4 from the Goodwill, is here. A
table, cast out by us when we moved to First Avenue South, is here. And
I am here. This morning I put a lock on the door, which had none. The
jakes is next door, but I haven't been there yet. There is another room like
this next door on the other side, but it is padlocked. Down the hall, toward
St Germain, are two lawyers and the Girl Scouts of America, and overlooking the street the realtor and insurance man's office: he is letting me
have this room for $16 a month because of his wife, he said, an admirer of
my work. Below me is Walgreen's; across Eighth Avenue—my window
looks down upon it—is Cy Brick's bar. Up the street is the cathedral.
Down the street is the courthouse. Across St Germain is the post office.
As you can tell by now, I am in the heart of things—the dead center, you
might say.

The room itself reminds me of Quincy College Academy: brown railroad paint on the door and mopboards; a silver radiator; one window
arched at the top; and light green walls, cracked and peeling and stained.
There are two mops and three rolls of toilet paper and some steel wool in
one corner, but I have permission to move these things out. In short, I am
all set—either to write during the day, something which is impossible at
home, or to go into the rubber-goods business. This is the kind of building the Clementines used to have their offices in in Chicago. I decided
yesterday, sitting here wishing the door had a lock on it, that I wouldn't
get pictures or do anything about the walls or floor—which is splintery and
worn. Only one object I desire: one of those old-fashioned watercoolers,
the kind you put ice in, and a big bottle of spring water, the bottle upside
down, and . . . the bubbles each time you draw one. It's the bubbles I'd
like to have. Otherwise I can stand it the way it is: the peace and quiet of
noises which mean nothing to me, traffic, bells, cries of fishmongers and
religious-goods butchers from the street.

This room is like a dirty bottle, but inside is the vintage solitude
which hardly anybody can afford nowadays, and I am sipping it slowly,
hoping to straighten out my life as a writer. I've done little or nothing
since returning from Michigan. We have a new woman who comes three

or four mornings a week, and she's a good one, and Betty too is hoping to accomplish something as a writer. The light, I've just noticed, comes into the room, falls upon the paper in the typewriter, just right. It comes from the west, though, and that could be awful in the summer—but then that, as you always say, is life. I must dash off a line to Ted.[1] After all, what I've managed to do here in No. 7—that is the number on my door—is only what he did in Elmira. I have more room, however—for what? For staring straight ahead, I guess.

All for now.

Jim

Why don't you tune in Bob and Ray, weekdays at 5:00 p.m., from the Mutual station in the Cities—it's above KSTP on the dial? I get them via Wadena.

HARVEY EGAN

From Number 7
March 25, 1957

Dear Fr Egan,

[. . .] You know that play I was telling you about? Well. And so to the novel. I am trying to work up some feeling for Fr Urban, his last night as a preacher, but don't seem to have the material I need. What I want is some examples of other men transferred as he has been, removed from the spot in the vineyard where it certainly did appear that they were doing awfully good work. Maybe it's in Newman. I have always remembered Fr Wulftange's remarks on Littlemore: another grey day at Littlemore, etc. Ah, well, I'm glad to be back with Fr Urban. We understand each other.

I made my trip to Urbana, Jacksonville, and Quincy, after 17 years away. The best thing was the visit I paid to Msgr Formaz, pastor at Our Saviour's in Jacksonville for 52 years, dean of the Springfield Diocese, and the man who rec'd my mother into the Church and baptized me. He is 82 and a delicious old man, civilized, subtle, wise, and witty. I stopped off at Springfield, at Templegate, booksellers, and was told stories of him by the proprietors, who also told me a good one about Waugh when he was there some years ago. Reporter: Is it true you don't care for American methods of heating? Waugh: What makes you say that? Reporter: Something I

1 LeBerthon.

heard or read somewhere. Of course I only know what I read in the papers, as Will Rogers used to say. Waugh: Will Rogers? He's dead, isn't he? Reporter: Yes. Waugh: Now he knows better.

I visited the cemetery in Jacksonville and noted all the Irish counties on the tombstones, more than I've seen since I looked over the graves in St Paul. The Powers lot is filled, only a few yards from the clergy, on high ground. I felt it was all a mistake, all these poor Irish immigrating—for what? Now *they* know better. Don and Mary over last night, my first social life in some time, in St Cloud. They had gone out to hear Fr LaFarge on racial justice. I was not up to it. Well, that's all I know this time. Write. I saw in the paper where we are jubilant about the changes in fasting regulations, we Catholics, I mean. T. Merton sent me his new book of poems. I can't see him as a poet. But that goes for about all the poets. And now your arch-author must leave you.

Jim

Jim had become friends at Ann Arbor with Michael Millgate, then a teaching fellow, later a biographer, critic, and teacher.

MICHAEL MILLGATE

509 First Avenue South
St Cloud
March 28, 1957

Dear Michael,

[. . .] I am writing this from my new office in downtown St Cloud. [. . .] I have no telephone, though things are really hopping here, what with lighting my pipe and going to the toilet and scratching myself. I am in the same building with the Girl Scouts, not a going concern in St Cloud, where the Camp Fire Girls dominate, with two attorneys, and something called the Western Adjustment and Inspection Company. I keep thinking this is just the spot for a small mail-order rubber-goods and pornography business and that I am the man for it.

I have just finished Angus Wilson's *Anglo-Saxon Attitudes*, which I enjoyed, and have just finished not finishing Iris Murdoch's *The Flight from the Enchanter*. It took me half the book to find out that it is worthless. Such books, and Nancy Mitford's, serve only to impress me with the genius of Evelyn Waugh. When they are bad, they are horrid.

Also Sean O'Faolain's book on modern writers, I've been going through. He does the job that has been needed on Faulkner and that no American, presumably, knows enough to do. It doesn't take much to make us pious. [. . .]

That horse whose name you were trying to remember that night at my place was Freebooter, I think. I have nothing for the National tomorrow, and if I did, I wouldn't know what to do about it. Very frustrating, life with the Lutherans. [. . .]

Jim Powers

KERKER QUINN

509 First Avenue South
St Cloud, Minnesota
March 28, 1957

Dear Kerker,

[. . .] Jacksonville was obsessed with basketball, but I did have a nice hour in the cemetery and several hours with the old priest who baptized me and who hadn't seen me since but who has followed my career as a writer closely. Quincy was worse. I spent five hours there, three in loneliness and two with the mother of an old friend. And so much for that.

Thanks again for your hospitality, and please let Chuck and Suzie know I appreciate that bash they put on for me.

Jim

And please tell Chuck that with a few choice words he ended my career, at least for a while, as a playwright.

Jim and Betty were told that St. Cloud State College would be taking the old red house by eminent domain. It was to be demolished and the land converted into a parking lot. Jim's story "Look How the Fish Live" is based on this. Around the same time, Jim suffered a severe attack of appendicitis and was rushed to the hospital, where he had an emergency appendectomy, the worst ordeal known to man, in his view.

509 First Avenue South
St Cloud
May 2, 1957

Dear Katherine Anne,

[. . .] We must soon move. We have hated it here in St Cloud, but we have loved being in this old house, which is now 101 years old, the oldest in town, painted red, barn red, with green trim, and owned by two maiden ladies, one of whom is failing in health and the other is living in California. First, ten days ago, an appraiser visited us, with no explanations except that he'd been sent by the owners' insurance agent. I wrote and rec'd reassurances that the house would be retained for some time to come. Ultimately, it would be consumed by the Teachers College across the street (they have made dormitories out of two imposing residences since we've lived here), and there is always something in the newspapers about their needing money to expand. Recently, the "Teachers" part of the name has been dropped, which makes it St Cloud State College, more in line with its true purpose, though preparing teachers is still an important part of its work, and this change is expected to aid faculty members in getting their books published—I am paraphrasing the press.

Well, yesterday we heard that Jan. '58 might be the latest we could occupy the house. This, in effect, with two children in school, means we'll have to move and be somewhere else in the fall. We are hoping it will somehow be put off, that we can stay here another school year, but it is not likely: there is the career of a young college president to be considered too (he is also president of the local chamber of commerce); the more he builds, the more likely he is to get the call to a better pulpit, say, Iowa State, and so on up the ladder. Of course I am prejudiced. If one could believe that what is going on across the street is education, it would be different. But here are country boys and girls continuing their high-school life, never, I think, encountering the idea of a university, or anything like it, in their entire education.

Well, we aren't the only ones soon to be ousted. The squirrels, both red and grey, go about their business with no thought of anything but their stomachs and next winter. There must be between ten and twenty squirrels resident on the property (the red ones were in the walls of the house until I came and fought them back and sank wire in concrete around all the porches, stoning, trapping, shooting, a man possessed for one whole summer). So much for that. We expect we'll take a terrible beating on appliances and furniture when we move, for we'll sell most of it. Probably we'll try Ireland again.

I rented an office downtown a couple of months ago and have been doing very well with my work there in the afternoons. I found that I could work then. I had got the idea that the only time was night for me, but this was due in great part to children, I know now.

I haven't been going down to the office since Saturday, though, for on Sunday I had to go to the hospital and have my appendix removed. I returned home on Tuesday and am still feeling the stitches and also the surprise and indignity of it: I have been lucky in the past, escaping the everyday illnesses and accidents. So my step is slow these days, and the Old World is ahead of me, and at times I don't feel up to it, to going abroad with four children, two more than last time, when I was five or six years younger, and settling down again. Still, I know it's the right thing to do. It is a terrible fact that there is no one I know and respect who, living here, in Michigan, Minnesota, Illinois, or anywhere else, isn't unhappy, an exile already, and becoming more and more of one as American society changes for the worse. All kinds of problems abroad, of course, but at least the children can get an education before it's too late: however much I wouldn't want mine to suffer needlessly, I would like to see them educated. Betty, who thinks she is more attached to things here than I am but sees the folly of remaining, has printed a card and put it over the doorway in the kitchen, to steady her. It reads:

In exitu Israel de Egypto,
domus Jacob
de populo barbaro

[. . .]
     Jim

Journal, May 31, 1957

DECAY: Old men, who a few years ago were wearing light canary and green and blue and white sport shirts of transparent nylon, I see this year are wearing caps of same hues. Bet they're nylon. Have strap in back like a wool cap. Wonder if they would wear a sign saying, "I'm an old Jackass." Give sign as premium as they used to give you a bat or ball when you bought a new suit at Myers Brothers.

Before leaving St. Cloud for Ireland, the Powers family traveled by train to Albuquerque to visit Jim's parents, his brother and sister, and their families. It was a bitter, unhappy time.

MICHAEL MILLGATE

June 3, 1957

Dear Michael,

[. . .] Your coming trip sounds brutal to me, but then you are young and can always console yourself with the thought that you're just passing through. Perhaps I'm unusually sensitive at the moment: we—Betty and I and the four children—are going to Albuquerque later this month, by train: what a way to die! My mother and father, brother and sister, live there. I hate the Southwest, the dust and disorder. Priestley, in *Journey Down a Rainbow*, is right.

Sorry you can't make it to St Cloud, but I think it may be just as well. Our life is breaking up here. The old house we live in is doomed, the lovely grounds probably scheduled to be a parking lot, all this part of St Cloud Teachers College's expansion program. We must get out by January 1958, but have decided our flight should not be in winter, and have booked passage on the *Britannic* leaving New York on October 3; next stop Cobh. We hope to rent a house with at least five bedrooms, not far from Dublin and on the sea if possible. I am formulating my ad for *The Irish Times*: *Immigrant returning requires* . . . [. . .] I had it planned that I should finish my novel and then go to Ireland. I love my little office. But it's not to be, and I must try to dissect the corpus of my novel for a story or two and still not kill the thing. This is old stuff for me, and I'd hoped I wouldn't have to do it again.

All for now, then, Michael. I hope to see you in Ireland. I don't know what my address will be there, but will drop you a line when we find a place. In any case, I am always to be found in the ten-shilling enclosure at Leopardstown Racecourse. A pint of plain is your only man.

Jim

509 First Avenue South
St Cloud, Minnesota
July 8, 1957

Dear Fr Egan,

Today I am 40, and so far no signs of life beginning. However, I was born around 5:00 p.m., as I understand it, and it's only about two now. Greetings, in any case. [. . .]

Now about this long journey to Albuquerque—don't ever do it. Very rough going on the Rock Island, failure of air-conditioning partway coming back, proximity of the little people hard to take, seeing what they eat and read, and returning on the Super Chief, which ain't nothing but a train except for the Turquoise Room and sweaty odors wafting through the sleeping cars. For the best in travel, I suggest the Enterprise, first class, running between Cork-Dublin-Belfast. You know I often eat a Clark Bar at 4:00 p.m., taking it with a glass of cold water, and called in vain for some on the Super Chief. In Ireland, I switch to Cadbury's Turkish Delight.

Suffering from the heat here, though we now have something approaching welcome relief. I spend my time at home waxing my trunks and remind myself of Noah somehow preparing for the Flood. We have three trunks and can use at least two more of the type (wardrobe); I find them at the Goodwill. I have washed off all the stickers except one: Shepheard's Hotel, Cairo.

I've said nothing about the main thing here: mosquitoes, the worst in the memory of men. I have bought a spray you pump up, have enough DDT coming to provide 400 gallons of fluid, and now, on top of this, we are having a professional do the place with one of those big machines. That was one thing, the one thing, about New Mexico: sitting out under the stars and not being bitten by anything. But I feel a little effete mentioning mosquitoes to you, for though you resent insects, you are still a Minnesotan—and I get the impression it's sort of chicken or something to give mosquitoes too much thought. But as it says on the first bottle of spray I bought: "Who enjoys your yard, you or the mosquitoes?" This struck me as a very powerful line, one upon which to act. But the bottle is all gone (and at $2.50 a quart), and I step very lively as I pass between house and garage; the children are kept indoors. [. . .] I must do justice to the mosquito in literature, for it plays a large part in our life here.

But I ramble. I trust you are finding your new assignment pleasant.[1] I imagine by now, a week there, you've got the place pretty well organized. Always a few things to iron out when you first take over, isn't that right? Now, I don't know how you fathers do it, but here's how I do it . . .

    Jim

HARVEY EGAN

St Cloud

August 1, 1957

Dear Fr Egan,

    No office today; too hot. [. . .] Del[2] has had it, from me. I sympathized with manager Glickman when he said, "Listen, Flanagan . . ." [. . .] All for now.

    Jim

1 Egan was assigned to St. Peter's Church, Mendota.
2 Del Flanagan lost to Gil Turner at Midway Stadium, St. Paul, July 25, 1957.

20

Scabrous Georgian, noble views of the sea, turf in the fireplaces

October 14, 1957–February 13, 1958

Hugh and Jim, Port of New York, 1957

The six-day voyage on the Britannic *was brutal, thanks to storms and high seas on the North Atlantic, seasickness, and the Asiatic flu. Jim and Betty arrived in Ireland in bad shape, mentally and physically. While still in the United States, they had arranged to rent St. Stephens, a furnished house in Greystones, for the time it would take to find a permanent place.*

BIRDIE AND AL STROBEL; BERTHA SEBERGER

Ireland

12:40 a.m., October 14, 1957

St Cloud

6:40 p.m., October 13, 1957

Dear Bertie, Al, G'ma,

Here we are with our dying fire, into our second bottle of Canadian Club (compliments of Doubleday & Company), and I've just finished, with much help from Betty, my ad for *The Irish Times*, which I'll be dropping off tomorrow when I go to Dublin.

> Wanted to rent house in possible surroundings for long period by unpopular author and family. Greystones to Dublin. 5/6 bedrooms. Cooker, immersion. View of sea? Require furniture, expect to have to collect it, but would consider furnished house if this would not mean eyesores, radiogram veneers, contemporary. State rent and other interesting details in first letter.

Well, there it is. It is calculated to catch the eye of that exceptional person who would not ordinarily reply to a blind ad but who, on reading this one, would suddenly decide to move out and rent it to us. [. . .]

As you can imagine from this, we are not in the best of spirits—I speak loosely—and whatever happens from here on can't help being better. We have had hard times ever since we left the *Britannic*, and the last two days on it, with each of the kids being sick with the flu and finally Betty in Cork, where we stayed another day, not according to plan, so she could recover. Even now, everyone isn't well, Hugh and Boz still very much off their feed. I haven't had a good night's sleep for three days on account of Hugh—the first night in Cork he started off in bed with me and then tired of me, as men will, I'm told, and I ended up on the floor between two comforters, short ones at that, with my head sticking out one end and my feet the other. (Betty, should your question concern her, was in the other twin bed, and very narrow twin beds they were, about what we'd call an army cot.) And so it goes. [. . .]

    Jim

You amaze us with your salesmanship. I refer to the way you've been selling our things. I am most impressed by the sale of the watercooler. I am the only person I know who would be tempted by it. [. . .]

MICHAEL MILLGATE

St Stephens, Victoria Road
Greystones, County Wicklow, Ireland
October 23, 1957

Dear Michael,

    Hoped by now that I'd be writing from a more permanent address, but we are still at the above, having arrived here on the 12th, with no prospect of improving ourselves. [. . .] I have more or less despaired of finding what I had in mind: a small Georgian residence in surroundings and view of the sea. I just sit here with the Telefunken. I celebrated Trafalgar Day on the Light yesterday, the return of the queen to London, and today listened to Victor Silvester and His Ballroom Orchestra, an old favorite of mine (he makes Guy Lombardo sound like Count Basie). And of course it's nice having *The Observer* and *Sunday Times* right after Mass on Sunday. Beauty we have too, the sea—snot green under the sun today—and Bray Head and the Sugar Loaf Mts. Stilton cheese and Double Diamond in this Crown Colony and Jersey cream. But . . . but this isn't it, Michael, and I'm not inviting you over. We would like to see you here when and if we find the place. (Betty is off seeing an agent now who advertises that he covers the waterfront. Words, words.) Let us hear from you.

    Jim

St Stephens, Victoria Road
Greystones, County Wicklow, Ireland
October 29, 1957

Dear Leonard and Betty,

Betty has given you a good picture of our life here. I can mention two more positive items. Haircuts are two bob (two shillings or 28¢); ¹⁄₆ (one shilling, sixpence) for lads like Boz. Do you want me to get an estimate on bearded gentlemen? The other thing is Jersey cream and Irish oatmeal. I haven't made oatmeal a feature of my life in the past, but here I look forward to it. Of course radio you know about, the highbrow 3rd Programme on BBC, of course, but I have a weakness for such music from "Grand Hotel, the Palm Court," which means "Tell Me Pretty Maiden" and "I Leave My Heart in an English Garden," medleys from Gilbert and Sullivan, "Zigeuner," and such, just the thing for the middle-aged tea toper . . .

I am full of questions about the Movement. I do hope you'll draw closer to it, Leonard, and not be the outsider you were, appearing only rarely at the smaller gatherings. Make a practice of dropping in on the Humphreys and O'Connells and others I want the latest on. Think of yourself as a routeman or roundsman, as the expression is here. If necessary, go to work for Jewel Tea or Watkins Products. You may not sell a lot, but you will get around regularly, and no one need know your real business—which is news, news, news! About payment, well, you name it. Maybe legman is the term for what I want you to be. Especially Don needs close covering. He's tricky, as everybody knows. Even when I was there on the spot, too much escaped me, and unless Mary is involved in the opposite point of view—unless it is to her personal advantage that the truth come out—you can expect little help from that quarter. Then, too, where you are concerned, she is inclined to be skittish, if you know what I mean. You are familiar, I hope, with the theory some of us hold that women are both fascinated and horrified by you. Mary is not the only one so affected; your wife is another; and there are others nearby. In fact, I can't think of a single one who doesn't qualify. You are the lion in that little jungle. There is a sudden stillness when you come nigh. My reports, such as they are, on Don haven't been much. I learn he is limping about; I learn he has worked Sputnik into his repertoire. The latter I had known instinctively. I still don't know what it is, what it's for, only that it somehow serves Don's ends on earth . . .

I was amazed to hear of Em's coming trip to Paris, having heard from him in the first mail today. (Incidentally, there is another advantage, two deliveries of mail in Ireland.) Burden him with commissions; perfume; pornography; the latest on the priest-workers. You should get some good evenings out of his trip. Let's hope it won't *all* be the kind of grist he can turn to CFM[1] purposes. I hope he manages to get drunk while there. I do not go so far as to wish him syphilis. But I do hope he has a good time. All for now. And please write. I was happy to have your letter, even though I could do with less detail on eye doctors (as you sensed, judging from your final remarks). You really must curb your interest in the physical, Leonard. Man does not live by homeopathy alone, you know. Do you need any seaweed?

    Jim

We had a call from one of Fr Fennelly's curates this afternoon. He disturbed me somewhat by repeatedly mentioning that I should call for him if I needed him. He asked what I thought of Fr F.'s practice of having the Mass explained from the pulpit as it's progressing, and I said I didn't care much for it but that I wasn't much of a missal man myself. "Nor am I," said he. We said we found eggs pretty high in Ireland, and he said, "Oh, keep a few hens." He also said that Greystones was the most Protestant town in Ireland except for Belfast. Yes, I said, we've been told that living here, we're not really living in Ireland. "Exactly," he said. I thought this might be a good thing but didn't develop the idea.

JOE AND JODY O'CONNELL

St Stephens
November 4, 1957

Dear Jody and Joe,

    [. . .] JF taking over here (Betty suddenly conked out and would like to turn in but is chary of cold sheets). Let me say too that I enjoyed the letter and the portrait,[2] and I wish you wouldn't apologize for either—not that anyone did apologize for the portrait. I am thinking of a large—about seven feet—frame for it, the thing being so small it would have to be widely matted, with hair, I think, old beard combings or, in default of those, horsehair such as pokes through our mattress and through the sheet. I

1 Christian Family Movement.
2 Drawing of members of the Movement.

always think of Leonard when I feel a sprig of horsehair at my backside. But be that as it may. Both of you should continue in your respective fields: the news of the Movement from Joe; sketches from Jody—and how about a few nudes? The subject could be the same—say, that one scene where the principal ingredients are horror and moonlight, call it "The Kill," or "Connubial Bliss."

Sorry—referring back to your letter—that it has come down to the Humphreys and the Bakers. Still, that is a lot, by our standards here. We see no one at all. We almost rented a house in the same borough Sean O'Faolain lives in, and from friends of the O'F.'s at that, and I suppose they'll hear about us from that encounter. I haven't got in touch with Sean, preferring to wait until we can appear in a better light, internally, that is. We have been pretty low and probably show it. We have rented a house, however, in Dalkey, which is up the line a piece, toward Dublin, once the home of G. B. Shaw, the town, that is, not the house we'll be in. We can't move in until December, though. It isn't quite what I had in mind (hardly anything is, I find), is large enough, imposing enough, with views beyond my expectations, but it won't give me the solitude I seem to require to do my own work. [. . .]

The bathroom is practically American, and we'll have the use of appliances such as vacuum cleaner, washing machine, and fridge. These are items you begin to covet when you live in a place like our present one: our toilet seat, for instance, is unfinished lumber that comes apart on one side like a jigsaw puzzle and has a leather hinge; the kitchen, to put it in understandable terms, would be fine for a blind sculptor to mess around in, has a concrete floor. [. . .]

Best,

Jim

P.S.: If Em wears a fedora and his mouton storm coat, won't he have to cut a hole for his eyes? Best. —Jim

St Stephens, Victoria Road
Greystones, County Wicklow
November 12, 1957

Dear Fr Egan,

I'm slow on the rebound, I know, but do you know what I've been through? Nobody knows the trouble: children seasick, flu in mid-Atlantic, Betty down in Cork, and more of the same here. This house has view of sea, Bray Head, railroad tracks, but prehistoric kitchen and bathroom (the toilet seat has a leather hinge), and when you pull the chain, it sounds like the Grand National field landing in Becher's Brook. [. . .] Around the first of December we'll be moving to:

Ard na Fairrge
Mount Salus
Dalkey, County Dublin

This house is 125 years old, four bedrooms, two living rooms, one of which will become my study, kitchen–dining room (the owners removed a wall after tasting life in America), a large room we'll turn over to the children, formerly a billiard room, at present site of a loom for weaving tweed. And wonderful views of Dublin and Killiney Bays; Dalkey Island with a small ruins said to have been the stamping grounds of St Begnet (I think that's the name). [. . .]

No theatre yet, haven't had the mind for it. Only managed the races last Saturday at Leopardstown. Very fine. I came home three or four quid to the good, thanks to being on the longest shot of the day—30–1. I do believe if I could just get away from the family long enough to concentrate, I could support them in style on my handicapping. I made one sentimental bet with you in mind: a horse called Four Roses ridden by a jockey named Egan. Ran way out.

Fr Fennelly going ahead with the liturgy. We arrived at the end of a week advertised as "the Greystones Pattern," devoted to "togetherness," culminating in a Gaelic football game visible from our back windows. Did you ever stop to think what the Communion of the Saints really means? It doesn't mean what you might think; not Communion and not Saints; Togetherness. We haven't spoken to Fr F., only to a new curate who asked me what I thought of the to-do at Princeton, saying he was for the man there because his bishop was supporting him. I mumbled something about Maritain being on the other side, but I gathered that bishops were trumps. I can never remember what's trumps.

We are lonesome for the North Star State and our dear brethren there. Even the snow we hear about sounds attractive now. Amazin', ain't it? Sometimes I wonder if old Abbé Garrelts with his monotonous line about the far-off hills always looking greener hasn't got a hold of something. What one needs is a pass on the airlines good all over the world. Some of the angels found heaven itself dull, didn't they?

I had a copy of *The Reporter* with my story[1] in it sent to you, and I hope—not that you actually liked it—but that it didn't make you pewk. The few reports I've had have been favorable.

All for now. Emerson Hynes, by the way, is in Paris at the moment, I understand, as aide to Gene McCarthy and a congressional delegation. That's the way to travel.

Please write all the news.

Jim

ART AND MONA WAHL; BIRDIE AND AL STROBEL;
BERTHA SEBERGER

St Stephens, Victoria Road
Greystones, County Wicklow
November 19, 1957
Postscript to Betty's letter:

Just a word of thanks, Birdie, for sending on the mail; I am always glad to know when I've written a good story and was cheered by your comments and by Nana's, and today by my mother's (who ordinarily has little to say but who loved this one) and by Chuck Shattuck's, sent in your letter rec'd today. He is one of the dedicatees of my first book, and my best critic, and when he says I've done my *most best*, as he does, I feel repaid a hundredfold. We haven't heard anything from Ruth Mitchell yet, and hope she was not disappointed, didn't expect something different: she only knew that it was about the house. Of course it is, but about much more.

It isn't often that I think about the old house. I don't like to think about it. I get upset and angry when I think that a year ago I missed the autumn there and little knew that that was the last one for me and for us there. We would all be happy back there, I know, but that chapter has

1 "Look How the Fish Live," *Reporter*, October 1957.

ended. We did not end it—and I trust whoever was responsible (aside from the circumstance of the college expanding, an incidental to the swift kick we got) is now satisfied. [. . .]

All for now. Please keep up the correspondence. I think I enjoy it more than anyone else, which is not to say that Betty doesn't enjoy it to the fullest; I just enjoy it more. Once more, in writing, my thanks to you and Al, to Art and Nana, for all your labor and concern in our behalf.

Jim

LEONARD AND BETTY DOYLE

St Stephens, Victoria Road
Greystones, County Wicklow
November 20, 1957

Dear Leonard and Betty,

We rec'd two communications today; your letter this morning and a royalty check for the British edition of *Prince* (1948): 67¢.

JF: Nine copies home, five export. Fourteen! Some sale!

Betty: Well, it's *up*, isn't it?

We are now nearing the hour of five, the light outside grows purple, the light inside is on, Betty is rustling *The Irish Times*, our glasses are empty (of Power's Dublin Whiskey), the coal fire glows at $30 a ton, and the two boys nap on and on, and on the radio from somewhere in the hills of Durham a Catholic seminary choir sings vespers. I pick up my Doyle and am moved to respond to your fine letter.

The girls (to complete the picture) are on a train somewhere between Greystones and Killiney, where they are now enrolled at a convent school run by the Sisters of the Holy Child Jesus, an order founded by a woman named Connolly whose husband, I understand, after instigating her higher vocation, reverted to the flesh and wanted her back; too late. Anyway, it is a good, expensive school where the standards are apparently high. Ours were tested and found "intelligent but very backward educationally."

The big news here is that the McCarthys[1] walked in on us Sunday, around noon. I was reading *The Observer*, Betty slumming around in the kitchen. They were our first visitors—except for the curate. At first I thought, seeing Gene suddenly before me, that Em would follow, but he didn't. He chose Rome over Ireland, tourism over the Movement—or so it

1 Eugene and Abigail McCarthy.

seems to me—and thereby showed himself for what he is. We had dinner with Sean O'Faolain and others at a good restaurant Monday night—this at Gene's invitation and expense. We had a good time. My regret, though, was that Em wasn't there. The McCarthys are out of touch with the stirrings in the Movement. Gene seemed a little hurt that I didn't consider him in it anymore. Let's just say the McCarthys are on leave of absence. I promised them that if Gene lost the next election and returned to the land, we'd return to *watch*. [. . .]

Speaking of Sputnik, the only people to mention it to me have been the barber and a shopgirl; the former thought we probably knew as much about it as the Russians but just hadn't put what we knew to proper use, and the latter wondered if I'd seen it pass over yet. I hadn't, and haven't. What time is it *on*?

I confess I was glad to hear things have been "grim" for you these last four weeks. Misery loves company—and it's hard to believe one doesn't lead the list these last weeks. [. . .]

Times are considered very hard in Ireland, much unemployment, and I can believe it. On the other hand, an Englishman who runs a café in Dalkey told me that nobody suffers in Ireland, not as he understands the term. The hardware man (Allie Evans) in Greystones said quite a few people here had left for America, mostly for Canada, but that he thought they'd be sorry. I agreed with him. We thought if a man could make a living at all, he'd be happier here. Anyone leaving Greystones for anywhere else will miss the scenery, I know. There are moments when the sun, filtered by the clouds, shines on the sea and on stone and on the green in such a way that I wonder if such moments aren't enough to make up for everything. [. . .]

Jim

At the end of November, the Powers family moved into Ard na Fairrge, a decaying Georgian house on Mount Salus in Dalkey, county Dublin. Betty discovered to her and Jim's horror that she was pregnant again.

Ard Na Fairrge
Mount Salus
Dalkey, County Dublin
December 3, 1957

Dear Cal and Elizabeth,

Glad to have your good letter and late word on your fellow immortal (this is a reference to Ted Roethke). I happened to hear from Buck Moon about the same time and passed the news (about Ted) onto him.[1] Buck was coming out of some kind of tunnel himself, but he didn't say what kind. I hadn't heard from Buck for years. He is now working for Curtis Brown, the agent.

This house we're in now is an improvement on the other. Scabrous Georgian, noble views of the sea, turf in the fireplaces, room for the children. Unfortunately, we aren't in the mood to appreciate it, having experienced some terrible misgivings about expatriation and yet with no place to live at home—and hating it where we were, a good old house.

Have no friends, have no plans for any. I may have to work. Either that or fritter and go down. I'm glad to hear you're operating as a poet again. You'll be better for the layoff, I think, but I am also hoping you will continue your autobiography, which struck me as the real thing, in your best comic vein and more.

Yes, I've always enjoyed reading Wilson,[2] only disappointed when he touches upon the spiritual and sounds like one of the little Blue Books published by Haldeman-Julius,[3] but even that, in a man otherwise so perceptive, is refreshing. I only hope he never gets religion on that level and daresay it isn't likely he will. I shook his hand in the *New Yorker* offices once and admired a tweed coat he was wearing and his overall grizzled look. The Scotch in him.

All for now. Write when you feel like it. I hope Boston still interests Elizabeth. I think you're right to be there, where you belong. There is a man living next door to us in a Georgian morgue, teaches at Trinity, high up in the Church of Ireland (layman), and I don't know whether he's the poet or not.[4] Seems to me Faber publishes a poet by the name of Stan-

---

1 Roethke had had a bout of madness but recovered quickly.
2 Edmund Wilson.
3 Cheap paperbacks designed to promote literature and rational thinking, especially in working people.
4 William Bedell Stanford (1910–1984), professor of classics, Trinity College.

ford, his name. Everybody (one or two people) has said we should enjoy his company. I spotted him this morning sitting in the window on the second floor, the open window facing out to sea (and England), reading a book, and looking like somebody in Henry James, or my idea of same.

Jim

DON AND MARY HUMPHREY

Ard Na Fairrge
Mount Salus
Dalkey, County Dublin
December 7, 1957

Dear Don and Mary,

A little slow in replying this time. One week ago, about to the minute—it is 3:15 p.m.—we moved into this house. In the past week we have gradually ordered our lives, though they are still rather chaotic by our standards in St Cloud. We are realizing more and more that we had a system of a sort there, though it was not satisfactory; it will take some time to equal it here—and the question before us is—is it ever possible in a rented house, subject to an owner's decisions? I think the answer is no, and when you have a lot of children, it is important not to have to start over at intervals. I realize this is something you, and others who own their own homes, have known for some time. My trouble is not wanting to settle for the life that seems to go with home owning, but I am coming to see the error of my ways, having paid and paid with these false starts and find the latest one harder than the one before it, right on back to Avon and St Paul. All this is not a prelude to our making a home in Ireland; I don't even mean that we'd like to do that. We wouldn't in our present mood, which is very odd. To us, anyway. We have been so busy with the material side of existence that we haven't been able to enjoy the advantages of living here. I get up in the morning, and it's almost an hour before I get the fires going, since we were burning only turf until yesterday; now we have some coal for the fireplace in the kitchen. [. . .]

My study has two impossible chairs, which we continue to sit in, however, and the best fireplace in the house, especially made for burning turf; there are two holes on either side, toward the front of it, connected with tile pipe which runs a few feet through the hall, and into an entryway from which it sucks cold air, just naturally does it, and this blows on the turf, making it burn beautifully. Turf makes a very pleasant fuel, but most of these fireplaces are too small for it, being designed for coal. Turf has to have room to be spread, and you have to introduce the fresh pieces to the rear of the fireplace, pull forward the hot ones. The odor is nice, and a good thing it is, for we get some very strong, wayward breezes up here so high, so close to the sea. I mention this because I've just come from the studio, eyes streaming, having had to transfer the turf from it to my study and give up on the fire in the studio for today; I think the chimney is too low for the wind we have now. [. . .] All for now. [. . .]

Jim

Journal, December 7, 1957

We have had a thorough shaking up. We no longer know what's best for us. I don't anyway—and this is a startling statement for *me* to make. Here it is past midnight now, and I am sitting here in the study, with the radio playing, alone. I might be back in St Cloud, St Paul, Milwaukee, Cape Cod, Greystones, or Avon—ten years ago—for all the change there has been in my habits. The radio station is German—but so it was six years ago in Greystones. I am not unhappy at this time of day—except now and then. But when the days pass as they have lately, I do feel the pressure of waste . . . This is the time to get on with my work. It will be hard, unless conditions change—unless we can find a way to order our family life—to make the months ahead mean anything for my work. Betty's probable pregnancy is the final turn of the screw—worse than ever before, this one, in these circumstances. We must somehow manage. We aren't far from the rocks, must somehow negotiate them. I have to be careful, to keep control.

BIRDIE AND AL STROBEL; ART AND MONA WAHL;
BERTHA SEBERGER

Ard na Fairrge
Mount Salus
Dalkey, County Dublin
Tuesday morning [Before December 13, 1957]

Dear Birdie and All,

While Betty is doing the dishes, I'll add a few lines to this letter that we keep neglecting to mail. Today there is a full gale blowing, and my study, which faces the sea, is taking in a certain amount of wind and water: the rain gets in somehow. But the kitchen and playroom are warmer, which may account for the presence there of Betty and the boys. For two days we couldn't have a fire in the playroom. The wind was wrong, and the place filled up with smoke. So it goes: all difficulties we can put up with but would not want to do so for a lifetime, I think. [. . .]

We had a good evening with the O'F.'s[1] the other night. They both thought that we'd be all right once we got some proper help. That may be. The mornings here are the worst time: getting up the boys, getting off the girls, getting the fires going. There are periods of almost solid comfort—when the wind is right, when the children are occupied or asleep. We are little by little, by hook and crook, making my study a place to hole up in. Here we have the radio, here is the best fireplace for burning turf, and the two chairs are improved by putting foam rubber cushions over the rup-tured springs (the foam rubber cushions from two other chairs in the living room). [. . .]

Thanks again to you and to Nana for all the kind words about the *Reporter* story. You were and were not in it, Birdie; it is the usual mixture of fact and fiction and should not be read for anything but entertainment. The requirements of art demand that you do violence sometimes to the facts as they took place, or interpret them differently, or make up inci-dents and conjure up characters that life itself, being such an erratic artist, seldom provides.

Jim

HARVEY EGAN

PHONE=84102
Ard na Fairrge
Mount Salus
Dalkey, County Dublin
December 13, 1957

Dear Fr Egan,

[. . .] Glad to hear—indirectly—that people are reading my books in your waiting rooms. Don't forget to order plenty of *Prince* in the Image edition for your vestibule, and tell your friends. Unfortunately, I am not available for autographing parties, but send my best to one and all.

It is getting dark, around four in the afternoon, and I have the

1 Ó Faoláins.

typewriter on a Schweppes case parked in front of the turf fire. This morning I made a stand for the Christmas tree, which is set up in the billiard room. We have bought one string of lights (twelve bulbs instead of the eight we know in the U.S.), a few ornaments, and probably will keep adding more to cover the bareness. Everything we do reminds us that we were awfully free with our hard-earned possessions, having given away our lights, stand, ornaments. I call it detachment. [. . .]

Sean and Eileen O'Faolain were over last Sunday evening, a good session, and Eileen has been working to find us a maid. It now appears we'll have one right after Xmas, use fill-ins until then.

We have been suffering from homesickness (without having a home), Betty and I, that is. The kids seem happy. The girls are gone from 8:30 until 5:00 daily; half day on Saturday; and are doing all right in school, after finding catechism and arithmetic very advanced at first. They wear green outfits and go by train to and from Killiney, where the school is (Convent of the Holy Child Jesus, apparently an order more English than Irish with laywomen—they call them "mistresses"—doing most of the teaching). Under the patronage of the Abp of Dublin (McQuaid). I am smoking Mick McQuaid tobacco.

For Xmas, I got them badminton racquets, etc., and think it'll be possible to play in the billiard room (it measures 38 by 14); Hugh a tricycle; Boz a large wooden train, a locomotive, that is, that he can sit on. Boz already has a chain-driven tricycle; Hugh a wheelbarrow. What Boz really wants is cords and plugs, the electrical equipment he had in St Cloud. [. . .]

Write. Merry Xmas from us all.

Jim

CHARLES AND SUSAN SHATTUCK

Ard na Fairrge
Mount Salus
Dalkey, County Dublin
Xmas 1957

Dear Chuck and Suzie,

Thanks for your soothing compliments on the story, Chuck. Nobody's mean so much to me. This is our address for the next year—it was to have been a three-year lease, but I got cold feet at the prospect—with no other prospects, however. Not at all pleasant to realize I don't know my own mind: however ignorant I am, I've always known *that* in the past. I have not taken to drink or anything, but I did subscribe to *Time* magazine, and I'd say that certifies me.

House large, Georgian, scaly-walled affair, with tremendous views of the sea, we have turf in the fireplaces, and I understand the cottage where Bernard Shaw lived is a block farther up this hill we're on, but I can't get up the strength to get up there and look at it. If you lived there, I think I might make it; Cyril Cusack, the actor, lives close by, according to the owners of this house (who have moved into a flat, not caring for the breezes), and is a friend of theirs, and we've seen Sean O'Faolain once, but there seems to be a shortage of outgoingness, if that's a word. I feel like the late Aga Khan toward the end, without his padding. Best to you both.

Betty and Jim

DON AND MARY HUMPHREY

Christmas 1957

Dear Don and Mary,

[. . .] A word about Christmas. I think Betty took it harder than I did, being away from home. Now and then I'd think of the old house—which waited all year to be in style, with its red and green—and feel a dart of pain, some scene, some room, some noise or other, gone, gone, gone. But I didn't encourage myself along these lines, and now Christmas is all over again—for good, I sometimes think, for me. The kids, I think, had a good time in their youth. We managed to get in quite a bit of stuff, toys and games, and tonight we all had dinner together (Betty and I have been eating in my study, not being able to stand the meals with them), and the plum pudding flaming with Jamaica rum in a darkened room was such a success that we had to do it three times. The turkey, unfrozen, was good; mushrooms and chestnuts in the dressing; and so on. I mention it because, as I said to Betty, I don't often have such a meal, not as often as I used to, hence my comparative thinness. I am still soft, Don—never fear—but I am thin-soft. Christmas, however, didn't really come. The weather has something to do with it: in the forties and fifties, some sun, some rain, some fog, some sun, and so on. Church was harrowing, very crowded, and constant coming and going to the Communion rail, no sermon, one song; not just uninspiring but depressing, like a bargain basement with more people than bargains.

I went out looking for an office the other day, in the next town, Dun Laoghaire, or Kingstown, as it used to be, and ran into a literary house agent, or auctioneer, as they're called here. He had a letter from Bernard Shaw on the wall of his office (having sold Shaw's cottage in Dalkey). We have an appointment for next week to look at a room over a bookmaker's premises, the bookmaker (P. Byrne) being the landlord—which could be expensive in the long run, I suppose.

All for now, Don. I don't have much incentive to write. We did receive one card (Palmquists) from the Movement and were glad to get it.

All for now.

Jim

Next day, Boxing Day. One year ago tonight we had our gala party. How long ago that seems now. Celebrated today at Leopardstown with Sean O'Faolain, who has a car and drove us to the races. Afterward tea and cake at his house and conversation, mostly about America. [. . .]

The next day (Dec. 27). I'm having trouble getting to the post office (which anyway was closed yesterday) with this, but I am glad. For this morning we hit the jackpot: letters and enclosures from Hyneses and O'Connells. I placed them unread at my right hand as I ate a good breakfast of bacon, oatmeal, fruit bread, and tea. Then I retired to my study, and bit by bit—taking about an hour—I got through them, savoring every line. Jody, using two mediums, made it all very vivid to us. And how I'd like to hear Em on Rome. His letter is full of it, and I am almost sold on going there—as a surprising result. I keep hoping, Don, that you'll somehow be able to make it over here this fall. All for now: I must get back to the letters, plenty of juice and deep-down goodness in them yet. My blessings, then, upon you one and all.

JOE AND JODY O'CONNELL

December 28, 1957

Dear Joe and Jody,

Here it is Saturday night with everybody gone to bed but me and the radio and the turf fire. [. . .] I am smarting from a card I rec'd today from my friend Haskins (who spoke up for the common man last summer, you may remember, one evening at our house), who, referring to my Christmas story in *The New Yorker*,[1] says: "A potboiler, no?" Such blindness, coupled with such impertinence, is hard to take. [. . .] One just doesn't

1 "A Couple of Nights Before Christmas," *The New Yorker*, December 21, 1957.

take up with such people, but having done so long ago, one doesn't just write them off. What one would like to do is cut off their balls, lovingly, that is, and shake their hand in friendship . . . [. . .]

Glad to hear Don made it out. There is something very good about Don coming, unannounced out of the night in winter. He used to scratch at the screen in my study. On the other hand, there's something awful about Don not showing up after announcing he's coming over, and never a word of explanation. So look out for that.

And now to Jody. We got a terrific lift out of her part of the letter, both the account of an evening in the Movement and her sketches. I call that talent, literary or not; the lovely still life. I do hope she continues along this line. I want the whole damn gallery. We had a letter from Em in the same mail with yours, and I find I can't get enough of that photo of him and the pope. I keep looking at it; pornography was never so sweet in my youth. Pope and Anti-Pope, I call it, or More Popish Than the Pope. We can all be proud of Em, and I meant to tell him so in my next letter, which will be coming very soon. Don't think I haven't lamented to Betty that we had to be away from the scene this fall. The Movement is really jumping. I hope you aren't so blind that you can't see that. You are very fortunate to be living in this time in that place . . . [. . .] Now I must close.

Jim

That winter, the weather was said to be the worst in Ireland in sixty years. Drafty, high ceilinged, and absent "a little thing called central heating," Ard na Fairrge possessed a deadly chill such as Jim and Betty (and the children) had never experienced.

Ard na Fairrge
Mount Salus
Dalkey, County Dublin
[early January] 1958

Dear Fred and Romy,

We were so glad to hear from you, and I know I thought many times of your living room during the Christmastime, of the trees I'd seen there and the one you probably had. It will be a sad day for you, if it ever comes, when you have to do with a commercial tree. [. . .]

This is a Saturday afternoon with a gale blowing, the sea looking like a picture in an old book of photographs, rough, grey, the only things missing a destroyer or two and a U-boat. [. . .] Betty has taken the last week pretty hard, the cold, I mean. It has been down to 25, which is quite an ordeal here, worse than 25 below in Minnesota—for, you see, we are heating by fireplace and in rooms with 12-foot ceilings (the one in the front hallway is as high as the house). Fortunately for all concerned, I don't have to get up as early as the others in the morning, when it's chilliest. [. . .]

Yes, Fred, do write and tell us of "a suitable house"—you know there isn't one. We do miss you all, as I keep saying, have raised you all to your proper heroic proportions as dear friends and gentle people in our imaginations, but there are differences between us, after all, the biggest one being that we are out and you are in—I won't go into the matter of which is better: there are disadvantages on both sides. But we are out in the picturesque cold. We don't know what we'll do. Best to you both, and please write.

Jim

JOE AND JODY O'CONNELL

Ard na Fairrge
Mount Salus
Dalkey, County Dublin
January 4, 1958

Dear Joe and Jody,

I must have a clock in my head like the Great Arcano, Master of Pace, for here it is Saturday night again and my thoughts turn toward you all, not that I haven't thought of you from time to time in the last week . . . I wasn't in the mood until tonight—and perhaps the mood is due to these little bottles of Mackeson's stout that I am consuming against the morrow, which is Sunday, always a tough day for me, even without a sermon—I haven't heard a sermon yet this time in Ireland, always drawing a curate, and they are, evidently, only trusted to read the announcements. Not a bad idea. It goes part of the way in the right direction. I don't get those attacks of Sunday Sickness that I used to get. Now you understand why, in my nonviolent fashion, I have always opposed the vernacular. I did listen to Macmillan, the prime minister, earlier this evening, and so, you might say, I've had it—and in English at that—for this week.

We are all pretty much as you would have found us last week, all but me in bed, the radio going, an Italian station, Radio Moscow having closed down. Listening to RM is like getting KUOM for me: obviously extremely decent people announcing, a note of concern in their voices, as if to say, you poor bastard, but we're for you, we're giving you this good high-class fare, not without stimulating lectures and news coverage and folk songs. I haven't listened to RM much this time but must try to remember where it comes in. I used to like to hear them bragging about their dam, when we were here the last time. I wonder whatever happened to that little old dam, the biggest little old best dam in the world. I suppose it's Sputnik now. [. . .]

Jim

DON AND MARY HUMPHREY

Ard na Fairrge
January 31, 1958

Dear Don and Mary,

[. . .] I do wish you could see something of the country; the furniture, silver, architecture, and what strikes me as the most impressive thing about Ireland: its stone walls, just everywhere you look, walls: man-hours that didn't go up in smoke or pass away somehow but are still here to be seen, marching into each other and off into the country endlessly. I have thought many times of building a wall, and perhaps I am peculiarly sensitive to what's involved; this vast achievement, much of it make-work in famine times, but a lot of it going right down into the sea and sound as if laid by God himself.

No word lately from any correspondent in the Movement. I would like to hear from someone of course, but I am not the mental case I was about it some weeks ago. Something died in me then. I look out at the cold, cold sea, and I realize it's going to be that way from now on, cold, cold, for old JF whether it's the sea or the land, Ireland or America. I had a bad accident last night. Half rising out of my easy chair to kill off a madrigal singer on the radio, I slipped somehow and came down on the side of the chair, the armrest (not well padded) injuring my ribs near my heart. Quite painful still, and I'm not as fast as I was at my tuning (the radio). But otherwise we are all more or less well—and you might say I was wounded in action. How about cutting loose with another letter, Mary? We enjoyed your last very much—and that goes for one and all in the Movement. How about a group picture?

    Jim

Journal, February 13, 1958

Reading J. B. Morton's *Belloc* and enjoying it. Must remember it when I begin next—family life—novel. For the high spirits—spirits, song, walks, people, conversation—which remind me how it was supposed to be when we got married . . . Hynes, if he ever really had this idea, confused it with the 4-H Club. But it needs handling in a book—and I think *Flesh* is the place for it. It will give the beginning—as a flashback—the foundation for contrast—that the book needs. And I want to do it. It gives me pleasure— sad pleasure—to think of it—this style we didn't keep up and even forgot—at least I did until I read the book last night. My theory is that marriage kills it or it becomes something else*—that Belloc made it work because he had no wife later. That may be the secret of George's success, too—at *this*.

* the Trapp family without music, or the awfulnesses we have in the Movement: ice cream and Coke and noise and children at four in the afternoon. The Baptism Party.

= Abigail considered it "immature" of us to go off to Madeline Island without our wives.

= Jackie Gleason apparently is indulging this feeling in his private life. Open house, his friends around him, plenty to eat and drink. What *is* it?

= Dick Keefe fell farthest, I sometimes think, *away* from this—whatever it is.

= I have despaired of it myself. But my standards have risen—am not so easily entertained now.

= Don H. is always ready for it. But cannot instigate anything.

= I can—but I want the real thing. Not Hynes in his county agent role.

= Fred Petters is good but compromised by his life—at least he thinks he is.

= Joe O'Connell, yes.

21

The office is in Dublin, on Westland Row

February 26, 1958—July 23, 1958

Jane (Boz and Hugh in background), Greystones beach

Jim rented an office in Dublin, which improved his spirits, although not his ability to write much aside from letters. He spent his time away from home reading newspapers, studying racing forms, fixing up his office, wandering around Dublin, attending estate auctions, and ministering to his purchases: rubbing unguents into leather-bound books and cases, gluing furniture, and pursuing woodworm with a hypodermic needle primed with poison.

HARVEY EGAN

Ard na Fairrge
Mount Salus
Dalkey, County Dublin
February 26, 1958

Dear Fr Egan,

[. . .] I have put off replying to your last with the intention of writing my first letter from my new office to you, as I did last year about this time from my office in St Cloud. I have been in possession of the office since the 22nd of the month, but not established there because I haven't been able to find the furniture. I sat through a whole auction unable to buy anything I wanted last Thursday. Today, however, I got the writing table—actually a dressing table—and a rug. I still lack a chair but hope to find one tomorrow in Dublin. I want a chair that I can rest in as well as work in: you might say that's the story of my life as a writer. Tonight I attended a night auction in Dun Laoghaire and got no chair but something I wanted without seeing its purpose clearly. A writing box, so called; brass bound, about the size of an overnight bag, wood, with a desk-like surface in it that unfolds; thirty shillings; and engraved on a brass plate on the outside: "Major Talbot." I have discovered that I take inordinate pleasure in auctions, even when I can't afford to participate actively. I like to look at this old furniture; nothing, I think, shows better how far we've sunk in the last two or three hundred years.

The office is in Dublin, on Westland Row, a few doors from where Oscar Wilde was born in 1854, a business district now, near the railroad station that serves the line that runs through Dalkey. I am on the top floor, back, with one window looking out in the direction of Trinity College; the top floor being the fourth and quite a climb. The previous tenant, a manufacturer's agent by the name of MacEgan, has a partner by the name of Egan, and they have moved down to the ground floor (just too much for them, the climb with their sample cases). The rent: £5 a month. This is about a third less than the going rate, and I am there with the understanding that I vacate if a proper tenant is found. I think this unlikely, with times so hard here. It's aesthetically the Dublin equivalent of my St Cloud hole. I have done practically nothing since coming to Ireland. The chips will be down from now on—or else.

We met Padraic Colum at Sean O'Faolain's house last Sunday night; a nice old gentleman. He (with his late wife) has a book coming out this spring, from Doubleday: *Our Friend James Joyce*. He said that Doubleday had wanted him to change the title because some of the salesmen thought it was likely to be confusing to booksellers—too close to *My Friend Flicka*. He didn't tell this as a joke. He is not changing the title, though. "A very popular book," he said, referring to *Flicka*, "about a dog, I believe." "A horse," I said, not having read it and still overwhelmed by the suggestion that he change the title for that reason. "A pony," Sean said. One card, Father?

Since I last wrote, our Abp[1] has been in the news. He nixed the votive Mass to open the Spring Festival (An Tostal, in Irish) because of two plays, one based on *Ulysses*, the other a new one by Sean O'Casey; Beckett, the dramatist famous for *Waiting for Godot*, then withdrew his contributions to the festival; and finally the whole thing—the drama part—was canceled. Plenty of people wrote to *The Irish Times*, including Kate O'Brien and Colum, but apparently the shooting is over; the odor lingers but is nothing new, I guess. The Abp, in theory, is in the clear. The trouble all began when some pious trade unionists petitioned for the Mass. The moral: never ask if you can't take no for an answer.

I was glad to hear that you liked the last story in *The New Yorker*.

I can't recall whether I made it clear that we have had the shakes about remaining in Ireland. [. . .] And—the payoff—we are going to have

---

1 John Charles McQuaid.

another baby in July. [. . .] How does it look from there? Bad, I suppose, but could be worse—and perhaps will be. I still have my aim, however. All I have to do is run the table. Rack 'em up.

Jim

HARVEY EGAN

29 Westland Row
Dublin
March 4, 1958

Dear Fr Egan,

Your letter came yesterday, having passed mine in the mails, and we were both very sorry to hear of your attack. It must have been very painful, and I do hope it won't color your outlook on suffering—which I personally do very badly but which, through associating with you, I have developed quite a good feeling for—in others. Let's just hope nothing ever happens to me, now that I've had my appendix out and my teeth fixed again. Anyway, I take it you're much improved and equipped now with good and holy reasons to enjoy yourself (this is a reference to the ban on milk) like a proper St Paul Diocese man. Better put that bag of beer I left in the front parlor in the fridge.

Well, I was an hour late coming down to the office today, having gone to Greystones with Boz for a haircut. It being about noon, I had some tea and buns nearby and then climbed up to it. Very pleasant here. Yesterday I patched the mahogany table my typewriter rests on, arranged the lamp with its pink shade (it hangs down directly over the typewriter, the best lighting I have had), and polished the copper of my electric fire. The little rug is down, with newspapers under it for padding, and the chair is a wonderful buy at 35 bob: a Victorian mahogany tufted one, with dark red leatherette cover, ripped in a few places. My back is to the one window, five feet off the floor and running up to the ceiling, which is only a little over seven feet, and so I have the best daylight too. I can hear the rumble of traffic from Westland Row (to the front of the building; I am to the back) and Nassau Street to the rear and sometimes pigeons nearby and sometimes gulls in the distance. I am at the head of the stair, and so there's no traffic at all outside my door; not much on the floors below, occupied by solicitors, engineering consultants, etc.

We get very little mail these days from the Movement (our colleagues in the St Cloud Diocese) and often wonder, if and when we return, how we'll stand it. You can have little idea of our dilemma—as to where we want to spend eternity on earth, the future, that is. What we couldn't do last fall—find a place to live—we won't be able to do next winter any better. I personally dislike this stretch of life ahead of me: the father of numerous children; the husband of a woman with no talent for mother-hood (once she's conceived); and with the prospect of making no more money than in the past. I see another office, spending more and more time in it and away from home, darting to the rescue at home, spanking this child, playing with that one, and finally gumshoeing the girls through their teens, tottering down the aisle with them when they marry and try-ing not to think about their husbands, who, I daresay, good for nothing else, won't even make money. Don will drop off, or live forever, and we'll all be on special diets. So what do I know for sure? Only that I'll have my art, and so I should pay more attention to it. Do not set a place for me at the church supper. Do not expect to see me running with the others in the stretch simply because I started with them at the beginning. I am looking for another course.

I bought my first ticket on the Grand National sweepstakes. First prize is £50,000. I wasn't able to tell Betty what I'd do with the money if I won.* That shows the state of my mind.

Saw the Earl of Wicklow crossing Westland Row to St Andrew's Church Saturday, but he didn't see me. He is one of Fr D'Arcy's converts, and we once had dinner together. When are *we* going to take a meal?

Jim

* Maybe I could bring myself to pay you what I owe, in that event.

JOE AND JODY O'CONNELL

Ard na Fairrge
Mount Salus
Dalkey, County Dublin
March 19, 1958

Dear Joe and Jody,

Very glad to have your letter yesterday: we had definitely given up on the Movement. For some time, in the past, I'd say to Betty, what do you suppose it means? Did it ever occur to you that we may not be liked at all by people? And Betty would say, Oh, that's true, of course, but I think they think they're busy. It isn't so easy for people to sit down and write, you know. But that was a long time ago. For some weeks, the Movement went unmentioned except for an occasional "Damn the Movement!" when the mail arrived, or didn't. We have been considering the idea of returning with a flinty eye—wondering if there could be anything worse than returning with no prospects of a home, billeting ourselves on Betty's relatives, probably having to split up our family because of its unmanageable size, and so on. There is only one thing to be said for returning, and that, of course, is the presence of people like yourselves—but we, in the circumstances I suggest, wouldn't be able to appreciate you, I think, and vice versa. The last time, we were almost a year finding a place to live, and we are even harder now to accommodate, to say nothing of the aesthetic side. We wouldn't care to live in the country. We have had our fill of pioneering—too damn much of it right now, here, in fact. Heaven for me would be never having to enter a hardware store again—and still I am fascinated by hardware. Well, anyway, whatever we do, you can be sure it will be done after much consideration.

Betty is already taking precautions against liking this house and situation when warmer weather comes, drumming it into herself, and me, that six months of the year in a freezing mausoleum just isn't it. She speaks of trying to find a warmer house. I have declared myself not a participant in this game. I have my office in Dublin now and must really bear down if we are to have money to do whatever it is we will do in the end. Except for a few days when I was still looking for furniture—a chair, a table—the weather has made it impossible to work in the office. Today I am staying home because I can hardly move: a recurrence of trouble with my back. Betty is in Dublin for an auction, where she hopes to pick up a chair that she can sit in comfortably during the rest of her pregnancy. *That*, as you might guess, was the last straw. So I thought until I found myself unable to turn over in bed—with visions of myself being lifted into an airplane and ever after being a blanketed invalid, but perhaps getting more work done.

I have a hot-water bottle strapped to my back and now must remove it for refilling. Thus I leave you for the time being.

March 21. Nothing to add to the above, I'm afraid. I go on suffering, spared only the gibes of those who can't see me as I am now, a bent figure tottering from bed to chair to radio. I enclose some clippings for you, Joe, and also Don—say, whatever happened to those people anyway? There were two of them—Mary and Don, I think they were called. Best to you.
      Jim

March 26, 1958

Dear Don and Mary,

I really shouldn't be writing to two such . . . as yourselves, but then I was ever one for returning good for evil. I am sitting here in my office—or "studio," as it's called in my lease—at 29 Westland Row, Dublin, thinking of you. I've just about got this place arranged so that I feel comfortable here: floor stained, rug down, table amputated so that I can type while sitting in my easy chair, a light suspended over the typewriter, pink shade, which brings out the lights in the mahogany table, and pipe cleaner drying on the shade: JF at his ease. I have a glass of porter in my stomach, having decided that it is better than having tea and rolls for lunch. I have an electric fire playing on my feet, for it's still chilly here (of late I've been sitting here with my coat and gloves on). There is a fireplace, but I am four flights up and would have to hire somebody to tend the fire and ashes, and I am trying to cut expenses. Oh, yes, I am smoking a new pipe—a bargain, or I never would've bought it. Before settling down here for the day, I "viewed" some articles which will come up for auction tomorrow at noon. A lovely set of demitasse cups and saucers; a card table with drawers for each player, also a place for his glass—but I can't quite see the use of these things for me. Still . . . [. . .]

—Now, I must leave you. What, if anything, can I send you? [. . .]

Jim

29 Westland Row
Dublin
Good Friday [April 4], 1958

Dear Fr Egan,

[. . .] Let me thank you for your kind invitation to return to America. I can't remember reading of anybody like myself (the Lord knows what Betty really wants; nothing for certain, I'd say) in this dilemma of where to spend my future. Today, for instance, the maid didn't show up at home, finally called and said she was too weak to rise, then said she'd tried three times before she found our number in the book (which isn't in the book yet), and so on, until Betty, not knowing whether she was really sick or not, said she should stay home. The last time it snowed (yes, it's snowing here today), the maid didn't appear for two days, not a word from her, and then one morning there she was. So that's the domestic scene. Fortunately, the girls are home all during April (vacation) and can help some.

So I get on the train at the usual time, around ten, and come down here, turn on the electric fire, and go out for a walk in the snow, or sleet, or whatever it is, waiting for the room to warm up. It's a bitter day in Dublin, most of the shops closed, a few men standing by excavations in the pavement, the postmen making their rounds, and small boys wheeling turf home in the family pram; the very poor are allowed so much free; and a baker's horse and cart going by: "Kennedy's Machine Made Bread," to show you how up-to-date we are. The pubs are closed. [. . .]

Still, as I was about to say on the other side of this page, I am pleased in many ways with these surroundings, seeing more of Dublin this trip, being able to walk out to secondhand bookstores and attend furniture auctions whenever the desire is on me to do so, or just to walk around looking at the 18th century. I do not consider myself terribly sensitive to my surroundings, but perhaps the most painful thing for me about America, about Minnesota anyway, is having to look at what I see around me, from wooden shack to concrete supermarket in 100 years, with very little in between, hardly anything in St Cloud. You could say that the automobiles here, in general, are easier to look at; people keep them forever; and those that aren't mere bugs, the economy models, are more or less appealing: I particularly like the ones with headlights as big as washtubs, the old Jaguars, Bentleys, and Daimlers. But of course all of this is by the way—not fundamental like my work to interest and survival—but then so much of life is by the way, don't you think?

I am way behind schedule in the novel. I should be nearing Grand Forks, but I am just leaving Cut Bank, Montana. Sometimes the train doesn't seem to be moving at all, and sometimes it appears that the engineer has got out of the cab and is fishing off a bridge with no thought of the job he's supposed to be doing. [. . .]

So much for that and me. [. . .]

Jim

Betty's Journal, April 11, 1958
Jim's first work in Ireland done today, 6 months & one day after our arrival, followed by his picking up "low ladie's chair" from auction.

April 15, 1958

Dear Michael,

Your letter rec'd, and the weekend of May 10 is fine—or any weekend, for that matter. Our only problem is how to entertain you in the custom of the country, for we just sit around and brood and hardly utter a brilliant word. But we would like to see you and hope you'll come. Just let me know when, exactly, and I'll try to meet you at the airport.

No, I'm not interested in teaching at Salzburg or anywhere else. And if I were, what would I teach? I gather education, in Europe, hasn't crumbled to the point where I could step in.

I have nothing to say about your marriage, if any, only hope she has money.

I am writing this from my office on Westland Row, where I have been freezing until lately. It is a lot like my office in St Cloud (in that I don't know who else would have it) but quieter.

Too bad you aren't here now, or sometime in the next ten days, for Edwin O'Connor, author of *The Last Hurrah*, is in town, and you could interview him. He has some good stories about Boston. One: Abp Cushing is showing ex–Lord Mayor Briscoe through a seminary and throws open a door to an auditorium where the seminarians are all assembled. "There they are," he says, "five hundred of the best anti-Semites you ever saw." Asked later what Briscoe said, the Abp said, "He took it very well."

Write, giving time of arrival. Until then, all best.

Jim

DON AND MARY HUMPHREY

April 29, 1958

Dear Don and Mary,

We were so glad to hear from you, and the fact that there has been a slight time lag since then doesn't mean a thing—except that we think it better that some of the delay be on our side. You would gladden our lives, however, if you replied at once. I don't have your letter at the office—where things are humming as usual—but I do remember that you, Mary, were busy with your sewing and that Don was busy with his haw-hawing. [. . .]

Very odd that you haven't had the pleasure of [the Hyneses'] company. I fear, too, that with the approaching warm weather they may seek to make amends by throwing one of their famous picnics in a public park. And what of the Doyle? He hasn't written to us, I think, in all the time we've been at our present address. Something I said, I suppose, without having a clue as to what. We spend less time than we did in imagining what you are all doing. This was a regular part of our life until recently. "Are they at Hyneses' tonight," I'd say to Betty. Or "I think Fred called, and they're going over there tonight. Don had to stop for cigarettes." Or "Hyneses came by, but Don wasn't there, and Mary had retired." We just don't get enough information to engage our imaginations these days.

Last year, about this time, it became clear that we were going to have to move, and I saw that the two, possibly three, years of economic security were not to be. And now, again, I am facing up to the same situation—the necessity to make some big money. It doesn't seem to be in the cards that we'll ever enjoy the small fruits of our labors. This, I'd say if it were happening to anyone else, and they were able to survive each crisis, as we've been able to do so far, would be a good thing, a device to prevent one from getting into a rut. But this too can be a rut. I think now I'd have been wise to stay on somehow in St Cloud and finish my novel in the office there—there would've been no change there. I have wasted months getting set up again, physically and mentally, and now that I have, I see it's not to be for very long, that it's starting up all over again. And this time, there isn't the objective there was, the feeling that if we could just get to Ireland, everything would be all right. The feeling now is that everything will not be all right, whatever we do, that hardly anything will be all right. Not a good spirit in which to advance toward the future.

[. . .]

Jim

HARVEY EGAN

Dublin
May 13, 1958

Dear Fr Egan,

Your letter came this morning, and glad to have same, to know that you'll welcome us back. At the moment, I have no very good prospects of making it back: cold in my nose, cold in my office, and so on.

KA is being confirmed by the Abp of Dublin today and expects a question: "I'm in the front row, and he asks those in the front row, and if they know the answers, he doesn't ask the others." I did *not* tell her to counter with a question: "Why don't you and O'Casey bury the hatchet?"[1]

The keys are cold to my touch this morning: it will not be a good day. I must go over to an auction and try to land a couple of elephant tusks. I got two the other day (supporting a dinner gong) and would like to get these today, which are unmounted, rough, as extracted. I plan to send the ivory to Don, who except for an occasional cue ball, is unable to procure the stuff for his work, mostly nodes on chalices.

[. . .]

Jim

Betty's aunt, Birdie, and her husband, Al Strobel, made a trip to Ireland. They came as part of a guided tour, which they left for a few days to visit the Powers family and see the new baby.

BIRDIE AND AL STROBEL

29 Westland Row
Dublin
May 31, 1958

Dear Birdie and Al,

[. . .] You are better off at the Shelbourne than at the Gresham (which caters mostly to Americans and is on O'Connell Street, which has always struck me as being like Broadway, full of little junky shops). There is a whole book about the Shelbourne, by Elizabeth Bowen. We wonder if it'll be possible to catch sight of you during those first days while you're still attached to the tour. I thought I might watch for you in the Shelbourne lobby—I wouldn't actually approach you—so I could at least tell Betty and the children how you were looking. Naturally, I would disguise myself. Anyway, we're all happy that you're coming, and looking forward to it. Don't worry about us putting ourselves out for you. It hadn't occurred to us to do so. You'll find plenty of work to do, inside, and Al can work around the yard. You can think of the time with us as a resting-up period for your ensuing travels. Well, I think that's all, and more, and so I'll close.

Jim

1 See Jim to Egan, February 26, 1958.

Ard na Fairrge
June 19, 1958

Dear Fred and Romy,

[. . .] It is seven in the evening. In the next few minutes, Betty will finish reading a book to the boys, and I'll go up to the bathroom and shove
them around for a while. No, Betty hasn't had the baby yet. No, not yet.
Wait a minute, I'll look again. No, not yet. When she does, we'll let someone know in the Movement. I won't develop this subject further. Except to
say that we're appalled by the prospect. Last year at this time I *thought* I
had trouble. I now think of last year as the English Channel and the year
ahead as the Atlantic Ocean. I know, you don't swim *that*; but that is
what I mean.

We are at home every evening, listening to the radio, reading. I smoke
while reading and Betty drinks. That's about it here. [. . .]

Jim

HARVEY EGAN

June 24, 1958

Dear Fr Egan,

It's in the early a.m., and somebody's charging batteries, and I can't
play my Telefunken, usually my solace when Betty and the children are in
bed. We were glad to hear you have a new typewriter—and to see that you
have—and I must say it's about time. You had the one before this about six
months, didn't you? I suppose it means something: some people wash their
hands and some change mates and some change typewriters. Me, well,
why go on? [. . .]

Somebody at *America* sent me that issue with the *Prince* review in it,
and so I saw the Waugh piece: too bad, why *America* can't do better, I
don't know; the ghetto mentality, as we in liberal circles used to say. Life
here much the same. Betty still with child, but the end shouldn't be far away.
Girls go swimming two or three times a week, as part of physical education, in the sea. They have tennis racquets too. Boz and Hugh go about their
business, building, farming, trains, shipping (we see boats of all kinds in
the sea below us), and I've just come from making Hugh's bed, which he had
stripped down to the springs, only to drop off, and then to wake up, mad
at the dirty trick he'd played on himself. Which reminds me that I must
teach the children short-sheeting, to round off the evening chaos. [. . .]

JFP Ltd is pretty quiet except in Germany, where, since coming to Ireland, I have had three little books published; the publisher is breaking up my two books and administering them in the form of spitballs. Well, I go down to the office six days a week, sit down, and prowl about Duesterhaus. For the last month I've been redoing the rec room—and can't seem to get the job done. Maybe tomorrow the ice will break (these metaphors I use are an author's stock-in-trade). A man tried to break in on me today, an agent with a client presumably interested in renting space in the building. Since the agent didn't seem to know I was there, but since I definitely was, I acted the part of the genuine tenant, a little outraged at this invasion of privacy. I have a deal with the owner of the building (£15 a quarter) for this hole I inhabit but would have to move out if he succeeded in interesting a regular tenant in my space; I have bet against this eventuality, in effect. In view of the luck I've been having, however, I suppose I shouldn't be surprised if asked to vacate. [. . .] All for now.

Jim

Betty gave birth to Jane Elizabeth Powers on July 2, 1958, at the Leinster Nursing Home in Dublin. Betty's journal, July 2, 1958: "8¼-pound daughter at 2:30 a.m. The news penetrates to me at one point and oh the relief of it. No pregnancy had felt so tedious, so completely unjust. But she is American, I'm sure now. The last product of the red house and my distress at leaving it."

ART AND MONA WAHL

Friday morning [July 4, 1958]

Dear Art and Nana,

[. . .] The baby, by the way, looks very healthy and less gnomelike than I remember the other children looking at this stage. We don't have a name, since it's a girl. I had wanted it, if it were a boy, to be Hjalmar. Now I must close, get this to Betty, and get back here to my office. I enjoyed your letter, Nana—the vision of you dashing off to coffees. I think of these last days for Bertie in St Cloud and am glad to be elsewhere; the pace must be terrific. I see Art and Al, like mechanics in the pits, changing wheels in a matter of seconds, while you and Bertie wait impatient to be off to the next coffee, and then the next, and so on. I see you as wearing crash helmets. I shouldn't bother you with these visions, I know. Incidentally, the boys and girls at home are doing very well under Mrs Kinsella's supervision. She has a real talent with children. All for now.

Jim

Betty's Journal, July 4, 1958

Five, five, five. How did it come about? I keep repeating Fr Egan—they are, in the end, the only thing that will have mattered. I believe it; I feel it. And yet they defy peace and order and what of art—of Jim's if not mine? Are we to make him into just another man who will die, his body rot, his possessions be dispersed, and his immortality all in heaven? God *does* intend there to be man-made beauty on earth. We are to make order of it all. Order and art.

MICHAEL MILLGATE

Baile Atha Cliath
July 5, 1958

Dear Michael,

First of all, excuse the envelope, but the J. F. Powers Corporation, Westland Row Division, is short of stationery at the moment. I write to tell you that Betty has produced a female child, weight eight and a quarter lbs, date July 2, and that we haven't decided on a name yet but lean toward Radio Train, as combining the best in both the Irish and American traditions.

Anyway, these have been hectic days, especially for me, traveling back and forth in the middle of the night, supervising our help at home (which has been supplemented by, of all things, a competent woman). Everyone well at home, including Jacobite Echo, the cairn terrier who belongs to the woman who is helping out. [. . .]

I saw Prof. Stanford twice clipping tall grass and said hello. Otherwise there hasn't been much of that famous brilliant conversation for which we are noted over here.

I wonder how you and Amis got along. All for now, and if you cross over, give my regards to Broadway.

Jim

29 Westland Row
July 17, 1958

Dear Don and Mary,

[. . .] We had a baptism party Sunday, lots of talk about "little Christians" and the traditional falling down and wetting of pants by children. I wish you could have been here. Speaking of all that, I see where the Hyneses are now able to tell parents how to sanctify vacation time for their children. My impressions are only impressions, of course, but it does seem to me that they are getting out of hand. Going a bit too far, if you know what I mean. I happened to see a brochure advertising a new publication by the Abbey Press in which this is presumably to be published, this sanctifying of vacation time. I also saw a picture of Betty's brother and of Jack Dwyer—what happened to his tie? I assume he's adapting to his environment. I see my compatriots without ties in the streets here, but most of them do wear a camera. All for now.

Jim

HARVEY EGAN

Dublin
July 23, 1958

Dear Fr Egan,

I was walking around in my office thinking my thoughts with a bottle of Pilsner Urquell ("The Only Genuine Pilsner"), product of Plzen, and a damn bad beer it is, inside me, when I looked up and there, staring downstage, from his place on the wall, was Fr Ed Ramacher[1] (in earphones) cranking a television camera, and I thought it might be well if I gave you a little description of my office.

There is one door, formerly black with fingerprints, now clean, and it opens in, and on the inside is one hook, on which hangs my Dunloe "Fills the Gap" raincoat. The floor is wide boards now stained mahogany, by me, because I decided against buying Egan's linoleum and that left only part of the floor stained. There is a small fireplace, but it isn't used except for debris: bottle caps, matchboxes, "The Friendly Match," and tobacco cartons. I have an electric fire with a copper reflector. The fireplace is to

---

1 Father Edward Ramacher (1917–2007), a tireless booster and promoter who mounted any number of celebrations and shows in partnership with the business community in the Diocese of St. Cloud.

my right, the one window to my back, which looks out, west, upon Trinity College and something called "Dental Hospital," on the sidewalk in front of which I have on occasion seen the blood of patients who didn't eat enough unbleached wheat. The window is the dormer, or starving artist's, type; all the roofs visible from it are slate.

I have this old sawed-off washstand for a desk—a really beautiful old finish, like a chestnut horse—and a Victorian tufted chair upholstered in one of the first imitations of leather and on the floor what appears to be an Oriental rug but is really only a bit of dyed burlap; this is under me and desk only. On the floor to my right are a number of empty bottles, witnesses to my cosmopolitan taste: Guinness, Mackeson's, Younger's, Ringnes's. To my left are some old books and priceless manuscript pages (my own) to be used to start fires at home. On the wall I look at, straight ahead, a calendar and Fr Ed; to my right Fr Pinky Doherty smiling at some laypeople of both sexes; to my left Fr Urban pointing a pencil at a photograph of a new building—this is really a man named Dexter M. Keezer, president of McGraw-Hill publishing company, but I cut him out of *This Week* last year, put collar on him, and he is Fr Urban. He keeps looking over at me. Yes, so I'd better leave you now and get back to Duesterhaus. Thanks for your kind offer in your last; I hope I won't come to that.

Jim

22

About Don, I haven't been the same since I read your letter

July 26, 1958—November 29, 1958

Don Humphrey (1912–1958)

Dick Palmquist wrote to say that Don Humphrey had been diagnosed with a tumor in his head.

DICK PALMQUIST

Dublin

July 26, 1958

Dear Dick,

[. . .] About Don, I haven't been the same since I read your letter, and know I never shall be, now. I do hope you are right in thinking he has a good chance. I don't know a thing about such cases—I don't even know what kind of case Don's is, beyond that he has a tumor—but I am praying he comes out of it all right. I am sick with this news, for which I nevertheless thank you. I wish you'd keep me informed, since I can't count on anyone else to do it, the way people are there about writing. Now that you've written once, perhaps you can go on doing it. I am tempted to call Mary long-distance, but I fear the consequences: fear it will not be the right time.

Until this morning, I didn't really know what I intended to do with myself and family, whether we'd return to St Cloud or not. Now I know that if Don pulls through all right, that is what we'll do. I guess I had thought of him as my best friend but had never realized until this morning how very much he means. I suppose you feel the same way these days, and many other people, to say nothing of his family. I will not pretend that I am hopeful. You can see anyway that I am not. This year has been a bad one. I pray God will redeem it by restoring Don to us and that I for one will get a chance to appreciate him again.

All for now. I know there's no need for this letter, for this kind of letter, but I am like a man buried in a mine, tapping, going through the motions of hoping—I *am* hoping.

Jim

This, if it is the end, would go too well with Don's poor, poor life. This is a tragic life. I pray it is not the end and that he recovers and that we both live as friends again. St Cloud without Don would have very little to offer me. I am already feeling what Don's death would mean. Such a life, though, figures to end in such a way.

JOE AND JODY O'CONNELL

August 1, 1958

Dear Joe and Jody,

Very grateful to you for writing so often these last few days, for there is nothing else on my mind but Don. We have been hoping that all this will come to nothing, and though your latest seems to be a step in this direction—I mean I regard it as hopeful that the doctors can discover nothing wrong—I don't feel much relieved. Too many people, in the last few months, have commented on Don's appearance. [. . .] How I wish I could go in with you on Tuesday. The picture of him enjoying himself with good food three times a day and visitors like Fr Egan, George, and Bp Cowley, well, that gives me great pleasure. If you should get this letter before you go to Mpls, please tell Don that I say, "Stop it. You're hoggin' the stage. First with your great reconversion and now this. Give someone else a chance." [. . .]

You ask how Ireland is. Well, there was our new baby, then a visit from the Strobels (during which time I rented a car and drove them around some, *not* my idea of fun), and then came the news about Don. So I go to my office six days of the week, and some days I sit here and brood, hardly turning a hand, and some days I go out to an auction. [. . .]

We are not definitely committed to returning, but I think that is what will happen if, as I say, I can produce the wherewithal. If I should fail, I suppose we might have to stay on here—and neither of us is at all certain we'd be worse off doing so. We do have a house here, although it's a freezing proposition in the winter, and I do have a life of sorts in Dublin, wandering about, plenty of newspapers, bookstores, auction sales, and, though I haven't felt easy enough in my mind of late to visit these, theatres and racecourses.

What I mean, Joe, is that it's more satisfying than dropping in at the bus station in St Cloud to see if they've changed the racks. When I think that Don may not be there anymore, the place gets really hard to take.

There are a few others—Fred Petters, Dick Palmquist—but they have other sources of pleasure than friends.* And there are you country people, but you all—you as long as you work—have ways and means of scotching discontent that either never worked for me or no longer do. These old eyes, though they are not the eyes of a painter or sculptor, have to be fed too. I think that's the hardest thing, the thing that's always hurting me in Stearns County whether I'm conscious of it or not: just having to look at the mess, the landscape, the offenses against architecture (which is a rather grand way of putting it, like accusing dogs of adultery). Ah, well. You know what I mean. Eyestrain, however, is a very great factor, as I define the term here.

All for now. Please keep writing. Best to you both.

Jim

* Like me.

KATHERINE ANNE PORTER

Ard na Fairrge
Mount Salus
Dalkey, County Dublin
August 21, 1958

Dear Katherine Anne,

[. . .] It is odd—to me—how as one grows older, memoirs become such an interesting form of writing. When I was young, working in bookstores, I could never understand why they were published at all. The British are great for memoirs, and I must say I never miss reading the reviews of them, of books by people I've never heard of usually. Harold Nicolson's *Some People* you probably know; fictitious memoirs, a way of getting at people and life that we Americans don't seem to have tried at all, as a form of fiction, I mean. Perhaps we don't see enough memoirs to play upon the idea. [. . .]

A few facts. Betty had a baby girl on July 2. We call her Jane, for reasons almost entirely euphonious. She is healthy. We plan to return to the U.S.—to what, we don't know—in November or December. I am in the act of earning our passage back these days—which is precisely where I was last year at this time. It is either that or look for another house here—one we can be warm in when winter comes, a full-time job and probably an impossibility anyway. The children are much better off in school here, I enjoy—as, say, a clam would—Dublin, but there are other considerations. Unfortunately, they do not outweigh the considerations for staying on, nor do those outweigh these for not staying. They balance out perfectly. We will not realize our mistake until we make it, and this, I fear, will continue as long as we live. We won't be in the least surprised either, each time it happens. We have not here a lasting home, is the text, but there isn't much satisfaction in that, is there?

Jim

JOE AND JODY O'CONNELL

August 23, 1958
Dublin

Dear Jody and Joe,

Your last came this morning before I left for the office, where I am now, and we are both very glad to hear that Don is holding on. We did hear from Em, a good letter but rather disturbing too in its description of the New Don (as he was before the stroke), which I guess is what you were saying too, only Em, of course, is well pleased with the results of so much tribulation. That is how I should be too if I thought I were going to die, I know. If Don does recover, though, I think we can count on a certain amount of backsliding—welcome relief, you might say. I would not care if he stopped a long way short of his Sputnik period (which I only heard about) but would not want him an Ade Bethune woodcut either, one-dimensional, illustrating some one virtue.

We also heard from Fr G., who expressed more confidence in Don's recovery than others have. He seems to be suffering from camp followers at the hospital—"all those people."

I have heard twice from Leonard, believe it or not, and mean to write him a suitable reply as soon as possible. He feels we have failed him and ourselves by not making a go of our venture in Ireland, and he may be right. I do not like to think of it as a mistake, but that is the word for it. It is also the word for whatever else we might have done at the time we did this. It is the word for coming back again. That is what I am doing to accept the idea that, so far as domestic arrangements are concerned, we cannot bring the fact into accord with the desire. There is too much against us, but still I do not intend to throw in the sponge. I may be seen emptying diapers, but I may be seen too at auctions looking for something to fill up one of the numerous gaps in my life, in the decor of the house I don't have. [. . .]

Leopardstown races today—Saturday—but I won't be there. October, I think. In October, maybe I'll feel more like it, I think. I am suffering from dry rot. I saw a fellow out the train window this morning whom I'd met at Sean O'Faolain's last winter—a novelist named Mervyn Wall whom I really liked—and he was getting on the train I was on, but I couldn't summon up the feeling to go and sit with him. I suppose for the same reason that I seldom have a drink at home: I don't want to set the stage, strike up the band, for nothing.

Now, when I was younger . . . I was blinder.

No, we didn't see Bucky[1] or his dome. It was on radio—Bucky chatting. He doesn't speak English—runs his words together like John Foster Dulles and pretty much sounds like a Consumers Union report: "snowload," etc. I'd say he comes halfway between F. L. Wright and the tool section in Sears's basement (before it burned)—*achievementwise*, to use what may well be one of his words.

Jim

LEONARD AND BETTY DOYLE

August 23, 1958

Dear Doyles,

I was raking through the debris here on the desk in the study, looking for a piece of paper so I could write to you, and what should I find but this letter already begun by another hand. Let me say, in passing, so that you'll better comprehend the foregoing sentence, that this desk is used almost exclusively by the woman of the house, a published arthur in her own right, my candidate for the Christian Mother of the Year, among other things. She is now slumbering overhead, among her troops, and I am listening to the BBC—the Light Programme, getting this week's top twenty. In this way, I keep faith with you all out there. To your letter then, Leon. (Why, I asked myself a moment ago, does no one call Leonard Leon?) [. . .]

Sometimes I think I ought to get together another collection of phonograph records and keep adding to them; same with books; same with everything, and keep busy that way. Takes money, though. Sometimes I think I should start collecting money, keep adding to it, keep busy that way—and in that way broaden my circle of friends, people of kindred interests. Perhaps you'd care to join me in this. [. . .]

1 Buckminster Fuller.

The home life is such that one often doesn't care to venture out, one feels he might be picked up, for blinking, flinching involuntarily, as if he were an escapee from an asylum rather than a good Christian Family type suffering from FF (Family Fatigue), which, by the way, is not going to go away but get worse and worse. Some of those white rats just don't answer *any* bell, in the end I imagine. With my office in Dublin, I escape a lot of this; I have to if I am to make a living; but I get a good shaking up before I leave in the morning and the first thing when I come home. Much of this wouldn't be true for a lot of other people, but I am not a lot of other people,* unfortunately—or fortunately if I am to go on unlike a lot of other people, making it as a writer, that is. But what the hell, Leon. I've told you enough. And much, much more than is necessary, since in a way I'm talking about your life. It's true I don't have to play pals with a lot of people I buy things from—people I don't know don't call me "Jim" here—and Dublin, for all its dirt, is much easier on the eyes than any place I've seen in America. [. . .]

Jim

* Which also applies to Betty.

Don Humphrey died 5:30 a.m., August 26, 1958.

Betty's Journal, August 26, 1958

Don died today . . . I am struck by the wastefulness of nature—can understand sea creatures laying millions of eggs so that most can be lost, but an artist like Don at the beginning of his career doesn't seem expendable. I felt of him much as I feel of Jim, destined by providence to fulfill role of artist, Don as accessory to priesthood, Jim as divinely inspired gadfly. Providence has always intervened in our favor at last minute in material matters, felt Calvinistically that a sign of being chosen. But this shakes my confidence.

Dublin
August 30, 1958

Dear Dick,

[. . .] We learned of Don's death with such feelings as *you* do not have to imagine. This has been the worst thing to happen to me, so far, and I know it is worse for Mary and the family—and worst of all for Don, looking at his life from this world, where he did accomplish much but only a small fraction of what he might have, with his gifts. Needless to say, his reward here was even more out of proportion. If his death was due to chemicals used in plating chalices, then that is indeed the final irony. That is my opinion, and I leave it to the others (of whom I'm sure there are many) to speak of how happy he must be in heaven. That I don't doubt, but what happened here on earth was just too bad, and I for one will not forget it, and in this I know I am not alone.

All best wishes.

Jim

Don Humphrey was buried at Jacobs Prairie, fifteen miles from his home in St. Cloud. The reason for this inconvenience was that some years before he had carved the altar lectern and font for St. James, the church there. As sole payment he had been promised three grave sites in the cemetery. The new priest attempted to renege on the agreement, but the Humphrey family prevailed.

HARVEY EGAN

Dublin
September 5, 1958

Dear Fr Egan,

Your letter came this morning at breakfast (tea, toast, scrambled eggs, prunes), and then Betty, it being a sunny day, took the boys to Greystones for haircuts, a job I need myself but cannot free myself to get. From my work, that is. This story-chapter will either ring the bell as I have seldom rung it before, or—it won't. Anyway, I am working without a net, so to speak, and am grateful for your offer, as before. I wake up in the morning, and gradually remembering who I am and what lies before me and all around me, namely responsibilities, I start to moan. It is not that erratic, blowing noise that you used to do in Beardsley (picked up from Fr Nolan, you said), which by the way I do a certain amount of here in my office, but a low, steady moaning, such as a man with an arrow in his ass (back in history) might make. Do you ever have that? Yes? Well, then you know what I mean.

Thanks for your account of the funeral. I had one from L. Doyle, very good, but not, of course, from the sanctuary side, where life is somehow headier.

I was glad to read (in L. Doyle first) that you and George and Bp Cowley and Fr Casey were there. Jacobs Prairie, though, that was more iron in the soul, not that St Cloud would've been better; where Don died, what was done thereafter didn't matter, though it was a lot of work for friends and family. One would be better off going down at sea. Yes, I must do something about my will—though I find that word preposterous in my case.

All for now. They're playing my music ("The Daring Young Man"), and I must go. Coming! Coming! [. . .]

Jim

[. . .] Out to buy some Parmesan cheese for tonight's spaghetti and was almost run down on Duke Street by the Earl of Longford, who was coming down the sidewalk with his wife; they look like Hardy and Laurel; but that's one thing you don't see too much of around St Cloud, earls and countesses, it occurs to me. A fellow needs a bit of that, and once he gets a taste of it . . .

LEONARD DOYLE

29 Westland Row
Dublin
October 7, 1958

Dear Len,

[. . .] We read about Fr Peyton's crusade[1] in your diocese, thanks to your thoughtfulness in sending the news story, and though I don't take this particular aspect of our religion as hard as some people do, it did give us a jolt. The part that gets me is the sudden appearance of people you wouldn't have thought it of, in the lineup. There was quite a lot of that in

---

1 Father Patrick Peyton (1909–1992), who led the Family Rosary Crusade: "The family that prays together, stays together." (It later emerged that the crusade in Latin America was funded by the CIA.)

Nazi Germany, I believe. I am thinking of working up a prelate whose motto would be "I Love a Parade." How would you put that into Latin? I remember a discussion which took place at my house a few years ago, when two priests were discussing the work of Fr Peyton, not very enthusiastically. Finally, one said: "Do you suppose he's even a Christian?" Oh, I liked the storm troopers coming to your house to collect your pledge. It's hard to be cool at such times, but that's the correct attitude, I believe. Of course, a beard helps too, keeps people off balance. [. . .]

Coolish these days in my office. I have on my electric fire, but it isn't very noticeable. Likewise at home. We always seem to land in places where little has been done about such problems, and we have the option of fixing matters up for the short time allotted to us in any one place on earth (by destiny, I mean) or shivering through it.

I have always felt pretty sure of myself, what I wanted to do, where I wanted to live, or at least where I didn't want to live. But the irony now is that this is no longer true. In the course of one day I change back and forth a hundred times, calling myself a fool to consider leaving Ireland and a fool to consider staying. Betty is doing the same thing. And so we are little help to each other. Fortunately, the children don't seem to care what we do. They fondly imagine that the moment they walk in, if we do return, when everybody is glad to see them, that moment will go on and on. We, Betty and I, at least know about *that*.

Jim

Jim and Betty, homesick and discontented in the usual way, decided to return to the United States.

HARVEY EGAN

Ard na Fairrge
Dalkey
October 21, 1958

Dear Fr Egan,

Sitting here torn between reading the next installment of Monty's war memoirs[1] and Orwell's *Road to Wigan Pier* (the latter in its original Left Book Club edition, which I bought secondhand for sixpence), I happened

1 *The Memoirs of Field Marshal Montogomery* by Viscount Montogomery of Alamein (1958).

to see an auction catalog on the table, and I then continued a discussion I'd been having with myself earlier: whether 'tis better to hope that we'll not only hear favorably but suddenly from *The New Yorker* or to get in immediate touch with Mendota[1] in case the Oriental rugs illustrated in the catalog are worth having and can be had at our price. [. . .]

The auction is next week, the rugs going off on Wednesday, but one need not have the total amount (a 25% deposit is required at time articles are knocked down) until the end of the week. If the rugs (and there are other items of interest to a householder) should run around fifty or sixty pounds, as I imagine they will, and we should get two of them, we would be pushed to the wall in the fiscal department. I maybe ought to tell you more. I am finessing from nothing. Fifty in the St Cloud bank, which is just rotting—not enough to send for—and $33 in my pocket (as personal identification in case of accidents), and forty or fifty pounds, more or less, in the bank here. But should the story be acceptable to *The New Yorker*, we would be back in the bazaars in a big way; if it shouldn't, it would be Doubleday, a source untapped for years, though available, and austerity—I would be in the bad position of drawing four or five hundred a month and having to produce accordingly on the novel. What's wrong with that? Nothing, if one is settled down with one's appliances and house around one, but if one is setting out for the New World with one's wife and family, one needs what we used to call "getaway money." So there you have it. A plan of many flaws, not the least of which is the intention to buy Oriental rugs while crossing the Delaware, as it were. [. . .]

We have made a deposit on the *Hanseatic* (German ship), formerly the *Empress of Scotland*, but we have misgivings even now. Betty was badly shaken when her aunt wrote about a place on a half lot, with oil heater in the living room, and said she could just see us in it—with the emphasis (we thought) on *us*. Mighty nice here now, with the wind off somewhere else, the fire making itself felt in the fireplace, the radio tuned to a German station, light opera. A gay company at my table [. . .]

Jim

---

1 Father Egan.

Dublin
November 1, 1958

Dear Fr Egan,

Bullion received, with thanks. Hectic days, these, with so much to do—which I won't go into. Except that these last weeks, if I continue at the present pace, will be entirely wasted so far as immortal literature is concerned. However, I am going to make a great effort to salvage some time for it. Not easy when one has to think of everything, as I do.

What really takes the bounce out of me is the thoroughly unpromising housing situation to which we return. Art Wahl, some months ago, offered Betty—let's be accurate—ten thousand to be applied on a house if we returned to Stearns. That is really all we're holding, the only card. I had thought, a year ago, that we would just make it to Ireland (sane, that is), and would crawl ashore and lie gasping in the sand, but that we would be at our destination. Now it seems that *this* lies back in the other direction (yes, I know in which direction it really is, but let's try to keep it in the park, huh?).

I confess the temptation to stay on still flits through my mind (about once an hour), but things have gone pretty far. People like us, with so many children, should stay at home, where our vulnerability wouldn't be so noticeable. I mean a man can keep working the sand up around his head, and surrounded by others doing the same thing, nobody is going to come right out and say: Hey, fellas, our asses are all out. But that is the feeling I have more and more. I used to think that the worst thing about Don Humphrey's parenthood was the indignity of it: something would happen in the neighborhood (a neighbor complaining about his cesspool or dry well, as he called it), and it would be crystal clear for a moment that he was considered a Jeeter Lester,[1] really the sort of fellow who shouldn't have moved to town. All this with reference to the house Betty's aunt picked out for us in St Cloud: oil burner in living room, no basement (just a dirt pit), three bedrooms (one with no window), bathroom back of the kitchen, and half a lot (nine feet from the alley on one side, twelve feet to the neighbors on the other, the house itself that distance, I mean). This doesn't mean I want you to look for a place, at least not yet. I am just trying to convey my feelings these days. (It should be said that Betty's father nixed the house I've just mentioned.)

1 The main character in Erskine Caldwell's *Tabacco Road*.

Meanwhile, I went to another auction (the one in Co. Offaly wasn't worth the long drive) and came away with six "lots," as we say in the trade: two old prints, a carving set, two Sheraton trays, and a Sheraton barometer: everything we'll need to set up housekeeping, as you can see. Lovely to look at, though, especially the barometer, which is inlaid with shell designs and of course doesn't work. By the time this reaches you, Gene McC. will be in or out. *Time* says he's running ahead of Thye in the polls but that "knowing Minnesotans" expect Thye to squeeze through.[1]

I am not picking 'em, since I assured my mother Siri would be the next pope; I just told her, as though there was no doubt of it, thinking it would be more telling that way.[2]

Jim

I tried to tell the girls you were in line for the papacy, but they were indignant at the idea. "He's not grand enough!" "He's not even a bishop!"

JOE AND JODY O'CONNELL

Dalkey

November 29, 1:00 a.m., 1958

Dear Cho and Yody,[3]

The last night in the old house, down to the furniture and lighting we found here, and finishing off the dregs, and Hughie, whose bed has gone on before him, crying out from the foreign couch, and Betty finally going off under a heavy load of John Power and Son Gold Label; me, I've had the last of the Black and White. I smoked a cigar earlier, dug out in the course of packing. I have the radio tuned to a German station. I wonder what it'll think of WJON, for we are taking it with us—leaving little behind, the baby's Moses basket and two siphons of soda, some corrugated cardboard (kind packers like), some coal, some logs, some turf, and so on.

We have been through all this before, but this is the worst time yet. Too much stuff, too many people. We have two little leather tags, and I found myself switching the little cards around tonight—rather, Betty did, and thought it all too ironic. On one side the cards say J. F. Powers, Greystones, Co. Wicklow, Ireland; on the other, c/o A. Wahl, North River Rd, St Cloud, Minn. The latter is showing now—among other things. We

1 McCarthy beat the incumbent Edward Thye for a seat in the U.S. Senate.
2 Angelo Giuseppe Roncalli was elected and became Pope John XXIII.
3 Stearns County pronunciation of "Joe and Jody."

have eleven packing cases, five trunks, and a number of smaller pieces. Fortunately, there is a worldwide shipping slump, and the rates are low. We may live in our packing cases, some of which are quite roomy. It now appears that the potty will have to be transported separately. [. . .] If it were wrapped in brown paper, it wouldn't be noticeable, we tell each other. How fair-minded can you get? Em and Arleen, yes, but they are immortal.

Sean O'Faolain was over earlier to bid us goodbye. He has been a great friend to us here, and he and his wife are sorry to see us go. But this is a feeling I cannot convey: setting forth under great difficulties and yet wondering how, if we did it again, we might do better, did return to Ireland, I mean. Whatever we do, though, in the future, it'll be with less furniture.

Tomorrow we take the Cork Express for Cork, stay there overnight, and embark at Cobh the next morning for the New World. We are fortunate to be sailing on the SS *Hanseatic*, which derives her name from the Hanseatic League, a medieval association of friendly German and other European towns. Externally, the *Hanseatic* presents a striking appearance . . . a modern bow and cruiser-type stern (kind men like) and black hull (I'm black and I'm evil and I did not make myself) with white superstructure (natch) topped by two modern streamlined funnels. Each class has an attractive Children's Playroom. The "Alster Club," which extends the full width of the ship, will be one of the favorite gathering places for tourist-class passengers. In the attractive St. Pauli Tavern tourist-class passengers will find the gay spirit of a stroll on the Reeperbahn in Hamburg. Here conviviality will reign in an exceptionally enjoyable atmosphere. For pleasant days and nights at sea the *Hanseatic* is your ship. Deck games, movies, dances, concerts, gang shags, entertainment, children's parties, fancy dress balls, and other events are included in the diversified program, which is arranged for the enjoyment of all, young and old alike. CFM groups meet under ideal conditions. Imbued with the spirit of Old Hanse, the sterling qualities of all the German personnel bespeak reliability. Taking pride in their jobs and the efficient performance of[1]

Jim

---

1 Joke—unfinished intentionally.

23

Back and wondering why

December 22, 1958—August 25, 1959

The Vossberg Building, suite 7, redux

Upon their return from Ireland, the Powers family stayed with Betty's parents, the Wahls, in their place on the Mississippi. The idea was to find a house to buy with the ten thousand dollars that Art had promised to give them for that purpose if they returned to the area.

KATHERINE ANNE PORTER
[North River Road, St. Cloud, Minnesota]
December 22, 1958

Dear Katherine Anne,

Back and wondering why, of course, and wishing I'd got this off to you in time for Christmas. We sailed from Cobh on Nov. 30, docked late in N.Y. (8:00 p.m.), which is no time to arrive with five children and nineteen pieces, including five trunks and five packing cases. There we were more or less slaughtered (our sensibilities and finances) by the porters and coopers and agents for the one "approved" transport company, all of whom struck me as members of the Mafia. A Negro customs inspector, however, proved to be a human being, by getting Betty and the children out of the place so they could get a cab to a hotel.

We had hoped to go on west the day we arrived, but the boat being late fixed that. I had tried for three weeks before we left Ireland to find out what would happen to my trunks and cases, especially *them*, when I docked, whether the railroad freight people would pick them up. I tried to find out what railroad we'd be traveling on when we got to New York. (My publisher, as it turned out, hired a travel agency to handle all this detail, and I was to be met by a man who would nurse us through customs, etc.) I called from Newfoundland, off Newfoundland, that is, to say we'd be late but didn't manage to get a word in edgewise; the girl at the publisher's kept saying DO NOT WORRY. NO MATTER WHAT TIME YOUR SHIP DOCKS, OUR MAN WILL BE THERE TO MEET YOU. Me:

"About the freight . . ." DO NOT WORRY. THAT'S IN THE PACKAGE TOO. "About the train, our Pullman reservations . . ." DO NOT WORRY. Me: "Well, thank you." THANK *YOU*! WE ARE CANCELING OUR CABLE TO YOU SAYING DO NOT WORRY. "Yes. Well, thank you." THANK YOU FOR CALLING.

As it turned out, I had to pay the Century Transportation Company for transporting my packing cases to, as it turned out, a trucking shipper; because of the airline strikes, there was trouble about the Pullman reservations, so that we were left with one unredeemable double bedroom ($25), my ship-to-shore call not having been conveyed to the travel agency; no allowance was made for "family plan" from Chicago to Minnesota ($25 loss); the [travel agency's] man left early, after being absent for the first fifteen minutes after disembarkation (picture man and wife and five children standing under the letter *P* not worrying).

Betty and children got out of it, though with no night clothing, and three hours later I followed, having had the worst time of my life. The cooper who axed into the packing cases in which I had things like a Sheraton barometer, Waterford glass decanters, and satinwood cane chairs cut his finger and therefore had to be adequately compensated for his injury: my heart broke to see how he nailed up the cases again (for which I had had stencils made which said FRAGILE and an arrow pointing up), but I was able to have them strapped with steel bands by paying the Mafia. I got a very good deal from Al of Century Transportation Company, who thought I ought to "take care" of Joe, who was writing up the tickets for the packing cases; Joe later thought I ought to take care of Al, who had given me a very good deal; and so on; and on.

I managed to borrow forty dollars the next day from a friend in New York, and so we left in a blaze of prosperity for Chicago. The train was an hour and a half late, and our plans went awry again. But we did get to St Paul ultimately, and then here by car. The barometer is on the wall in this knotty-pine basement room, and an 18th-century print also, both fruits of my attendance at auctions in Dublin, and the trunks, which went as baggage, finally arrived, after a week of not worrying about them. (I relaxed Sunday afternoon in N.Y. and forgot to redeem them at Penn Station and arrange that they be sent on as baggage, relaxed with Betty and my friend and his wife over some of our duty-free Irish whiskey, that is.)

Oh, the joys of travel! And yet, unless we find a house we can stand to look at here, which seems unlikely at the moment, I see no course open but to set out for somewhere again. Meanwhile, we swarm all over this little rambler house, and I don't even *think* of working. The prospect isn't promising, but I suppose I at least will have to pull myself together and start working pretty soon somehow. *Now* how are you? Happy New Year.

Jim

Art and Money left for their place in Florida, planning to return in April, by which time everyone expected that Jim and Betty would have found a place of their own. Happily, Jim was able to rent his old office in downtown St. Cloud.

HARVEY EGAN

St Cloud

January 5, 1959

Dear Fr Egan,

The last words typed by this typewriter originated in my office on Westland Row. I am now writing from my old office above Walgreen's—which is somewhat singed from the fire next door, but then aren't we all? It was not my intention to write to you today, or tomorrow for that matter, for there are times when silence is the better part, but something just happened—something so symbolic that I thought you ought to know about it. You recall King Alfred's hard times, don't you, when it was a spider who gave him strength, inspiration rather, to go on. I seem to remember that Bruce, or Douglas, had a similar experience. Well, in my case, it is a ladybug. It was lying half frozen against the sill, and then the sun trickled in, shining first on the diocesan exchange building, which is a power-house of Catholic Action, and then, having nothing better to do, shining in here on me and the ladybug (we are both wearing orange-red, by the way). Now the ladybug has gathered its strength and is walking around the envelope which I intend to put this letter in. I'd say the bug, if it watches itself and sticks close to the radiator, will be all right. As for me, I anxiously await inspiration, wondering if I've already had it and if I need a stronger charge than Alfred and the others.

Let me telescope it for you. I've spent fifty on the car and a certain amount of time waiting on the garageman. I've been to several affairs sponsored by members of the Movement up here: no change except for a little ram's wool in Leonard's beard. The Wahls left for Florida yesterday. The girls are enrolled at Holy Angels school, and by a singular combination

of circumstances I drive them to school (today is the first day): school begins at 8:15 a.m. We have found one house that just might do, though I
personally feel very shaky about it (and about the whole picture—as does
Betty, I think, but she is slower to entertain thoughts of turncoatery).
Anyway we are now prepared to entertain you and George anytime you
care to venture up. My radiator gives off a keening sound, and I must
draw closer to it. This building has only about a year to live. My shirt is
threadbare, and my cushions are dead. Our bishop gave a talk on TV yesterday (Alexandria station), only a half hour, all too short.

Jim

What does a ladybug eat? Clark Bars.

Journal, January 5, 1959

First day in office. Radiator cooling at 2:00 p.m. . . . Money short. Friends
depressed and depressing. Houses nonexistent . . . Truth is I hate wooden
houses and especially white ones . . . Last month probably the most miserable in my life. Ladybug like me—half frozen, wearing orange-red. Will
it be here tomorrow?

Journal, January 6, 1959

Yes, it's here. I tried a crumb of milk chocolate on it, but it wasn't interested.
I wonder if it's seeking the cold and doesn't enjoy the sun, knowing it's winter.

Journal, January 7, 1959

So far I'd say returning has been a mistake. Keep coming back to Don.
What's wrong? I ask myself, and topping the list is that . . . Ladybug still
around.

Journal, January 8, 1959

No work yet. Am hoping to start pretty soon now. Always hard to begin
again, and this is as hard as any time I can remember in the past. About
all this—house, staying on, etc.—I feel no better. Discovered girls have
been wearing no sweaters under their coats—just their blouses. Mary
home sick today. Suppose KA will be next. I don't know—at this point,

with the weather near zero every morning—what it means. Nothing in my history enables me to understand them at their ages—or Betty, for that matter. A strong strain always tending toward absolute confusion. Haven't seen the ladybug around today.

Journal, January 9, 1959

Trying to get started—still. No sign of ladybug, but haven't really looked for it.

Journal, January 12, 1959

The family-life novel seems more and more possible. (Perhaps the account of our arrival off the *Hanseatic* cd be in it, for I now see the novel not ending with our departure from St Cloud.)

Journal, January 14, 1959

I drove out to Jacobs Prairie—looked for Don's grave. I think I found it in a corner. Very odd standing there where he is buried—hard to believe—and I'm afraid I'm such a poor Christian that I get mad at him for dying.

HARVEY EGAN

February 11, 1959

Dear Fr Egan,

[. . .] We haven't found the social life here quite what we'd hoped it would be. I finally got Doyle to come out last night, having spent one night at his house watching the children go to bed for three hours; they kept reappearing to have a dish of cereal and to pat the cat. The Doyles are considered strict disciplinarians by most people, I understand.

I have my Dublin office furniture here now, but the work, I must say, isn't getting done. It is now 10:00 a.m., and I've been here about two hours and am beginning to think about opening up my sandwiches and thermos of tea. *The Mpls Tribune* is out of the way for another day.

I got pretty interested in the Del-Dupas[1] contest, reading up on it before and after. Watching it on TV, though, I got that old feeling. I don't

---

1 Del Flanagan versus Ralph Dupas. Del won.

think I gave Del a round. Just shows you how much you can miss watching a show on TV. I thought I heard your voice ring out at one point.

In short, I am trying to take an interest in the life around me. Not easy, is it?

Del drank too much water before the fight. He wants title shot. If ever a guy deserved it, Del does. Maybe with the International Boxing Club dissolved, he'll get it. Well, let's hope so. But if so, I hope he remembers to train for it, and doesn't get too fine, and doesn't drink water to excess when he's drying out, and all the rest.

Jim

Jim whose address is:
c/o A. Wahl
North River Road, Rte 2
St Cloud

Journal, February 21, 1959

I was asking what it is my present life seems to be saying to me—I think it is that I must work willy-nilly and abandon all hope of living as I'd like to, forget what I like to eat, who I'd like to see, where I'd like to be, etc., and think of myself as just having been given a stiff prison sentence: if I should ever get out, it would be nice to have a book or two to show for the time. I'll not get out either until I have a book that makes me some money. So what, my life is a plot against living, but perhaps a good thing for my work—if I can ever get around to it. If I can stop trying to think of *other* ways to escape the trap I'm in. Stoicism then . . .

HARVEY EGAN

March 6, 1959

Dear Fr Egan,

I just rec'd the following wire here at my office: THE TROUBLE[1] SHOWING CBS LOOK UP AND LIVE SUNDAY MORNING MARCH EIGHTH MANY THANKS AND CONGRATULATIONS = ANNE FREMANTLE. So I wanted you to be the first to know. The only

1 One of Jim's early short stories, made into a play.

thing is that CBS in Mpls–St Paul isn't carrying the program. [. . .] They are on tape, so maybe we'll see them someday somewhere. Naturally, I am excited about my debut on TV, though there's no money in it and it's, unfortunately, invisible.

How they going?

I hear conflicting reports. That Del will meet Martinez on St Patrick's Day, and since Vince is so heavy, Del will not have to train down (and so, it follows, will not have to drink so much water); but this morning Sid Hartman, that ace reporter, reports Del and Vince will never meet because Del isn't ready.[1]

Joe Dever writes that Hollywood is nibbling on his last. Some talk of Crosby, Sinatra, and Dean Martin (now crooner, late of Martin and Lewis) all wanting priest parts. How about you?

Jim

Journal, March 24, 1959

Opened the window for a little air—and a few minutes later I saw the ladybug going up the windowpane. Hello again.

Art and Money returned from Florida at the end of March. Although they never complained or showed resentment about sharing their house with seven Powerses, the couple did not understand Jim and Betty's insistence that they would not even consider a rambler, most especially one in a new development. Jim found the living situation at the Wahls' increasingly intolerable. He accepted an invitation to a writers' conference at Grinnell College in Iowa and planned to stay briefly with Egan on the way there or back.

HARVEY EGAN

North River Road
April 1 (ha ha), 1959

Dear Fr Egan,

Yours rec'd and glad that you were able to shuffle the cards so as to make space for me on your tight schedule. I sometimes wonder if Pope

1 They didn't meet.

John knows what our American pastors are going through (and I'd be interested in his reaction). If I am ever to receive recognition at the Vatican, now is the time. Well, no, I didn't realize that Fr Bandas was succeeding to Msgr Knox's seat at the Round Table.[1] Do these things just happen, or is this the divine humor? [. . .]

Betty exclaimed during the course of changing diapers, getting milk for the baby, trying to quiet boys, etc.: "Suicide would be better than this. No, I shouldn't say that." But I'm afraid that's about it. How's it with youse?

Jim

ROBERT LOWELL AND ELIZABETH HARDWICK
c/o A. Wahl
North River Road
St Cloud, Minnesota
April 13, 1959

Dear Cal and Elizabeth,

On returning to this, the Granite City, yesterday, I found a summons from what may be one of your publishers, to meet you people in New York toward the end of April. Nothing was said beyond that, but I take it that you have a book coming out; Betty says that you are on your way to England, remembers something to that effect in one of your letters. If the former is true, there's nothing I can do for you. But if the latter is true, keep an eye out for a place for me, my wife, and five children. [. . .]

I am just back from Grinnell College, where Howard Nemerov and I were visitors for the writers' conference. I must say I liked him very much. He is like you in conversation—a kindly, murderous approach. I'm sorry I can't make it to New York in April, but you tell them how it is with me. I imagine you've been as happy as I have to see that Ted Roethke is finally being recognized. I am hoping they don't make him wait too long for the Nobel Prize.

Best to youse.

Jim

---

1 Bandas had been appointed to the forty-member Pontifical Academy of Theology, a position Knox had held before his death in 1957.

c/o A. Wahl
North River Road
St Cloud, Minnesota
April 21, 1959

Dear Katherine Anne,

As for housing, I'm afraid our luck is no better than yours, and here we are four months later (than when I last wrote) and still where we were, with Betty's father and mother, who have had three months in Florida in the meantime. The one house I could imagine us living in was rejected by Betty's father, who, of course, has the money with which we were going to operate; too big, taxes too high, he said, and he's right, but I fear that means we won't find a place. We are *not* going to move into a three-bedroom rambler and fix up the basement (one of his suggestions). There is little direct communication between us and him. Betty has gone on for years without intimidating him—he is a builder of large buildings—by her different outlook on life. To me it seems odd, for my parents knew from about the time I got out of high school that I was not going to follow in their steps, i.e., make earning a living my primary concern. [. . .]

The atmosphere is clear of trouble. That is the really remarkable thing, that the two of them can stand to have us and our five children around. I know I, in their position, couldn't go it at all. Meanwhile, we sleep in fear of the baby's waking in the night and get through the meals sometimes with hardly a mumblin' word——and I am in the worst spot I've been in yet, which is saying something. We run ads for lake cottages; we write letters to people who have suitable ones—the majority of cottages in these parts aren't fit for man or beast. You have to be from Chicago to believe you're experiencing the best that nature can provide. As a resort area, it is not of the first class or even of the second. And still we can't find a place to rent for the summer. What we'll do in September, I don't know. The thought frightens me, but I think we may go abroad again. I have all summer to pan the necessary gold. [. . .]

All best.

Jim

O'er Walgreen's
Suite No. 7
St Cloud
April 24, 1959

Dear Fr Egan,

[. . .] I walked around St Paul that morning I left you, and I kept getting the feeling that the city had been bombed. St Paul Stationery now looks like one of the Horder office supply stores in Chicago. The public library has been all switched around inside so that the contents no longer match the words carved in stone over the various doors. Field, Schlick appeared about the same. But my opinion is that the same rats who are gnawing down the good old buildings here—the Highway Department leads the pack—are at work in St Paul. It didn't seem much like home to me. I did not go up around the cathedral, fearing perhaps I'd find a cloverleaf in its place.

Now, as you know, I have considered from time to time the title *Morte D'Urban* for my Duesterhaus novel. Whether that will be it, I don't know, but in any event I intend to play upon the idea of dying to this world, a phrase I seem to recall from the writings of several saints. [. . .]

We are getting nowhere at all with our quest for a summer cottage. I keep thinking that anyone else of my eminence would know somebody who would say, "Oh, go use our house in Maine. We didn't intend to open it at all this year." I peer into the eyes of each passerby, but not a one stops and says anything like that to me.

[. . .] Jim

Journal, April 25, 1959

Yesterday call from Ken McCormick saying there was a nibble for "Defection of a Favorite" for television, which could mean as much as $2,000 to me . . . Now what happens—nothing, I suppose. In any case I suppose the money would be applied on my debt. But it was, for a while, before I thought of *that*, pleasant to think that I had passage money coming in from out of nowhere.

Journal, May 4, 1959

A hard weekend for Betty and me—absolutely nothing accomplished, and the morning the worst ever so far as the children are concerned. No mail for days. No word from Ken as to that TV sale. I must bear down—as never before.

HARVEY EGAN

Suite 7
May 4, 1959

Dear Fr Egan,

[. . .] I was sure when I read that Del had spent the night before the fight[1] chatting with a few close friends that he'd be waterlogged again, but no. It must be as some of the scribes say, if we could just see into Del's mind, we'd know what to expect. Anyway, more power to him!

These are ulcerous days around the ranch, with one chance after another fizzling out on us: to get out from under, that is. The only possible house (the one I mentioned to you) was sold last week, and that, we've decided, is it so far as St Cloud is concerned.

If I had my life to live over, I'd join the Clementine fathers.

Jim [. . .]

Journal, May 12, 1959

Last night we looked at the Colbert house on Third Ave. South and decided to rent it for June–July–August. $100 per mo. Fabulous clutter. But we can do no better. Betty, desperate to be somewhere else, is unhappy to be moving into the place. I understand her feelings. I had the same ones when I was walking around in the place. I couldn't see a place to sit and read except on the porch—which figures as a crying room for the children in Betty's plan, I learned. So it goes.

HARVEY EGAN

Suite 7
Tuesday, 10:00 a.m. [May 1959]

Dear Fr Egan,

[. . .] We found a place for the next three months, beginning in a week or so, over in the old neighborhood, students overhead, clutter where we'll be, but . . . Betty still holds out in her heart for better places than this. As for me,

---

1 Del versus Jimmy Martinez. Del won.

I have cut away every last bag of sand and will begin on the members of my family if that is necessary to stay aloft, if you follow my imagery. [. . .]

Jim

Journal, May 18, 1959

Out of gas—creatively . . . I feel absolutely powerless these days to prevent financial ruin. Ideas for stories don't come.

Journal, May 26, 1959

Now living at 424 Third Ave. S. So far it has been very tough going. Betty and I never so out of harmony. Today I am back in my office for the first time since Saturday. I have the feel of the golf course story—came to me finally during Mass on Sunday—and am girding my loins to write it. Everything depends on it. The only things holding me back from Ireland now are leaving my parents and living with Betty under unsettled conditions. Perhaps if we went by air this time, we'd be in better shape when we got there. It will be killing, I know—but what is this here? What of the furniture? And so on? Into storage, I suppose. Money, money, money—this is the answer to every question confronting me.

HARVEY EGAN

June 9, 1959

Dear Fr Egan,

I am in receipt of yours and am pleased to provide you with our new address, namely: 424 Third Avenue South, St Cloud. Although the men on the radio persist in calling these days perfect days, comfortably warm, I do not find them so. In suite 7 the climate is intolerable, but I work on and on, whiskers growing longer, garments gradually falling apart, eyes reddening, and am in short a sort of walk-up beachcomber. But enough of that. I don't know what to think of the coming Del go.[1] You have the promoter's old car and so perhaps know more than most of us. I do know, having read it in George Edmond, that it won't be a decision. I suppose you'll be there with your flask in Del's corner. I have decided not to try to follow this one, being busy these days up in Duesterhaus. [. . .]

1 Versus Joey Giardello.

My eyes are holding up, but everything else seems to be slipping, especially the old get-up-and-go that we Americans are just dead without. [. . .]

Jim

HARVEY EGAN

June 18, 1959

Dear Fellow Fan,

Del had a pretty good battle plan laid out for Joey,[1] but his one mistake was in not following through on it. Del isn't the first fighter to have his well-laid strategy blow up in his face. It happens all the time in boxing. Nobody says that Joey landed a lucky punch, but the bout was too brief to prove anything. Del has made St Paul the fistic capital of the U.S., the talk of the country. So you might say he deserves a chance to redeem himself in the eyes of St Paulites, not all of them his well-wishers, by the way. If a rematch between these two topnotchers could be staged, would it prove anything? It just might. A lot of people might be surprised if Del could just get dried out or beefed up, could get proper sparring partners, and could come in at his best fighting weight, either 150 or 160, or both. Just one man's opinion, of course. What's yours?

A Real Ring-in-the-Nose Flanagan Fan

HARVEY EGAN

Suite 7
July 7, 1959

Dear Fr Egan,

Assuming you read this on July 8, it might interest you to know that I was born on that day, 1917, around five o'clock in the afternoon—in time for cocktails—and that I have been going ever since, but I have now reached the point where if success does not come soon, I'm afraid I will have seen the show. I have been working hard for the last five or six weeks and need a rest. I have a few days to go yet, but the story-chapter is in the nets, all except a paw or two. Now what can you offer me? I crave life, laughter: Do you suppose we could find a theatre where they still have a mighty Wurlitzer and still have the audience sing along to the bouncing ball?

---

1 Joey Giardello. Del was knocked out.

Otherwise I have nothing to report. [. . .]
Jim

Journal, July 21, 1959

Mailed off letter to Killiney nuns.[1] . . . So now it appears we are pointed toward Ireland again. Of course everything depends on my story being accepted by *The New Yorker*.

Journal, August 5, 1959

Hot, humid—sitting in my office looking out the window, wanting to remember this scene and the people and the weather—so I'll never be silly enough to wish I were back, for it is now almost certain we are returning to Ireland. Bats, the latest thing at home to keep us from getting any rest at night. This miserable, miserable summer. I now see our whole married life as a search for a home, and every child making the need more pressing and the prospects less likely . . . I hope this will be the last harvest I will reap of the failure of Betty to educate her parents and others in the meaning of her calling and mine (as writers, artists) and the few prerogatives attending same.

Journal, August 14, 1959

The startling news when I came home yesterday that the Dickehuts[2] were moving out of the flat at Strobels'. Betty *saw* evidence of an immediate move—and Birdie *told* KA that she's had two shocks that day. 1. D's moving. 2. Our plan to go to Ireland.

JACK CONROY

424 Third Avenue South
St Cloud, Minnesota
August 21, 1959

Dear Jack,

I came across a note among my effects (as we published authors say)

---

1 The school Katherine and Mary had attended in Ireland.
2 Tenants.

from you, dated Dec. 8, last year, and I wonder if I was going to reply to it or if I actually did. Anyway, you ask if we are still in Ireland, and the answer is no. But should be, on consideration of all we've been through since coming back: looking for a house and not finding one and meantime living with Betty's family and—for the last three months—in a house owned by an undertaker who summers up the river, possibly because he can't stand the heat and bats at home, we now think. So that's it, Jack. We are now in the process of readying ourselves for another shot at Ireland. If we do not go, you may be sure this will not be known to us until we've got everything crated up for shipment, including ourselves. [. . .]

All for now,

Jim Powers

The Strobels offered to rent Jim and Betty the two-floor apartment above their own in their large house on the Mississippi in St Cloud. The plan to return to Ireland was canceled.

Meanwhile, skulduggery was afoot at St. John's, where the new Abbey Church designed by Marcel Breuer was being built. A number of architects had been considered, but Breuer was the one promoted by Frank Kacmarcik,[1] who, apparently, collaborated with him on the design. Breuer and Kacmarcik decided they wanted a window in keeping with the brutalism of the church and tried to reject the agreed-upon design by Bruno Bak. They failed, and the Bak window was installed.

HARVEY EGAN

St Cloud

August 25, 1959

Dear Fr Egan,

You've been pretty quiet lately, and all kinds of news has been breaking that, frankly, I think we ought to have your ideas on. What about this third major league?[2] I think that Branch Rickey (a great friend of St Paul, by the way) is the best thing that's happened to it so far. Why should or shouldn't the Minneapolis team play half of its schedule at Midway?

---

1 Frank Kacmarcik (1920–2004) taught art and print design at St. John's, also painted and designed graphics himself; collected works of art in Europe after the war and brought them to St. John's.
2 The proposed Continental League, which never came to be. The existing major leagues expanded.

What about football—this new league, the American League? The players are available for it, as they aren't for another baseball league of the highest caliber, but you know what the expenses are in football and how the weather can play hob with the gate, especially here in Minnesota—where, however, the winters aren't as bad as the summers. [. . .]

Yes, it does appear that we will be staying on here for a time, the flat at Strobels'—overlooking the river—having fallen vacant a week or so ago. About seven rooms, including the third floor. Girls heartbroken, but there are too many things pending—my work—which I don't care to transplant just now. So rejoice, and tell all my good friends in St Paul and environs that I will remain and am always on tap for good talk and good fun and all that's worthwhile. Let's make the most of my presence while we have it.

    Jim

[. . .]

The big scandal is the infighting going on at St John's, to get the big window—at this late date, after okaying sketches, after ordering all the glass—away from Bruno Bak. Frank.[1] I gather Breuer has begun to fear that the window will kill his building—kill the powerhouse effect for which he is so famous. This of course is off the record.

Good news, that, if true that Del is planning a comeback. I'd like to give this boy of mine Joe O'Connell a shot at him. Any chance of Glen making a comeback?[2]

1 Kacmarcik.
2 Glen Flanagan, Del's brother, also a prizefighter.

24

The J. F. Powers Company: "The Old Cum Permissu Superiorum Line"

September 19, 1959—June 14, 1960

"In the days of Dwight D. Eisenhower, when he was chief, there lived a mighty preacher of the Order of Saint Clement, and Urban was his name."

The Powers family moved into the top two floors of the Strobels' house, a place almost directly across the street from the site of the old red house, now a sandlot used for parking. Jim was desperate about money and infuriated by the chaos of family life; still, he was immensely pleased to be in his old office, and just being there buoyed his spirits.

He crept ahead on the novel and, at the office, adopted the ironical conceit that he was running a going concern, "coming and going like a businessman in sheep's clothing, or vice versa," issuing any number of spoof letters "From the Desk of America's Cleanest Lay Author" ("Pledges Administered * Pious Lobbying Undertaken * Fig Leaves"). These exercises went some way toward defusing the frightening reality of his situation.

HARVEY EGAN

Suite 7
September 19, 1959

Dear Fr Egan,

It has been a tough fight, moving this time—the worst ever, and only two blocks away. I had known things were bad with us, confusion, possessions, etc., but the payoff is when I look for my manuscript, when the air is beginning to clear, and find it is missing. I had two chapters in a plastic container—sort you businessmen use when you go to the bank—but it is nowhere. An ad appears in the Lost & Found section of *The St Cloud Times*, starting today. I'll never get the manuscript back if it falls in the hands of the St Cloud clergy. You see I have this parrot, who lives in a rectory, and says: God love you!

Otherwise, well, the kitchen is small, tortuously so, but the living room is good, and the bedrooms look out upon the Father of Waters, as we all call the river up here. I am making a fire screen (for the fireplace) today,

343

out of old iron picked up at Gopher[1] and copper screening: impossible to find one ready-made here except at exorbitant prices. I have been gluing furniture—in short, preparing myself for my old age as a sexton and chauffeur for some lucky pastor.

Boston College wants me to come and lecture once, for $250 and expenses, but I've decided against it. Even if I had you write my talk, I'd have to change planes at Chicago and New York to get to Boston—and I don't think I should be risking my life just to swell the procession of big names on the BC lecture roster (Frost, Warren, O'Faolain are others). I know this will please you. [. . .]

Jim

KATHERINE ANNE PORTER

412 First Avenue South
St Cloud, Minnesota
October 20, 1959

Dear Katherine Anne,

I have your postcard and will answer your questions: we are here at the above address (which overlooks the Mississippi), and we are pretty well. We were going back to Ireland in September (and had arranged for the girls' reentry into school there and paid for it) when this place fell vacant. Why it should be offered to us with five children is easily explained: it is owned by Betty's aunt and uncle. And also why we, who know we must leave it, probably in a year, decided to take it; we just weren't up to another transatlantic move so soon. It would have been into the dark again, with no housing and this time with one more child to make housing even more difficult and with less money in hand than we had the last time we tried it, when I had the *Kenyon Review* fellowship money. And so, for all these reasons, and because this place became available, here we still are. Each night I find I'm stranded. A good friend died while we were in Ireland last year, and I knew St Cloud wouldn't be the same without him—I had expected to spend my declining years in argument with him, before a good fire—and it isn't. There is no news. Let me hear from you—*not* on a postcard. If you've published anything anywhere, or are about to, please let me know.

Yours,

Jim [. . .]

1 Salvage and surplus outlet.

412 First Avenue South
St Cloud
October 22, 1959

Dear Fr Egan [. . .]

All fairly well here. No word on the coming story. It may be this week, or may not—nobody tells me anything. I read my Reidar Lund and Hennessy,[1] but I don't seem to get any better for it.

I couldn't have asked for more: Glen Flanagan's comeback and Del off to Bangkok.

Jim

This envelope was opened by mistake, contents noted, and clumsily re-sealed. J. Edgar Hoover.

Donald McDonald, a writer for The Catholic Messenger, *the newspaper of the Diocese of Davenport, Iowa, wrote to Jim saying that he would like to interview him. Jim agreed but for months heard nothing more. In his letters, Jim turned the affair into a satire on an author's eagerness for publicity. He also found material for epistolary capers in his friend Joe O'Connell, who had written a book review, an unlikely undertaking for this gifted artist.*

December 7, 1959

Dear Fr Egan,

[. . .] Thanksgiving would've been murderous if I hadn't been called upstairs periodically (it was celebrated below, at Strobels'), but what could I do? Nobody invited me out for dinner. There should be an organization that would make it possible for family men to spend holidays away from home—instead of inviting a serviceman to dinner, why not ask a family man? [. . .]

Brought the vacuum cleaner down here yesterday and used it, and now the office fairly sparkles. Discovered among my papers one of the

1 Sportswriters.

chapters I considered lost and am happy about that, though—let's face it—a little dismayed to find that it doesn't read as well as I'd been imagining. I haven't heard a word from McDonald of *The Catholic Messenger* and don't know what to do. Do you think it would be all right if I write and ask him in a nice way when he intends to interview me? I don't want to crab my act, of course, but I desperately want to be interviewed. I have so much to say. Maybe a Christmas card would be the thing, with a friendly note. If I can get him to interview me, I'll do what I can to get him to interview you. Well, that's enough of that.

    Jim

Joe O'Connell has written a review of Van Zeller's book on art, for *Worship*, and that's all he can talk about—*his review*. I think he'd like me to stage a party at which, by candlelight, he'd read his review. Watch for it, if you get *Worship*; it occurs to me that you're about the only person I know who doesn't review. What's the matter?

CHARLES AND SUSAN SHATTUCK

412 First Avenue South

St Cloud, Minnesota

December 20, 1959

Dear Chuck and Suzie,

    I am cutting down on Xmas cards this year and so will tender my usual greetings in this more businesslike form. I am in my downtown office, a quiet place, having extracted myself from the arms of my loving wife and family and all their endless cookie making. I have a clear plastic sheet nailed over the one window, and this, with my new calendar from the Great Northern Railway, my world map (I like to know where I am), my postcards and newspaper photos—of Dick Clark and Nelson Rockefeller and other heroes of our time in smiling poses—makes the office a warm and restful haven. We are living on the second and third floors of Betty's uncle and aunt's house on the west bank of the Mississippi, just across the way from where we used to live, now a parking lot. We have a fireplace and five children, and I hope that sets the scene for you. Betty doesn't have time to work at writing, since we have no help except a cleaning woman once a week, and she,* of all people, is subject to thoughts of returning to Ireland. Me, I keep watching the world map, but nothing lights up on it. We don't think we're long for this hemisphere, however. All right so we're nuts. Now how about you? [. . .]

Jim

* Betty, that is.

MICHAEL MILLGATE

Boxing Day 1959

Dear Michael,

Very happy to have your avant-garde Christmas card and to know where you are—still with the same landlady, I wonder. I am down here at the office—the J. F. Powers Company is the only one working in the building today—enjoying the cleanliness and comfort of it. I was busy for several days constructing a puppet theatre,[1] and until this morning, when I vacuumed it, the place looked more like Santa's toy shop than the hard-hitting business office that it is. I am having a cup of tea at the moment.

Now, I understand Allen Tate is back at the University of Minnesota with a new wife, but I have not seen him and probably won't. I remember your saying in your last that you'd had the impression that I didn't like Allen. That isn't true. I like him well enough but haven't known him very well. I think he's a fine essayist. I knew Caroline Gordon somewhat better. What I don't like (and it isn't very important) is this Legion of Honor role Allen plays, dinner at the Walker Art Gallery in Mpls, hobnobbing with the wives of chain drugstore magnates (soon to be heading for Mexico and landscape painting), everybody acting as if it's literature and not drugstores that really matters. [. . .][2]

Otherwise things are pretty dull. No new children, by the way. [. . .]

Jim Powers

1 For the children for Christmas.
2 Jim to Betty, November 26, 1956: "My fervent desire, as you should know, to have all the symphony orchestras founder, all the books go unread, for there to be nothing but trash in every branch of art and entertainment—if people can't see the real thing, feel the need of it as of food and drink; anything but that *they* feel humanitarian about *helping*. That is burning incense before a god which doesn't exist—and that is what? I don't want to be party to it anyway."

412 First Avenue South
December 26, 1959

Dear Fr Egan,

This ought to get some action. You, by the way, are the friend I refer to in the body of the letter. All for now, have to get this across the street. jf

Dear Mr McDonald,

Your files will show that you wrote to me last fall with the idea of interviewing me on tape and possibly using the interview in a published book (as well as in the Davenport *Messenger*). Since then, though I expected you all through November, I have heard nothing from you or your office. Word has recently reached me that you are leaving the employment of the *Messenger*.

What I'd like to know is where does that leave me? I have been expecting to be interviewed and have told my wife and various friends, including clergy, *that I would be interviewed*. What am I to tell these good people?

I have not entirely given up hope of being interviewed, but I do think that we'll have to work fast if this is to come to pass before you take up your new employment, assuming you are to begin it soon, possibly at the start of the second semester. I stand ready, as before, to cooperate with you in every way possible (that is consistent with ethics and my reputation as a published arthur). I don't know that I'm prepared to come to Davenport, but I might meet you halfway, say, at Prairie du Chien. If you could come as far as the Twin Cities, that, though not what you originally suggested, would be better than my traveling farther south. I think I can promise you a meal and a room suitable for interviewing not far from St Paul where I have a friend, himself eminently interviewable, and no stranger to the intricacies of tape-recording. He might even be able to furnish the machine and tape. Perhaps we could make it a double interview—such as Ed Murrow sometimes does on his TV program. I think this might very well be just what your series needs. Be that as it may, I want you to know that I mean to hold you to your original proposition, or know the reason why not. Please write to me at the above address, or perhaps a wire would be better, as to your plans regarding me.

Sincerely yours,

J. F. Powers

Journal, February 5, 1960

At Fred Petters's last night with big crowd to see Dorothy Day. She talked of people at the CW, especially Ammon Hennacy, and was very interesting. I was bothered, though, by the tacit consent given to her by everybody present. I was moved to make my own position—that of an artist with a wife and a family with little faith in the common people to save themselves from themselves—clear, but I didn't, feeling that it was her evening and not for me to interrupt with my personal feelings and also feeling that she would know whatever I had to say anyway. The usual reaction is one of guilt, I think, on hearing Dorothy or Ammon—but I do not have this. I am trying, so to speak, to get from A to B to C as a writer and parent—and it is all I can do now.

HARVEY EGAN

Lincoln's Birthday 1960 [February 12]

Dear Fr Egan,

[. . .] For a long time I have been seeking a way to give my family the finer things in life. Could this be it? This synod Pope John called[1] evidently means to require all visiting priests to wear cassocks and round hats while in Rome. What about a deal whereby clergy would purchase same from me (the J. F. Powers Company—the old "cum permissu superiorum" line) here in the States, using U.S. dollars, and simply pick up same on arrival in Rome, with my representatives meeting clients at the airport and railway stations?

Ammon was here, or was that before your last visit? Then Dorothy. There was a big evening with her (many present, that is) at Petters's, and a small one at our place. I think I got her straightened out in one regard: better to take the train than the bus when traveling to Fargo.

I'm afraid that's about it. Except, of course, that I was a little surprised to see where Del is booked to fight in England (today's *Pioneer Press*). I hope he doesn't come in too fine.

—Jim

You'll be interested to know that Dorothy was going to Milwaukee to be taped by Donald McDonald. I heard this on two occasions while she was here and didn't have the nerve either time to pursue the matter with her

1 Second Vatican Council.

(she mentioned it to other people both times, as it happened), for fear of letting her see that I'd been let down and was still suffering the effects. Did I do the right thing? I kick myself, in a way, that I didn't find out more from her. Perhaps all is *not* lost! I mean, if McDonald is still taping, why . . .

Ted LeBerthon, Jim's friend and onetime roommate at the Marlborough in St. Paul, died at the age of sixty-seven.

HARVEY EGAN

St Cloud
February 19, 1960

Dear Fr Egan,

I just wrote to Ted's wife, care of the *Register*, the only address I know that might reach her or Ted's daughter. I, so far, have heard from nobody out there. God bless Ted. I hope to see him in heaven someday. "Little more coffee, Ted?" "Blaaaack. Jim, what's your thoughts on . . ."

I might come down for a pre-Lenten spree. I must first find out when Lent begins, though. I am so wrapped up in liturgical observances that I can't keep the seasons sorted out—and of course we are all under considerable pressure to make the Lennon Sisters,* brought here by that old friend of showbiz Pere Ramacher, a sellout. No adults, however, will be permitted into the concert hall. The program, so the reports say, is suitable for preschool children, high-school and college students; no adults. I say, could you make a hole in another pint? No, I'm buying.

I'll be in touch with you in the next few days. The J. F. Powers Company is rather busy at the moment—one more letter to write before I can get to the *Pioneer Press*: the last one to my Polish publishers, who want to publish *The Presence of Grace* (one of my early books) and pay me under the "IMG program"—whatever that is. Since *Prince* did very well in Poland and I made about $150 out of it, I think I'll just have them send it to me (next time) in hams, by way of Duluth. You know (who better, eh, pastor?) the ham and sausage supper season will soon be upon us. I could market these hams to hard-up parishes or give them to people for whom a ham would make a suitable gift, beginning with the hierarchy in church and state. [. . .]

The opus is not going. I lie prostrate on the floor, with nothing between me and the bare boards but *Pioneer Presses* and *Minneapolis Tribunes*, and moan. I am going over the falls this time, and without a barrel.

No word from Donald McDonald, either.

Jim

* Featured with Lawrence Welk.

JOE O'CONNELL

Nihil Obstat
The J. F. Powers Company
"The Old Cum Permissu Superiorum Line"
Suite 7, Vossberg Building
St Cloud, Minnesota
February 22, 1960

Dear Joe,

In confirmation of our conversation of last night, I enclose a copy—my master copy—of the letter. I trust that you'll not feel left out. I don't know how your name happened to be left off the list, but I have asked that it be added, and I think it's safe to say that should there be other letters to writers and reviewers, you'll get yours. (Do not try to correspond with me at the above address. For some reason letters so addressed are returned to senders: just another handicap for the small businessman to overcome.)

Jim

February 4, 1960

Dear Mr Lund,[1]

You scarcely qualify as a writer in the limited sense I give the word, but I often read your column, and today, after noting what you say in it— "Incidentally, some gimmick will be decided upon soon on how to pick a name for the team . . . and it will probably wind up in a contest of some kind"—I decided to send you a copy of my letter to my fellow Minnesota writers and to ask you to do all you can to suppress such news until we—we Minnesota writers—can consolidate our forces and name our team according to the plan outlined in my letter. Get Joe Hennessy to lay

1 Reidar Lund (1910–1961), who for the last two years of his life was the sports editor of the *St. Paul Pioneer Press*.

off. If what you say in today's column appears as one of Hennessy's Tips of the Morning in the next few days, I will know that I was too late.

Sincerely,

J. F. Powers

[Enclosure]

January 30, 1960
412 First Avenue South
St Cloud, Minnesota

Dear Fellow Writer,

As you must know by now, our area will field a team in the National Football League in 1961. Some there were who said it couldn't happen here (and some there are who say we'll never acquire a baseball franchise in one of the major leagues), but be that as it may, we will have a team representing us in the National Football League in 1961.

Fellow writer, this team of ours must have a name, and I think it is up to us writers to see that the name chosen is a worthy one. Doubtless there will be those (secularism being what it is) who will rise up and say, "Why should these ~~fuckin~~' writers be the ones to name our team?"—and that is why I am writing to you today. At this very moment there could be taking shape in some businessman's ~~head~~ twisted mind a plan to run a popular contest to name our team, with prizes and a tie-in on season tickets, with all the usual boring ballyhoo and sad results. (I'm ashamed to say that the baseball team in my town, a granite-producing center, is called "the Rox.") We must, therefore, act at once to assert our authority in this matter. Let's stop drifting! It is no exaggeration to say that most people seldom give us a thought nowadays. Some years ago, in Minneapolis, T. S. Eliot, the prominent poet, attracted a crowd of 14,000 and much favorable comment from people in all walks of life, but we have not gone and done likewise. I might add that in the great days of the quiz shows of television it was eggheads in general, rather than writers, who were looked up to.

This, then, as I see it, is a splendid opportunity to let the people know of our continuing presence among them, and, what is much more, *to do our job*. In the matter of naming our team, we should see ourselves as surgeons performing a delicate, dangerous operation—and so, let us hope, the people will see us and draw back at the very thought of wielding the scalpel themselves, i.e., of naming our team.

I have some excellent names in mind for our team—the Paul Bunyans, or Buns, the Blue Oxen, or Blues, the Twins, Swedes, Vikings, Eskimos, or Zeros—and perhaps you'll be able to think of others as suitable—but that must come later. Here is what must be done first. We must announce that we are united and prepared, in our special capacity, to think of a name for our team; then, from time to time, word should leak out that we are pondering away in our studies and on our long walks; then that we are gathered in solemn enclave in some likely place—Schiek's Café or Izatys Lodge, up north; then, *finally*, would come the chosen name. In response to popular demand, we would run out into the field with the players at the start of the first game, or crawl out, as the case might be.

Before any of this can begin to happen, however, we must unite—under one name and one letterhead. What say you, fellow writer? I'd be glad to hear.

J. F. Powers

HARVEY EGAN

April 12, 1960

Dear Fr Egan,

Thanks for the clipping on Del in London: I'd missed that one.[1] If he keeps on, I'll write his biography. The next snipe hunt he puts on, we must attend. I think he would have been great anyway, but the St Paul sportswriters have done their part. Joe Hennessy writes that Del's in peak form, training as never before, and then Joe goes to Vero Beach and does the same kind of job on the Saints: Looks like Slugger Howard will be assigned to St Paul and will make the club a threat; Howard to Spokane. [. . .]

On the sunny side of the street: Donald McDonald back in the picture with new date for taping (May) to which I have naturally consented. Bring plenty of tape, I told him. I intend to attack everybody but Pope John.[2] [. . .]

Jim

1 Match with Phil Edwards in London, March 8, 1960. Decision: no contest. Referee disqualified both in seventh round for "persistent holding."
2 The result appeared in *Critic* 19 (October–November 1960).

JOE O'CONNELL
ST CLEMENTS HILL RETREAT HOUSE[1]
ON BEAUTIFUL HOLY SPIRIT LAKE
NEAR DUESTERHAUS, MINNESOTA

Date: June 14, 1960

Dear Mr. O'Connell,

It is our intention to sponsor a Spiritual Writers' Conference at the Hill this summer. Doubtless you have heard of writers' conferences, but unless I miss my guess, you will not have heard of one like ours— A SPIRITUAL WRITERS' CONFERENCE. This means exactly what it says: we will cater to writers engaged in work of a spiritual nature and to those who are thinking of entering this rewarding field.

Naturally, I am writing to you in your professional capacity. It is my hope that you will be a member of our staff and will take charge of "Reviewing." You will also be expected to give one public lecture or chalk talk. You may be interested to know that I am writing to other well-known writers (among them Emerson and Arleen Hynes, Leonard and Betty Doyle, J. F. and B. Wahl Powers), and I have every reason to believe they will accept. I understand that your wife is *not* a writer, or I'd invite her too.

Since this is to be a spiritual operation in every sense of the word, I will not bother you with material details save to say that you will, of course, be provided with a place to sleep and will be fed at our expense during your stay at the Hill. Our fare is plain, but outsiders tell us it's good and nourishing. We have our own bees.

The dates set for the Conference are August 7–12. (Please try not to arrive before Aug. 7.) I trust you'll give this invitation every consideration. We want you with us, Mr. O'Connell. The world needs reviewers of your stripe. I might add that a stock of published work by the staff will be on sale during the Conference and the public will be strongly urged to buy. Expecting to hear from you in the very near future, I am,

Sincerely yours,
Father Wilfred, OSC
Rev. W. Bestudik, OSB

---

1 The place to which Father Urban was exiled in *Morte D'Urban*.

J. J. O'Connell
R.R. 2
St Joseph, Minnesota

P.S. His Excellency Bishop Bullinger has given us reason to hope for an address from him in connection with a Field Mass.

25

No money is the story of my life

July 6, 1960—April 3, 1962

*Shanedling Building, room 5, next door to your friendly Household Finance
Corporation*

As was the case in 1956, the prospect of the Democratic and Republican National Conventions, in all their televised grotesqueness, drove Jim to purchase a television for the Powers household.

412 First Avenue South
St Cloud, Minnesota
July 6, 1960

Dear Jack,

Good of you to write, and, yes, I'm still here, two or three blocks away from where I was when I last wrote: old rockin' chair's got me, you might say. That doesn't mean I've deteriorated *physically*: I am ready to serve, if elected, but I don't expect it to come, if at all, until about the 28th ballot. I hope you can control your delegation. We need an arthur in the White House—and a Catholic arthur at that. I will not take second place. It occurs to me Kennedy is an arthur, and I don't want you to think that's what I mean. I am nonpolitical and always have been. I was laughed at when I suggested an Earl Long–Hubert Humphrey ticket some months ago (when Humphrey was still running for president), but it begins to look better now, doesn't it? Enough of that, except to say that I wish I had the price of a TV set, for I do enjoy the sight of those cotton-pickin' faces at conventions.

I wasn't surprised to read about your trip turning out as it did. It seems to me I've had other letters, in the past, from you to that effect. Why do you travel, Jack? People are pretty much the same all over. I am writing from my downtown office, in the heart of things, and don't have your letter, but I remember you did what you could to encourage me by quoting from the *TLS* and Bernard Malamud, for which I thank you. I feel more and more like a back number. It has been some time since I saw myself included among the important arthurs of our day, but then that happens to the best of us, doesn't it? Probably I have achieved what immortality I'll have. I continue with the novel, parts of which have appeared in *The New Yorker*, and hope to finish it this summer, when my advance royalty payments run out. There are times when I wish I'd gone into oceanography as a youth and were presently on an expedition somewhere. I think a lot of money as I grow older, and as my children do. [. . .]

All for now. Write.

Jim

Journal, August 4, 1960

Saw Bishop Sheen on TV the night before last, for the first time I can remember—"Why the Gloom in Modern Literature?" Appalling spectacle. Obviously knows little and cares less about the subject. Down on Graham Greene—who, it seems to me, uses Sheen's palette. No Americans mentioned, though for a moment I thought he meant me when he pronounced Proust as PROWST. He wrote an odd mixture of names on the blackboard he uses (after writing JMJ[1] at the top): Beauvoir, Sagan,[2] and Camus—only the last was written and pronounced "Le Camus." Only names to be mentioned favorably were Claudel[3] and T. S. Eliot. They, he said, had their hands against the dike, holding back the tide of gloom. He is the personification of gloom himself, Sheen, and it depresses the hell out of me to think of his success, considering what he does to earn it. "Ham what I am"—all the way. I had thought Fr Urban beneath him. Not so, by a long shot. The other way around. That voice, those gestures, and those red eyes. All ham and pride.

The 1960 expansion of both the National Football League and baseball's American League brought the Vikings and the Twins (the former Washington Senators) to Minnesota, each playing its first season in 1961.

---

1 Stands for Jesus, Mary, Joseph—inscribed at the top of written work by the pious.
2 Françoise Sagan (1935–2004).
3 Paul Claudel (1868–1955).

August 10, 1960

Dear Fr Egan,

As I see it, our team could be called many things—Eskimos, after the old Duluth entry in the NFL, but that would call undue attention to our climate, as would Zeros. Mosquitoes, though apt, would call attention to an aspect of our life that has been overstressed. Vikings wouldn't be fair to our whole population. Likewise Swedes. Millers has special connotations that wouldn't appeal to some of us. What it comes down to, in my opinion, is Lakers and Huskies and Maroons. The first and last have much to recommend them, but historically smack of failure. Looks like Huskies, therefore, to this observer, and I am giving that name my endorsement. However, I would support Lakers and Maroons, particularly the latter if A. A. Stagg would be available as coach. Any thoughts on the subject?

All well here.

Lack Tux and Will Not Travel . . . so come up and see us sometime.

Jim

Plowboys, do you think? Snowmen? ~~Reefers?~~ Northerners? Maybe you can give a thing like this too much thought, but Reidar did say recently that we ought to start turning it over in our minds. We now lead the nation in turkey production. Turkeys? Gobblers?
HUSKIES CLAW GIANTS 21–7
SNOWMEN ICE STEELERS 14–0
FROZEN TURKEYS BOW TO BEARS 28–21 (game played in snow)

Journal, September 19, 1960

If I were to begin another book today, I don't know whether it would be the Movement Book (beginning with Bellocian walks and eating and drinking à la George) or *NAB*.[1] Former seems more interesting at the moment—perhaps because of news that Leonard Doyle is planning to leave next summer for other parts: one more loss, or one more clinker dropping through the grate.

---

1 *NAB* (Nationally Advertised Brands), a novel in which a "supermarket derby" and a "bureau of conscience" were to figure.

412 First Avenue South
October 10, 1960

Dear Fr Egan,

[. . .] As for our team being called the Vikings, I am hoping to see something negative on this in Archbishop Brady's column soon; not representative of the whole community, etc. Since my name is Norman, I do not feel entirely out of it. [. . .]

Jim

CHARLES AND SUSAN SHATTUCK

Christmas 1960

Dear Chuck and Suzie,

Sitting up here in the office, contemplating the past and so on, I thought of you and seemed to remember that I'd written to you last year about this time, perhaps on this day. I find I'm worse off this year than last at this time, novel within three chapters of being finished, but nothing in the bank, advance royalties at an end, no stories out or in the works, and one week more in this office—the building to come down then. I am the last one here, and there wouldn't be heat but for a fly-by-night toy store downstairs (formerly Walgreen's agency) and the barbershop in the basement. Not so long ago I moved among lawyers and insurance agents and their secretaries here on the second floor. I don't look forward to finding another place. There is something about the J. F. Powers Company that doesn't gladden the hearts of businessmen with offices to rent. I pay $15 a month here and work out of a Victorian easy chair and off a low table—and, though I am perhaps one of the better writers in town, there isn't the interest here that there might be in me or my work. I'll let you know next year how it all turned out. Betty is well, though desperate with caring for our children, and would like another go at Ireland. I don't know. I tend to think in terms of great sums of money rather than far-off places as the answer to our problems. I realize this letter is all about me, but then what do I know about you? Or anybody?

Happy New Year.

Jim

St Cloud, Minnesota
December 30, 1960

Dear Michael,

Glad to have your card. Your handwriting isn't easy for me, but I gather you are now married (on which I'll have nothing to say except God help you both) and are coming out in a paperback[1] and may visit these shores in a year or so. We have no plans to go abroad. We have none to remain here. [. . .]

Now about politics, which I see is still with you, I took no part in it, as usual. I did not, and do not, like Kennedy. That doesn't mean he's no better than Nixon. If I permitted myself to entertain serious thoughts about politics, I'd be sorrier than I am that Adlai lost out. Gene McCarthy nominated him, as you doubtless know, in the best speech of the convention. Too bad it isn't Gene instead of Jack, if we have to have a Catholic. I understand Pope John's already packing. I think we can use him, too. What this country really needs is a monarch, as you people* keep telling us, and why not Farouk, whose interests are surprisingly American? All for now. My blessing upon you both.

Jim

* Malcolm Muggeridge, if not Martin Green.

Jim, forced to move out of his beloved office, managed to find another one, also in downtown St. Cloud.

HARVEY EGAN

January 9, 1961

Dear Fr Egan,

You will remember me, probably, as the occupant of room 7, the Vossberg Bldg, over Walgreen's. Well, today I moved, of necessity, since they are going to demolish the building soon, and now I am on the next corner, east, in what was formerly known as the Edelbrock Bldg, but is now better known as the Shanedling Bldg (pronounced Shanley, or Schaneedling, which I frankly prefer); room 5, second floor, next door to your

1 *William Faulkner*, part of Writers at Work series.

friendly Household Finance Corporation. The rent went up to $25, from $15 at the Vossberg Bldg, and I should be paying $45, but will move should a legitimate tenant covet my space. I have 200, or 300, square feet, I forget which; two telephones (disconnected); a place to brush my teeth (with a leaky pipe), i.e., a lavatory sans jakes, alas. With jakes and a bed, I don't know that I'd complain. I also have a fluorescent fixture for lighting, but I am hoping I'll be able to rig up a lamp of some kind. That's about it from here. [. . .] I know it's weakness, but I loved that old place and had to take myself in hand, leaving it. It was more my sort of thing.

 Anon.

 Jim

KATHERINE ANNE PORTER

412 First Avenue South
St Cloud, Minnesota
January 11, 1961

Dear Katherine Anne,

I got your card, for which thanks, and today your letter. [. . .]

I want to tell you how much I enjoyed your stories in the *Atlantic* and *Harper's*; I'd like to read more about Eliza, who dissected her food and said "Hum."[1] The ending is very fine in that one. The other story, "Holiday," is one of your finest on another level, a level you have all to yourself. No one else can go there. It is a great piece of writing, and I hope it has been recognized as such, though I doubt it. [. . .]

 Best,

 Jim

One of the amazing things about "Holiday," and one I was following with you bit by bit, going over the same ground after you, like another explorer, is the insight into Germans. I have been surrounded by people of German descent all my life, it seems—this is another German town—but I can never believe that what I feel to be true of them is enough to account for them as human beings. I had a German grandmother (on my mother's side) who worked all her life, and saved, and finally had to spend her last years with the mind she'd never really used, her body at last failing her, and it was very sad to see. She used to compliment me on the fine head of

---

1 "The Fig Tree."

hair I have, as if it were money in the bank. One day, when I was in my early twenties, she showed me a dollar bill and said, "He was our first president, wasn't he?" and then said she *wanted me to have it*, that dollar bill. At Christmastime, she got out old scraps of cloth and wrapped them up and presented them to members of the family—always a great thing for my father, who, I think, saw himself vindicated as a non-saver at such times. Well, you know all that, but you haven't let it go at that in this story, and what you have is so much more.

HARVEY EGAN

January 25, 1961

Dear Fr Egan,

I have been hoping for a miracle in the mail, that I'd get some money from somewhere, but rather than wait until the 11th hour, I've decided to apply to you for a loan of, say, $500, or less if that is too much for you, and save a little wear and tear on Betty's nerves (and mine). I have begun a story that has possibilities, I think, if I can end up with what I have in mind. In a month I should know about that and also have enough of the novel typed up for Doubleday to deal with them. I exhausted my advance royalties at the beginning of December but should be good for more if they can get a good chunk of manuscript in their hands. I fear my reputation isn't of the best, as a producer, and unlike Del—the J. F. Powers of boxing—I can understand why. Anyway, let me know how you are holding, and don't hesitate to tell me if you are strapped for funds. [. . .] I gather, from accounts of the fight, that Del did *not* slice up Lee like country ham. [. . .] All for now from the Schaneedling Bldg.

Jim

Gene McCarthy vs Barry Goldwater tomorrow night on TV—that might be good.

HARVEY EGAN

February 10, 1961

Dear Fr Egan,

Just to thank you for the check. I have a lot of time to think, or at least take a lot of time to think, but I don't come to any conclusions that strike me as good enough to act upon, with regard to the future. Our "nut" is too big here: $110 for rent at home, $25 for my new office; the schools are lousy; camaraderie is at an all-time low; but. Even if I were rich, though, I don't think I'd know which way to turn, to get out. Meanwhile, I work on this story as if everything depended on the next few words, work in the dark, unsure that I can make it come out, that I'll reach the last page . . . I see Del is going on in Rochester on a twin bill. [. . .] Baudelaire tells us that April is the cruelest month, but what about February?

Jim

HARVEY EGAN

412 First Avenue South
St Cloud, Minnesota
April 19, 1961

Dear Fr Egan,

Yours rec'd yesterday but read only once, and here I am at the office remembering you said something about the Twins and the Solons.[1] I couldn't possibly make it down there this weekend, much as I'd like to, and I am interested in the Twins. I think of the Griffith clan[2] as hillbillies somehow, but Cookie[3] looks good to me. We used to get a Cuban now and then down in Jacksonville when I was a boy, usually a pitcher for the other team. We had these Sunday games with Ray Zelle pitching for the Indees (us) and Clark behind the plate (when he could get out; he was a patient at the asylum). I was just a boy then, but my mind was formed, or touched, by it all. Ray looked awfully good—a tall pink-skinned lad with platinum hair—but they used to get to him in about the third inning. Ah, well, little you care about this, you with your Association ball and highfalutin ways. [. . .] I wish I could send Katherine Anne in my place for the game. She's nuts about baseball, and I don't know whether I approve or not. I don't want her to end up playing pro ball with some team in Gary, Ind . . . but I will be in touch with you. Do you get a new magazine called *Country Beautiful*?

Jim

1 Washington Senators.
2 Clark Griffith (1869–1955) and Calvin Griffith (1911–1999), successive owners of the old Washington Senators, which became the Twins.
3 Cookie Lavagetto (1912–1990), Twins manager.

Journal, May 16, 1961

Want to finish this book—then do *NAB*—then family-life one: latter appeals to me, the contrast between Bellocian life—wine, food, ideas, walks, travels—and what, in fact, happens to you in this country if you live in a place like Collegeville, have a lot of children, teach at a place like St John's . . . Dangerous idea—this Bellocian one—for someone like me. People like the Hyneses, who you might think are with you, don't get hurt. They work with a net under them; they live that way, I mean.

HARVEY EGAN

August 19, 1961

Dear Fr Egan,

I must tell you I rec'd word this morning that *Esquire* wants the story ("Twenty-Four Hours in a Strange Diocese") but will pay only $750, this although I sent my special jacking-up letter when I sent the MS. I can't do better, though, and so I must ask you to carry me on the books a while longer. Now, I know you'll do this with a smile, and probably don't even like to hear about it, but still I feel I must report in from time to time. We will now buy shoes and so on and probably get through October, by which time I trust my book will be finished and I can get back on Doubleday's relief rolls. [. . .]

Jim

Journal, September 22, 1961

No money even before I started writing for a living—no money is the story of my life.

In the autumn of 1961, the Doyles moved to Angola, New York, for a year, where Leonard taught at Calasanctius Preparatory School. While away, Leonard provided Jim with a Latin translation for a passage in Morte D'Urban. *Emerson Hynes and his family were living in Washington most of the time, where Emerson was Senator Eugene McCarthy's legislative assistant.*

October 21, 1961

Dear Leonard and Betty,

I don't know whether you remember me or not, but at one time I was prominent in apostolic circles in these parts. I have since fallen out of favor with just about everybody, and though there is a tendency in me to sulk and to think ill of myself simply because others do, and—what is worse—to think ill of others, necessity demands that I write and ask if you'll do some Latin for me, for which I'll pay you, say, $25, when I can afford to; at the moment, I can't. [. . .]

Nothing has happened since you left—nothing at all.

Jim

LEONARD DOYLE

412 First Avenue South
St Cloud, Minnesota
November 4, 1961

Dear Leonard,

Your wire rec'd yesterday, and your translation today—for which very many thanks. [. . .] When I can, I'll try to reward you in part anyway for the time and trouble. Times have been hard for me for a couple of years now. At the moment they are the hardest, with Xmas and all that coming on and the mail disappointing me daily. Still, I have finished the book, and for me at least that is something. I am now rewriting the early chapters, which have proved a sore disappointment to me.

I feel you'd be happy if I could fill you in on the local scene. I feel that you must think *something* must be happening, as I did when I was away, but I don't think a thing has happened since you left. [. . .] Whether you are missed by others, I don't know. It is a moot question whether anybody can be missed in this life we all lead. The O'Connells we see about once a week. Joe is still going back and forth to Mankato. He may do the jacket for my book. Hyneses, of course, were here in all their reflected glory, reflecting it. Em has written me a line since, saying Dick Keefe—remember him?—was in our nation's capital doing good work for education, as well he might, and who better, considering what *it's* like. Fred Petters, Dick Palmquist, Joe, and I went out one afternoon and put up Don's tombstone, but I understand it's loosened up in the meantime, in its foundation cement. I haven't seen Mary Humphrey for months. Fr Egan is returning from a couple of months abroad, looking into the cathedral situation with the idea of building one of his own. What else? The Gophers beat the Spartans[1] this afternoon, a stunning upset. Buses, I understand, a dozen or so every Sunday, come to St John's with students, nuns, et al., to see the new church, as it's called.[2] Our home life is all children and their fights and falling-outs. Let me know, if you find out what you're living for, but do not give up. The Baks, it seems, have taken your place on the highways, Hetty delivering children to various schools all day long. Now I must sign off. Best to youse both.

Jim

LEONARD AND BETTY DOYLE

St Cloud, Minnesota
December 7, 1961

Dear Leonard and Betty,

Whatever you say, there is something nice about getting a Christmas letter from me—something that might not happen to you if you weren't away from home—if that is what we have here. Myself, I'm afraid we have here no lasting home, any of us, except the Hyneses, of course, who have the marvelous faculty of being away from it without really leaving it (to hear them tell it), so there isn't the onus of treason or desertion in their case such as there's always been in ours. [. . .]

Joe is getting on with the job. He is also working on a jacket for my book. Jody has a new dog whose name is Mac. Joe has had a couple of feelers from St John's, one small job, one in Puerto Rico—you get the feeling they feel guilty about freezing him out and now that Frank[3] has been "fired" again are not afraid to approach Joe. Oh hell, don't ask me why Frank was fired—it would take *you* to get it all straight, and, of course, he isn't really fired. It happened before the Walker Gallery showing of the new church plans, pictures, etc. The payoff on this (the Walker show) was Bruno Bak being invited with other notables to the private showing and walking in with the abbot, and Fr John, and others—and then seeing that Breuer had made up some glass for the occasion. No sign of Bruno's work. We're told (by the Baks, though) that the abbot was humiliated by the situation he found himself in, as was Fr John, and that the Walker people

1 University of Minnesota Golden Gophers versus Michigan State Spartans.
2 St. John's Abbey Church, designed by Marcel Breuer.
3 Frank Kacmarcik had undermined Joe in the past.

were disgusted, too, by this kind of dirty pool (Breuer's men, presumably, arranged the exhibit), which, I think, has the odor of Frank about it. Ah, well. If I never hear another word (happy thought!) about that church, I'll be happy. There are times when I think I may have to immortalize them all there. I am not sure, though, that even if I did it as it should be done, they'd recognize it, or themselves. Intellectually, and aesthetically, they just don't burn with a hard gemlike flame. Have to go out there on Sunday, however, so as to escape the pledge taking that will go on everywhere else. [. . .]

Jim

HARVEY EGAN

December 26, 1961

Dear Fr Egan,

I got your note, and thanks, but I wasn't myself for a few days, including yesterday; nothing serious, just not able to take nourishment, and had my hands full chauffeuring Betty and the children up and down the river.[1] [. . .] The last I saw (on Xmas Eve), people were circling around other people with flashbulbs and cameras, and that was all I saw yesterday when I called for Betty and the kids (I stayed in the car). "Ever think of pornography?" I said to them out of the side of my mouth on the first night. [. . .]

I heard our bishop's midnight Mass address last night on radio (a playback): pretty strong stuff. He figures the nation's leaders, and not only this nation's leaders but other nations' leaders, are about ready to take the Bethlehem lesson to heart, having tried everything else, and if not now, then in centuries to come. By the way, he traded in the baby-blue Cad for a black Continental . . . [. . .]

Word reaches me that Fr Godfrey[2] was hard-hit by Pope John's words on vernacular (or Latin), set "us" back fifty years.[3] "Send 'em *Worship*! Send 'em *Worship*!" he cried, meaning *Time* magazine, and not Pope John, oddly enough. Ho, ho, ho, and a bottle of rum. This pronouncement (of Pope John's) changes *nothing* in my book. Could it be that I, of all people, am in touch with the mind of the Church?

Jim

1 To Art and Money's house and attendant festivities.
2 Father Godfrey Diekmann, a monk at St. John's and one of the prime movers in liturgical reform and the vernacular Mass.
3 Pope John XXIII spoke in favor of Latin being preserved as the teaching language of the Church.

412 First Avenue South
St Cloud, Minnesota
February 1, 1962

Dear Leonard and Betty,

Your letter rec'd and passed on to the O'Connells. I feel that it requires an answer of some sort—that you ought to be kept in touch with the situation here. But, as we say in the spiritual life, you can't give what you don't have yourself, and I am not in touch myself. The truth is, of course, there's nothing to be in touch with. But for what it's worth:

Mary Humphrey, at Fr Fehrenbacher's behest, had an evening at which, as it turned out, we not only got to meet a Hindoo but got to hear him lecture—for about an hour and a half, immediately after which I gave Betty the high sign and we got the hell out of the house. When we arrived, Mary was on the phone (you won't like it, Susie told me when I inquired what was going on), calling *The St Cloud Times*, saying she had an Indian from India and an Indian from Onamia, and wouldn't the paper like to photograph them together? Yes, a little while later, in comes Myron Hall and acts as though he expects everything will stop (by everything I mean the lecture) so he can get his picture. It didn't stop, and I shook his hand (quickly) on the way out as I was leaving and expressed sympathy, for he had to sit there an hour with his camera hanging out before he could consummate his business. So much for that: the worst deal I've been exposed to, of its sort, and that is saying something. [. . .]

Jim

In February, the production company MCA (Music Corporation of America) offered Jim a thousand dollars for a seven-year option on his short story "Defection of a Favorite" for a segment in its Going My Way *TV series. Jim turned it down, saying he wanted control and a percentage of the profits. MCA doubled the offer to two thousand dollars and reduced the time to three years. Jim turned it down.*

Journal, February 26, 1962
P. 545 Dictionary: firefly, any of several winged beetles whose abdomen glows with a phosphorescent light; the larvae and wingless females are

called *glowworms*. Would be good description of women and children in family-life novel.

Journal, February 27, 1962

15 below o. Car trouble, coming as it usually does, it seems—when we're scraping the bottom. New battery, new spark plugs, and possibly more. This is a bad time—and I don't see how we'll get through it unless money comes from out of the blue . . . I feel completely out of touch with sources of possible income—and very close to sources of expense: car, rent, food, and so on. No mail again.

Journal, February 28, 1962

29 below o. Had to call tow truck again this morning . . . Pinch is really on—in several ways: my work, my finances, my future. This has been a mean month.

The galleys of Morte D'Urban *arrived on March 21, 1962.*

CHARLES AND SUSAN SHATTUCK
412 First Avenue South
St Cloud, Minnesota
April 3, 1962

Dear Chuck and Suzie,

[. . .] I often think that if I'd had someone like you to push me around, editorially, I might have accomplished much more, but then I can see it wouldn't have been much of a life for you. Anyway, let me say, now that *Accent's* gone[1] (something I didn't know until I went to St Louis), that I am very grateful to you, Chuck, for your help and all-around kindness—at which point I think of that tar I tracked into your house on my first visit to Urbana and of the big party you gave for me on my last visit, and thank you, too, Suzie.

Yes, I too am glad the novel's over. I was through with it last December but had to take my place in line at Doubleday. A couple of other big authors ahead of me, Dick Nixon and Herman Wouk, were pushing the

1 Last issue was in 1960.

presses to the limit. It was not, [. . .] I was told, that they were better known than JFP, but just happened to be there ahead of him. Well, the book has some rough places in it, such as it wouldn't have if you'd seen it, or if more of it had been published in *The New Yorker*, but I am not unhappy with it. I feel pretty sure it's immortal—just *how* immortal is the question. [. . .] Just*

Jim

* Cribbed from Fr Urban, the hero of my novel.

26

The day was like other days, with the author napping on the floor in the middle of the afternoon

April 12, 1962—September 1962

Jim and Morte D'Urban

Journal, April 12, 1962
Could I, by next year at this time, be working on family-life novel?

Jim and Betty went to Minneapolis to hear Robert Lowell read at the Walker Art Gallery (Walker Art Center) and spent an evening with him, Elizabeth Hardwick, John Berryman, Allen Tate, James Wright, and others.

ROBERT LOWELL

412 First Avenue South
St Cloud, Minnesota
April 21, 1962

Dear Cal,

Very good of you to write and to say such nice things about my work: it is not as good as you say, of course, but as you or Ted[1] (I don't remember which one) once said, after a long discussion of Faulkner and K. A. Porter, What the hell—it's only prose. [. . .]

Betty and I both thought you read very well—I love that somewhat wheedling tone you use when taking the voice of the people as in "Skunk Hour"—and your comments were quite printable: I wonder, though, as I tried to tell you, how many can savor that sort of thing, not that you can do anything about it and many people, to bring *them* together, I mean. I wonder if you know how you sound and look in such a gathering as the one at the Walker Gallery, very foreign, I imagine: Betty remarked how alike the people and the pictures were. I can't get used to seeing people wearing blue jeans, and in shirtsleeves, and I think it's going out, thank God. I see one of those bastards, with a beard, and tricked out like that, and give

1 Roethke.

thanks I'm not teaching creative writing. That is what I'll have to do, though, if the book doesn't do well. I have even thought of going out on tour, playing the Catholic college circuit, exhibiting myself as Tom Thumb, or the Biggest Horse in the World, lecturing on Evelyn Waugh, the Prairie Years, Graham Greene, A Crash Program for God, and Luke Hart, Friend of Prelates. That is all I've been able to work out in my mind, so far (and Luke, by the way, is Supreme Navigator, or something of the sort, of the Knights of Columbus).

Everything depends on the success of the book—our getting out of here, the kids getting an education, and so on, everything—but I wonder. I had hoped that with a novel I could have a different feeling about Doubleday, for instance. I get ecstatic notes every month or so, but no replies to my questions concerning typography, revisions, and money, and then more ecstatic notes. I would like to ask, again, if the changes I made on the galleys will be carried out (a ridiculous question, you might think), but I can't; I break down and sit staring into space. I am on a desert island, and I am down to my last bottle: I don't know whether to send my last message today, tomorrow, or maybe next month. Oh, well, but that is my state of mind. [. . .]

About a blurb, Cal, nice of you, or mighty white of you, as Father Urban says in the book. (I have Fr U. get into a small car accident and have his car repaired at Cal's Body Shop, which I thought might appeal to you: I don't know why.) But you haven't read the book, and you might not like it all together, and if you wrote a blurb and I sent it to Doubleday, they would lose it or use it on somebody else's novel, and so I'll send you a copy of the book when it's ready, and if you feel moved, and not just from kindness, at that time, we'll see.

Let us hear from you again, and, yes, if I come to New York, I'll stay at your place. My best to Elizabeth and Harriet, and tell them to stop picking on each other.

Jim

Journal, April 25, 1962

Visit from a Joan Thomas at the house this morning, author of ten novels, with agents, creative writing courses, and so on—unpublished—and wanted *me* to help her . . . Needed money, she said, and seemed to think it could be got from publishers. I said she was fortunate not to have children—and she quickly assured me that children are a blessing. It all added up. She said Fr Casey is her "spiritual director." She is one of those, I think, who feel the facts of life and art are two different things and is out of touch with both.

Jim had struggled for weeks trying to write a review of Gordon Zahn's German Catholics and Hitler's Wars: A Study in Social Control (Sheed & Ward, 1962) and found himself contemplating again the German character, one of his preoccupations.

Journal, May 12, 1962

Wondering if I could someday (if I live long enough) write a *War and Peace* novel about the 2nd World War, with the main characters Germans, rise of the Nazis and fall of what good there was in German politics—very little, I think. I must try to understand the position of the army—a holy order of men, to the Germans, it seems. In a world of bullies, may God bless ours—is all it comes down to, I think. Fear, fear, fear.

LEONARD AND BETTY DOYLE

[May 1962]
St Cloud

Dear Leonard and Betty (if I may be so bold),

[. . .] St Cloud State is spreading out. It has played hell with what was the best part of town, and though the editor of *The St Cloud Times* keeps talking about the increase in payroll, it does seem too bad. Still, very few people realize it, and the student body must be humored, which I guess is the best reason to do away with trees and greenery, to make the terrain more and more like where the students come from. There is now a turnstile in the library, for checking users in and out, and that has made me reluctant to be seen there (I used to go there and read *Publishers Weekly* and *Variety*).

I did a review of Gordon's book for *The Reporter*, but it was, after being set up in galley proof, returned to me: it was believed I was being too hard on the German hierarchy, a grand bunch of fellows if ever there was one, and there were many, in Hitler's Germany. Review then went to the *Saturday Review*, on Gordon's suggestion, and was returned to me with a printed rejection, the first of those I've had in fifteen years or so. I am now thinking of submitting it to Fr Egan for his church bulletin. Very frustrating to one of our best loved, to say nothing of immortal, authors.

What else? My book is scheduled for September 21,[1] is not, so far as I know, being sought by major book clubs, the movies, or Broadway. [. . .]

Jim

JACK CONROY

412 First Avenue South
St Cloud, Minnesota
July 23, 1962

Dear Jack,

Glad to hear from you. I did get your jeering postcard from Moberly. I was never one to underestimate the strength and cunning of the Greyhounds, but then the Hawks, when the backfield was sober, weren't so bad in their day. Myself, I was never a student of Quincy College* but only of the Academy (we were known as the Little Hawks), and so did not play against the Greyhounds. I have shed blood in Missouri, though, in three sports, baseball, football, and basketball—in Hannibal and Monroe City. Actually, I never did very well in Missouri, come to think of it—or, come to think of it, anywhere else. Oh, a star, yes, but nothing like the star I am in our literary firmament. About my book, I don't know whether it'll win, lose by a short head, or run way out of the money. For the last year, I thought I'd really pulled it off—done almost as well as I'd hoped I would—but lately I've begun to doubt it. Maybe it's too odd a world I describe, to go over big. I don't know. [. . .] Just — Jim

---

* Our colors were brown and white, on account of the Franciscans.

HARVEY EGAN

412 First Avenue South
St Cloud, Minnesota
July 27, 1962

Dear Fr Egan,

Glad to hear you like the book—gladder perhaps than you would

---

1 It was actually published September 14.

think, for though I would still back it against your "Pass this one" or "Not today," I would prefer to bet with you. In the past week, I have had several good signs, word of a favorable comment from Evelyn Waugh, which Doubleday will doubtless be using; a nice long paragraph in *Publishers Weekly*, in their forecast department, although it does say the book is too underplayed for mass appeal; and your comment. At least it will not be left at the post, the book. I'll simply tell No boy (my jockey) to see that the horse doesn't get bumped at the start and boxed in at the eight pole. Anyway, your note made me feel pretty good.

The seats for the Yankees look good to me. How far will Roger Maris be standing from Mickey Mantle? That is what Hughie asked me today (he wants to see Maris, he says, more than Mantle). We have a new bat autographed by Mickey, but it seems to be a little heavy for the boys, and so I've just purchased another, autographed by somebody who calls himself Crackerjack. [. . .] Katherine should've been a boy as she has a lot of power at the plate. As for me, my arm is pretty well gone, but I have a lot of savvy and am getting by on that and luck. [. . .]

Jim

EVELYN WAUGH

412 First Avenue South
St Cloud, Minnesota
August 14, 1962

Dear Mr Waugh,

I didn't realize you'd been sent galleys and am all the more grateful for the favorable comment.[1] No, I haven't been on Christian-name terms with you in the past, and, to answer your question, it was the bishop's ball that broke Fr Urban's old spirit. I hope you don't mean I should've gone into the medical aspects of his case—injuries to the head (and spine) are very hard to diagnose, and though this would have been easy enough in fiction, I preferred to skip it. Perhaps you mean more than that. As I saw it, and see it, the change in Fr Urban had to come from without—a *rude* wind. Perhaps the book loses by it, the involuntary quality of the change, but otherwise there could have been none in Fr Urban, in my hands. I'm afraid you're right about my being more of a short-story writer than a novelist. I know I don't like to think of taking on another novel, though I

1 Waugh gave Doubleday a quotation.

must. Some of my devoted readers among the clergy have been after me to try a nonclerical book, and maybe I will. [. . .] Best wishes.

Morte D'Urban *was published by Doubleday on September 14, 1962.*

JACK CONROY

412 First Avenue South
St Cloud, Minnesota
September 18, 1962

Dear Jack,

Thanks for sending on your review (and the one from the *Tribune*, about which I won't say more). You were good to me, Jack, and you wrote a beautiful, creative review, doing everything you could for me in the space and doing it so that it was a pleasure to read as writing. [. . .] The *Mpls Tribune* man slugged me good on Sunday: I think he regarded the book as a threat to earnestness in business and the arts in Mpls, and humor with a capital *H*, as in HA HA, and so he called it banal, said I eschewed "rugged plot"—what the hell, I wouldn't mention it, but people see me on the street here and look away as if I'd been taken in adultery with a chicken. The *Sunday Visitor*, Catholic weekly, the other organ of book reviewing that enters St Cloud, also blasted me. [. . .]

Jim

HARVEY EGAN

Between the Bookends
September 1962

Publication day was marked by two events, a phone call at 4:00 a.m. from Johnny Berryman, poet, critic, University of Minnesota professor teaching this year at Brown, in his cups, and reading the book, and saying he'd phoned (from Providence) to tell me that a night letter was coming, which did, in fact, arrive. The day itself was like other days, with the author napping on the floor in the middle of the afternoon, and then in the evening there was a surprise party preceded by any number of telltale clues, Betty not going to bed at her usual time, having her hair combed, and wearing shoes, plus the porch light being on, and somebody had even flushed the toilet. A gay evening, Guinness mixed with beer. Today no mail at all, and so it goes. I am much cheered by your predictions of success and would still not bet against the book, but let's face it, it's being slammed into the rails on the turns. Still nothing from *The New Yorker,* and so I'm not moving from my cabin door. Sometimes I think I'm dead—ever get that feeling? All for now.

Jim

27

As a winner, let me say you can't win, not on this course

October 23, 1962—August 29, 1963

Jim and Leon Edel, National Book Award ceremony, 1963

The novel was badly handled by Doubleday. The text was rife with mis-prints, and breaks in the narrative were not indicated. Bookstores didn't get the number of copies they ordered, and in the coming months the book kept going out of stock. Jim's letters to Ken McCormick, his editor at Doubleday, became increasingly bitter: "If you weren't out of stock on publication day, you were so close it must have gladdened the hearts of the men who worry about the high cost of warehousing . . . I pray that my book isn't out of stock for periods between now and Christmas, as it's a long, long time between Christmases." (It was, in fact, unavailable in places for periods before Christ-mas.) Beyond that, Doubleday's advertising department was too late in getting ad copy to many of the journals in which the book was to be publicized and bungled the wording of Evelyn Waugh's expression of admiration.

Journal, October 23, 1962

After yesterday's incredible news of a blockade on Cuba, I don't know what to think about the future, already depressing enough.

CHARLES SHATTUCK

412 First Avenue South
St Cloud, Minnesota
November 6, 1962

Dear Chuck,

Good to hear from you, to see that you still can't type, are safely back in captivity, and to know that you do like the book. I wish you might've read it in manuscript, but otherwise I have no regrets, which is rather surprising: it is as if I've been packing a bag to catch a train and actually got everything in. Well, I did wish I'd made Dr Fish Dr Jass (the name on the door in the old offices of the Clems), but for reasons only an old musician might appreciate and small ones at that. (Perhaps you know the old tune "Dr Jazz," where the man calls out, "Hello, Central, give me Dr Jazz!")

I gather the book doesn't come off to the extent I hoped it would, for you and others, and whether this is actually the case, due to the fact that you've read parts as stories (as you say), to the fact that I am not a novelist, or, what I sometimes think is the same thing, lack patience, or have an 18th-century mind, or no mind at all, I don't know. I had hoped—and had some reason to hope, going by first reports, not only from Betty and friends, but from booksellers—that the book would be a bestseller, and perhaps it will be, over a twenty-year period, but so far it hasn't made its move. In six weeks, it has sold about 12,000 copies (that is the total sale, rather, for there was a pretty good advance sale). This is more important to me than in the past, since this is a novel—it is the novel I was assured would make all the difference in the world—and not another collection of stories, and I do not think I'll do better. If I can't make it with this one, I'll have to give up the idea I've lived with and on so many years—short-story writer, no, novelist, yes, economically speaking. The book was published last Thursday in England, and I'm hoping it will be less of a puzzle there. [. . .] Best to you both and to others there.

Jim

Journal, November 7, 1962
Scotty (the typewriter man) brought back my typewriter almost completely refurbished and would take nothing. I was thinking a while ago what, in a very few words, my trouble has always been and still is: a desire to associate excellence with eminence. This is the rub that keeps me thinking (in my fashion) and writing.

Birdie Strobel, Betty's aunt, died on November 16, 1962.

Morte D'Urban *continued to be plagued by what Jim considered Doubleday's incompetence, most especially its small print runs and failure to supply enough books to stores during the gift-buying season. He was also disappointed by the reading public's lack of enthusiasm for the novel. By December 11, 1962, it had sold 13,864 copies, half of what Jim had hoped for and, indeed, expected. His journal makes melancholy reading, as do his letters to his editor at Doubleday, Ken McCormick: "What am I doing you ask, and the answer is suffering. I have written (and sold to* The New Yorker, *fortu-*

nately) a fine long story,[1] *but mostly I have been sweating it out, watching my hopes for the future disintegrate."*

Journal, December 14, 1962

Both bookstores in town are out of stock on my book and awaiting more copies—but I doubt they'll arrive before Xmas . . . Al [Strobel] left for Idaho today,[2] for Christmas. Who would have thought this the last time I drove him to the train?

JACK CONROY

412 First Avenue South
St Cloud, Minnesota
December 18, 1962

Dear Jack,

Let this be my Xmas letter and card to you (I do not plan to purchase any of the latter this year). [. . .] The book is still alive, Jack, and just might come on stronger, but as of now I have to call it a flop—by my expectations and perhaps even by Doubleday's. I am pretty well disorganized in my mind as to my future, whether 'tis better to be a novelist or a short-story writer, for in my case there really isn't a great difference in the payoff, unless, of course, the novel is going to put on the longest come-from-behind stretch run in history. Whether we stick it out here, or I take a job teaching, or we go abroad again—this depends on the book's sale. [. . .]

You will not send me a copy of *The Disinherited*, Jack.[3] I'll buy one—and that is that. If you send me one, I'll return it to you autographed. That is the form failure has taken in my case, Jack. I autograph every book I can lay hands on, this to compensate for the great success I might have had, and am now watched when I enter the public library here. All the textbooks my daughters bring home from school I've autographed. Ever hear of a case like this, Jack? . . . Yes, I heard from Herman Kogan,[4] who

---

1 "Keystone," *The New Yorker*, May 18, 1963.
2 Where his daughter and her family lived.
3 *The Disinherited* was being republished with an introduction by Daniel Aaron, the author of *Writers on the Left* (1961), among other works, and one of the founders of American studies as an academic discipline.
4 Herman Kogan (1914–1989), Chicago journalist.

asked me to do a short piece for the book page, and I said I might—and thought I just might a month ago—but I am miles away from such thoughts now. I am only interested in writing my name these days. That is all, Jack.

J. F. Powers

J. F. Powers

J. F. Powers

Al Strobel died on January 22, 1963, only a couple of months after the death of his wife. The Powers family had to vacate the house they had been living in for over three years.

HARVEY EGAN

January 24, 1963

Dear Fr Egan,

[. . .] Al Strobel died Tuesday evening, in bed, from a heart attack. Bertie, I think I told you, his wife, died in November. This is a knockout blow, their deaths, the end of something. The children—wife of dentist, a physician, an optician, and a newspaperman—are on the scene now. The funeral is tomorrow. Al was a very good and gentle man. He grew flowers, had nails and screws of all sizes, and never got excited. The children, though he didn't work at winning them over, loved him. I used to think of him as a typical small-town businessman, really only the husband to Bertie, but for several years I have known better and have respected him. He is someone I hope to see again. I was the last one to see him alive and, fifteen minutes later, the first one to see him dead. I shouldn't be telling you this, I know, but that is what's on my mind. No news otherwise.

Jim

Jim, filled with gloom about Morte D'Urban's *prospects, wondered how to make a living. One moment he would resolve to take the next good teaching job offered him; the next he would turn down just such an offer.*

On February 10, 1963, the six leading contenders for the National Book

Award were announced. In addition to Morte D'Urban, *they were Vladimir Nabokov's* Pale Fire; *Katherine Anne Porter's* Ship of Fools; *Dawn Powell's* Golden Spur; *Clancy Sigal's* Going Away; *and John Updike's* Pigeon Feathers, and Other Stories. *Publicity was hampered by the New York newspaper strike (which ran from December 8, 1962, until March 31, 1963). Jim was pleased to be nominated but believed that Nabokov would win.*

HARVEY EGAN

St Cloud
March 2, 1963

Dear Fr Egan,

[. . .] I turned down a chance to lecture at Columbia University ($500), and also to teach this spring at the University of Chicago, and also to teach at Purdue ($10,000). On the other hand I was trying on a pair of used dress rubbers at the Goodwill a while ago: impossible to find cloth-lined dress rubbers, did you know that? I picked up an old 78 Victor record at the Goodwill which I'm looking forward to hearing this evening (we fell heir to the Strobels' radio-phonograph), a little thing called "Sahara (We'll Soon Be Dry like You)" from Monte Cristo Jr., which played at the N.Y. Winter Garden. It is sung by Esther Walker, whoever she was. On the flip side is "Nobody Knows (and Nobody Seems to Care)," also sung by Esther, composed by Irving Berlin. All right, so it doesn't look like much of an evening. But that's life in St Cloud and perhaps everywhere. [. . .]

Jim

Morte D'Urban *won the National Book Award, presented on March 12, 1963, in New York—where the newspaper strike continued. The judges were Elizabeth Hardwick, Harry Levin, and Gore Vidal. The prize was a thousand dollars. Jim was happy, except for having won over Katherine Anne Porter, who had done so much for him.*

412 First Avenue South
March 10, 1963

Dear Jack,

The book has won the National Book Award, and I am leaving for New York tomorrow. [. . .] I travel by train—Great Northern, Burlington, New York Central, and back—and should be returning through Chicago on Friday. I'll give you a ring at your office. Sam Gadd mentioned that your novel would be out by now, and I hope to get a copy in New York— that is another reason to leave this town, where *Morte D'Urban* and *Happiness Is a Warm Puppy* are the bestsellers. [. . .] Through two deaths in my wife's family we will be losing our perch overlooking the Mississippi here. I wish you could be in the Americana Hotel on Tuesday (the cocktail hour) to hear my acceptance address. It starts out like this: Down in the Lehigh Valley/Me and my pal Lou . . . [1]

Jim

I'll call you when I arrive at LaSalle Street Station, in the morning, on Friday—unless of course I am held up in New York, in *any* sense.

CHARLES AND SUSAN SHATTUCK

412 First Avenue South
St Cloud, Minnesota
March 15, 1963

Dear Chuck and Suzie,

Very good of you to write, Chuck. I am only just back from the Big Town, where I was wined and dined and pleasured in general but where I behaved myself as a holy founder should: your name, too, came up every now and then, and that kept me on course, but never fear: in all my interviewings I never once mentioned you or in fact anyone much but me, me, me. My acceptance speech was a little gem of cool conceit, a thing writers should display oftener on such occasions, I think, since they have nothing to lose anyway. It now belongs to the ages, my speech, but *The NY Times Bk Review* will pay me to use it in the event papers are published again in the Big Town (oddly enough, I was about the only one

1 Joke.

there using that term; I did not meet Walter Winchell).[1] I did meet Hedda Hopper, though, and except for our age difference, and maybe not that, we have a lot in common besides our publisher.[2] "Did Doubleday send you my book?" she asked (this after she said that she did indeed believe my success was due to hard work, clean living, and large advances). "No," I said. "That's Doubleday!" she cried, and there we were again, hitting it off. "This man won the fiction prize, Hedda," said a famous newspaper editor, "but I think you should've had it." Then we were parted, Hedda and I—it was impossible to talk with the *Life* people riding herd on Hedda—but later she asked to see me again, and I was soon standing before her, hitting it off again. "I wanted to say goodbye," she said. "And I," I said. "Goodbye, then," she said. "Goodbye," I said, "and—" "Yes?" she inquired, her hat inclining dangerously toward me. "Just stay as you are," I said in a husky tone. She smiled back, and then she was gone. The truth was I liked the old gal—and, really, 75 isn't so old . . .

I called on Bob Henderson, who said he'd had a bad fall of sickness but looked fine. He asked how you'd liked the book, mine. [. . .] Blamed whatever faults it has on you because you failed to read it in the manuscript. Well, there was a lot more I might tell you, for kicks, but except for the thousand dollars there are no *clear* gains: I did feel, however, that my reputation is growing and not just in my own imagination. I was a longshot choice—a good show bet, and I am sorry if KAP will be at all disappointed, as perhaps she has reason to be (I still haven't read her novel); I hate the role I've been cast in, or will be, say, in *Time*, assuming, of course, the story appears there. (The *Time* interviewer, after finishing with me, said, "Now I'm off to Little, Brown." "*Is* that the story?" I asked. "That's the story," I was told.) [. . .]

The date for the awardees to appear on the *Today* program on TV was suddenly called off, our appearances, with only this by way of explanation and this only by hearsay: "Who's heard of 'em?" This, after my poor wife, children, and bloodthirsty friends were all alerted to the time and channel. And had to be de-alerted, long-distance, late at night. In these matters, I am strictly eye for an eye and will quietly await an opportunity, coast-to-coast and prime time, to tell the nation. Hugh Downs, who represents all that's best in our thinking today, is the emcee of the *Today* program and

1 Walter Winchell (1897–1972), newspaper-and-radio gossip reporter; habitually called New York "the Big-Town."
2 Hedda Hopper (1885–1966), gossip columnist for the *Los Angeles Times*. On JFP: "A charming shy man, I imagine he's quite lonely at times."

provided one of the lines in my book (speaking of Islamism), "That's one of the world's top religions." Enough of this, Chuck and Suzie.

Love,
Jim

JACK CONROY

412 First Avenue South
St Cloud, Minnesota
March 19, 1963

Dear Jack,

Thanks for the clippings. Joe Diggles also responded, and so I'll be able to send one pair to my folks in New Mexico. About the Kogan story, Jack, never fear: I would never see you in the role you've been cast in, as you are one of the last gentlemen on earth, and since very few people, if any, would take exception to the idea that you shaped my career, since few would know otherwise, well, what the hell? I only wish you'd had more to do with it, that I'd known you earlier—and, of course, you remain the first published arthur I ever laid eyes on. In fact, in rereading the above, I only wish I had a career. [. . .]

I rec'd an invitation today from Mrs R. Ferguson of the Friends of Literature to attend the 32nd Annual Shakespeare Birthday Program and Award Dinner on Saturday, April 27, 6:30 in the Walnut Room of the Bismarck Hotel, but she don't say nothing about giving *me* an a-ward, just talks about spending the evening with kindred spirits, and nothing about transportation either. It don't sound like my kind of thing, Jack. Once you get a taste of an a-ward, Jack, you want it all the time.

STOP SENDING ME THOSE DAMNED LEAFLETS AS I AM SAVED.

Best wishes,
Jim

HARVEY EGAN

St Cloud
March 21, 1963

Dear Fr Egan,

[. . .] I do have a lot of mail, as a matter of fact, but not as much as you'd think, and it is already tapering off. Nothing is different—and the prospect ahead gives me the shakes. By which I mean the exodus. I find, at this point, I have no needle on my compass.

I'd be glad to tell you of my adventures in the Big Town, actually not so exciting, since I was bent on staying vertical and in fact managed to do so. High points: Hedda Hopper, Ed Skillin (who I hadn't met before), my acceptance speech, the hit of the evening, my dazzling performances with the interviewers, my relentless affability—so that I became thoroughly sick of myself and was glad to get the hell out of town. [. . .] I was decent all the way, telling Doubleday I'd rather wait and see before signing on for more advance royalties. It will come to that, of course, in time. As a winner, let me say you can't win, not on this course, and perhaps not on the next. Anon.

    Jim

Journal, March 29, 1963

Word today from Ken McCormick that I, if willing, can have honorary degree from Adelphi College on June 12, with Leopold Stokowski, Mary Martin, and William Schuman. I don't think so.[1]

KATHERINE ANNE PORTER

St Cloud
April 11, 1963

Dear Katherine Anne,

[. . .] The award [. . .] made my life difficult where you were concerned. Your letter of congratulation relieved my mind, but I hated my part in the business, though God knows I needed something of the sort. I had counted on my novel to sell enough to give me a house of my own in Ireland, or somewhere, and a couple of years. I was insane to think this could happen, people told me in New York recently, said I was lucky to have done as well as I had with the book. Well, if so, I don't know how to look the future in the face, for I don't expect to write a better book and certainly not a more salable one. [. . .]

    Yours . . .

    Jim

1 He declined.

Jim won the Thermod Monsen Award from the Society of Midland Authors, presented in Chicago on May 24, 1963.

HARVEY EGAN

May 3, 1963

Dear Fr Egan,

[. . .] Boz thinks the Kralick-Perry trade is a good one for our Twins.[1] I don't know myself (know thyself, right?), but I do not think Cal[2] will ever put our welfare before his own. About a day at Met,[3] I'll have to go down sometime, I know, but dread it. Maybe by bus or train, with cab to and from Met. I wish, as always, Betty could drive and bear more of the burden. Marriage isn't a 50–50 affair, I know, before you sic your curate on me.

Big fund-raising campaign beginning here, with out-of-town strong-arm men masterminding it. One thing they plan is to make anyone who doesn't come up with it wear a scarlet *A* back and front. Fortunately, they will accept payment in livestock, agricultural products, or old manu-scripts. [. . .]

Word from Chicago is that the affair will be in the King Arthur Room of I've-forgotten-which hotel and that some of the men will wear black tie. I plan to wear white sneakers with brown rubber soles and a towel around my shoulders. [. . .]

Jim

HARVEY EGAN

May 7, 1963

Dear Fr Egan,

[. . .] I hate this lousy heat, which is all very well when you're wheeling around in a monastery garden, with your sandals on and the swallows twit-tering around your toes. On St Germain Street it's murder, and I often think, yes, this is how I'll go: down on the pavement, with the butts and Popsicle sticks and Mr Goodbar wrappers, to the music of hillbilly music in the passing convertible, farewell, Household Finance, S. S. Kresge, Three Sisters, it was good while it lasted—or was it?

1 The Twins traded the pitcher Jack Kralick to Cleveland for Jim Perry.
2 Calvin Griffith.
3 Metropolitan Stadium for a Twins game.

Boston, judging by this column[1] I enclose, sounds like a much better place to live, or do I mean die?

Jim

CHARLES SHATTUCK

412 First Avenue South
St Cloud, Minnesota
May 27, 1963

Dear Chuck,

Thanks for the letter. I am glad you like the story[2] as you are the highest court I recognize in such a matter. [. . .]

I played Chicago last Friday night, the King Arthur Room of the Sheraton-Chicago (actually the Medinah Athletic Club), and, as usual, knocked them in the old Kent Road with my speech. For the first time in my life, I wore a tuxedo (rented) and liked my looks so much that I sat up for hours, after the ball was over, just admiring myself in the mirror. I mean to get one first thing when I am rich. I don't know what it means—secret hankering for order, holy orders, great wealth, you name it. This was in connection with the Monsen award given by the Society of Midland Authors, $500. I was sorry I missed the Pulitzer, as I'm told it's good for sales. My sales, however, have been good since the National Book Award, have now reached 23,000, which is just a little less than half of what I'd hoped for about this time last year, before the book was published. It is going as well now, though, as it did at any time last fall, and I hope it continues so I can get out of the field entirely and into something more remunerative, something, perhaps, that would require that I wear evening dress. Am I entering a new period—my "Raffles" phase?

We still don't know where* we're going by summer's end, or perhaps before if the house we're living in is sold out from under us. I think I told you deaths in Betty's family will require that we move on.

I have had some good job offers but have turned them down.

Best to you both . . .

Jim

* Betty is for Ireland again.

1 George Frazier praised *Morte D'Urban* in his column in *The Boston Herald*, April 22, 1963: "On the basis of a single novel, Mr. Powers seems to me the most gifted fiction writer in America today."
2 "Keystone," *The New Yorker*, May 18, 1963.

412 First Avenue South
June 29, 1963

Dear Jack,

Thanks for the publication with my picture (and the other NBA winners) in it: I don't mind being from St Cloud, Illinois—it may lead to a clarifying footnote in years to come, and it may change my luck. [. . .]

I was sorry not to see you in Chicago but needed the time I might have used for a decent meal with you, needed it for my speech, which turned out all right but gave me a lot of trouble and worry until it was over. I didn't meet Hoke Norris[1] (whom I'd met in N.Y.) but did see Van Allen Bradley[2] again and met Herman Kogan for the first time. I had the feeling that I was better known to them than to the ordinary membership, but I am used to that: my fame and fortune, if any, will be posthumous, I fear. [. . .]

I'm sure Wharton[3] would've done a better job than the Jesuit: *he* had no idea, of course, that the book would create the stir it did and was only doing what he could to downgrade it, a thing that happened to me here and there, with a certain amount of malice aforethought. Why, I don't know, for to know me is to love me.

If I live long enough, and don't find another, better way to make a living, my next book will have little or nothing to do with the Church . . . and we'll see how they like them apples.

I've read most of Algren's new book,[4] and find some good lines and touches and a point of view that holds up, but the book misses in too many places: things like his Ked Gavilans,[5] for God's sake. On the other hand, I enjoyed his treatment of Mailer and Baldwin, neither of whom I know, but both of whom make my arse tired, they themselves rather than their work, though I did find Baldwin's last novel unbelievably bad. But all of them, including Algren, still believe in Santa Claus, which I guess is the distinguishing mark of the American, writer or not.

---

1 Hoke Norris (1913–1977), literary editor of the *Chicago Sun-Times*.
2 Van Allen Bradley (1913–1984), literary editor of the *Chicago Daily News*.
3 Will Wharton, a.k.a. Wallie Wharton, had been business manager of *The Anvil*, the literary journal founded by Jack Conroy.
4 Nelson Algren, *Who Lost an American?* (1963).
5 Kid Gavilan, Cuban boxer.

May large birds defecate on the heads of most of the reading public for not buying the works of J. F. Powers.

I am, sir —Jim

J. F. Powers

HARVEY EGAN

August 6, 1963

Dear Fr Egan,

[. . .] I am crazy with the heat, and so is my typewriter, which, ever since Scotty, of Scotty's business machines downstairs, fixed it, hasn't been the same. Instead of a twenty-dollar gold piece when I die, so the boy'll know I was standing pat, I want my typewriter in the coffin with me. I love this little machine.

I have decided on the first word of my new novel. It is "I" and now for the second one. [. . .] Anon.

Jim

Jim's hope that Morte D'Urban *would bring financial salvation and a place to live was finally extinguished. The novel sold only twenty-five thousand copies in hardcover, and so, he wrote, "the great experiment with the great American (and British) reading public is over, so far as I am concerned."*

JACK CONROY

412 First Avenue South
St Cloud, Minnesota
August 29, 1963

Dear Jack,

[. . .] We are hauling ass for Ireland soon. I am apprehensive, but that is the only place that lights up at all on the map, if only dimly. [. . .] I am trying to get into a new novel, nonclerical, but not doing so well at the moment, what with all the commotion of packing and disposing (again) of worldly goods. In the words of Lead Belly, I am, like the boll weevil, lookin' for a home. We have here below no lasting home, we all know, but in my case there seems no margin for error to build on. I keep having to get rid of furniture and sets of books that were going to adorn my estate after which the collected edition of my works was going to be named, but perhaps it's just as well. We sail from New York on September 13, on the *Nieuw Amsterdam*. Anon, then, Jack.

    Jim

28

Ireland grey and grey and grey, then seen closer, green, green, green

September 23, 1963—Christmas 1963

Sailing to Ireland aboard the Nieuw Amsterdam, *September 1963*

The Powers family traveled to New York by train and sailed on the Holland America Line's Nieuw Amsterdam ("easy voyage and bad food"), arriving in Ireland on September 19. From the United States, they had arranged to stay in the Trenarren Hotel in Greystones as paying guests for the rest of the month. After that, the proprietors were moving to England for four months, during which the Powers family would have sole occupancy. That was the plan, but it was not how it worked out in the end. It became a dismal affair.

DOYLES, O'CONNELLS, PALMQUISTS, PETTERSES

Trenarren Hotel
Greystones, County Wicklow
Ireland
September 23, 1963

Dear All,

[. . .] Let me say at the outset that nothing has been gained so far and nothing lost. I do not find myself any clearer in mind than I was a month ago. The trip, as regards weather and children, was better in the first and about what I expected in the second. Arriving in St Paul, we went to the St Paul Hotel, got the children to bed—all of us in one big room, with two bathrooms—and Betty and I went down for a drink in the Gopher Grill, Carlsberg beer, and then back to the room, where the ten o'clock news was coming on. I began to watch Channel 4 for what I thought just might be the last time when Fr Egan showed up. He regaled us all until the children dropped off, and then I took him to his car, which, a Mercedes diesel, I am to inherit on his death.

The trip down the river the next morning on the Builder[1] was beautiful in a way I've seldom seen in the Middle West: raining slightly, with fog

---

1 The Empire Builder.

hanging over the river and in notches in the little mountainous hills, with grey herons set out like lawn furniture at suitable intervals, literally hundreds of them. Chicago was humid and eightyish and no place to shop for salami, cheese, pickles, bread, beer, and canned soft drinks, with only an hour to do it in, which was what I did, but fortunately I know my way around the Loop and have plenty of money for cabs. This stuff we ate and drank in our compartments so we didn't have to appear en masse in the diner on the 20th Century.[1] (By now you will have noticed that we were following in the footsteps of Fr Urban, from Builder to Century.)

New York was also humid and eightyish the next morning. We were compelled by our numbers to take two cabs to our hotel. We then quarreled for a while, the whole family, and some of us took baths, and some went out to see the Empire State Bldg, I leading this group and, one thing leading to another, actually going up and paying money to do so and glimpsing the *Nieuw Amsterdam* at her berth in the distance. I returned and called various people in publishing and show business such as Al Jolson and soon, as luck would have it, was out on the streets again leading the same group as before (Jane, Hugh, Boz) from Schrafft's for sodas to Hoffritz's for a brass compass to Gimbels for a very good buy in lead soldiers and a paddle and ball, all of which we needed, with our baggage, like yet another hole in the head. But as you might guess, I was fighting for my life by this time.

That evening we dined and wined at Robt Lowell's apartment, and the next morning he saw us off at the boat. The ship sailed easily except late on the first day and once or twice for short intervals, but the food was a large disappointment to all and particularly to Fatso, who had been looking forward to a gastronomic bash. In the end, she consoled herself with innumerable Holland gins at ten cents a throw and little Dutch cigars. I spent hours on the deck in my chair and blanket and wondered at the meaning of life aboard ship. Everywhere I looked I saw Hedi and Bruno living it up and, having traveled on American, German, and British vessels before, thought there was really no way to escape the sight of same. One man and his wife were particularly hard to stomach: he was handsomely grey with a sabre scar on his left cheek, à la Heidelberg, and she was long-legged (in yellow slacks) and leathery of visage, and when separated by other acquaintances they were busily striking up in all directions would call and wave and smile to each other sweetly from time to time. "Blow it

[1] 20th Century Limited.

out!" I'd say to myself from time to time, resorting to this nautical term, although the navy was not my branch of the service.

We saw *The Leopard* in the cinema aboard and enjoyed it more for the scenery and for what it might have been than what it was. The last night, as we approached Ireland, there was fog, and consequently thoughts of immortality. The name *Nieuw Amsterdam* struck me as just right for a sea disaster, doubtless because of Hopkins's poem about the wreck of the *Deutschland* or something. Ireland grey and grey and grey and then seen closer, green, green, green: the same old tender coming out to meet us, the same old fat man employed by American Express, and the wonderful consideration shown by porters and customs men and baggage men, as always, which is why, when you travel in the other direction, you are almost killed by New York.

Train to Cork (from Cobh), from Cork to Dublin, and on to Dun Laoghaire, and then by cab ("You must have a very big trunk—boot, that is—to get all that luggage stored away"—"Vauxhall has a very big boot, sir") to the Trenarren Hotel in Greystones. It is not, we saw right away, the hotel we had in mind. It is dumpy in its furnishings but excellent in its cuisine, miraculously so, and we'll be all right, I guess, for the next four months. The boys went to school today, Christian Brothers, and seemed to fare very well, and this I regard as a blessing from God, as I feared this aspect of our trip as much as any. We had tea with the O'Faolains this afternoon. They say we could buy a house with only a little down, but, though this is news to me, I don't know. I have been so busy cursing Doubleday and the American reading public for not giving me a bestseller that the idea of lighting a candle is strange to me. Now I'll close with gratitude to you all—for your various favors, especially the ladies.

Jim

FRED AND ROMY PETTERS

Trenarren Hotel
Greystones, County Wicklow
October 7, 1963

Dear Fred and Romy,

[. . .] For the last five or six days we've been running the hotel by and for ourselves. This, in the former respect, mostly means Betty, who even now is down in the kitchen—one of them—scraping grease off the wall behind the stove—one of them. I want you to understand what I'm saying but can only bear to look in for moments at a time in that region: there are what we would call four or five large rooms down there, all parts of the cooking setup: a room with stoves in it, one with a sink, one with a refrigerator, and so on, so that Betty gets plenty of exercise whenever she prepares a meal.

I am writing this from my office in the unused half of the hotel, somewhat away from the madding crowd. I have a distant view of the sea and a much better one of a filling station where there are Mobiloil and Castro signs, the latter being some kind of gas or oil, I guess. [. . .]

What I should've said right away is that you don't have to send a money order for the car; in fact, you don't have to pay for it immediately, or even soon. [. . .] Here was what gave me constant trouble: the hubcaps. Do not remove them unless you have to, and if you do, be sure you have them on just so or they'll come off—they depend entirely on those little metal flanges which get bent and oh, what the hell . . . [. . .] Be very careful, in this connection, Fred, or you'll have missing hubcaps, and if there is anything that looks bad, it is a car with missing hubcaps, I think. Better you lose your manhood than your hubcaps. [. . .]

Jim

JOE AND JODY O'CONNELL

Trenarren Hotel
Greystones, County Wicklow
October 8, 1963

Dear Jody and Joe,

[. . .] Boz asks me when we're alone, walking down the street, why I don't buy a house, and I tell him or I don't, depending how I feel, but in a day or so or a week it happens again, and he is very gentle about it, and quite hopeless, I sense, that I'll be able to pull it off. I see myself as an alcoholic at such times—not a bad person, really, but one from whom little can be expected. That, in outline, may be my problem. [. . .]

You are there and we are here. I can see the sea out my window, about two blocks away, and it is municipal-swimming-pool green close to shore, with low whitecaps, and deep green on the horizon. Right across the road from the hotel, as I told Fred and Romy in a letter yesterday, is a filling station with Mobiloil, Shell, and Castrol signs, and not Castro signs, as I reported yesterday. My electric fire is on (and my own fires are banked), and I still have some wiring jobs to do on lamps if I decide to spend the evening hours here instead of in our bedroom, where we have an electric fire, Scotch and Irish (his and hers), and Boz's transistor radio. We have been absolutely nowhere socially—tea once with the O'Faolains. The Dublin Theatre Festival came and went. We get *The Irish Times* delivered daily, and *The Observer, Sunday Times*, and *Telegraph* on Sunday, which, with churchgoing, pretty well takes care of that evil day. [. . .]

We have just had lunch, Betty and I, tea, roast beef (not good) sandwiches, and several kinds of cheese, with nobody home but us and Jane and Terry. The latter is our dog. Only on loan, fortunately, the property of the hotel owners, who thought they wouldn't be able to find accommodations for all three of them (they have no children) in London. Terry is a woolly dog, spayed (I believe the term is), with the body, or flesh consistency, of a woman, to the touch, that is. This I noticed this morning, when searching for fleas (we all seem to have bites). He (I refer to Terry) is a pleasant enough dog, has very intelligent brown eyes, and the kids love him. I can't look at him, though, without wanting to clean him up, beginning with Murine for his eyes, which are suffering from erosion at the corners. Betty really has to take care of him: take him out at night, remove his collar, tuck him under his blanket in what is known as the Smoking Room here at the Trenarren.

Here there are Aer Lingus schedules for the summer of 1962 (take one) and a small so-called billiard table, with holes into which you try to get the balls to drop (it is like a pinball machine, not a pool table, though covered with good green felt). I must say I looked forward to a game when, on the first night here, the proprietor invited me to take the children into the Smoking Room whenever I felt like it, for a game of billiards. But you have to put in a sixpence, in order to open up the holes, and get about ten minutes of play. This, as you might imagine, can mount up with a family the size of ours all waiting to use the table and nobody but Betty and Himself with the slightest idea of the relationship there is between a sixpence piece and real money. There is a humming noise while the ten minutes are running out, and everybody seems to feel that this adds to the fun—a noise from somewhere in the table. What I was going to say, though, is that wherever Terry goes, there is a slightly doggy odor, and a layer of lanolin, too, and he goes everywhere, following the sun from bed to bed, room to room, during the day. I guess that ought to fill you in, along with what Betty will tell you in her letter. [. . .]

We are glad to hear that Romy was delivered of her baby and that all is well.[1] We hadn't heard until your letters came. Now, for the love of life, why don't you get Fred drunk and back him into a lathe or something? What about Dr D. in the role of the disbarred famous surgeon, asked to do a job, and actually turning in a whale of a performance for a half-pint? While you, Joe, and Dickie, and Dick Palmquist, and Leonard play cards in the next room, a candle in a bottle, and Jody is stalking around in a coat from Petters's Furs? Somebody switches on the TV (updated from radio), and there we see the president of the United States (played by J. F. Powers) just completing a fireside talk on crime when suddenly, seen through the window, there are headlights—commercial here—and more headlights—and oodles of monks* pouring out of squad cars—too late, though, to prevent the operation. Titled *Tragedy in Hardon County*.

Cheers, and do write.

Jim

* And sisters, including Carmelites.

The owners of the Trenarren returned from London and took up occupancy in a few rooms of the hotel. It was not part of the agreement and led to a great deal of unpleasantness and, eventually, to Jim's story "Tinkers." ("So far it is writing itself. And also killing me.")

DICK PALMQUIST

Trenarren Hotel
Greystones, County Wicklow
November 13, 1963

Dear Dick,

[. . .] You are lucky enough to have a friend who thinks enough of you to celebrate your birthday with a gift of champagne. As I recall, even when you provide same, it is hard to get anybody to come over and celebrate in St Cloud. It is the same the world over, though. I have always wished to be part of a going concern whose day-by-day existence makes for a few laughs, with our own stationery, office equipment, calendars, branches, and branch managers, perhaps a lake in Ontario where we go

1 Catherine Petters, born October 2, 1963, their seventh (and last) child.

to relax (further) from time to time. You don't have all those things, but you do have some and much more. So hang on to your job.[1] Word is that Speltz will be the auxiliary, if that's the way it's spelt.[2] Get that old suction pump going the moment he walks through the door—some of Mary's pâté de foie gras gift wrapped in money might not be taken amiss. Talk down Alfrink's heretical suggestion that laymen should do the office jobs at the Vatican and not the bishops.[3] Stick up for Ottaviani.[4] He is one of the first to talk against the bomb. His father was a baker, his mother a swan, hence his neck. Deny me and all my pomps. So much for good counsel, Dick. [. . .]

I am, sir, as always.

Jim

HARVEY EGAN

Trenarren Hotel
Greystones, County Wicklow
November 15, 1963

Dear Fr Egan,

[. . .] After three weeks in London, the proprietors of this small hotel descended upon us, taking up residence in the wing where I had been assigned a room as an office. Nothing was said by way of explanation. And since in the lease there is a clause saying the proprietor might have access to two rooms on our side of the hotel, both kept locked, at any time, we thought at first that he was simply taking advantage of this clause (it was explained to us by Sean O'F. that the proprietor might exercise this privilege for one, two, or, at most, three nights in the four months we'd be tenants), but said proprietor, a drunk, and his wife, a coarse-grained golfer, have been here since October 26, with dog, which we looked after while they were in London.

Well, since nothing was said and the situation is so ridiculous, proving more so by stages, it wasn't until yesterday that I decided to go to the house agent who contracted our lease and say I wanted out if we could find another place before our time was up here. [. . .] Sean was outraged

---

1 He was working at the St. Cloud Diocese's chancery.
2 George Henry Speltz was not appointed; he became coadjutor bishop of the St. Cloud Diocese in 1966.
3 Cardinal Bernardus Johannes Alfrink, who was Dutch, promoted liberal ideas at Vatican II.
4 Cardinal Alfredo Ottaviani, an Italian, championed the conservative position at Vatican II.

when he heard the proprietors were in residence, which fact we managed to keep from him until the other day, and wanted to throw them out, but I forbade him to get involved: the worst thing about such a deal is the wear and tear on your mind, just thinking about it, I mean. [. . .]

We went up to see Sir Tyrone Guthrie in Co. Monaghan last week and spent a day with him, his wife, and Tanya Moisevitch, the stage designer, who was staying with them and working on paper models for next season's sets. (She'd like to lay hands on 500 fox furs for *Volpone*.) We liked all three of them, and Sir T. said he'd be happy to have me spend the period of my Ford Fellowship in Mpls if the foundation (Ford) approved the idea, either for the coming season or the one after. I have written to the Ford people asking that I be given this assignment with the date left open [depending on] the housing situation in Ireland and the direction taken by my work, if you'll pardon the expression.

This, too, I'd wish you to keep to yourself, as I don't want to beat the gun so far as the Ford Foundation is concerned—for all I know they make a point of sending people to places they'd rather not go, like Texas, in which case I'm afraid I'd have to say no and claim my rights to your car prematurely and go into the taxi business. Let's face it. I'll have to find work pretty soon, work that I can do until I shuffle off this mortal coil. My fast one is gone. They are hitting my other stuff. Remember Frog Maranda.[1] Remember Old Blue.

And now, with a sigh of relief, to *your* problems. 1. Let the sisters run the school. 2. Try to be out even more, if possible. 3. Don't fight Frank[2]— even in his sleep he talks against those who oppose him (and God). 4. Change your position at Met Stadium, get out from under those echoing steel tiers and up into the sky where you can see the countryside. 5. Moderate your interest in pro football. 6. Chicken out in the interracial area. (Pope John is dead.) 7. Pray for Gene McCarthy. 8. Pray for me.

Anon.

Jim

---

1 Georges Maranda (1932–2000), who was born in Quebec, pitched in the majors only two seasons: 1960 for San Francisco and 1962 for the Twins.
2 Kacmarcik.

JOE AND JODY O'CONNELL

Trenarren Hotel
Greystones, County Wicklow
November 18, 1963

Dear Joe and Jody,

We were very glad to have your letter on Saturday and to hear of the sales of the prints. You don't really say, but I suspect you have been having hard times, and the business with George hit you very hard: he is my friend, but I must say he has a way of handling people which has made him a lot of enemies.[1] He has always wanted to play the grand patron, and you have to give him credit for imagination there anyway, but he hasn't had enough money to pull it off—and will have less now than he's been accustomed to in recent years, now that he is pastor of a parish that won't support itself, let alone support the Newman Club, or so I'm told. I'm sure he'll come through where you're concerned, which I know still leaves out the time element, the big when. [. . .]

If you really want to know what kind of dump we're in, see Fr Walter. He was here at the hotel, in the doggy lounge, and he also used the chain-driven toilet. Tell him I said it was all right to talk. [. . .]

Betty, as usual, is in Dublin. I don't know what she does there, but as long as I don't find any lipstick on her collar, I won't worry: you know how it is, Joe, when you're married to a woman who smokes cigars. [. . .]

November 20

[. . .] Sometime soon I should write vividly of our new life in the Old World. I know you expect that. It is as Betty says in her letter, though— very dull, St Cloud without comfort and without friends, but then I expected it would be. As a writer, I am even less here, if possible—have yet to see a copy of my novel in a bookstore. I suppose it would be the same in Paris, where the novel has just been published, or Italy. We are sick of *The Irish Times*, though it seems to be the conscience of all Ireland, just tired of the daily fodder: Will there be a general election in the new year? Will the government fall because of the so-called turnover tax (2½% added onto the price of everything)? Will the Grand Canal, one of the neglected beauties of Dublin, be filled with sewage pipes and closed up? Will the exhibit of Irish goods at Lord & Taylor in New York stimulate

---

1 Garrelts had commissioned a carved wooden panel from Joe for the Newman Center at the University of Minnesota. After having Joe deliver it and leaving him waiting—first he was out, then he was on the phone—he tried to get out of paying for it.

exports? It is like party designation and industries for the Iron Range in *The Minneapolis Tribune*. You just get tired.

The future [. . .] doesn't seem to be any clearer today. One regrets the loss of time, time in which one might have worked (but probably wouldn't have anyway), but having had very little choice (so it still appears), one can't very well regret the decision to do what we've done. I have learned nothing I didn't know about traveling with children—or about the impossibility of living with them in other people's houses. Were it not for them, we wouldn't be here, which is not to say we are martyrs, Betty and I, but would-be survivors. Last night I had to remove the radio from Katherine's bed (listening to Radio Luxembourg, which is as close to WJON as you can get here). So we don't expect a complete cure, but just hope to give the girls more of a perspective. The young men look positively cretinous here, and all dress like burglars. And yet . . . but as Betty says, there is no more depressing sight on earth than Irish snazzy.

She also said at breakfast that there was some talk at the girls' school of a tour of Greece in the summer, and my first thought was: "Summer! My God! Will we still be *here*, living like *this then*?" Why not? For years I have lived on the hope that Time would, just by passing, someday, somehow, provide an out (I do not mean death, or at least didn't), but how wrong I've been. It is still my best bet, though, such as it is. What do I want? I can no longer describe it except in general terms—a million dollars, or even fifty thousand—and thus I leave the decision to later. The motto of the J. F. Powers Company is *Shoot high and don't miss*, but it is one I can only hope to achieve in my work, if there, and seems more and more out of the question in my life, in which, alas, I still take an interest. So much for today's gospel. Just trying to help you understand us. [. . .]

Jim

LEONARD DOYLE

Trenarren Hotel
Greystones, County Wicklow
November 29, 1963

Dear Leonard,

[. . .] We were floored by the crimes in Texas. I realized I'd been too hard on Kennedy in my own mind and hadn't given him credit for using the best kind of people, to the extent that this is possible (it isn't possible in the arts), to run the ship of state. Ireland and England were in deep mourning. Our PP, perhaps the only liturgist in Ireland in communion with Collegeville, only stalked the aisles during the memorial Mass on Tuesday, commenting on the Mass and whatever else occurred to him, and in the end praised Kennedy for four things and said we should write them down when we left the church: "edgication, *self*-edgication, social-minded, and parish-minded." On a call recently, he told Betty that there was only one place in the U.S. that he wanted to visit and that was Minnesota because of St John's, the liturgical capital of the world. Even if I weren't anti-laical (and of course anticlerical), I think I'd give thanks for the old guard in Rome, after divine worship with our PP calling the shots from the pulpit—a kind of triple dialogue Mass, celebrant and people patiently waiting to get a word in edgewise and the latter urged at the same time to speak up, say the prayers in any language they please, and, for the love of God, to pull themselves together and try to be more edgicated.[1] [. . .]

Jim

DICK PALMQUIST

Trenarren Hotel
Greystones, County Wicklow
November 30, 1963

Dear Dick,

[. . .] I try to keep in touch with reality by listening to the Armed Forces Radio from Germany—spot announcements telling me to turn down my radio, to install seat belts, to give blood, and to drive carefully. I followed the terrible events in Texas for several days (AFN had access to all three networks in America), and now that it's over, I still don't understand it, and I guess that is as it should be, sound and fury signifying nothing. [. . .]

It is late. AFN's Mr Midnight, a very romantic fella, has gone to bed. The wife and family have gone to bed. The only ones up are me and the Germans (on the radio), who never seem to go to bed. And now I'm going to bed. [. . .]

The following morning. Frosty today, for the first time, a harbinger of the cold-assed days ahead, as we say in the writing game. [. . .]

The house we'll be moving into is comparatively new (1933) and

1 Irish pronunciation.

consequently is snugger than we're used to in Ireland. It has several rooms that appear to be quite livable—not perhaps as you would use the term, or I, ideally, but by the standards that apply here, at least to our income and experience. [. . .] Best to you both from us both.

Jim

JOE AND JODY O'CONNELL

Trenarren Hotel
Greystones, County Wicklow
Christmas Night 1963

Dear Friends,

Just because this letter comes to you mimeographed,[1] do not think it does not come from the heart. Well, another year has almost ended, and once again, as I sit here before my fire (electric this year), my thoughts range back through the days gone by, gone but not forgotten. There was much to be thankful for, more than I have space for here, but here are some of the highlights that come immediately to mind. January and February, so far as I can tell from my diary, were taken up, as were the previous six or eight months, with correspondence with, and dark thoughts about, my publisher. March, as some of you may recall, was the month I won the National Book Award for *Morte D'Urban*, now available in paperback at 60¢, and went to New York City to be honored by the publishers, book manufacturers, booksellers, and gentle readers of America. Unworthy though I was, I could see no way out and tried to conduct myself like a good arthur and family man should, and in this I think I can say I did good. April passed without an award, but in May I went to Chicago, that toddlin' town, for another. June was unsensational, as were July, August, and September until we kissed St Cloud goodbye. The rest you more or less know, and that brings us up to Christmas. I received the following gifts from members of my family: napkin ring (Mary); talcum powder, with built-in deodorant (Katherine); diary (Boz); socks (Hugh); pipe cleaners and clothes brush (Jane); and Drambuie (Betty).

The latter hit the hay at 8:45 p.m. tonight, which may be a new record, but then the poor kid carried the rest of us through the ordeal of Christmas, no little thing in our present circumstances.

We were very glad to get your letters, for which we waited and waited,

---

1 Joke.

which is not to say that we do not understand the many reasons for the delay. One you don't mention, namely the busy and exciting life you lead. By our standards, I'm not kidding. NOTHING HAPPENS HERE. Well, yes, Boz did lean on a window in the lounge yesterday, and getting it repaired, or perhaps repairing it myself, may keep me occupied for days in this town, where nothing is easy, where a piece of glass 38" by 36" may mean a trip to the next town (Bray), and this on a bus, if you can picture us, me and the glass and probably a strong wind blowing. [. . .]

The panel for George looks good under my magnifying glass—and all I can say against it is the medium, wood, which always has a way of looking wooden, particularly when new. Or so I think, and seem to recall you do. I pray it all ends well, with you and George, and I think it will. And right here I knock out ashes from a pipeful of #400, specially blended for Rev. Urban Roche, which I smoke on feast days and great occasions or would if there were any of the latter. I am down to about 4 oz. of #400 and two small packages of Brindley's and have bought my first Irish tobacco at the going price of $1.40 for 2 oz. I am rationing out the other on those dark nights of the soul which come a bit oftener than formerly, as I take up the eternal subject of dirt, disrepair, folly, and waste with myself. [. . .]

I loved "a heavily insured bag of nuts," and Dickie should have used longer tacks.[1] It's all too easy to use short tacks and hit them harder, but where does it get you in the end? When I was a householder, and a goddamn good one too, I always kept a plentiful supply of tacks in assorted sizes. I checked my stock regularly to see that I wasn't running low, and I also checked against rust spores, which have a way of getting into a nest of tacks, and if anything plays hell with tacks, it is rust. Keep plenty of tacks on hand at all times, and don't let rust get to them lest there be hell to pay. Keep tacks on a high shelf, under lock and key, away from children. [. . .]

We often think of you. I don't know when we'll go back to America, or where we'll go when we do. We have literally no plans.

Jim

Epilogue: I once knew a writer (before I was married) who had a wife and four children, and he was always traveling around with them and his manuscript of the moment, which he kept in a metal file, which he carried, and when this writer came into a hotel dining room with his wife and children and the metal file and the violin case (one of the children

---

1 Dick O'Connell, Joe's brother, sent a package that fell apart in the mail.

played the violin), he'd turn on you in anger and say, "What's everyone looking at?" That has since become the story of my life, except that I have *five* children (none of whom, however, plays the violin) and a *leather* case for my manuscript, and I *don't* ask what everybody's looking at.[1]

J. F. Powers, 1963

1 *Milwaukee Journal* questionnaire typescript, July 1963.

Afterword: Growing Up in This Story

Katherine A. Powers

Katherine Anne Powers

This volume ends with 1963. There are enough letters, further removals, and more ocean crossings *en famille* to supply at least another volume, but the novel Jim might have written concludes here. What lies ahead, years ahead to be sure, is a certain resignation. "It's as if the story of my life has been badly cut, like a film, and what's left has those specks and scratches on it from too many showings."[1] But what lies directly ahead—the near future, that is—is not suitable material for Jim's gift.

His children were becoming adolescents and, infinitely worse to his way of thinking, teenagers. The presence all around him of burgeoning consciousnesses, of egos to rival his own, and, most harrowing, of his two older daughters' growing fascination with the opposite sex was too much for this author to control and defuse through comedy. In 1963, he hadn't yet come to see his children as people possessing identities and destinies separate from his own—that revelation was years away—but he was having trouble maintaining the illusion that his was the central point of view. Add to that the older children were beginning to be infected by popular culture, and not just any popular culture either, but that of what was becoming the sixties. This he viewed with appalled incredulity, and the move to Ireland in 1963 was made in part to stem the contagion. I cannot say that in this respect it was a roaring success.

Growing up in this family is not something I would care to do again. There was so much uncertainty, so much desperation about money, and so very little restraint on my parents' part in letting their children know how precarious our existence was. Our terrible plight—as it was always painted—was made all the more so by how particular, not to say impossible, our requirements were in the realm of housing and style of living.

Reading these letters, I found myself becoming sad and occasionally angry at what could be described as a folie à deux. What really shocked

1 Jim to Joe and Jody O'Connell, December 19, 1971.

me was seeing more clearly what my mother had taken upon herself in joining her life to this man's. Jim had warned her repeatedly before they were married not to expect an ordinary life ("sometimes I get to thinking you don't know me at all, don't know what you're getting into, and if you do, you think changes can be made which, as a matter of fact, won't be made"). But Betty, who loved Jim and believed that he was an exceptional being, a true artist, also believed that he would be rewarded as such if only he would knuckle down and stop wasting time. He wouldn't or couldn't, but she did.

Betty wrote almost every day on a strict schedule, hoping to bring in some money—which she did, though nothing like what the situation required. She published a number of stories in magazines, including *The New Yorker*, and in 1969 her one novel appeared, *Rafferty & Co.* Published by Farrar, Straus and Giroux while Jim was trying desperately to get out of a multibook contract with the despised Doubleday, it was based in a gentle way, far too gentle, I would say, on life in Ireland with a man something like Jim. Aside from that, she cooked every meal from scratch and sewed most of our clothes; she went to her parents for aid; she scrimped, rationed, and cobbled together the wherewithal for our survival.

But to return to Jim's letters. In the end, their wit and drollery and festive turns of phrase won me over. A distance developed between me, the person actually present in the predicament the letters describe, and me, the reader. And indeed, in selecting the letters to tell this story, I increasingly felt I was bringing order to a situation where there was little. With that came satisfaction and a certain amount of peace.

My sister Jane, on the other hand, found reading the letters more troubling. She was bowled over by the early ones, by Jim's expressions of love for our mother. But the feeling aroused by the whole twenty-one-year run of them was one of overwhelming, inalterable sadness. "All that energy, all those plans, all that crazy idealism in the beginning: it somehow turned in on itself to make something—our family, our way of life—that was always contrary and constricted. There are hints of JFP's truculence in the early letters, and they make me uneasy and unhappy, as they pierce through the beautiful fabric of his prose like little daggers. Also, he was so hopelessly impractical: How could it ever have turned out well?"

The last word will be Jim's, from Ireland (again), some seven years further down the road. We find him having recently acquired a pair of "Tall Man" pajamas, now transformed into yet another emblem of the human condition of which he was always an appreciative victim.

Dear Fred and Romy,

[. . .] I was interested to see [from Betty's letter] what it is we are doing, or will be doing (finishing our books and making a pile and coming back), as we don't often discuss such matters and I often wonder what it is we are doing, or will be doing. As for lonely, well, all men are lonely. I am myself lonely, always have been, and never more than when in my new pajamas. I think of myself then as the last man on earth, as Tall Man. My sleeves extend four inches beyond my fingertips, one of my legs is, for some reason, narrower, the stitching overlapped for a few inches before rejoining the main stitching, like a service road, and I bag in the back, I'm told. However, I am well and working, and hope you are the same.

    + TALL MAN

Appendix: Cast of Characters

Jim and Zella, Jim's parents, on their wedding day, 1915

Jim's sister, Charlotte, and her husband, Bill Kraft, 1944

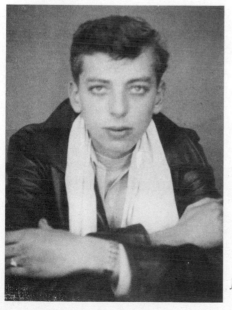

Jim's brother, Dick

1946: The Wahls plus
Jim. Left to right:
John, Betty, Jim, Art,
Money, Pat, Tom

Friends

Quincy College
Academy Little
Hawks, 1934–1935.
Jim, middle row, far
right; Garrelts next to
him; Keefe, same row,
middle

Back row, left to right:
Emerson Hynes, Harry
Sylvester, George
Barnett, Jim; front
row, left to right: Don
Humphrey, George
Garrelts, John Haskins

Jim and Seán Ó Faoláin, 1958

George Garrelts and Dick Keefe (whom Seán Ó Faoláin called "a complete cynic with, deep in the blubber, a heart of ambergris")

Joe and Jody O'Connell

Leonard and Betty Doyle, 1949

Fred and Romy Petters

Arleen and Emerson Hynes

Dick and Mary Palmquist

The Writer and His Wife

James Farl Powers (1917–1999): Called J. F. Powers for all published work; informally called James, Jim, JF. Born in Jacksonville, Illinois. Author of three books of short stories, *Prince of Darkness* (Doubleday, 1947), *The Presence of Grace* (Doubleday, 1956), and *Look How the Fish Live* (Knopf, 1975); and two novels, *Morte D'Urban* (Doubleday, 1962) and *Wheat That Springeth Green* (Knopf, 1988).

Elizabeth Alice Wahl Powers (1924–1988): Called Betty. JFP's wife; born in St. Cloud, Minnesota; graduated with a BA in English from the College of St. Benedict, St. Joseph, Minnesota; author of a number of published short stories and one novel, *Rafferty & Co.* (Farrar, Straus and Giroux, 1969).

Their Children

Katherine Anne Powers (1947–): Called KA. Became a barmaid, cook, archivist, literary critic, and columnist.

Mary Farl Powers (1948–1992): Became a prominent artist in Ireland, a director of the Graphic Studio in Dublin, a founder of the Graphic Studio Gallery, a member of Aosdána (the Irish academy of arts and letters), for which she served as a *toscaire* (delegate).

James Ansbury Powers (1953–): Called Boz. Became an artist.

Hugh Wahl Powers (1955–): Became a photographer.

Jane Elizabeth Powers (1958–): Became a garden writer, photographer, and columnist.

The Powers and Wahl Families

James Ansberry Powers (1883–1985): Called Jim. JFP's father; born in Jacksonville, Illinois. See Introduction.

Zella Routzong Powers (1892–1973): JFP's mother; born in Seward, Nebraska. See Introduction.

Charlotte Powers Kraft (1920–1999): JFP's sister; born in Jacksonville, Illinois; married 1944; three children.

William Kraft (1921–1994): Called Bill. Charlotte's husband; engineer in the nuclear weapons industry in Albuquerque, New Mexico.

Richard Powers (1931–1993): Called Dick. JFP's brother; born in Quincy, Illinois; became a professor of political science at the University of Victoria, B.C., teaching international relations; married Laura Daniel in 1955; two children.

Arthur L. Wahl (1893–1973): Called Art, Papa. Betty's father; born in St. Cloud, Minnesota; his father, a builder for whom he and his brother worked, went bankrupt in the second decade of the twentieth century, and the brothers immigrated to Alberta, Canada; raised horses and worked as casual farmhands; both returned to the United States, and Art became a successful building contractor.

Romana Seberger Wahl (1900–1991). Called Money, Mona, Nana. Betty's mother; born in St. Cloud, Minnesota; taught school until marriage in 1922.

Patricia Wahl Bitzan (1927–): Called Patt; Patty; Pat. Betty's sister; seven children.

Donald J. Bitzan (1926–): Called Don. Pat's husband; watchmaker; eventually established successful jewelry store.

John Arthur Wahl (1930–): Betty's brother; construction company manager and owner.

Irene Sticka Wahl (1931–): John Wahl's wife; three children.

Thomas Peter Wahl (1931–): Called Tom; religious name Caedmon. Betty's brother; Benedictine monk and priest; ordained, 1958.

Bertha Seberger Strobel (1891–1962): Called Birdie; Bertie by JFP. Betty's maternal aunt.

Albert Strobel (1880–1963): Called Al. Birdie's husband; successful optometrist.

Albertine Muller Seberger (1865–1957): Called Bertha; called Grandma Seberger. Betty's maternal grandmother; born in Stillwater, Minnesota; married Peter J. Seberger (1864–1935).

Friends in the Movement (or Otherwise Associated with St. John's)

Bronislaw Bak (1922–1981): Called Bruno. Painter, printer, stained-glass artist; taught art at St. John's University; designed stained-glass window of St. John's Abbey Church.

Hedi Bak (1924–2010): Called Hetty. Bruno Bak's wife; artist; three children.

Carlos Cotton (1913–2001): Sculptor; taught at St. John's.

Mary Katherine Finegan Cotton (1916–1992): Carlos Cotton's wife; sister of Elizabeth Anne Finegan Doyle; Catholic Worker; eight children.

Leonard J. Doyle (1914–1970): Taught English at St. John's Prep; translator for St. John's Liturgical Press; his beard, a subject of great interest to Jim.

Elizabeth Anne Finegan Doyle (1918–2011): Called Betty. Leonard Doyle's wife; sister of Mary Katherine Finegan Cotton; Catholic Worker; nine children.

Donald Humphrey (1912–1958): Called Don, Hump, Humphaus. Artist, sculptor, and chalice maker; Catholic Worker.

Mary Alice Frawley Humphrey (1912–1992): Don Humphrey's wife; seamstress of baptismal robes; weaver; Catholic Worker; eight children.

Emerson Hynes (1915–1971): Called Em. Professor of sociology at St. John's; at center of Catholic rural and family-life movement in the area; became Senator Eugene McCarthy's legislative assistant in Washington.

Arleen McCarty Hynes (1916–2006): Emerson Hynes's wife; ten children; became Benedictine nun after ten years a widow.

Eugene McCarthy (1916–2005): Called Gene. Taught at St. John's, 1940–1943; novice for nine months, 1942–1943; married, 1945, and lived in a Catholic agricultural commune in the area for a while; later U.S. representative (1949–1959) and U.S. senator (1959–1971).

Abigail Quigley McCarthy (1915–2001): Eugene McCarthy's wife; writer and journalist; four children.

Joseph O'Connell (1927–1995): Artist, sculptor, and printmaker; taught at St. John's in mid-1950s; later, artist in residence at St. John's and St. Benedict's.

Joann Wiley O'Connell (1930–): Called Jody. Joe O'Connell's wife; five children.

Richard Palmquist (1922–2005): Called Dick. Worked for the Chancery of the St. Cloud Diocese; later owned insurance agency.

Mary Pluth Palmquist (1927–): Called Mary Jean. Richard Palmquist's wife; teacher; six children.

Fredric Petters (1926–): Called Fred. Owned a fabric and fur shop in St. Cloud; later worked at the Liturgical Press at St. John's.

Rosemary Boyle Petters (1925–): Called Romy, Rome (only by JFP). Fred Petters's wife; potter; seven children.

Other Friends and Correspondents

George Barnett: Called Barnhart by JFP. Friend; was at Sandstone with him.

Jack Conroy (1898–1990): Proletarian writer, best known for his 1933 novel, *The Disinherited*. Good friend.

Father Harvey F. X. Egan (1915–2006): Called Mon pere, Detachismus. Ordained in 1941; JFP's great benefactor, dispenser of frequent loans.

Sister Mariella Gable, OSB (1898–1985): BWP's college teacher; editor of collections of Catholic fiction; critic. Introduced JFP to BWP.

Father George G. Garrelts (1918–2003): JFP's classmate at Quincy College Academy; close friend; ordained, 1942. Was a Detacher in early years; later president of the Newman Clubs of America. Left the priesthood in 1970 and got married.

John Haskins (ca. 1918–1977): Called Hask. Classmate at Quincy College Academy; best man at JFP's wedding; became music critic for the Washington *Evening Star* and *The Kansas City Star*.

John Howe (1913–1997): Called Jack. Draftsman for Frank Lloyd Wright; JFP met him at Sandstone Federal Penitentiary.

Richard Keefe (ca. 1917–1980): Called Dick. Close friend; JFP's classmate at Quincy College Academy; expelled from the seminary for "worldliness"; became dean of St. Louis University and host of a TV show.

Ted LeBerthon (ca. 1893–1960): Journalist and columnist; reported on racial inequality, migrant workers, from 1930s on; associated with *The Catholic Worker*; JFP's roommate in St. Paul in 1945.

Robert Lowell (1917–1977): Called Cal. Poet; JFP met him at Yaddo, 1947; took road trip together in 1947.

John Marshall: Called Marsh by JFP. JFP met him at Sandstone Federal Penitentiary; became a physician.

Michael Millgate (1929–): British biographer, editor, critic, teacher; teaching fellow at Ann Arbor, 1956, when Jim met him.

Seán Ó Faoláin (1900–1991): Irish short-story writer; extremely helpful in practical ways and as a friend in Ireland from 1952 on.

Katherine Anne Porter (1890–1980): Short-story writer and novelist; championed JFP's work.

J. Kerker Quinn (1911–1969): Editor at *Accent* magazine; accepted JFP's first short story and a number of subsequent ones.

Theodore Roethke (1908–1963): Called Beast; Champ by JFP. Poet; JFP met him at Yaddo in 1947.

Charles Shattuck (1910–1992): Called Chuck. Married to Suzie; editor at *Accent* magazine and professor of English at the University of Illinois at Urbana; Shakespearean scholar; was extremely influential in editing Jim's work.

Harry Sylvester (1908–1993): Short-story writer and novelist; attended JFP's wedding; an informal rivalry existed between him and JFP for position of top American Catholic writer; later rejected the Church.

Evelyn Waugh (1903–1966): English writer and novelist; championed JFP's work.

Harvey C. Webster (1906–1988): Called Clocker by JFP. Professor of English at the University of Louisville; JFP met him at Yaddo; a frequent companion at the Saratoga Springs racetrack.

Gordon Zahn (1918–2007): Sociologist and writer; conscientious objector during the war; critic of the Catholic Church's position on war; best known for *In Solitary Witness: The Life and Death of Franz Jägerstätter* (1964).

Source Notes

Letters

To Jack Conroy: Jack Conroy Papers, Roger and Julie Baskes Department of Special Collections, Newberry Library, Chicago

To Father Harvey Egan: Powers family collection

To Sister Mariella Gable: Sisters of the Order of Saint Benedict Archives, St. Joseph, Minnesota

To George Garrelts: Powers family collection

To Charlotte and Bill Kraft: Powers family collection

To Robert Lowell: Robert Lowell Papers, MS Am 1905, Houghton Library, Harvard University

To John Marshall: Mrs. John Marshall collection

To Ken McCormick: Powers family collection

To Michael Millgate: Michael Millgate collection

To "the Movement" (Doyle, Humphrey, O'Connell, Palmquist, Petters): Collections of the families

To Katherine Anne Porter: Special Collections, University of Maryland

To Betty Wahl Powers: Powers family collection

To Kerker Quinn and Charles Shattuck: University of Illinois Archives: Charles H. Shattuck Papers, 15/7/39; J. Kerker Quinn Papers, 15/7/30; George Scouffas Papers, 15/7/38

To Wahl and Strobel: Powers family collection

To Evelyn Waugh: Alexander Waugh collection

Other

J. F. Powers's and Betty Wahl Powers's journals: Powers family collection

Milwaukee Journal questionnaire typescript: Powers family collection

Illustrations

Frontispiece: Drawing by Joseph O'Connell for *Morte D'Urban*: Powers family collection

pages xiii, 1, 23, 53, 63, 77, 123, 147, 161, 181, 193, 231, 253, 267, 289, 323, 375, 401, 417, 425, 426, 427 (top two): Powers family collection

page 27: Archdiocese of Saint Paul and Minneapolis Archives

page 87: Photograph by J. F. Powers: Powers family collection

page 107: *Minneapolis Star Tribune*

page 135: *Minneapolis Star Tribune*

page 201: Photograph by J. F. Powers: Powers family collection

page 209: Drawing by Jody O'Connell: Powers family collection

page 217: Photograph by Russell Roe: Powers family collection

page 253: Photograph by Lee Hanley: Powers family collection page 307: Humphrey family collection

page 323: Photograph by Lee Hanley: Powers family collection

page 341: J. F. Powers's montage for writing *Morte D'Urban*: Powers family collection

page 357: Photograph by Donald Black: *Minneapolis Star Tribune*

page 385: Photograph by Herb Snitzer: Powers family collection

page 427: O'Connell family collection

page 428 (top left): Doyle family collection

page 428 (top right): Petters family collection

page 428 (bottom left): Saint John's University Archives, Collegeville, Minnesota

page 428 (bottom right): Palmquist family collection

Acknowledgments

The greatest thanks for this book belong to the late Fr. Harvey Egan, who not only preserved over a half century's worth of Jim's letters, but also provided him with an exceptionally congenial correspondent. Great thanks, too, belong to those members of the Movement, Jim's good friends, living and dead, who did the same: Leonard and Betty Doyle, Don and Mary Humphrey, Joe and Jody O'Connell, Dick and Mary Pluth Palmquist, Fred and Romy Petters. Beyond their number, I thank Jim's other friends and correspondents, whose letters gave him such pleasure and who, in return, didn't throw his letters away.

I am most thankful for the valuable assistance of one sort or another given to me by Daniel Aaron, Mike Aquilina, Rich Arpi, Robert Barros, Michael Bitzan, Pat Bitzan, the late Tom Brown, Christopher Carduff, Chris Cotton, Justin Doyle, Katherine Doyle, Kevin Doyle, Rosemary Hugo Fielding, Rachel Humphrey Fischer, Roland Fischer, Anita Fore, Susannah Humphrey, the late Sister Nancy Hynes, OSB, X. J. Kennedy, Elizabeth Knuth, Jim Kraft, Sister Mary Kraft, CSJ, Hilary Bracken McGhee, Mrs. John Marshall, Michael Millgate, Cassandra Nelson, Jody O'Connell, Mary Pluth Palmquist, Catherine Petters, James A. Powers, Julianne O'Connell Restani, Peggy Roske, David Scott, Susan Stepka, Bob Tholkes, John Thorn, Michael True, Nicole Luthman Turnbull, Alexander Waugh, and Sister Mariterese Woida, OSB.

I also thank my agent, Andrew Blauner, and editor, Sean McDonald.

Much more than thanks belongs to my sister Jane and my brothers, Boz and Hugh; to my sons, Hugh and Thomas Blaisdell; and to my particular friend, Bob Groves.

Index

Page numbers in *italics* refer to illustrations.

Bellow, Saul, 139, 247; *Seize the Day*, 247 and *n*1

Benedictines, 25, 28, 34, 46, 59, 228*n*3

Bennington College, 115, 120

Benvenisti, J. L., 94 and *n*2

Berlin, Irving, 391

Berra, Yogi, 236

Berryman, John, 377, 382

Best Sellers, 90

Big Spunk Lake, Avon, Minnesota, 79

bingo, 216 and *n*2

birth control, 215*n*1

Bitzan, Donald J., 429

Bitzan, Michael, *147*

Bitzan, Patricia Wahl, 63, 79, 142, 426, 429

Blackfoot Indians, 186

Blades, Ray, 81 and *n*2

"Blondie-Dagwood myth," 73

Bloomington, Indiana, 183

Blue Books, 278 and *n*3

"Blue Island," 214 and *n*2, 215 and *n*3

Bonn, Fr. John Louis, 155 and *n*3, 156

Bontemps, Arna, xvii, 89, 90

Book of Kells, 173

Books and Brent (radio show), 155*n*1

Boston, 103, 126, 278, 298

Boston College, 156, 344

Boston Herald, The, 397*n*1

Boswell, James, *Life of Samuel Johnson*, 213

Bowen, Elizabeth, 300

boxing, 151, 152, 329 and *n*1, 330, 335 and *n*1, 336, 337 and *n*1, 340 and *n*2, 353 and *n*1

Boxing Day, 244, 245, 246, 284

Bradley, Van Allen, 398 and *n*2

Brady, William Otterwell Ignatius, 226 and *n*1, 227 and *n*2

Brent, Stuart, 155 and *n*1

Brentano's, xvii

Breuer, Marcel, 339, 340, 369 and *n*2, 370

Brewster, Massachusetts, 80, 81

Britannic (ship), 269, 270

British Columbia, 203

Brooklyn Dodgers, 17*n*4, 213 and *n*2

Brown, Curtis, 278

Browning, Elizabeth Barrett, 173

Browning, Robert, 173

Brown University, 382

Bruce Publishing, 81

burlesque, 131 and *n*1

Busch, Joseph F., 191 and *n*2

Caedmon, Fr., *see* Wahl, Fr. Thomas Peter

Caesar, Sid, 242

Caliri, Fortunata, 92 and *n*1

Camus, Albert, 360

Canada, 141, 277

Cape Cod, 80, 81

Capote, Truman, 212

Carr, Mr., 234

Carrington V. C. (film), 230

cars, 71, 77, 86, 89, 100, 127, 145, 150, 151, 198, 222, 297, 372, 403, 406

Casey, Fr. Marion G., 71, 214, 316, 379

Catechetical Guild, 137, 138

Catholic Action, xvii, 327

Catholic Action News, 178–79

Catholic Church, xvii–xviii, xix, 25, 31 and *n*1, 33, 91–92, 116*nn*1–2, 139, 149, 320 and *n*2, 370 and *n*3; in Ireland, 164 and *n*1, 166, 167; JFP's views on, xvii–xviii, 17, 25, 59, 67 and *n*1, 97, 166, 186, 220 and *n*3, 223, 224, 243, 260, 272, 349 and *n*1, 413. *See also specific reform movements*

Catholic Digest, 27, 154

Catholic Herald, 168

Catholic Messenger, The, 345, 346, 348

Catholic rural life movement, xvii, xix, 25, 119*n*3, 224

Catholic Times, The, 168

Catholic Worker, The, xvii, 15 and *n*2, 114, 119*n*3, 145, 220 and *n*2

Catholic Worker movement, xvii, xix, 4, 8, 16, 25, 26, 41, 50*n*1, 85, 119*n*3, 200*n*1, 215*n*6, 349

Catholic World, 97, 119

CBS, 330, 331

Century Transportation Company, 326

Chaucer, Geoffrey, 236

Chesterton, G. K., 59

Chevrolet, 77, 86, 89

Chez Show (radio show), 155

dogs, 407
Domino, Ruth, 91 and *n*2
Domrese, Walter J., 14*n*1
Dos Passos, John, 142
Doubleday, 60, 68, 89, 94, 112, 115, 137,
183, 196, 219, 221, 224, 226, 227, 255,
269, 292, 318, 365, 367, 372, 378, 381 and
*n*1, 382, 387–90, 393, 395, 405, 420
Downs, Hugh, 393
Doyle, Elizabeth Anne Finegan, 112, 354,
367, *428*, 430; JFP's letters to, 271–72,
276–77, 313–14, 368–72, 379–80, 403–5
Doyle, Leonard J., 99 and *n*.1, 112, 179,
299, 316, 329, 354, 361, 367, 428, 430;
JFP's letters to, 178, 271–72, 276–77,
313–14, 316–17, 368–72, 379–80, 403–5,
412–13
Dryden, John, 103
Dublin, 157, 163–65, 168, 180, 188, 269,
273, 274, 277, 291–305, 309–21, 326, 405,
411
Dulles, John Foster, 313
Dumfries, 174
Dunphy, Fr., 223
Dupas, Ralph, 329 and *n*1
Dwyer, Jack, 304

Earley, Sister Eugene Marie, 50 and *n*1,
59
Ecclesiastical Directory, 30
Edel, Leon, *385*
Edinburgh, 174
Edwards, Phil, 353*n*1
Egan, Fr. Harvey F. X., xxvii, 17, 28, 29,
37, 47, 51, 56, 58, 59, 60, 66, 97, 138, 203,
244, 368–69, 403, 431; JFP's letters to,
17–18, 25–26, 49, 81, 89–94, 109–14,
118–20, 138–40, 143–45, 149–60, 163–80,
183–84, 186–92, 195–97, 200, 206–7,
211–16, 219–30, 239, 241–45, 248–49,
258–60, 265–66, 274–75, 281–82,
291–305, 315–19, 327–32, 334–40,
343–53, 361–67, 370, 380–83, 390–99,
409–10
Egan, Madge, 29
Egypt, 238
Eisenhower, Dwight D., 230, 341
El Greco, 41

Eliot, T. S., 11, 102, 188, 352, 360; *The
Rock*, 8 and *n*1
Elmira, New York, 101
El Paso, Texas, 33
England, 139, 174, 175, 211, 219, 220, 237,
238, 247, 279, 388, 412
Esquire, 15, 367
Evans, Bergen, xvii
Evening Mail, The, 177

Falque, Fr. Ferdinand C., 223, 224, 225
Family Rosary Crusade, 316*n*1
Fandel's, 55 and *n*1, 57, 58
Farina, Fr. Louis, xviii, 8 and *n*2
Farrar, Straus and Giroux, 420
Faulkner, William, 117 and *n*1, 261, 363,
377; "A Rose for Emily," 117; "Spotted
Horses," 117
FBI, 91
Federal Writers' Project, xvii
Fehrenbacher, Fr. Henry, 215 and *n*6, 371
Fennelly, Fr. John, 167 and *n*1, 169 and *n*1,
171, 172–73, 177, 180, 272, 274
Fiedler, Leslie, 246 and *n*2, 247
Fielding, Rosemary Hugo, xvii*n*
Fifield, William, 5 and *n*1, 7
Fighting Flanagan Brothers, 151, 152
films, 68, 184, 230, 405
fish, 80, 81
Fitts, Dudley, 104
Fitzgerald, Barry, 184*n*1
Fitzgerald, F. Scott, 42–43, 116; *The
Crack-Up*, 116; *The Great Gatsby*, 116;
Tender Is the Night, 116; *This Side of
Paradise*, 42
Fitzgerald, Robert, 100
Flanagan, Del, 151, 152, 266 and *n*2, 329
and *n*1, 330, 335 and *n*1, 336, 337 and *n*1,
340, 345, 353, 366
Flanagan, Glen, 151, 340 and *n*2, 345
Flaubert, Gustave, 173
Florida, 187
food, 69–70, 131, 139, 164, 167–68, 169,
185, 188, 204, 205, 221 and *n*3, 240, 270,
271, 283, 284, 404
football, 32, 114, 180, 241 and *n*2, 274,
339–40, 352–53, 360–62, 369
Ford, John, 184*n*1

horse racing, 92, 120, 140, 143, 144, 152
    and *n*1, 153, 154, *161*, 170, 171, 174, 180,
    191, 213, 264, 274, 284, 313
"The Hotel," (unwritten novel) 50
Hovda, Fr. Robert, 215 and *n*6
Howe, John, xix, 4, 7 and *n*1, 9 and *n*1, 45,
    104, 105 and *n*3, 431
Hughes, Fr. Philip, 200 and *n*5, 206
Hughes, Riley, 90
Hugo, Fr. John, xviii, 8*n*2, 214
Humphrey, Donald (Don), 26, 28, 29, 36,
    39, 41, 44–46, 55, 57, 72, 102, 151 and *n*1,
    172, *181*, 186, 213, 216, 222, 224, 228, 249,
    271, 273, 285, 288, 307, 309–15, 319, 426,
    430; illness and death of, 309–10, 312,
    314–15, 329, 368; JFP's letters to,
    279–80, 283–84, 287–88, 296, 298–99,
    304
Humphrey, Hubert, 178, 359
Humphrey, Mary Alice Frawley, 29, 36,
    71, *181*, 188, 200, 212, 214, 309, 315, 368,
    371, 430; JFP's letters to, 279–80,
    283–84, 287–88, 296, 298–99, 304
Hungary, 238
Huntington Hartford Foundation, 221
    and *n*1
Huxley, Aldous, 33
Huysmans, Joris-Karl, 19, 33
Hynes, Arleen McCarty, 25, 219, 321, 354,
    367, 428, 430
Hynes, Emerson, 25, 34, 57, 59, 84, 90, 96,
    102, 112, 216, 219, 245, 273, 275, 276, 277,
    284, 285, 288, 298–99, 312, 321, 354,
    367, 426, 428, 430

Idaho, 389 and *n*2
Illinois, xvi, xvii, 31, 65, 259
Indiana, 207
Institute for Sex Research, 207
International Boxing Club, 330
Iowa, 198, 331
IRA, 157
Ireland, xvi, xix, xxi, 30, 31, 46, 47, 51, 59,
    121, 122, 154, 157, 158, 163, 184, 186,
    187–88, 191, 199, 204, 238, 239, 249, 256,
    260, 264, 265, 269, 291, 309, 338, 339,
    344, 362, 399, 403; Catholicism, 164 and
    *n*1, 166, 167; Powers family in, 163–80,

183, 269–88, 291–305, 309–21, 403–16,
    419, 420, 421; press, 168
Irish Hospitals' Sweepstakes, 152 and *n*1
Irish Times, The, xxi, 168, 199, 264, 276,
    292, 407, 411
Irving, Washington, 32
Israel, 238

Jacksonville, Illinois, xvi, 31, 259, 261, 366
Jacobs Prairie, Minnesota, 315, 316, 329
James, Henry, 117, 188, 279; "Lesson of the
    Master," 116
Jansenism, xviii, 17
Japan, 74
Jarrell, Randall, 120 and *n*2
jazz, 3
Jehovah's Witnesses, 60, 126
Jensen, Rosemary, 112
Johnson, Lonnie, 3
Johnson, Dr. Samuel, 213
John XXIII, Pope, 320 and *n*2, 331–32,
    349, 363, 370 and *n*3
Jolson, Al, 112
Joyce, James, 102, 138, 171, 198; *Ulysses*,
    292
Judge, Fr. Paul, 119 and *n*3
Juvenal, 103

Kacmarcik, Frank, 339 and *n*1, 340, 369
    and *n*3, 410
Kansas, 141
Kansas City, Missouri, 154 and *n*1
Keefe, Richard (Dick), 60, 90, 112, 156,
    179, 191, 229, 242, 288, 426, 427, 431
Kelly, Fr. Patrick, 50–51, 59, 60, 74, 221
Kennedy, John F., 359, 363; assassination
    of, 412–13
Kennedy, X. J., 241 and *n*1; "Epitaph for a
    Postal Clerk" (poem), 243 and *n*3
Kentucky Derby, 140 and *n*3
Kenyon College, 101, 102, 103
Kenyon Review, The, 103, 125
Kenyon Review Fellows in Fiction, 255,
    256, 344
"Keystone," 388, 389 and *n*1, 397 and *n*2
Kinsey, Dr. Alfred, 207
Knox, Msgr. Ronald, 332 and *n*1

Noone, Jimmie, 3
Norris, Hoke, 398 and *n*1
Northwestern University, xvii, 33

Oakmont, Pennsylvania, xviii
O'Brien, Kate, 292
Observer, The, 168, 251, 270, 276, 407
O'Casey, Sean, 292, 300
O'Connell, Dick, 415 and *n*1
O'Connell, Joann Wiley, 427, 430;
   caricature of Jim by, 209; JFP's letters
   to, 272–73, 284–87, 294–95, 310–13,
   320–21, 403–8, 411–12, 414–15
O'Connell, Joseph, 288, 340, 345, 346, 427,
   430; JFP's letters to, 272–73, 284–87,
   294–95, 310–13, 320–21, 351–55, 403–8,
   411–12, 414–15
O'Connor, Edwin, 298; *The Last Hurrah*,
   298
O'Connor, Flannery, 256; "Greenleaf,"
   256
O'Connor, Frank, 157, 168, 169
Ó Faoláin, Eileen, 282
Ó Faoláin, Seán, 157, 168, 169, 171, 173,
   200, 204, 220, 261, 273, 277, 281, 282,
   283, 284, 292, 313, 321, 344, 405, 407,
   409, 410, 427, 431
O'Hara, Maureen, 184*n*1
O. Henry Award, 256
Ohio, 95*n*3, 101, 102
O'Neill, Marty, 140 and *n*1
Ong, Walter, 219 and *n*2
Oregon, 203, 204, 205
Orwell, George, 211; *The Road to Wigan
   Pier*, 317
Osaka, Japan, 74
Ottaviani, Card. Alfredo, 409 and *n*4
Our Father's House (anthology), 5 and *n*3
Oxford, England, 247

pacificism, xviii, 9, 27*n*1
Palmer, Joe H., 140 and *n*4, 143–44
Palmquist, Mary Pluth, 284, 428, 430;
   JFP's letters to, 403–5
Palmquist, Richard (Dick), 284, 309, 311,
   368, 428, 430; JFP's letters to, 309, 315,
   403–5, 408–9, 413–14

Parcheesi, 91 and *n*1
Paris, France, xvi, 275, 411
Partisan Review, 142
Pater, Walter, 19
Penitentes, 160 and *n*2
Perón, Eva, 175
Perry, Jim, 396 and *n*1
Perspectives (magazine), 225
Petrarch, 103
Petrek, Fr., 178
Petters, Catherine, 408 and *n*1
Petters, Fredric, 288, 311, 349, 368, 428,
   430; JFP's letters to, 286, 301, 403–6,
   421
Petters, Rosemary Boyle (Romy), 408, 428,
   430; JFP's letters to, 286, 301, 403–6,
   421
Peyton, Father Patrick, 316 and *n*1, 317
Pickwick Papers, The (film), 230
Pirates of Penzance, The, 180
Pontifical Academy of Theology, 332 and
   *n*1
pop culture, 419
Pope, Alexander, 103
Porter, Katherine Anne, 103, 104–5, 110,
   114, 121, 195, 235, 236, 377, 391, 393, 431;
   "The Fig Tree," 364 and *n*1; "Holiday,"
   364; JFP's letters to, 130, 256, 262–63,
   311–12, 325–27, 333, 344, 364–65, 395;
   Ship of Fools, 391, 393, 395
Portland, Oregon, 203, 204, 205
Pound, Ezra, 102, 116, 122, 131
Powell, Dawn, *The Golden Spur*, 391
Power, Jimmy, 152
Powers, Elizabeth Alice Wahl (Betty), xvi,
   xix, xx, xxi, 19–21, 23, 55, 63, 181, 217,
   401, 426, 429; Avon house of, 85–86,
   107, 109–19, 158–59; courted by Jim,
   19–21; death of, xxi; early married life,
   79–85, 89–105, 109–21, 125–33;
   engagement to Jim, 21, 25–36, 39, 39–51,
   55–61, 65–74; Fr. George Garrelts and,
   72–74; in Ireland, 163–80, 183, 269–88,
   291–305, 309–21, 403–16, 419, 420, 421;
   JFP's letters to, 26–36, 39–51, 55–61,
   65–74, 82–85, 93–104, 128–33, 152,
   158–59, 184–89, 203–7, 233–52;
   marriage to Jim, xix, xxi, 63, 73 and *n*1,
   74, 79, 125, 294, 336, 411, 420;